a hard way
to make a war

a hard way to make a war

the italian campaign in the second world war

IAN GOODERSON

CONWAY

© Ian Gooderson, 2008

First published in Great Britain
in 2008 by Conway,
an imprint of Anova Books Ltd.,
10 Southcombe Street,
London W14 0RA
www.anovabooks.com

Ian Gooderson has asserted his moral right to be identified as
the author of this work.

The analysis, opinions and conclusions expressed or implied
in this book are those of the author and do not necessarily
represent the views of the JSCSC, the UK MOD or
any other government agency.

British Library Cataloguing in Publication Data:
A catalogue record for this book is available from the British Library

ISBN: 978144860593

Editing, design and map illustrations by DAG Publications Ltd

Printed and bound by Cromwell Press Ltd, Wiltshire

Endpaper illustrations:
Front, Aerial bombardment of Cassino by the Allies.
Back, American troops, using bicycles and mule carts, move
up towards the front line through the town of Vittoria,
Sicily, 1943. (Conway Picture Library)

CONTENTS

For Remy De Roover,
in fond gratitude for early encouragement

ACKNOWLEDGEMENTS

For their often painstaking assistance in the past I would like to thank the staffs of the National Archives at Kew and of the Imperial War Museum, and of the library of the Joint Services Command and Staff College of the UK Defence Academy. I owe a debt of gratitude to publisher Roderick Dymott who, at that time with Brassey's UK, gave his initial support to this book and made it possible, and to Alison Moss at Anova Books who subsequently took on the project and whose forbearance with a part-time writer is beyond praise. I am also grateful to David Gibbons of DAG Publications for his valuable suggestions. The readers of this book will note from my references and from the bibliography the many published sources consulted, and I am conscious of a debt to their authors who, by so ably leading in their interpretations of the Italian campaign, have made it possible for me to follow in their wake with my own. As a lecturer with the Defence Studies Department of King's College London, at the Joint Services Command and Staff College, I have been privileged to tutor officers from the UK and overseas studying the Italian Campaign when reading for their MA in Defence Studies during their Advanced Command and Staff Course. It is wholly appropriate that I express my gratitude to them, and acknowledge that I have learned from their insights as much as they have ever learned from mine.

Ian Gooderson

INTRODUCTION

'There must be more ... training in the elements of initiative and responsibility, in ability to meet unexpected situations, and in acting on sound decisions made on individual responsibility. No one in our outfit expected to meet the situations we encountered in Sicily ... One thing, we have got to stop belittling the fighting ability of the German. The enemy is vicious, clever, and ruthless. It's going to take leadership of the highest order to whip him for good and all ...' — US Infantry Battalion Executive Officer, August 1943[1]

The heartfelt warning from an American infantry officer was recorded in August 1943, the day after the fall of Messina and just at the end of the brief, but hard-fought, campaign to capture the island of Sicily that had begun with the Allied landings on 10 July. Sicily had been a tough challenge for the American, British and Canadian troops as they fought their way inland from their landing beaches and then overcame a series of German defensive lines thrown across the path of their advance. The terrain, well suited to such a defence, bore little relation to what experienced Allied troops had encountered previously in North Africa, while several of the Allied formations involved possessed no combat experience at all; for them Sicily was a learning experience, often a painful one. The fact that the Italian defenders of the island, their country on the point of overthrowing its Fascist dictator Benito Mussolini and defecting from the Axis, mostly melted away after the initial beachhead battles made little difference. If anything, the awareness of their ally's unreliability spurred the Germans on the island to fight all the harder, with a grim determination to make the Allies pay as dearly as possible for every yard of their advance, knowing that the island must ultimately and inevitably be relinquished to their enemies. For the first time in the Second World War, soldiers of the Anglo-American alliance engaged the German Army fighting on the defensive on ground that was, to all intents and purposes, Europe, and fighting desperately to hold that ground for as long as possible. Many German soldiers knew by this stage of the war that to inflict delay was the

11

only victory they could hope for. It was a sobering experience for Allied troops to meet their enemy fighting under this imperative; but a greater challenge, and worse experience, was to come.

On 3 September 1943, British and Canadian troops of General Montgomery's Eighth Army crossed the narrow straits of Messina and landed in Calabria in southern Italy. A British army stood once again on mainland Europe. This time there was no question of Italian resistance. Mussolini had been deposed, and the successor government of Marshal Pietro Badoglio was seeking an armistice, though vainly trying to disguise the fact from the Germans both within and beyond Italy for as long as possible. As Eighth Army waded ashore in Calabria, Italian soldiers greeted them on the beaches and helped them unload their landing craft. The thin screen of watching German troops in the overlooking hills disdainfully fired a few rounds of artillery and moved away inland, leaving demolitions, road blocks and small rearguard parties covering the terrain's natural bottlenecks in order to hold up the British advance. Their Führer, Adolf Hitler, had not yet made up his mind about how to react to events in Italy, and for the moment they were under orders to withdraw to the north, not to stand and fight. On 8 September, as the unconditional surrender of Italy to the Allies was announced by radio, General Mark W. Clark's United States Fifth Army, composed of US and British divisions, prepared to land to the south of Naples in the Bay of Salerno, straight into a hornets' nest and one of the hardest, most critical, and closest-run battles that US and British troops experienced against the Germans in the entire war.

The speed and ferocity of the German reaction at Salerno was a shock to Fifth Army that reverberated throughout the Allied command. In an eight-day battle Clark's troops clung desperately to their narrow beachhead, as strong battle groups of German infantry and armour, supported by their artillery well placed in the hills dominating the bay, fought just as determinedly to throw them back into the sea – and very nearly did so. Heavy naval gunfire support and the intervention of Allied air power on a massive scale, adding to the tenacious resistance of troops who had little more than the sea at their backs, gradually turned the scale in favour of Fifth Army. The German soldiers who broke off the battle and moved away to the north may have been sullen at their lack of success, but they certainly did not consider themselves defeated. They had suffered heavy casualties, but they had also inflicted them. The British Eighth Army was gradually, but surely, approaching them from the south and, moreover, they were still under orders to pull back from southern Italy. As before in Sicily, they lived to fight another day. Their chastened opponents recovering in the beachhead did not consider the Germans defeated either. What had become the Italian Campaign might not, after all, be the occupation of the country in the wake of the retreating Germans that had been initially anticipated, not without reason, by the Allies when the strategic decision to land forces on mainland Italy had been taken. Within a month they knew very well that it would not be.

At Salerno, Field Marshal Albert Kesselring, commanding the German forces in southern Italy, and General Heinrich von Vietinghoff, commanding the German Tenth Army, had shown Hitler what they could do. In early October Hitler finally decided upon his course of action in Italy, and abandoned the policy of a northward withdrawal. Instead, he would hold Italy south of Rome, and henceforth every yard would be fought for. Impelled by the enthusiastic energy of Kesselring, who had advocated this course and who was appointed as Army Group commander throughout Italy, the Germans began to prepare a series of defensive lines across the Italian peninsula, not to delay the Allied advance but to stop it. When the Allies learned this through their signals intelligence, there was consternation. Hitler's decision had altered the entire nature of the campaign in Italy and sealed the fate of thousands of Allied and German soldiers. Yet there could be no question of the Allies remaining static in Italy, thereby surrendering the initiative to the Germans and, metaphorically if not literally, remaining under their guns. They had to maintain their advance in Italy, because until the launching of the main second front in North-West Europe, Operation 'Overlord', it was only in Italy that the Anglo-American Allies were engaging the German army. It was imperative to maintain Italy as an active, and therefore offensive, theatre, both to draw German strength away from France as a means of assisting 'Overlord', and to demonstrate to their ally, the USSR, unquestionably bearing the brunt of the war on land and ceaselessly demanding the opening of the 'Second Front', that they were engaging significant German strength. A passive theatre in Italy was both militarily and politically unacceptable, but the consequences of this strategic reality for the Allied troops in Italy were appalling. Between the autumn of 1943 and the final defeat of Germany in May 1945 they were almost continually on the offensive. While maintaining the ability to attack, they had to cope with difficult terrain for which their largely mechanized formations were unsuited and which negated their preponderance in armour. They had to cope with extremes of weather, from the bitter cold, drenching wet and cloying mud of the Italian winter, to the heat and dust of the Italian summer. They had to become proficient in amphibious landings and beachhead battles, in mountain warfare, in urban fighting, in clearing defended river lines.

Above all, they had to defeat their enemy, the German soldier in Italy. Unquestionably he fought a remarkable defensive campaign: a model of its kind and worthy of study for that reason alone. His divisions were never at full strength, and like his Allied opponents, he had to fight starved of resources because for him too Italy was always a secondary theatre, subsidiary to the campaign on the Eastern Front and later that in North-West Europe as well. His difficulty in obtaining replacements for his battle casualties was greater than that facing the Allied armies; he lacked the scale of their equipment and firepower; and in sharp contrast to them he fought the campaign without the benefit of air superiority. It was rare for him to see one of his own aircraft flying to his support, whereas he lived, moved, and fought both at the battlefront and beyond under the continual threat of Allied air attack. He possessed some advantages. His military organization was generally more flexible than that of his enemies. He could be rapidly organized into an ad-hoc battle group formed of units from widely differing parent formations in a way that would have been impossible in the British and American armies, and he would fight effectively in it. His reaction capability was phenomenal, and against those Allied soldiers who had not yet come to know him well, and who were not prepared for him, his counterattack could be devastating. He did not possess anything like the numbers of tanks and anti-tank guns of his opponents, but those he did have were generally better in performance, if less rugged, and his opponents were always prepared to acknowledge, at the time and since, that he certainly knew how to make the best use of them. For a while, until they learned how to cope with him, he was their superior in tactical skill and battlecraft. In Italy, his skill at military engineering and his lavish use of concrete and steel, mines and wire, his eye for ground and for fields of fire and his knowledge of the use that could be made of terrain and natural obstacles, enabled him to confront the Allied armies with defensive positions of a strength rarely encountered in war. Yet the Allied armies overcame them, and they defeated the German soldier in the field – of that there can be no doubt.

The campaigns in Sicily and Italy are studies in the gaining of operational and tactical proficiency, of innovation and sometimes of experimentation as the Allied armies and the air forces and naval units that supported their operations assimilated and applied their hard-won experience. It is a study of joint warfare, as the various services learned to integrate their operations, and a study of combined warfare, as the Allies learned to work together to fight the common enemy rather than to obstruct each other. It is also a study in command, of the pressures of decision-making at the operational and tactical levels of war.

The operations and individual actions examined in this study have been reconstructed from a wide range of sources. However, in the concluding chapter I have tried to let the Allied soldiers of the Italian campaign speak for themselves, in the voices of 1943–5 unaltered by time and unaffected by the distortions of subsequent perceptions of events and the vagaries of memory. Among the more important sources consulted were the contemporary interviews, mostly anonymous, of soldiers of all ranks who had recently been in action and whose experience and comments were urgently required by their own training organizations. These young soldiers of the Italian Campaign, some of them not fated to survive it but who had become battle-hardened veterans, speak with an authority that cannot be gainsaid. Their words are a vivid evocation of a campaign now long over and part of the past. The weapons and equipment about which they talk are museum pieces now; the principal battlegrounds to which they refer with easy familiarity have become the quiet cemeteries where all too many of them rest. Yet their words are a testament to their achievement, a military achievement perhaps not even now accorded by historians its due acknowledgement. The greater strategic controversies of their campaign,

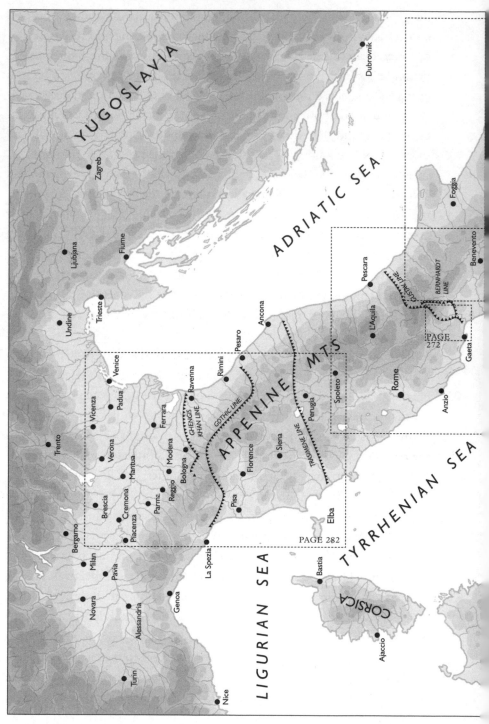

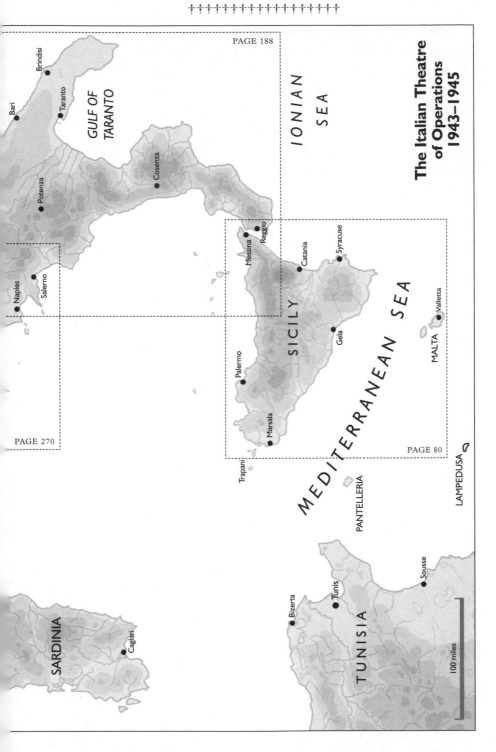

The Italian Theatre of Operations 1943–1945

PAGE 188

PAGE 270

PAGE 80

IONIAN SEA

MEDITERRANEAN SEA

GULF OF TARANTO

SICILY

SARDINIA

TUNISIA

MALTA

LAMPEDUSA

PANTELLERIA

Brindisi

Taranto

Bari

Potenza

Cosenza

Naples

Salerno

Messina

Reggio

Catania

Syracuse

Gela

Palermo

Marsala

Trapani

Valletta

Caglari

Bizerta

Tunis

Sousse

100 miles

the undoubted mistakes that were made have tended to obscure the quality and combat-tested battle professionals that these soldiers became. That quality and proficiency will emerge in the pages of this book, and with it a resonance beyond the purely historical. For how armies cope with the unexpected, how they assimilate and apply their battle experience, how they make use of innovation and experimentation when resources are scarce, how they keep fighting when the advantages of terrain and weather are against them – all these have a more than historical relevance.

1

THE STRATEGIC CONTEXT OF
THE ITALIAN CAMPAIGN

A campaign on Italian homeland territory became a certainty with the decision to invade Sicily, taken at the 'Symbol' Conference held at Casablanca between 14 and 24 January 1943. Codenamed Operation 'Husky', the invasion of Sicily was a logical follow-on for the Anglo-American Allies once they had finally brought the North African campaign to a successful conclusion.

As British Prime Minister Winston Churchill and US President Franklin Roosevelt and their Allied Combined Chiefs of Staff [1] met at Casablanca, the German-Italian Panzer Army Africa under Field Marshal Erwin Rommel fell back, about to relinquish Tripolitania and drawing closer towards Tunisia, continuing the long withdrawal begun after its defeat at the second battle of El Alamein in October 1942. In pursuit was the British Eighth Army under General Sir Bernard Montgomery, and above him as Commander-in-Chief Middle East was General Sir Harold Alexander. The North African coastal plain, the see-saw battleground of two years, was now left behind for good. But in Tunisia another battleground awaited.

In reaction to Operation 'Torch', the Anglo-American landings in French North West Africa in November 1942, Hitler poured reinforcements into Tunisia. So too did Mussolini.

It was imperative for them to retain a bridgehead in North Africa for as long as possible, to keep the Allies at maximum distance from southern Europe and the Balkans, so vital to the Axis war effort with its resources, and from Italy. With North Africa lost, Fascist Italy would be in the front line, vulnerable to Allied attack not only through intensified aerial bombing but also at risk to the threat of Allied amphibious invasion. The fall of North Africa would exacerbate Italian war-weariness and increase Italian disaffection with the Axis. Mussolini's own hold on power, already tenuous and under threat, might break altogether. Hitler was well aware, and had been since early in the war, that the Axis alliance with Fascist Italy would not long survive without Mussolini.[2] Therefore sizable German and Italian land and air forces arrived at Tunis and Bizerta by sea and air, the comparatively short distance from Italy and Sicily enabling them to win the race for Tunisia against the Anglo-American 'Torch' forces and the French formations that had joined them.

Rommel, falling back from Cyrenaica and Tripolitania, linked up with these Axis Tunisian forces, By Febuary 1943 he had been given overall command of the newly-formed Army Group Africa, comprising the Fifth Panzer Army under General Jürgen von Arnim in Northern Tunisia and the Italian First Army, which included the original German Afrika Korps, under General Giovanni Messe. High quality German and Italian troops, and equipment, were sent to Tunisia to buy time, while Rommel's troops were also veterans. The 'Torch' forces opposing them, the stretched British First Army (General Kenneth Anderson) with one corps in the line and the US Army's II Corps (General Lloyd R. Fredendall), were still learning their trade – and learning it the hard way against proficient battle-experienced troops and their equally experienced commanders. The French were keen but lacked the equipment necessary for a modern campaign. There was every induce-ment for Rommel and von Arnim, both aggressive commanders, to strike out offensively at the forces trying to close in on them, especially as the Allies' most experienced army, Montgomery's Eighth Army, was hampered in reaching Tunisia by over-extended supply lines as it followed in Rommel's wake, a situation which Rommel's demolition of the port of Tripoli did much to prolong. In February the Axis went over to the offensive in limited but sharp attacks, dealing hard blows physically and psychologically at the Faid Pass, El Guettar, Gafsa and the Kasserine Pass before breaking off. They left few illusions about the work still required for inexperienced Allied troops and their commanders to attain battle proficiency. Nor could there be much doubt that, however certain ultimate Allied victory in North Africa might be, it would come neither easily nor cheaply.

At the Casablanca conference the duration and nature of the Tunisian campaign could not easily be foreseen, but until it was won and its forces and commanders released there could be no further major offensive move in the Mediterranean. The Allied command team in the Mediterranean faced with the Tunisian campaign combined the managing of theatre-level direction of coalition warfare with experienced operational direction. The American General Dwight D. Eisenhower, selected by Churchill and Roosevelt for the role in 'Torch', continued to prove his even-handed skill as a coalition Supreme Commander and retained his post. The fact that he lacked operational experience was offset by his three distinguished senior land, sea and air commanders all having plenty, much of it pertaining to operational level command recently gained in the Mediterranean theatre. They were Alexander as commander of the 18th Army Group (First and Eighth Armies), Admiral Sir Andrew Cunningham commanding the Allied Naval Forces and Air Chief Marshal Sir Arthur Tedder commanding the Allied air forces. Threatre command was exercized through Eisenhower's Anglo-American Allied Force Headquarters (AFHQ), organization of which mirrored American practice, while Alexander's 18th Army Group headquarters organized according to the British system, coordinated the operations of the two Armies. The overall functioning and liason was smooth. In the Mediterranean the Allies had a major campaign under way, a hard fight on their hands and a functioning and experienced command set-up. Ongoing campaigns generate their own momentum and often follow-on strategic and operational opportunities. These would prove to be important factors, though would not be the main determinants, in the Allied strategic decision to pursue a Mediterranean campaign by invading Sicily once North Africa was finally secure.

The context of the 'Husky' decision was controversial. Soon after the United States became a belligerent in what had become a global war, following the opening of the Japanese offensive in the Far East and Pacific with the attack on Pearl Harbor, the British and Americans agreed their overall war strategy. At the 'Arcadia' conference held in Washington just before Christmas 1941 they endorsed a view already reached during Anglo-American staff discussions held earlier that year. These identified Germany as the principal enemy, and the Atlantic theatre therefore as the most decisive. In the event of the United States entering the war and Japan also becoming a belligerent, the Allies should concentrate first on the defeat of Germany; the lynchpin of Allied strategy must be 'Germany first'. This was adopted at 'Arcadia'.[3] In a paper largely reflective of a

British strategic outlook, they agreed to close a ring around Germany – in effect a strategic noose encompassing the Black Sea to the Arctic, which would gradually close and tighten in preparation for the major assault that would bring Hitler to final defeat. This assault, the Allied Combined Chiefs believed, would occur in 1943, and options were open as to whether it would take place principally through southern or north-western Europe.[4] While the entry of the United States into the war and its immense military and industrial potential promised ultimate victory over the Axis powers, this potential had yet to mobilize for total global war, and in the meantime the immediate strategic outlook was grim. The Japanese were on the rampage with little to stop them. 'Germany first' meant the allocation to the Far East and Pacific of forces sufficient to 'contain' Japan, but the Japanese offensive momentum was only beginning; Australia and India were under threat. Even the Pacific coast of the United States was potentially vulnerable to attack. China, fighting a Japanese invasion since the 1930s, might collapse, releasing further Japanese forces. In Europe Hitler controlled the coastline of western Europe from occupied Norway to the border of neutral, but generally pro-Axis, Spain. Southern Europe and the Balkans were firmly in the Axis grip. The USSR, invaded by the Germans in June 1941 in the momentous Operation 'Barbarossa', was still in the fight, but the Red Army and Air Force had suffered massive defeats and colossal losses. Their recuperative ability was phenomenal, but the British and Americans could hardly be confident that the USSR would last for long into 1942. Indeed, it was imperative that she should do so, to impose an Eastern Front on Hitler that would continually drain German strength. If the USSR collapsed, as she had once before under a German onslaught in 1918, there could be no doubting that Hitler would be master of Europe and in a strategically unassailable position. This was the underpinning logic of 'Germany first' – plus the continual demands of the surly and incalculable Soviet leader Joseph Stalin, so unlikely an ally of the British and American democracies. For the western Allies to assist the USSR by opening a 'Second Front' against Germany could not be ignored. The Soviet Union was the principal existing land front against the European Axis, the Red Army confronting the main strength of Hitler's Wehrmacht together with forces contributed by Germany's allies and satellites. Only in

North Africa did a small army of British and Commonwealth divisions, supported by the Royal Navy and Royal Air Force in the Mediterranean, engage a handful of German divisions – Panzer Group Africa – and the Italians.

The strategic imperative to assist the USSR was the catalyst in 1942 for a dissonance between British and American views on how to implement their strategy against Germany. Roosevelt's endorsement of 'Germany first', despite its strategic logic, was politically courageous given the strength of American feeling against Japan after Pearl Harbor; it needed rapid justification by results. This, added to the need to assist the USSR and an assurance given by Roosevelt to Stalin's Foreign Minister, Vyacheslav Molotov, in Washington in May, that major action against the European Axis would occur in 1942, drove American thinking to implement a strategy of decisive action before the end of the year. While Roosevelt was open-minded about where such action might take place, and was receptive to Churchill's own wide-ranging enthusiasm for seizing offensive opportunities, his professional military were not. To General George Marshall, the US Army's Chief of Staff and Roosevelt's principal military advisor, who faced the challenge of focusing American military strength against escalating demands for resources across the theatres of global war that threatened to dissipate it, it soon became apparent that the best means of implementing 'Germany first' was by a concentrated blow directly at the heart of Germany.

This meant an Anglo-American invasion launched across the English Channel to open an offensive front in France. Marshall accepted the view, articulated by the then Brigadier-General Dwight Eisenhower of the US War Plans Division, that only by using Britain as an offensive base could the Anglo-American Allies concentrate the full weight of their sea and air power for a campaign that strategic logic demanded should be conducted in North-West Europe. While acknowledging the need to secure North Africa and the Middle East, American military opinion looked askance at the concept of the Mediterranean and southern Europe as a decisive theatre. Too far removed geographically from the principal enemy, Germany, and impossible to deploy there the full weight of Allied striking power, there was also the inescapable fact that Germany's southern frontiers were natural defensive bastions protected by mountains. The plain of North-West Europe was not. Moreover, the build-up of American forces in Britain would concentrate Allied naval power to protect the vital sea communications, enabling the defeat of the German U-boats and the sustaining of Britain's population and war effort. Winning this 'Battle of the Atlantic' was at the heart of Allied strategy and would release naval and merchant shipping for further offensive operations.[5]

By April 1942, Marshall adopted the concept of a build-up in Britain of American forces that year coupled with an aggressive harassing of the Germans across the Channel, codenamed 'Bolero', to be followed in 1943 by the cross-Channel invasion operation, 'Round-up' in April 1943. Endorsed by Roosevelt, the 'Bolero'-'Round-up' plan also found qualified approval with Churchill and the British Chiefs of Staff when put to them in April 1942, subject to the need to ensure Britain's position in the Mediterranean and Middle East against the Germans and Italians, a theatre vital to Britain for its air and sea communications to the Far East and its access to oil and to secure the Indian Ocean area against Japan. The strategic dilemma of 1942 soon arose with the need to assist the Soviet Union with a significant offensive effort against the European Axis before the end of that year, whereas 'Bolero'-'Round-up' demanded the husbanding of resources and a tight rein on offensive enterprises for a 'Round-up' in 1943 employing an envisaged 48 divisions and nearly 6,000 combat aircraft.[6] For Marshall and the American Joint Chiefs of Staff the only solution to the dilemma lay in a compromise, which they knew very well was unsatisfactory and which would hardly be welcome to their British ally. Included in 'Bolero'-'Round-up' was a contingency plan, 'Sledgehammer', for an emergency cross-Channel operation in 1942 for implementation in the event of an imminent Soviet collapse, a high-risk operation to forestall such a strategic calamity. Alternatively, in the extremely unlikely event of an imminent German collapse, it would be an exploitative rather than a sacrificial operation. Given the state of American mobilization, 'Sledgehammer' in 1942 would have to be primarily a British operation.

Another alternative, which Marshall and the Joint Chiefs looked at with some alarm, was a concept about which Churchill was enthused. This was 'Gymnast', a British scheme originally for an invasion of France's North-

West African colonies with the idea of bringing France, or at least her colonial forces and resources, back into the Allied camp and securing the entire North African coast. Possible American participation, a factor likely to increase French acquiescence if not active support, widened the concept in scale to 'Super Gymnast'. The concept worried Marshall and the Joint Chiefs, and Admiral Ernest J. King, the Chief of US Naval Operations, in particular because this operation in its demands upon shipping and forces would hamstring 'Bolero' and spell the end of any chance of 'Round-up' in 1943. King, his attention never far from the Pacific theatre and its demands, would only support a decisive direct line of attack in Europe. 'Super Gymnast' would divert American strength away to the Mediterranean theatre. What also worried Marshall and the Joint Chiefs was that Churchill had managed to enthuse Roosevelt about 'Super Gymnast' as well, not least as a major operational debut against the Axis for American forces. Therefore, in July 1942, following Roosevelt's directive to reach agreement with the British on a theatre of action, Marshall and King were in London in a forlorn-hope attempt to sell 'Sledgehammer' to the British Chiefs of Staff in the form of a viable operation – the seizure in the autumn of 1942 of a peninsula in Brittany and the port of Cherbourg as a bridgehead for a 'Round-up' in 1943.[7]

As they discovered, and almost certainly were already prepared for, there was not the slightest chance of the British agreeing to this concept. It ran counter not only to the traditional guiding principles underpinning a British approach to war strategy but also to the bitter British experience of fighting the Germans during 1914–18 and 1940–2. The thought of prematurely taking on the Wehrmacht before it had been sufficiently weakened and the risk of opening an offensive front in France that might become an attritional stalemate (if it even survived that far) represented an appalling and unacceptable military risk. Britain's armed forces were simply not yet ready for this challenge – and certainly not for taking it on for the most part alone. Churchill had already prepared Roosevelt for this during the 'Argonaut' conference in Washington in June, pointing out the impossibility of a British government sanctioning an operation for which no responsible British military authority could come up with a plan offering any chance of success.[8] He also warned the Soviets bluntly that an

Allied disaster would be of no help to them, and there remained the consideration that a cross-Channel invasion was strategically a 'one-shot' enterprise. If the Allies attempted it and failed, there would be no telling when they could try again, if at all.

Nor could the British seriously consider crossing the Channel while their strategic positions in the Middle East and Far East were under threat. The British people had also had their fill of disasters. In February 1942 had come the fall of Singapore, thought to be an impregnable imperial base, to the Japanese. In June the Libyan port of Tobruk, which had defied an Axis siege for eight months in 1941, fell to Rommel without a fight. Both Churchill and his chief military advisor and Chief of the Imperial General Staff (CIGS), General Sir Alan Brooke, were with Roosevelt and Marshall in Washington when they received the shattering news of Tobruk's fall, and both would recall the support and understanding extended to them by their hosts and war allies on that difficult occasion. Singapore and Tobruk were not only serious military defeats they were also blows to British prestige, and scandalous in their nature. In early July 1942 Churchill faced, but survived, a parliamentary vote of censure debate on the higher conduct of the war.[9] It was no time to contemplate opening a front in France.

When Marshall and King reported the British refusal to accept 'Sledgehammer' to Roosevelt they were instructed to lay it aside and reach agreement. Roosevelt would not countenance threatening his ally with an American revision of emphasis towards the Pacific at the expense of 'Germany first'. That left 'Super Gymnast', which was agreed and which Marshall and the US Joint Chiefs, their strategic disappointment set aside, entered into wholeheartedly. At Churchill's suggestion the operation was rechristened 'Torch', and, as part of the emphasis placed upon American participation, Eisenhower, by then commanding US forces in Europe, was appointed its Supreme Commander. Planning under the codename 'Rutter' continued for a cross-Channel attack in 1942 on the lines of a major raid of a day's duration. This led ultimately to the ill-fated Operation 'Jubilee' in which a landing force comprising mostly Canadian troops suffered heavy losses in attacking the port of Dieppe on 19 August 1942, an operation that showed all too clearly the Allies' lack of experience and skill in planning and executing a major amphibious assault.

From an American military perspective 'Torch' with its threat of extending the campaign in the Mediterranean theatre, was dangerously reflective of a British 'peripheral' approach to strategy in contrast to their own propensity for concentrating resources against the principal enemy. It was a question largely of strategic experience and the culture it generates. Britain, a sea power unable to challenge directly the military strength of a major Continental power, had in its wars conducted its strategy in combination with a Continental ally (or allies) to offset the enemy's strength, while deploying its own sea power and limited striking forces to hit the enemy's identified weak points with a strict economy of force in the aspiration of disproportionate strategic gain. The commitment of mass armies to a Continental war of attrition between 1915 and 1918 and its human and material cost had seared the generation that had experienced it; it was an aberration that should not – indeed could not – be repeated. The period without a major ally between the fall of France in 1940 and Hitler's own invasion of the USSR a year later starkly revealed Britain's strategic impotence: Britain alone had no means of striking effectively at Germany itself or of even remotely shaking the German hold on Europe. Nevertheless, an offensive opportunity had occurred with Mussolini's entry into the war in June 1940 – but in the Mediterranean.

Even before the outbreak of war British and French strategic planners had identified Italy as the potential 'weak link' in the Axis and a probable liability to Germany in war. Hitler would have to prop up Mussolini's own power base and sustain Italy's war effort, for, despite Mussolini's bombast, Italy was unready for a prolonged modern war and there were serious equipment deficiencies in her armed forces. This was known through intelligence sources, and it was confidently expected by British and French planners that while against Germany in Europe they must remain on the strategic defensive until strong enough, there would be opportunities to strike at Italy.[10] This was a means of eroding German strength and Germany's strategic position. Britain alone in 1940 followed this same path by default. Limited strength but highly proficient British and Commonwealth forces conducted successful campaigns in North and East Africa in conditions ideally suited to their levels of equipment and competence, overcoming Italian forces superior to them only in numbers. In

1940–1 these successes demonstrated that Italy was indeed a 'weak link' in the Axis, and that pressuring Italy would draw a German response. Mussolini's disastrous invasion of Greece in October 1940 opened the door to British support of the Greeks and the possibility of extending British influence in the Balkans.

All this, of course, proved counter to British strategic interests, as Britain alone in 1941 could not withstand Hitler's riposte. German intervention to prevent the fall of Libya and the arrival of Rommel in North Africa overturned British successes against the Italians; British forces were driven out of Greece and Crete by a German invasion intended to secure southern Europe and the Balkans before 'Barbarossa'. Strategic overextension had followed from initial dramatic successes against the Italians, and the consequence exposed Britain's own military weakness and strategic vulnerability in the Mediterranean and Middle East. Nevertheless the legacy in British strategy remained one of pressuring Italy to undermine Germany, and a perception that the Mediterranean was a theatre of offensive opportunity against Italy with the ultimate goal of knocking her out of the Axis and out of the war, with dire consequences for Germany's war effort in southern Europe and the Balkans. 'Torch' was seen not only as a means of securing North Africa but also as a step on this strategic path against Italy. Realization of this British view worried the Americans considerably, for it was a path diametrically opposite to that of the direct attack. It was in effect 'Italy first', not 'Germany first'.

With 'Torch' accomplished and the conclusion of the North African campaign in prospect, Allied strategy needed firm direction. Following the 'Torch' decision and the sidelining of 'Round-up', the American Joint Chiefs tended to the view that the European war had lost offensive momentum, and the balance of deployed American forces began to favour the Pacific, a trend that seriously worried the British Chiefs of Staff and Churchill once they were appraised of it. The purpose of 'Symbol' at Casablanca was to put Allied strategy back on track – for the British, to gain confirmation of 'Germany first' and a decision on where after North Africa the Allies should pursue their offensive strategy in 1943. As far as Brooke and the British Chiefs of Staff were concerned, the strategic choice was either to continue along the Mediterranean path or to close down the theatre and concentrate forces for a cross-Channel assault. They had some difficulty in convincing Churchill of this stark choice, as he firmly believed that a 'Round-up' was possible in 1943 in addition to exploiting further opportunities against Italy in the Mediterranean. In Moscow in August 1942 he had assured Stalin as much, and he wanted very good reasons indeed to present to the Soviet leader if in fact this could not be so. His own conviction was that in 1943 German difficulties in the USSR might well make 'Round-up' possible. His belief that Hitler would find himself in serious trouble in the Soviet Union would prove vindicated by the destruction of the German Sixth Army at Stalingrad early in the year and the problem the Germans had in restoring their front. These events augured a new note in the higher levels of Allied strategy; apart from assisting the USSR, Churchill and Roosevelt were also under an increasing imperative to demonstrate that their forces were 'pulling their weight' in the war to a resurgent Soviet ally that was now achieving significant victories of its own.

At the end of 1942, however, Brooke and the British Chiefs of Staff, provided with assessments by their own Joint Planning Staff, could not accept Churchill's dual strategy for 1943 of attacking in the Mediterranean and across the Channel as well. The Chiefs of Staff, drawing heavily upon an assessment by their Joint Planners, pointed out that the strongest force that could be assembled in Britain for a 'Round-up' in August 1943 would be thirteen British and twelve American divisions, of which there would be sufficient specialized amphibious shipping to organize only four British and two American divisions for assault landings. Not only was this force considerably less than the 48 divisions originally envisaged when the 'Round-up' plan was first devised; since then German defences in France had been strengthened. It was a wholly inadequate force with which to try and break into Hitler's 'Fortress Europe' in the West. Moreover, to enable the concentration of even this force would require foregoing all possible amphibious operations in the Mediterranean, the build-up of bomber forces in Britain and a projected amphibious operation against the Japanese in Burma. The time lapse, some eight months, required between the necessary closing down of the Mediterranean and launching the cross-Channel attack would be of greater benefit to the Germans by giving them a reprieve and releasing them from the threat of attack in the south. They would therefore be able to redeploy forces to the East and to Western Europe. In effect, if 'Round-up' in 1943 could only be attempted, and at great risk, at the expense of Mediterranean operations, as opposed to being a surer operation launched in combination with them, then to make the attempt in 1943 made no strategic sense at all.

The alternative was to exploit 'Torch' and the ongoing momentum of offensive in the Mediterranean, directed primarily upon Italy. The eventual conquest of North Africa would enable further amphibious operations against Sardinia, Corsica, Sicily or the mainland of Italy itself. The Eastern Mediterranean, the Dodecanese Islands and Crete, might also offer offensive opportunities. There would be no need to curtail the build-up of the heavy bomber forces in Britain, while the reduced 'Bolero' build-up, although insufficient for a 'Round-up', would still have the effect of fixing significant German strength in the West, up to some 40 divisions, for fear of an Allied attack. Operations in Burma could go forward. The principal factor was the intelligence prediction that if Italy were knocked out of the war, then a potentially crippling increase in commitments would be imposed upon Germany. Hitler would have no choice but to cover the loss of Italy and of Italian garrisons in the Balkans. If, at the same time, he attempted to hold the existing length of front in the USSR, he would find himself short of what he needed by some 54 divisions and 2,200 combat aircraft. Moreover, he would have a particular logistic and transportation difficulty imposed upon him, for while a highly developed and efficient lateral railway system enabled the Germans to switch forces across Europe between the East and the West, there was no such system to the south – only two lines into Italy and one into Greece, all of them potentially vulnerable to disruption by bombing.[11]

It was a compelling argument. During a Chiefs of Staff meeting on 16 December 1942 attended by Churchill and the Foreign Secretary Anthony Eden, Brooke presented the case for the Mediterranean instead of 'Round-up'. Churchill pronounced himself finally convinced. 'I think he is now fairly safe,' confided a relieved Brooke to his diary, 'but I have still the Americans to convince first, and then Stalin next!'[12] In fact Brooke's relief proved premature, for Churchill made one more try for 'Round-up' in

1943 later that same month. This was in response to a sharp reminder from Stalin to both himself and Roosevelt that they had promised a second front in the following spring. The US Joint Planning Staff also forwarded a proposal for the closing down of the Mediterranean once North Africa was secured, and the transfer of forces from there to Britain for a cross-Channel operation. Churchill wanted the British Chiefs of Staff to pull his political-strategic 'chestnuts out of the fire' and honour his promise to Stalin. But they remained adamant to their strategic concept, and to this he finally had to bow.

Marshall in late 1942 was alarmed at the likely cost in men, shipping and resources of further Mediterranean operations and unconvinced of their strategic worth, and wanted to strike at the Germans in France in 1943 with all available forces. He still wanted to focus Allied strategy where he believed it would hurt Hitler most and where it would be of the most help to the Soviets, by opening a front in North-West Europe. Both the escalating demands in the Pacific and those likely to arise in the Mediterranean were undermining the direct line of attack on Germany. He wanted the Mediterranean closed down before it was too late to check its momentum, fully realizing that this would become progressively more difficult and perhaps eventually impossible. His was the dominant interpretation within the US Army planning staff and the US Joint Chiefs. Nevertheless some American planners, mindful of the Dieppe raid experience and faced with the facts about the available forces and shipping, began to share the view of their British counterparts and to doubt whether crossing the Channel was after all a viable military proposition for 1943.[13] By the end of 1942, therefore, Allied strategy was veering off track and losing coherence; it required re-focusing at the highest level.

It took two high-level conferences between the British and Americans in the first half of 1943 to establish the strategic framework that would direct their resources and efforts to ultimate victory. Although concerned with the waging of their global war, the importance of the Mediterranean theatre and of Italy in their strategy was central to both conferences. The result was that by May 1943 the Allies were set on course to land armies in Italy. They were also committed to mounting a major cross-Channel operation in the spring of the following year, 1944, a concept for which the name 'Round-up' was dropped and replaced with 'Overlord'. Although Marshall sustained a defeat in his wish to close down the Mediterranean, he did achieve a firm commitment to the direct line of attack and the prioritization of Allied effort. While the British Chiefs of Staff won their case to pursue opportunities in the Mediterranean directed upon Italy, they had to accept the reality of doing so with strictly defined and limited resources and in the knowledge that, whatever opportunities did exist, they had to be regarded in the light of a secondary theatre to the main line of attack. This was compromise as strategy. Although compromise served the purpose of bringing agreement on fundamentals and coherence back into Allied strategy, it would later generate dilemmas and shortfalls of its own.

Churchill and his Chiefs of Staff went to the 'Symbol' conference at Casablanca determined to reassert 'Germany first' and to establish a definite agreement on exploiting the eventual gaining of North Africa. Their plan was for 'Husky', an invasion of Sicily. The British had not themselves firmed-up upon 'Husky' without considerable debate prior to attending at Casablanca. Only on the very eve of departing did Brooke win his case for Sicily over the contending concept of 'Brimstone', an invasion of Sardinia. To invade Sicily would secure the Mediterranean sea passages, obviating the long route around the Cape for Allied convoys necessary to avoid Axis sea and air attack. Moreover, it was considered a far more powerful blow, possibly a decisive one against Italy, and an operation of sufficient scale and strategic merit to present to what would be an inevitably disappointed and cynical Stalin, balked yet again of his promised 'Second Front' in the West. Sardinia, on the other hand, offered what promised to be a less risky amphibious operation, a not insignificant factor in the wake of Dieppe, one that required far less planning and preparation and which could therefore be mounted earlier. It was not 'big' enough, however.

The British went to Casablanca with their arguments well prepared – indeed they astounded the Americans with the extent of their preparation and the staff machinery that accompanied them. The Americans for their part were willing to be convinced of a viable strategy that would bring significant strategic gain without dissipating resources unnecessarily. Roosevelt was still receptive to the Mediterranean possibilities, and Marshall, despite his preference for crossing the Channel, was beginning to appreciate its difficulties in 1943. Although he would warn of the 'suction pump' effect of Mediterranean operations draining forces from the direct line of attack, he was willing to countenance an invasion of Sicily as a definable step from North Africa that offered in strategic terms a positive calculable return. Given that Allied strategy was dependent upon shipping, he was also impressed by the fact that securing Sicily and opening the Mediterranean would release a million tons of British capacity. Beyond Sicily, however, he was not willing to look. With the requirements of planned operations in the Pacific assured, King was willing to support a worthwhile operation in the Mediterranean – which to him meant Sicily rather than Sardinia. General Henry H. 'Hap' Arnold, representing the United States Army Air Force (USAAF), was aware of the value of airfields in the Mediterranean for intensifying the bombing of Germany and, particularly, of enabling raids on targets beyond the range of bombers based in England. These included the oilfields in Romania. At Casablanca Churchill also met General Ira C. Eaker, commanding the USAAF in Britain. At Arnold's urgent request he had flown out to Casablanca in order to persuade a hitherto sceptical Churchill of the feasibility of the USAAF conducting daylight raids on Germany from England, which in tandem with the RAF's night raids would enable a round-the-clock bombing offensive. Following the meeting, Churchill withdrew his objections to the American plan and his request that the USAAF join the RAF in night bombing.[14]

It took five days of intensive and sometimes difficult debate between the Combined Chiefs of Staff to reach agreement, but eventually the principal argument as earlier outlined by Brooke to Churchill was accepted. The Combined Chiefs' Memorandum, C.C.S. 155/1 'Conduct of the War in 1943', reflected the strategic pull of ongoing essential operations and, in regard to the Mediterranean, of a theatre in which considerable forces and effort had already been invested and which was by now generating a momentum and logic of its own. As a first priority was the need to defeat the U-boats, everything as always depended upon this. The Allies were to maintain the maximum possible supplies to the USSR by convoys. Their offensive effort, however, would be in the Mediterranean with an invasion of Sicily, the declared objectives of which were to secure the Mediter-

ranean lines of communication, divert German effort from the Eastern
Front and intensify pressure upon Italy. The strategic bombing offensive
against Germany would also intensify, while the 'strongest possible force'
would be built up in Britain to be held 'in constant readiness to re-enter
the continent as soon as German resistance is weakened to the required
extent'. In the Far East and Pacific, operations were to continue with the
forces allocated in order to maintain pressure upon Japan and to regain the
initiative.[15]

The military professionals were reasonably content with 'Symbol'. The
British Chiefs of Staff had achieved their objectives, though like Churchill
they would have been happier if more assurance could have been obtained
from their American counterparts as to exploiting Mediterranean opportunities after a successful invasion of Sicily. This was impossible, as beyond
'Husky' the Americans would not look. Indeed, from their perspective a
successful invasion of Sicily appeared a logical cut-off for Mediterranean
operations. It offered solid gains, of which they allowed themselves to be
persuaded, but they were not inclined to look favourably at what could
only be the logical steps onward from 'Husky' in the Mediterranean – a
campaign on mainland Italy or the Balkans.

Churchill and Roosevelt were unconvinced that invading Sicily was a
substantial enough operation against the Axis when set against the scale of
the Soviet effort, and they would be receptive to increased efforts in 1943.
They were locked into the strategic straitjacket of ongoing campaigns and
their drain on time and resources, shipping constraints and timelines
required for the planning and preparation for further offensive operations,
but they were not prepared to sit under this passively. While General
Eisenhower was notified that he would be the Allied Supreme Commander for 'Husky', and directed to plan for a July invasion, it was made quite
clear to him that every effort must be made to bring forward the operation
to June. Large-scale action was wanted, and quickly. In the meantime, the
'Symbol' conference ended with an equivocal message of Allied political-
strategic intent.

To a gathering of press representatives and with Churchill at his side,
Roosevelt announced that the Allies would accept nothing but the 'Unconditional Surrender' of Germany, Italy and Japan. Their aim, he made clear,

was not the destruction of the German, Italian and Japanese populations, but 'the destruction of the philosophies in those countries which are based on conquest and the subjugation of other peoples'. This avowal of Allied commitment to prosecute the war to the fullest extent was aimed not least at Stalin. In this it was timely, for as evidence has subsequently revealed, the Soviets were in this period keeping their own options open and were engaged in moves towards the Nazi leadership to sound out the possibility of a separate peace.[16]

'Unconditional Surrender' may not have demonstrated Allied commitment to the same extent as landing armies in France would have done, but there could be no doubting the extent to which at the political-strategic level it tied the hands of Churchill and Roosevelt and their governments. They were both far too politically experienced and astute not to realize this, and in the case of Germany and Japan they accepted it. The potential benefits from the signal given by 'Unconditional Surrender' were significant. It imparted a sense of moral crusade to the war and its sacrifices to their own populations. Stalin could hardly thereafter question British and American resolve, while his Allies' avowal of 'Unconditional Surrender' made far less attractive, and far more difficult to justify, any Soviet attempt to reach terms with Hitler. To the subject peoples enduring Axis occupation it offered hope; and to the peoples of Japan and Germany it signalled the grim determination of their enemies to dispose of the leaders who had led them into the catastrophe of war. And in this latter lay the problem. For while a successful German revolt against Hitler, or a decisive swing within Japan against those in power committed to the war policy, were hardly conceivable near-term possibilities, this was not so in Italy. Indeed, the thrust of Allied strategy in the Mediterranean, and one of its principal justifications, was to promote a collapse within Italy where the overthrow of Mussolini was known to be feasible.

Both Roosevelt and Churchill had originally doubted the wisdom of including Italy in 'Unconditional Surrender' because it might compromise the chance of separating Italy from the Axis; that it might send precisely the wrong signal to, and undermine the efforts of, those Italians in a position to act. Churchill put this point to his War Cabinet from Casablanca by telegram, but received the unequivocal reply in favour of the declaration, and that there could be no exceptions: it must apply to all the Axis powers without distinction.[17] In effect, Churchill and Roosevelt had to accept that crusades did not allow exceptions, and in the wider interest of Allied unity and commitment to the war the British and American governments would effectively limit their own options with regard to Italy. It is conjecture to suggest that had the Allies made a distinction in the case of Italy this might have seriously embarrassed the Mussolini regime and greatly encouraged its opponents in Italy, perhaps enabling a more coordinated Italian action when the final split in the Axis came. What is certain is that including Italy within 'Unconditional Surrender' at least risked the Allies being unable to fully exploit the effects of the very strategy they were pursuing in the Mediterranean. Later there would be complications.

In the interest of ensuring agreement, 'Symbol' postponed the decision on what in the Mediterranean should follow an invasion of Sicily. By May 1943, with the impending end of the Tunisian campaign, such a decision was urgently necessary, indeed overdue. Churchill pushed for a further high-level meeting with Roosevelt, who agreed, and this was held in Washington during 12–25 May 1943, the 'Trident' Conference. Point was given to the urgency of a decision, in terms of planning and preparation, when at the opening of the conference General Alexander's signal arrived announcing the victorious conclusion to the Tunisian campaign. By the time of 'Trident' it was quite clear where Allied strategy in the Mediterranean was headed: since the 'Torch' decision, its self-generating logic and momentum had been inexorable, and after Sicily it could only be the Italian mainland or the Balkans, or both. These, the American military were now determined to resist. They had strong reasons for doing so. Marshall was appalled by the fact that the Americans in the Mediterranean by now totaled some 388,000 men and 37 Combat Air Groups, a force achieved at the expense of 'Bolero', whereas there were no more than 59,000 American troops in Britain. If there was to be the remotest chance of a direct line of attack across the Channel in 1944 this trend had to be reversed, and quickly. Moreover, the American Joint Planning Staff, in assessing the availability of American manpower for total war commitments, arrived at a suggested total of 100 divisions (some 8¼ million men) for the US Army in 1943 and 1944, a considerably revised figure from the

334 divisions that had been mooted in late 1942. This gave urgency to concentrating effort where it mattered; Marshall's concerns since late 1941 about the likely calls upon American manpower and the need for a clear strategic focus were fast being vindicated. The projected peaking of American mobilization and war production in 1944 demanded the earliest possible defeat of Germany in order to be able to concentrate against Japan. The US Joint Chiefs, while prepared to consider exploiting 'Husky' in the Mediterranean, were only willing to do so with a reduced scale of effort. They would not compromise the cross-Channel offensive in 1944; the Mediterranean would be clearly subsidiary.[18]

Churchill deployed all his eloquence and the British Chiefs of Staff their arguments for the advantages of 'the great prize' of knocking Italy out of the war, the principal ones being the German difficulty of holding their front in the USSR while trying to hold the Balkans. It was a strong case, and a very great deal had already been invested by both the British and Americans in the Mediterranean; too much for them not to benefit from its eventual returns. Yet the case was no longer such as would be allowed by the Americans to undermine 'Overlord'. British arguments that Mediterranean operations prepared the way for, and were therefore directly linked to, 'Overlord' by weakening the Germans were not altogether convincing to the Americans. In any case, if such operations were pursued to the extent that they absorbed resources, it could only be at the expense of the forces needed for 'Overlord', and the cross-Channel attack was itself too risky an enterprise to have anything less than absolute first call on resources. There could be no gainsaying this. The balance in Allied strategy-making had now swung to the Americans.

After a fortnight's debate, the British gained agreement to exploit what was possible from Allied efforts thus far and those forthcoming in the Mediterranean. General Eisenhower was directed 'to mount such operations in exploitation of "Husky" as are best calculated to eliminate Italy from the war and to contain the maximum number of German forces'. Nevertheless, he would do so with reduced forces, for seven experienced Allied divisions, four American and three British, and considerable shipping and air power would be withdrawn from the Mediterranean for 'Overlord'. 'Trident' saw a timely and rigorous stock-taking by the Allies of their resources. For operations in the Mediterranean subsequent to 'Husky' the Allies would have a total of 27 divisions; nineteen British or British-controlled, four American and four French.[19] Moreover, each specific operation Eisenhower proposed would be subject to the approval of the Combined Chiefs. 'Trident' gave no commitment to land in mainland Italy after 'Husky' – no firm decision about Italy at all.

To rectify this, Churchill with Roosevelt's endorsement, flew to Eisenhower's headquarters in Algiers. With him went Brooke and, released by Roosevelt at Churchill's urging, a somewhat reluctant Marshall. In a number of meetings from 29 May to 4 June with Eisenhower and his senior commanders Churchill strongly urged that 'Husky' be exploited by landings on the Italian mainland. Eisenhower was favourable to the possibility of a rapid exploitation of 'Husky', a 'rush into' southern Italy, gaining the port of Naples and the airfields around Foggia, but Marshall would not commit himself. While not opposing such plans, he insisted that a final decision wait upon the success of the forthcoming invasion of Sicily. It was the best Churchill could get, indeed the most he could reasonably have expected following the 'Trident' agreement. 'I felt that great advances had been made in our discussions', he later wrote, 'and that everybody wanted to go for Italy.'[20]

That Allied forces would land in mainland Italy following the securing of Sicily was virtually assured. So was the fact that such landings would have to be carried out by limited forces, appropriate for a 'rush into' Italy against little opposition but not for an invasion against a strong defence. Moreover, rapid exploitation from Sicily indicated landings in the south of Italy, all very well for an advance in the wake of a retreating enemy, but if that enemy stood his ground then the Allies would be fighting their way up the peninsula against the 'grain' of the country, with its mountainous terrain against them. This was hardly the type of campaign to mount on the shoestring of resources decided during 'Trident'. Marshall's caution was well-founded: there were many uncertainties ahead. What awaited any Allied forces landed in mainland Italy, no one could as yet tell. That would be for Hitler to decide. In the meantime was 'Husky'.

2

'HUSKY':
COMMANDERS AND CONTROVERSY

'Husky' was an amphibious invasion on an unprecedented scale. In terms of geographical setting, terrain configuration, the necessary coordination of air, land and sea forces and in the factoring-in of considerations that determined planning options, the problem posed by 'Husky' was immense. There was very little experience within the memory of the serving generation that touched upon it, and a good deal of what there was emphasized the considerable risks inherent in such operations. Events on the Gallipoli Peninsula in 1915–16 were still close enough in time to exercise the minds of those British and American planners aware of them, and they gave small cause for comfort. The recent bloody shambles of the Dieppe raid gave even less. Neither 'Torch', nor the American landings at Guadalcanal in the Pacific in August 1942, was comparable in nature to 'Husky', and in neither case had the landing force met strong initial opposition. Sicily, in addition to its own unique characteristics as a military problem, was also Axis homeland territory, the first the Allies would invade. It was reasonable to expect that the Italians might fight hard in the defence of their territory. The sort of reaction to be expected from a German presence on the island, especially if it were one of some strength, no one could doubt.

Shortly before the 'Symbol' conference at Casablanca the British Joint Planners set down to tackle the 'Husky' problem. It meant an invasion of the largest island in the Mediterranean, separated from mainland Italy only by the Strait of Messina, some two miles wide, but distant from North Africa and Malta by 90 miles and 55 miles respectively.[1] At the time of the Casablanca conference, during the course of which an outline 'Husky' plan was completed for the Allied Combined Chiefs of Staff under time pressure, there were few certainties upon which the planners could build. There was no immediate prospect of an end to the campaign in North Africa, no certainty as to what forces would eventually be released for 'Husky', no guidance as to how the invasion would relate to subsequent operations. Above all, there could be no confidence about the likely pres-ence of German formations on the island, their strength or dispositions. This question of the German element in an Axis defence of Sicily would torment Allied planners considerably during the early months of 1943.

Inevitably the outline plan produced for the Combined Chiefs hinged upon known certainties and reflected a theoretical interpretation of the 'Husky' problem. The logic that emerged was sound, but it had no valid-ation against such practical factors as the conditions imposed by terrain and weather and how they were likely to influence the fighting on the island; nor could the plan offer detailed guidance on how the campaign should develop subsequent to the landings. The known certainties were distances to Sicily from Allied embarkation ports and airfields, the combat radius of Allied single-engine fighter aircraft and their duration over Sicily when flying from their airfields in North Africa and Malta, the logistic needs of an invasion force, and the number and location of ports and air-fields on Sicily.

Given that a single army division required some 500 tons of supplies daily, and an air force squadron some 30 tons, it was imperative that suf-ficient port capacity be secured quickly in order to ensure the supply and build-up of the invasion force. Sicily offered four ports known to be capable of handling 1,000 tons or more daily; Messina (5,000), Palermo (2,500), Catania (1,800) and Syracuse (1,000).[2] Their location, in theory, allowed for Palermo, along with the minor ports of Marsala and Trapani, in the west of the island to supply half the invasion force while Syracuse and Catania, along with Augusta, in the east supplied the other. Smaller harbours could be utilized to help supply the forces in their immediate vicinity. Logistics therefore drove the requirement for landings in both the west and east of the island, which in turn dovetailed with the likely North African embarkation zones of the bulk of the invasion force. American formations sailing from Algeria and Morocco logically constituted the western force that could be directed upon an early capture of Palermo; the British sailing from Egypt, Libya and Tunisia could form the eastern force directed upon Catania as an early objective.[3]

Mindful of the Dieppe experience and its severe warning against attack-ing a defended port head-on from the sea, the planners ruled out direct seaborne assaults upon the main Sicilian ports because of their defences. There was also the air to be factored in. Sicily lay at the extreme range of Allied single-engine fighters whose pilots would be flying from airfields in Malta and North Africa; their time over the island would be limited, and they would be anxiously watching their fuel gauges throughout. Palermo, Catania and Messina were effectively beyond their range, and in any case the latter lay in the strongest Axis defence zone on the island, covering the vital communications artery with mainland Italy, the Strait. Any Allied landing here logically required a complementary landing across the Strait in Calabria to isolate the Axis forces on Sicily, but apart from the strength of the defences this meant an invasion of mainland Italy which lay quite beyond the planners' remit. Indeed, this option was never pursued for this reason, and because of the risks involved. The Allied air forces would heavily outnumber the Germans and Italians in the air – indeed Axis air strength covering Sicily, Sardinia, Pantelleria and southern Italy was estimated at only some 1,560 combat aircraft (810 German) – but there could be no doubting that initially the Allied air forces would be disadvantaged by distance.[4] This might enable the Axis air forces to pose a significant threat to the invasion shipping and landing forces. Planning had to take this threat very seriously indeed.

The air factor demanded that the landing forces relieve the distance problem for the Allied air forces by the earliest possible capture of the Sicilian airfields. This would ensure the air superiority necessary to protect the invasion shipping and enable an increase in air support. The airfields were clustered in three groups, all about fifteen miles inland: in the east around Gerbini, the south-east at Ponte Olivo and Comiso, and in the west at Castelvetrano, Milo and Palermo. Only Castelvetrano for the Americans, and Ponte Olivo and Comiso for the British, looked to be feasible early landing objectives, though in the British case only with a widely extended landing front. The ruling-out of direct assaults on ports, added to the need to secure airfields for the rapid fly-in of Allied squadrons and the availability of shipping, indicated staged landings for both the eastern and western forces. In the first they would establish themselves ashore and capture airfields from which Allied fighters, having flown in, could operate in support of the next phase, the capture of the ports.[5]

The plan projected widely dispersed seaborne landings, all of limited strength, staged over three days and dependent upon a tight schedule of shipping availability and timings. It envisaged simultaneous landings by the eastern and western task forces, the British landing three divisions on D-Day in the south-east to capture Syracuse and Augusta and the nearby airfields. The Americans would land a division at Sciacca to capture the airfields there in preparation for a landing by two divisions on D+2 near Palermo to seize the port and airfields and link up with the Sciacca force. On D+3 the British would strike towards Catania with a further infantry division, an airborne division and a brigade group. Further reserves would follow through Catania and Palermo once captured. The plan envisaged a total Allied force of some ten divisions with supporting arms, necessary to overcome an Italian garrison of eight divisions, but which could be reinforced by a further five divisions before D-Day, two or three of which might be German.[6] There was also the potential for the Axis forces to be reinforced through Messina at the estimated rate of one-and-a-half divisions per week once the invasion was under way, so the Allies needed to conclude the campaign as rapidly as possible to deny the Axis opportunity to build-up on the island and impose an attrition deadlock. Their options determined by logistic and air factors, and working very much in a vacuum clouded by strategic and operational uncertainties, the Joint Planners were well aware of the risks inherent in their plan. They warned the Combined Chiefs that 'Husky' would be a doubtful proposition against a garrison which included battle-ready German formations, and at this no one demurred.

General Eisenhower, already the Allied Commander-in-Chief in the Mediterranean, was notified of his appointment as Supreme Commander for 'Husky' shortly after the Casablanca conference. His directive from the Combined Chiefs of Staff was to set up the necessary operational and administrative staffs and plan for a target date in July when the darkness still offered sufficient moonlight to assist an amphibious operation. If at all possible, he was to bring forward 'Husky' to a similar moon period in June, though on this score the ongoing campaign in Tunisia gave little cause for optimism. With the directive came the outline 'Husky' plan produced for the Combined Chiefs, which was inherited by the British-American planning staff set up at Eisenhower's Allied Force Headquarters (AFHQ) in Algiers.[7] Known as 'Force 141', this was headed by Major General C. H. Gairdner as Chief of Staff, posted in from Field Marshal Sir Archibald Wavell's command in India.

In the operational planning of 'Husky' the Allies were about to encounter some serious problems. The most fundamental was that the planning and execution of a major operation was entrusted – though imposed upon might state it better – to an in-theatre command team whose members had no time to spare to consider it closely. Yet the 'Husky' concept as it stood in early 1943 needed close scrutiny, and it needed it urgently if this massive enterprise were to be carried out in July. The campaign in Tunisia was proving to be hard-fought and militarily frustrating, as the Allies struggled to overcome not only an increasingly desperate enemy and difficult terrain but their own inexperience. The American Army formations in action for the first time against the Axis, and the British First Army, were learning their trade. They were learning it the hard way against troops, not just German but Italian as well, who were adept in attack and stubborn in defence. These Allied formations and their commanders needed careful handling and vigilance if their battle proficiency and confidence was to progress, and this was a burden that fell particularly upon General Sir Harold Alexander, commanding the 18th Army Group. Neither he nor Eisenhower could long take their eyes off the Tunisian battle. That the Allied Commander-in-Chief and his senior land forces commander had their hands full in Tunisia boded ill for 'Husky', as their roles were to be replicated in that operation and Alexander held overall responsibility for its planning. A similar situation existed for the senior Allied naval and air commanders. Admiral Sir Andrew Cunningham and Air Chief Marshal Sir Arthur Tedder both held theatre-wide responsibilities in the Mediterranean in addition to closely watching the air and sea blockade of the Axis in Tunisia, and in Tedder's case particularly the ongoing campaign against Axis air power and coordinating Allied air effort with that of the land and sea forces. The practical result of this situation was that Gairdner and 'Force 141' had the problem so aptly described by General Sir William Jackson as 'absentee landlordism', working for senior commanders who operated from widely dispersed headquarters and who had little time to consider their roles in 'Husky' and who were not on hand to give guidance.[8] Meetings were problematic to arrange, firm decisions hard to secure.[9]

There was also a good deal of potential dissonance within the Allied Mediterranean command structure. At this stage of the war it was the British who possessed the theatre operational command experience. The appointment of Alexander as Eisenhower's deputy had been a deliberate high-level decision pushed by the British for this reason. Eisenhower, as Brooke observed, had been placed where he could deal with political and inter-allied issues, while Alexander handled the military situation.[10] In Tunisia, Eisenhower had to contend with a sometimes fraught British-American relationship. For the most part it concerned the land environment, far less so the air and maritime realms where the professional bonds between British and American airmen and sailors were strong from the start. The campaign saw a good deal of British condescension towards the Americans manifest at various levels, and a sometimes unconscious, and a sometimes not so unconscious, tendency to regard and treat the Americans as junior partners gaining their apprenticeship. This generated considerable resentment. Eisenhower proved his stature as an alliance commander-in-chief by dealing shortly with prejudice and negative attitudes wherever they came from, and Alexander too learned during the campaign to take account of American susceptibilities that had been initially too-little considered in the planning and execution of operations. Nevertheless, sensitivities were raw in the final months in Tunisia and during the run-up to 'Husky', with considerable American determination to no longer play second fiddle and to make sure that they would have the chance to demonstrate just what their Army could do.

This was an undercurrent to a more serious problem which, because of the command set-up, Eisenhower was not well placed to influence. Sitting like the chairman of a board over his senior British land, air, and sea commanders-in-chief, each of whom had considerable command experience and stature, Eisenhower depended upon them to function together smoothly. If they did not, there was little he could do, little authority that he could realistically exert, and over 'Husky' they fell out seriously.[11] It began straightforwardly enough when the senior commanders had the opportunity to look at the Combined Chiefs' outline plan. It struck Alexander as unsound at first sight because of its dispersal of effort and 'penny packet' use of ground forces, both of which had once characterized the employment of British formations in North Africa and which had allowed Rommel to defeat them in detail. He and Montgomery had put a stop to this when assuming their respective commands in Egypt in 1942.[12]

In fact, from the soldier's point of view the plan bore little relation to actual experience gained thus far in fighting the Germans. In denuding the various landing forces of concentrated striking power and leaving them widely dispersed beyond mutual support, the plan also ran counter to the reality of an amphibious operation when viewed from the same perspective. An offensive on land normally begins at maximum power, declining in strength and momentum over time in relation to the resistance it encounters and the losses it sustains, as well as the extent and nature of the ground over which it moves. This is not so with an amphibious operation, which necessarily begins with limited power, determined by the strength of forces and equipment that can be landed from the sea in its initial stages and which is subsequently reinforced as rapidly as the rate of follow-up landings and shipping turn-around allows. An amphibious invasion, if successfully established ashore, still necessarily takes time to attain its full offensive striking power and momentum, and until it does so it is at risk, vulnerable to a determined and strong enemy counterstroke. Widely dispersed and limited-strength landings, the break up of fighting formations into sub-units with reduced battle cohesion and fighting power, all dependent upon a staggered rate of reinforcement in an extended and complex shipping timetable, looked like asking for trouble. Against the Germans it could mean disaster.

Alexander would have preferred both the British and American landings to be concentrated in the south-east of the island, but the planners pointed out that this was logistically impossible. He chose not to overturn the existing 'Husky' plan by pushing his case; in the light of subsequent events this may have been a mistake. Alexander was likely to have secured the support of Tedder and Cunningham once the soldiers' concerns were put to them, instead of which he appears to have stifled his own doubts.

On the other hand, the plan found favour with both the senior airman and
sailor because its emphasis upon seizing airfields promised to counter the
Axis air threat. Certainly no Allied naval commander could lightly accept
the air risk to hundreds of Allied transports, assault ships, supply ships and
warships concentrated off the Sicilian coasts, especially as Tedder's air
forces would be hard put to protect them until some airfields on Sicily
were at their disposal. Cunningham also felt that the plan reflected the
advantage of an amphibious operation in striking at the enemy in unexpected locations and dispersing his strength, the dispersed landings also
reduced the density of shipping concentrations. For his part, Tedder could
not long tolerate the situation whereby his squadrons had to support
'Husky' at the limit of their range. These were, of course, valid concerns
and could not be overlooked; the 'Husky' dilemma in the making was that
these imperatives ran counter to the soldier's imperative of getting ashore
early in concentrated strength. Alexander's input to the plan at this stage
was to do what he could to offset the weakness of the landing forces. He
directed that the airborne units, intended to assist in the capture of inland
airfields, instead be used in more direct support of the seaborne landings,
and he also directed that fighting formations should not be broken up any
more than absolutely necessary.[13] On 13 March Alexander, Cunningham
and Tedder recommended the plan and, in the light of their advice, Eisenhower gave his approval.

Alexander, highly experienced and the senior Allied soldier, and his
Commander-in-Chief, also a soldier though not, admittedly, an experienced operational commander, had both let the 'Husky' plan through
without serious questioning of the intended handling of the ground forces.
Alexander had done so with some demur, and almost certainly against his
own better judgement. Yet, while unity and the need to have an agreed plan
in place and in time were both important considerations, the ground fighting aspect of the plan demanded some critical examination and questioning. There remained only two soldiers of sufficient standing to do this, the
designated commanders of the 'Husky' invasion armies. For the Americans (Force 343), this was Lieutenant General George S. Patton; for the
British (Force 545) it was Montgomery. Patton, an experienced armoured
soldier from the First World War and now commanding US II Corps in

Tunisia, did not yet have an authoritative voice in Allied counsels; nor was it in the tradition of the US Army for a commander at that level to challenge an agreed plan. That left 'Monty'. Once having seen the plan, he would have none of it. His Eighth Army would provide the formations of Force 545, the eastern invasion force, and he had no intention of seeing them used in such a way. On the very day the plan was approved, 13 March, Montgomery urgently signalled Alexander that it broke every commonsense rule of practical battle-fighting and should be completely recast.[14] Monty was about to blow the 'Husky' plan to pieces and compel Alexander to take action.

The response to Monty's blast initially amounted to tinkering with the plan, not recasting it. His argument was that the drive from the south on Syracuse would require more strength, an extra division, but this could only be at the expense of the landings at Gela and Licata, also earmarked for a Force 545 division, and this in turn meant foregoing the early capture of the Ponte Olivo airfield group. This was examined at a meeting on 18 March, and the unsatisfactory consequence of 'absentee landlordism' could be seen in that, while Tedder, Cunningham, and Major General C. H. Gairdner of Force 141 were present, the Force 545 case was put by General Sir Miles Dempsey, normally the commander of Eighth Army's XIII Corps but temporarily serving as Monty's Chief of Staff, and the Force 545 naval commander, Admiral Sir Bertram Ramsay. The senior soldiers, Eisenhower, Alexander, and Montgomery, were not there to add their voice or authority – they were fully involved in the forthcoming Mareth Line offensive in Tunisia. Tedder sympathized with the army's need for greater strength to secure Syracuse but pointed out that failure to gain the Ponte Olivo airfields would leave the south-east landings exposed to an unacceptable air risk and that to ensure the success of 'Husky' air superiority had to be secured in the first 48 hours – in effect that the air requirement had priority in time.[15] The 'Husky' commanders were now facing up to the planning dilemma between concentration of force on land and the early capture of airfields. There was no easy solution as to whether the risk should be borne in the initial strength of the landing forces or in the initial securing of air superiority.

When appraised of the situation, Alexander's suggestion was to reallocate the British division earmarked for Gela/Licata to the east coast landings instead, to increase the strength of the Syracuse thrust. An American division detached from Patton could carry out the Gela/Licata landing under Montgomery's command. However, shipping availability meant that no solution in one sector could be found without penalty in another, and in this case the American landings at Sciacca and Marinella would have to be scrapped. This in turn meant no early capture of the Castelvetrano airfield group, needed for the support of the Palermo assault and which, as Patton reasonably pointed out, were as important as those around Ponte Olivo. This drove the further suggestion that the American landings at Palermo should be delayed for several days so that when they went in, they could be supported by aircraft flying from airfields captured by Montgomery in the south-east. The problem with this, as Tedder warned, was that the supporting fighters would then be operating from airfields in the south-east about twice as far away, while the Castelvetrano airfields would also be left, at least temporarily, in enemy hands, posing a threat to the Palermo landing force and shipping.[16]

It looked as though this would have to be the compromise, and the implicit risks accepted. No one was satisfied. Montgomery still lacked the concentration he really desired; Eisenhower was very concerned at the delay to the Palermo landings. So too was Patton, whose operational schedule would be disrupted and whose forces were likely to face greater risk. The air situation pleased neither Tedder nor Cunningham. Unsurprisingly, American conviction that their role in 'Husky' was to be subordinated to Montgomery began to take unshakeable hold. Gairdner and the Force 141 planners had their own concerns, balanced between an awareness of the original plan's limitations and the consequence of later tinkering. The British Chiefs of Staff intervened to allocate an extra British division from North Africa for the south-east landings, but the problem remained that of shipping availability and turn-around. A delay in the Palermo landings until D+5, and the scrapping of the Sciacca/Marinella landings seemed inevitable. On 5 April this amended plan was agreed, and issued by Eisenhower on 10 April, the doubts once again stifled – though not by Montgomery. On 7 April his attempt to secure Alexander's agreement to yet further changes that would give the south-east landings greater concentration met no response. Alexander was too involved with the Tunisian offensive, and Gairdner had departed for London to secure high-level endorsement of the plan. His deputy informed Montgomery that no further changes would be possible if 'Husky' was on for July.[17]

Montgomery was by now concerned about time on his own account. For a July 'Husky' his Eighth Army formations needed soon to be released from the Tunisian battle for their essential preparation, including training for an amphibious assault, re-equipping, the waterproofing of vehicles, and the assimilating of battle casualty replacements into their units. Yet to both Alexander and Eisenhower the release of Eighth Army was unthinkable until the success of the Tunisian offensive and final victory were assured. The battle experience of his army and its undoubted indispensability to the Tunisian battle, and his own standing since his victory at El Alamein, made Montgomery a force to be reckoned with. Nor was it an unreasonable assumption at the time that he and his Eighth Army would be required to play the lead role in 'Husky'. He would not rest content with the existing 'Husky' situation.

In the meantime, Eisenhower had to contend with sharp intervention on 'Husky' from the highest level, and it reflected a potentially dangerous dissonance existing between the in-theatre command and those responsible for the strategic direction of the war. Once agreed at Casablanca, the Allies were committed to 'Husky' – there certainly could be no backing away from it. On 7 April Eisenhower reported to the Combined Chiefs that his planners considered 'Husky' to have little chance of success if there were substantial numbers of well armed and fully organized German troops. He added that he, Alexander and Cunningham concurred with this view, and by 'substantial numbers' was meant more than two German divisions. This was a legitimate military appreciation, for against an amphibious invasion of Sicily and especially one as envisaged in the existing plan, two battle-ready German divisions would be enough to give the soldiers good cause for concern; more than two divisions would constitute a very serious threat. This was no more than a reflection of the original warning issued by the Joint Planners, but under the circumstances Eisenhower's warning was an unwitting bombshell, and the explosion came from Churchill.

On learning of Eisenhower's warning, he sent a furious memorandum to the British Chiefs of Staff condemning 'pusillanimous and defeatist doctrines' and an attitude on the part of Allied commanders that would make them a laughing stock. It was true enough that the Allies could not afford the impression to either friends or foes that the presence of a limited number of German troops was sufficient to stand down a major Allied operation supported by superior sea and air power. It risked giving the Germans a psychological ascendancy that might well compensate for their lack of numbers. Moreover, Churchill was too old a hand at the business of war not to recognize, even from a distance, that something was seriously wrong with 'Husky'. That the Allied in-theatre command team was deeply unhappy about the operation resulted in a palpable aura of pessimism.[18] Something needed to be done. Churchill was particularly sensitive to how Stalin would view what to him would surely appear as British and American dilatoriness and, more seriously, unwillingness to come to grips with the German army. Already the chance of a June 'Husky' was fading as the Tunisian campaign dragged on, now the senior Allied commanders in theatre seemed reluctant to carry it out at all. It had been presented to Stalin as a major Allied effort, an alternative to a Second Front in the West that year. It had as one of its primary objects the assisting of the Soviet Union, for which, to release the necessary shipping, the Soviets were to accept a suspension of their supply convoys. Churchill's frustration was evident in his closing sentence: 'What Stalin would think of this,' he thundered, 'when he has 185 German divisions on his front, I cannot imagine'.[19]

The British Chiefs of Staff and the US Joint Chiefs could read the implications of the warning as well as Churchill, though it was his reaction that prompted their thunderbolts directed at what must have been a surprised Eisenhower and AFHQ. Their messages left Eisenhower in no doubt at all that the tone of the warning he had passed on was unacceptable. The risks associated with 'Husky' were known and accepted, they informed him, and there was no question of the operation being abandoned. They pointed out to him that with the Sicilian coastline defended by mainly Italian troops, and with German strength on the island limited, they considered the chances of success outweighed the risks. The Germans would be unable to counterattack in strength at all points simultaneously, an assessment clearly based on the existing invasion plan.

Eisenhower hastened to repair the damage and allay whatever misconceptions existed at the higher levels of Allied command: 'Husky' would be prosecuted with all the means available, he replied to the Combined Chiefs of Staff. 'There is no thought here', he averred, 'except to carry out our orders to the ultimate of our ability.' It was an incident potentially damaging to the confidence of both the Allied theatre commander and his political and military superiors.[20] But at least Churchill's blast of 8 April had ensured the removal of any lingering doubts there may have been in the Mediterranean theatre about whether 'Husky' was an agreed operation, or an option for discussion.

In the meantime the in-theatre planning approached crisis. Montgomery, in his own frustration at getting sense out of no one, once again turned 'Husky' upside down. In mid-April he was desperately trying to alert Brooke in London to the fact that no single commander was providing direction. He warned on 12 April that unless Alexander and his 18th Army Group, which were immersed in the Tunisian battle, soon got down to 'Husky' the Allies would be in for trouble. Three days later he signalled Brooke that no senior commander was handling 'Husky' and that he could obtain no decision on important matters from anyone.[21] It was not only Montgomery who was concerned. Brooke received a similar warning about the state of the 'Husky' planning from the equally worried British Commander-in-Chief in the Middle East, General Sir Henry Maitland Wilson, who even tentatively suggested that Brooke might wish to 'send someone out there to sort things out'. Brigadier C. J. C. Malony in the British Official History states only that: 'Sir Alan Brooke decided to let things be'.[22] There was little alternative. To have sent out a further senior commander, providing a suitable one could be found, would probably have only exacerbated the already complex and sensitive Mediterranean command set-up. In any case it must have seemed a reasonable expectation that the theatre Supreme Commander, proven in his role since 'Torch', and his highly experienced senior air, land and sea commanders, could agree upon and implement a workable 'Husky' plan. Brooke could have been forgiven for thinking that if they could not, no one could.

As if he and Eisenhower did not have enough trouble, they each at this time had to fend off a quite determined onslaught by the Combined

Chiefs and Churchill advocating a descent upon Sicily to coincide with the end of the campaign in Tunisia. The idea was to exploit the effect upon Italian morale and also to forestall a German reinforcement of Sicily. But in practical terms the scheme seems to have taken little account of planning, preparation and shipping requirements for an amphibious operation. Eisenhower pointed out that he had as yet only sufficient shipping to carry a single division and only enough assault craft to land the equivalent of an American regimental combat team (or British brigade). With considerable understatement, influenced no doubt by the reaction from the Combined Chiefs to the earlier Force 141 warning, he gave as his opinion that an attack on Sicily by less than two divisions would be 'too great a risk'. There was certainly little reason to suppose that such a coup de main type operation could hope to succeed, even if the practicalities of mounting and supporting it by air and sea could be overcome. Brooke's diary for 17 April 1943 recalls his being telephoned at home that evening by Churchill, enthused by a signal from Marshall about the scheme. While Churchill considered it 'a high strategic conception', to Brooke it was 'quite mad and quite impossible' and they had a half hour row over the telephone.[23]

On 19 April Montgomery met Alexander and Eisenhower in Algiers and secured their agreement for part of his Eighth Army Staff to leave Tunisia for Cairo to take over the planning of Force 545. This would be under his regular Chief of Staff, the newly promoted Major General Sir Francis de Guingand. After arriving in Cairo and examining the 'Husky' plan, de Guingand signalled to Montgomery his own concerns about the dispersion of forces, as well as the lack of intelligence about the enemy; he suggested Montgomery should come in person without delay to see the details for himself and discuss the plan with Admiral Ramsay.[24] This Montgomery decided to do, having a few days in hand with an operational pause in Eighth Army's drive in Tunisia. By now, as his biographer has observed, he was under the impression that he had been delegated authority by Alexander and Eisenhower to run the planning of 'Husky' or at least that of the south-eastern sector of the invasion.[25]

Montgomery could hardly disregard the reservations about 'Husky' now being voiced by his own Chief of Staff and corps commanders as they gained sight of the plan. The proposed weak and dispersed landings on

Sicily were completely contrary to Eighth Army's tried and tested battle methods. They were also well out of tune with the tough and desperate fighting that Eighth Army was coming up against in Tunisia, not only from German but also now from Italian troops. In this latter respect the Wadi Akarit battle in early April had been an eye-opener, with Italian troops turning in a battle performance that shook whatever complacent attitudes Eighth Army had about them. The obvious implication was that if they could fight as tenaciously as this to hold a position in Tunisia, they would certainly do so to defend Sicily. To assume otherwise would have been militarily irresponsible. Montgomery took matters into his own hands. On 24 April he signalled Alexander what amounted to an ultimatum, telling him that he was prepared to carry the war into Sicily with Eighth Army but must do so in his own way. This meant the way he had been employing Eighth Army successfully since he became its Commander, concentrating its striking power for the maximum offensive blows calculated to overwhelm any opposition. Eighth Army may not have been at its best when called upon for a rapid and mobile exploitation, as Rommel's slipping away after El Alamein indicated, but in the opening stages of that battle, and in the dogged Tunisian fighting still under way, once Eighth Army had teed itself up for set-piece attack it had proved itself unstoppable. This was precisely what Montgomery wanted in order to establish his lodgement on Sicily and ensure his progress inland. His corps and divisions must land in mutual support, with the maximum naval and air support concentrated for their assault. In practical terms, this meant landings focused on the beaches near Avola and Pachino to the south of Syracuse, and forgoing the proposed landings at Pozallo and Gela. This ruled out the early capture of the airfields around Ponte Olivo and Comiso. Montgomery emphasized the importance of securing the initial lodgement against what he believed would be fierce enemy resistance and a 'prolonged dogfight' battle, of a type Eighth Army's methods were designed to win, following the initial assault landings.

He had, he signalled Alexander, ordered his planners to proceed on these lines and that Admiral Ramsay was 'in complete agreement'. Ramsay did agree, though had been initially reluctant to have this quoted in the telegram, suspecting with good reason how this would be viewed by his naval superior, Cunningham. Montgomery also insisted that the air plan 'should provide close and intimate support for the Eighth Army battle', adding that he must have Air Vice Marshal Sir Harry Broadhurst, commander of the RAF Desert Air Force, 'and his experienced squadrons'. Montgomery had good working relationships with Ramsay and Broadhurst, and the Desert Air Force had become a close partner in Eighth Army operations. Nevertheless, referring to Ramsay and Broadhurst in this way spared little thought for the command protocols as they would be viewed by Cunningham and Tedder, let alone the wider issue of how Montgomery's action would impact on the entire 'Husky' plan. He had presented Alexander with a fait accompli, and the fact that Eighth Army was now working to a completely different 'Husky' plan from everyone else.[26] Montgomery had effectively subordinated 'Husky' as an Eighth Army operation.

Alexander was not the man to take a hard line with Montgomery and order him to adhere to the plan agreed on 5 April. As his military biographer has written, 'Among all his many virtues, Alexander did not possess the iron of a ruthless commander.'[27] Besides, Montgomery, fêted as a British national hero following his victory at El Alamein, was in an unassailable position. His name was synonymous with Eighth Army – to remove him from its command was unthinkable – and in any case it would have taken a decision at the highest level to do so. It would also have been the only alternative, for it seems unlikely in the extreme that Montgomery could ever have been brought to agree to a plan he was convinced would fail. He unequivocally warned Alexander that to go ahead with the dispersed plan, which in his opinion – erroneous as it happened – could only have been based on an assumption of slight Axis opposition, would 'land the Allied Nations in a first class military disaster'.

Alexander could hardly have failed to have been in sympathy with Montgomery's solution; it too closely mirrored his own earlier suggestion of February. In fact he had got there before Montgomery but had not insisted upon a revision of the ground force role; the gentlemanly diffidence within Alexander's personality was doing his own military experience and judgement little justice, and it cannot have been lost on other Allied senior commanders that Montgomery was now showing him scant respect. Had Alexander stuck to his own guns in February he might well have achieved a revised 'Husky' plan by bringing Tedder and Cunningham fully on board with him and ready to back a plan in which they had contributed as a team. He certainly would not have antagonised them as Montgomery had now managed to do. When Tedder and Cunningham had sight of Montgomery's signal, the result was a planning deadlock, for they would not agree. Montgomery's high-handedness in overturning the agreed plan and his presumption with regard to naval and air command seniority hardly produced an atmosphere in which Tedder and Cunningham were disposed to consider Montgomery's plan dispassionately and in a team spirit.[28] In any case, they were opposed to his concept.

Alexander convened a meeting in Algiers on 29 April in an attempt to reach agreement. Neither Montgomery, now ill with tonsillitis, nor de Guingand, concussed as a result of the plane intended to fly him there having forced-landed, could attend. Instead, General Sir Oliver Leese, XXX Corps commander, was sent at short notice to present Eighth Army's case. No transport awaited him on arrival at the airfield in Algiers, and he had to hitch a ride on a truck to reach a lions' den of very senior officers, few of whom were feeling well disposed towards his Army Commander. Alexander was prepared to accept Montgomery's plan from the land perspective, but this meant little; although it was the soldiers who had to go in and win the land battle on the island there could be no ignoring the fact that 'Husky' would be a major inter-service and inter-Allied operation. Tedder made this clear by his reminder that the land part of the eastern landings could not be considered unrelated to air and naval aspects, or to the operations of the western (American) Task Force; Cunningham rejected the plan because it looked to attack Sicily at one of its most strongly defended points. But the real problem remained the air threat. Concentrated landings demanded concentrated shipping, and without the capture or neutralization of the Axis airfields the risk to the ships offshore was to him unacceptable. This was Tedder's province, and he made his rejection equally clear. With thirteen Axis airfields left in enemy hands, the task confronting the Allied air forces based on Malta would be impossible, besides which the airfields were needed by Allied squadrons from which to support the western Task Force. Patton, remaining mostly on the sidelines of what amounted to a dispute between British commanders, pointed out the wide distance Montgomery's plan would leave between their respective forces and the increased air threat to his own landings when they went in near Palermo.

In fact Montgomery's proposal threatened to make completely unviable the role of the western landing force as it stood in the existing plan. Montgomery was aware of this, but was so far holding his hand on suggestions for the American role in 'Husky'. The meeting broke up without agreement, but with considerable frustration at Alexander's apparent inability, or unwillingness, to take a firm hand. Tedder sent Air Marshal Sir Arthur Coningham, commanding the Allied tactical air forces and who had worked closely with Montgomery in the Western Desert, to accompany Leese on his return to put the counter-argument and find a way out, but Montgomery remained adamant.

Montgomery himself suggested a further high-level meeting, and Eisenhower agreed, for 2 May. Both Eisenhower and his AFHQ Chief of Staff, General Walter Bedell Smith, were by now anxious at the time being lost for detailed planning and preparation. Time was running out if 'Husky' were to take place in July. This time Montgomery turned up, ready with his notes for the meeting and a further proposal, but neither Alexander nor Coningham could reach Algiers, weather in Tunisia grounding their aircraft. Cunningham and Tedder would not agree to a conference without Alexander. Had it not been so serious, the situation would have been farcical. Montgomery went off to find Bedell Smith and encountered him in the AFHQ lavatory, where he gained a hearing for his proposal, albeit in an unorthodox setting. Bedell Smith warned him of the urgent need to reach a decision for 'political reasons', meaning the imperative to launch 'Husky' in July, and Montgomery apparently rejoined that it was 'far more important to do so for military reasons', offering to provide 'the answer to the problem at once'.[29] This was to cancel the American landings near Palermo altogether and instead have the entire western Task Force land in the Gulf of Gela. This would secure the airfields considered vital by Cunningham and Tedder and provide a more cohesive invasion, the British and American Task Forces landing side by side.

Apart from the fact that Bedell Smith and Eisenhower needed a rapid solution to the planning deadlock, Montgomery's proposal fell on fertile ground, as the Palermo landings, delayed in the plan agreed on 5 April, were already viewed with concern. Eisenhower agreed to Montgomery's proposal after discussing it with Alexander on the following day, 3 May. Tedder and Cunningham acquiesced but were still concerned at the number of airfields in the west of Sicily and around Gerbini that would be left initially in Axis hands. Patton came off worst. His Task Force planning for the Palermo landings all went for nothing; his forces in the new plan now had a role mainly supportive to Eighth Army; and his supplies, without securing a major port would have to come through Syracuse in the Eighth Army sector. He was not consulted but loyally stood by Eisenhower's decision without protest. The unfortunate Gairdner of Force 141, also not consulted, found his own position impossible and offered his resignation to Alexander. This was accepted, though Alexander, as Brigadier C. J. C. Malony acknowledges, blamed himself.[30]

Ultimately the importance of a concentrated landing was allowed to outweigh the other considerations. Montgomery had ensured that his Eighth Army would land in maximum strength as the invasion's principal striking force. His methods and personality were far from conducive to coalition warfare, and made him enemies; however, circumstances appear to have given him little choice but to upset the planning apple-cart, especially after Alexander's decision not to challenge the original plan despite his own misgivings as a soldier. If the 'Husky' planning fiasco – this does not seem too strong a word for it – indicates anything beyond its historical context then it is that a joint plan which leaves one of its components deeply unsatisfied and its imperatives sacrificed to those of the other components will ultimately have to be recast, and the sooner the better – for merely to tinker with it will end up satisfying no one. Somewhere there will have to be compromise and certainly risk, but precisely where they should sit within the plan needs to be identified, and agreed as early as possible between those commanders expected to carry out the plan; for this they need an early and very firm grasp upon the planning process.

In this latter respect the ongoing Tunisian campaign, itself at a critical stage, and its consequent demands upon the Allied command team had much to answer for. 'Husky' was the undoubted victim of the campaign in Tunisia, its effects being perhaps a vindication of Hitler's decision to make a stand there. And for 'Husky' there was altogether too much disparate planning going on in too many dispersed locations. Apart from Britain and the United States being centres of planning for the forces that would sail direct from there, there were also disparate headquarters scattered all over the Mediterranean involved in the planning: Algiers (AFHQ), Rabat (Force 343), Cairo (British Middle East Headquarters and Force 545), and operational headquarters for Alexander and Montgomery in Tunisia, as well as separate air and naval headquarters.

Setting hindsight aside and acknowledging that whether the original plan would have worked can only be conjecture, then, despite the air risk worrying Tedder and Cunningham, the final plan looked sounder as an amphibious invasion than one of widely dispersed landings. If simplicity is a virtue in a plan, then it benefited from that too, as Patton himself admitted.[31] It was also better suited to Eighth Army's methods. The reliance up to then placed upon Eighth Army as the main battle-winner in the Tunisian fighting could justify its precedence as the principal striking force in 'Husky'. It would be up to Patton and his soldiers to redress that particular imbalance when the chance occurred in Sicily.

3

'HUSKY': PLANNING
THE ALLIED INVASION OF SICILY

The Allied invasion of Sicily was a successful, but deeply flawed, operation. While there was little to fault in the fighting performance of their naval, air and land forces, the Allies' operational conduct of 'Husky' indicated significant problems. The integrated planning and execution between the various air, land and sea components, and between Allies, necessary to exploit success and to create and exploit opportunities for decisive action, were lacking. While there were tactical-level successes, the command machinery of welding these into a cohesive operational pattern had yet to be perfected. The initial Allied landings established an unshakeable foothold on the island, but soon afterwards the momentum of the Allied campaign broke down. The operational initiative passed to the Germans, who carried the burden of the defence once the principal Italian formations on the island had been spent in battle or had disintegrated. While the German operational cohesion was impressive, tactically their options were restricted to fighting stubborn delaying actions followed by withdrawals. Nevertheless, in the terrain of Sicily this generally allowed them to dictate the pace of the Allied advance, and permitted them to stage a well-planned and executed evacuation of their forces across the Strait of Messina in good order. This the Allies proved unable to prevent, despite their unchallenged superiority at sea and in the air.

The Invasion Plan and Practical Amphibious Planning

The final 'Husky' plan provided for a cohesive and simultaneous amphibious invasion employing formidable combat power. Two of Eighth Army's corps (XIII and XXX) were to land abreast. XIII would land to the south of Syracuse with the 5th Division directed upon Cassibile and then north towards Syracuse and Augusta. The 50th Division was directed on Avola and the high ground dominating the coast road and covering the west and south-west of the beachhead. The landings in this sector would be preceded by an airborne operation in which the 1st Air Landing Brigade in gliders were to capture the Ponte Grande bridge over the River Anapo just to the south of Syracuse, and to deal with coastal gun batteries. XXX Corps would land astride the Pachino Peninsula with the 51st (Highland) Division to capture Pachino while the 1st Canadian Division and 40 and 41 Royal Marine Commandos would secure Pachino airfield. The 231st Infantry Brigade was to cover the right flank and push out towards Avola. The Canadians were to link up with the US II Corps at Ragusa. Held back in Eighth Army reserve were the 46th and 78th Infantry Divisions.

Montgomery's success in securing 'his' plan was marred, and his already strained relations with the other senior Allied commanders further soured, by his suggestion that Eighth Army should run 'Husky' with the US forces, a reinforced corps, under its command. Given that 'Husky' had already become more of a Montgomery-Eighth Army show than anyone had originally envisaged, this was understandably too much for the Americans to swallow. American participation had to have equal status with that of the British in this full-scale Allied operation, and Marshall, following a suggestion from Eisenhower, decided that once landed the US forces would become the US Seventh Army, with Patton therefore elevated to becoming an Army Commander. Both Eighth and Seventh Armies would come under Alexander's overall 15th Army Group Headquarters, which had been organized for the invasion and subsequent campaign.

Seventh Army was to land its II Corps under Lieutenant General Omar Bradley at Gela, while a force based around the US 3rd Infantry Division under Major General Lucian Truscott landed at Licata. II Corps, with the 45th and 1st Infantry Divisions, plus Ranger troops, the equivalent to British Commandos and armour in support, were to land and capture the airfields at Gela, Ponte Olivo, Comiso and Biscari and to make contact with the Canadians in the area of Ragusa and Comiso airfield. Ahead of II Corps landings, the reinforced 505th Regimental Combat Team of the US 82nd Airborne Division would land by parachute to secure the high ground to the east of Ponte Olivo covering the 1st Infantry Division's beaches against counterattack from the east and west. The 3rd Division and two tank regiments of the US 2nd Armored Division were to land and capture the small port of Licata and the airfield nearby. A floating reserve of one regiment of the 1st Infantry Division and the remaining half of the 2nd Armored Division was to be on hand for Seventh Army, but shipping afforded no more. After the initial landing phase, both armies were to push inland, Eighth Army's XIII Corps to capture Catania and XXX Corps to advance on Vizzini, and Seventh Army to a line generally east to west from Vizzini through Mazzarino out towards Agrigento.

'Husky' was an immensely complex amphibious challenge. Cunningham's naval forces had to provide escort and covering protection for the assault and follow-up convoys sailing from their embarkation ports in North and North-West Africa. In addition the US 45th Division sailed direct from the United States on 28 May, to link up with forces sailing from Algiers and Oran; convoys transporting the 1st Canadian Division and British Commando units departed Britain between 20 June and 1 July and would take them direct to their invasion beaches.[1] The number of warships, assault craft and transports involved would total nearly 2,600 and the coordination and timings of naval forces and convoys required a major feat of organisation. Nothing like it had been seen before.

Inevitably there were frustrations for all concerned in the organization and planning, and the staffs of Allied formations and their naval counterparts encountered many problems. Shipping availability remained uncertain to a late stage, and there were complications because among the various formations there was a mix of amphibious landing methods, vessels, and varying levels of amphibious warfare training and experience. With the exception of the 51st (Highland) Division and US 3rd Infantry Division landings, the Allied troops would be landed by the ship-to-shore method, meaning that they would be transferred from ships to landing craft for their final run in to the beaches. Truscott's 3rd Division and the Highlanders were to land shore-to-shore, landing direct from the vessels that had transported them. To confuse matters further, there were different loading procedures in place between those formations that would arrive in theatre direct from the United States and Britain, and those already in theatre. In all cases, equipment, vehicles, and vital supplies had to be assembled, checked, waterproofed if appropriate and loaded according to a correct sequence to ensure they appeared on the beaches where and when needed.

In the weeks leading to the invasion, life was dominated by orders of battle for the assault and loading tables, which to everyone's frustration could change frequently according to short-notice alterations in shipping availability. A British observer from Combined Operations Command, accorded every facility by his American hosts and attached to Truscott's force, saw this frustration, which affected all the Allied forces to varying extent, at first hand. He noted a pattern whereby every decision seemed to depend upon another decision which could not be taken in default of still a third decision that had yet to be taken. The solution he witnessed was time-consuming but necessary: staffs developed alternative sets of plans, one of which would be selected once sufficiently firm data became available.[2]

The early planning by corps and divisional staffs was also bedevilled by lack of data on the assault craft, as yet unseen, such as their capacity for combat-loaded troops and equipment. For example, the British observer with Truscott's force was able to provide his American hosts with some information on American-built equipment about which they knew little, simply because he had recently come out from England.[3] Such data short-falls were not only frustrating; they cost valuable time. A later digest of reports on 'Husky' lamented the lack of exchange of technical information between theatres, and urged that it be made a priority.[4] While there were considerable and largely successful efforts to obtain reliable intelligence upon the nature of the proposed landing beaches and on the strength and dispositions of Axis forces, its dissemination among the assault formations was patchy, and in some cases even confusing. It did not help that in the final weeks of planning the Army and Navy were each presented with separate and quite different sets of beach intelligence; as both adopted the age-old military method of planning for the worst case, no real harm resulted.[5] Rather more serious were such problems as, in Truscott's case, that as late as D–5 (five days before the landings) no one could tell him with any confidence whether he should expect to encounter ten, twenty, thirty or forty thousand Axis troops on D-Day.[6] On the other hand, the US 82nd Airborne Division's 505th Regimental Combat Team tasked with securing the high ground inland of the Gela beaches were deliberately kept in the dark about the known presence of the German Hermann Göring Division near their drop zone: this information had been obtained through

Allied signals intelligence, and there was a risk paratroops might be captured and inadvertently indicate that German operational security had been compromised.[7]

The 'Husky' invasion force would be beach-dependent, not only during the landings but for a considerable time afterwards until ports were captured and functioning. Beaches fully matching the suitability criteria for large-scale landings were hard to find anywhere, and rarely existed where they were needed most, on the stretch of coastline offering swift access to such important objectives. Likely beaches had to be identified, a task requiring extensive aerial photographic reconnaissance. The results of many sorties were then pored over by photo-interpreters trained to identify signs, perhaps only shadows on the print, indicating natural obstacles such as sandbars, and the scale and type of the enemy's defences and fortifications. Then close physical examination of selected beaches would confirm their suitability, a hazardous clandestine task. In the British case this was conducted by Beach Reconnaissance Parties, sometimes termed Combined Operations Pilotage Parties, small joint teams of officers and men of the Royal Navy and Royal Engineers landed at night in collapsible canoes from a submarine. They provided the answers to such questions as whether landing craft would have an unobstructed run right up to the beach, or whether their lowered ramps would still leave a gap of water that troops and vehicles would have to negotiate; whether there were underwater obstacles, natural or contrived by the enemy, that did not show on aerial photographs; and whether the beaches were firm enough for a landing operation.

To land a mechanized army from the sea required beaches accessible from the sea with offshore anchorages deep enough for large vessels, but free of strong tides or currents against which smaller craft could not contend. The beaches had to be wide enough for deployment, and deep enough for the accumulation ashore of troops, artillery, tanks and other vehicles, and stores. Uneven, shifting sands, marshy ground or mudflats would bog down vehicles and heavy equipment. Rock-strewn beaches would hamper and delay movement. Not enough exits and too many cliffs and steep gradients would make it difficult, if not impossible, for the troops and vehicles to get off the beach and advance inland rapidly. This was vital, for the only combat troops of the assault and follow-up waves who could afford to stay on the beach were the dead and wounded. The others had to push on quickly to widen the beachhead, secure the initial inland objectives and, especially, the commanding ground from which to repel likely counterattack. This demanded the earliest possible landing and bringing forward of heavy supporting weapons – artillery, anti-tank guns and tanks. To secure the vital ground inland of the beaches amounted to a race against time and the enemy, for its occupation by the latter would enable them to seal off of the beachhead and dominate it by fire. Only costly attacks would then dislodge them from it. Hence the important role accorded to airborne forces in the initial stages of the invasion.

Aerial reconnaissance photographs and data obtained by clandestine beach reconnaissance did not always immediately provide the answers required by the planners at unit level. To find them required painstaking detective work and logical deduction, the effectiveness of which depended upon the most experienced photo-interpreters able to deduce from the often scanty evidence before them. Such personnel were in short supply and were spread as widely as possible throughout the Allied formations. Two examples indicate their work and its importance, and that luck also played its part. Colonel Darby's US Rangers, trained to a high pitch on the lines of British Commandos and combat experienced from Tunisia, had the specific task of capturing Gela itself. They had no data on whether the beaches adjacent to the town were mined, but a last-minute pre-invasion aerial photo reconnaissance caught fishing boats lying up on the stretch of beach directly in front of the town, a good indication that the boats were in regular use and that the beach was not mined.[8] A similar case occurred with pre-invasion aerial reconnaissance of the British sector. Careful scrutiny of a low-level photograph revealed what appeared to be women bathing on one of the beaches assigned to the 51st (Highland) Division, much to the relief of its Intelligence staff who could at least note that particular beach as mine-free and having no dangerous anti-personnel obstacles.[9]

Confounding Axis Defence: Allied Strategic Deception

Despite the revised plan with concentrated landing strength, the original Joint Planners' warning remained valid. 'Husky' stood little chance if, before it was launched, the Germans turned Sicily into a fortress. While

This photograph taken in Algiers shows the Allied Supreme Commander General Dwight D. Eisenhower and his senior command team for the invasion of Sicily, Operation 'Husky'. From the left in the foreground are Eisenhower, Air Chief Marshal Sir Arthur Tedder, General Sir Harold Alexander and Admiral of the Fleet Sir Andrew Cunningham. In the background from the left are the Hon. Harold Macmillan, Churchill's political representative at Allied Force Headquarters, Brigadier General Walter Bedell Smith, Eisenhower's Chief of Staff, an unidentified naval officer, and Air Vice Marshal Wigglesworth, Senior Air Staff Officer to Tedder. (IWM CNA 1075)

Lieutenant General Sir Bernard Montgomery commanding the British Eighth Army addresses troops at a camp in Malta before Operation 'Husky', the invasion of Sicily. During the planning of 'Husky', Montgomery caused considerable controversy within the Allied Command as a result of his insistence upon concentrated landings; arguably his influence was critical in ensuring a sound plan. (IWM NA 4078)

A photograph taken shortly after dawn on 10 July 1943 – 'D-Day' for Operation 'Husky'. Troops of the 51st (Highland) Division (XXX Corps of Eighth Army) are unloading stores from LCT (Landing Craft Tanks) as beach roads are prepared for vehicles. Initial opposition to the landings was light. (IWM A 1719)

Opposite page, top: The success of Operation 'Husky' depended upon the Allies securing air superiority, a task successfully accomplished by the Allied Air Forces during an intensive air campaign in the weeks leading to the invasion. Once the landings had taken place, the earliest possible fly-in of squadrons to operate from the island was also essential to ensure air support for the invasion force. Here the first RAF Spitfire to land on the island approaches an improvised airstrip cut out of a wheat field, watched by Sicilian farmers. (IWM CNA 1098)

Above: In the difficult terrain of Sicily Allied troops made much use of improvised transport to support their advance and maintain supplies. Mule teams proved of vital importance, especially in the mountains, and there were never enough of them. Here a British mule team passes through the rubble-strewn street of Adrano, devastated by bombardment, in August 1943. (IWM NA 5782)

Left: In early August 1943, the 38th (Irish) Brigade of the British 78th Division captured the mountaintop town of Centuripe, stubbornly defended by German paratroops, in a remarkable feat of climbing and fighting, earning fulsome praise from Montgomery. Here troops of the 6th Royal Inniskilling Fusiliers search houses in the town during mopping-up operations. The solid stone buildings and narrow streets indicate just how formidable such towns could be when turned into a defensive zone held by determined troops. (IWM NA 5388)

Opposite page, top: Strong and stubborn German defence positions barred Eighth Army's advance towards the port city of Catania and defied its attacks throughout July in some of the heaviest and costliest fighting on Sicily. The city was not taken until 5 August, when this photograph was taken of British infantry scrambling over the rubble of one of its devastated streets. Catania, like many other towns in Sicily, was subjected to heavy Allied bombing. However, as the German defence zones were rarely in the towns themselves, the bombing was of only limited assistance to the attacking Allied troops. (IWM NA 5335)

Opposite page, bottom: This photograph was taken on 3 September 1943, the day when Eighth Army crossed the Straits of Messina from Sicily to land on the Italian mainland. C Company, 2nd Battalion, The Northamptonshire Regiment, part of the 17th Infantry Brigade of the British Fifth Division in XIII Corps, are shown waiting on the quayside at Catania to embark on the landing craft that will take them to Italy. Note the kit carried by the infantrymen and the nearest platoon's Bren light machine-gun on the Quay. The photograph also imparts a sense of the scale of amphibious assault shipping necessary to support a landing operation and upon which Allied strategy in the Mediterranean depended. (IWM NA 6284)

Above: The beach activity following an amphibious landing is evident in this photograph taken on the morning of Operation 'Avalanche', the landing at Salerno by the British X and US VI Corps of Lieutenant General Mark Clark's Fifth Army on 9 September 1943. Taken from the deck of a Landing Craft (most probably an LCT), the photograph shows a DUKW amphibious vehicle loaded with stores driving on to the beach. The availability of the DUKW considerably eased the problem of ship-to-shore transporting of supplies during Allied amphibious operations. (IWM NA 6636)

A patrol of American Rangers advancing uphill under the cover of smoke in the mountains near Naples in September 1943. Rangers, along with their British allied counterpart, played an important part in securing and retaining high ground covering the Salerno beachhead. (IWM NA 6999)

the Allied offensive strategy in the Mediterranean was intended to assist the USSR by drawing German strength to the south, the Allies had to ensure that such strength was not sent to Sicily. That meant Hitler and the OKW had to be persuaded to send it somewhere else, and to achieve this required an elaborate and highly credible deception operation.

The credibility challenge was formidable. Sicily might well look from the Axis perspective to be the obvious next choice after North Africa, especially as the Allied securing of their sea communications would logically demand its capture. The Allies could offset this obviousness by exploiting the fact that Sicily was only one part of a very much wider strategic whole that Hitler needed to defend – always the importance of the Balkans and its vital oil, chrome, bauxite and copper figured highly in his calculations. 'A' Force, the Allied deception organization in the Mediterranean whose main controlling headquarters was in Cairo but which had an advanced headquarters at Eisenhower's AFHQ and a tactical headquarters with Alexander's Army Group, faced the task of exploiting this and diverting attention away from Sicily.

To support 'Husky', the 'A' Force planners were able to build upon two existing and successful deception schemes in place since the autumn of 1942 and the beginning of 1943, Operations 'Warehouse' and 'Withstand'. These, intended to fix German and Italian forces in Greece and the Balkans and prevent the further reinforcement of Tunisia, raised Axis fears of an imminent Allied invasion of Crete and the Dodecanese Islands. The judicious planting of rumours by agents, the evidence of amphibious forces located in Cyprus and eastern Mediterranean ports, the manoeuvrings of British armoured units in Syria within striking distance of the Turkish border, and the wide deployment of dummy tanks and vehicles to give a false impression of strength – all were intended to play upon Axis sensitivity to the Balkans. Further credibility was lent to these operations because it was known that the Allies were keen to induce Turkey to join them as a belligerent. Thus 'A' Force could convincingly blend the actual facts known to the enemy with fiction to create a successful deception. Throughout the early months of 1943 the Allies were able to monitor through their signals intelligence the extent to which their schemes were deceiving Axis appreciations.

Most important was that they managed to feed the Axis a completely inflated Allied order of battle for the Mediterranean. Had German and Italian intelligence sources possessed a more accurate picture of Allied strength, particularly in shipping, which they knew was limited, they would have been far more discerning and hard to convince. With the decision taken to invade Sicily, 'A' Force developed and put into effect Operation 'Barclay'. This was intended to heighten by similar methods Axis fears for the Balkans by indicating it as the Allied Second Front for 1943. This was a logical and believable strategy. It was depicted by the fictional British Twelfth Army in Egypt poised to invade Greece in the early summer; Turkey was to be brought into the Allied camp and an offensive opened against the Axis in Bulgaria, linking up with the Red Army advancing from the southern USSR. A diversionary attack would go in against Crete, while further diversionary operations to fix German strength were to be made against both northern and southern France, the latter under the command of General Alexander and involving the British Eighth Army. An American attack would go in against Corsica and Sardinia under the command of General Patton. The Allies had decided to bypass Sicily and mainland Italy, which would be the target of a heavy bombing campaign, for which the Allied Mediterranean air forces were being heavily reinforced. This entire deception scheme was intended to convince the Axis that the Allies had firmly rejected an invasion of Sicily, and of mainland Italy with its risk of a 'laborious advance through the mountainous terrain' with 'the formidable barrier of the Alps at the far end' – rather ironic in light of later events.[10]

This scheme had sufficient credibility to make the Germans and Italians at least question the obviousness of Sicily. Most importantly, it ensured that the arguments of those within the Axis command who were convinced that Sicily was the next Allied objective would not be able to prevail over competing claims for reinforcement. A further move consolidated the veracity of the picture the Axis were being encouraged to piece together and was ingeniously calculated to make the Germans believe that they had achieved an intelligence coup. Operation 'Mincemeat' involved the deliberate planting by British submarine, on 30 April, of a body off the Spanish coast purporting to be that of a major in the Royal Marines killed in an air crash while carrying important documents as a high-level courier. These documents were in a briefcase attached to the body, and there were also personal items giving life and individuality to an entirely fictitious man. All had been meticulously fabricated. The documents indicated that the Allies would land in Greece and Sardinia, and evidence pointing to Sicily was only part of a cover plan. As expected, when the body was discovered by the Spanish the documents were copied and passed to German Intelligence (the Abwehr), who forwarded them upwards through appropriate channels in the direction of Hitler and the OKW, with the view that they were genuine. This was accepted. That the body and the documents might be a 'plant' was, of course, considered but rejected, not least because they offered further confirmation of what was already suspected. 'Mincemeat' was a successful deception because it induced German intelligence to believe not only that it had been *lucky*, but that it had also been *clever*. They had found another piece of the jigsaw, and it fitted well. [11]

Between them 'Barclay' and 'Mincemeat' ensured that whatever German forces could be found to reinforce the Axis southern flank went to the Balkans. In March 1943 there were eight German divisions there, but by July there were eighteen, with the number in Greece increased from a single division to eight. Two divisions were sent to reinforce Sardinia and Corsica.[12] Luftwaffe strength was also stepped up, with fighter, bomber and dive-bomber units sent to the Balkans, mainland Italy, Sardinia and Sicily. The German ground strength on Sicily remained comparatively meager: two divisions at less than full strength; the Hermann Göring Panzer Division, a reconstituted Luftwaffe field formation (the original of which had been lost in Tunisia), and the 15th Panzer Division, later redesignated as a panzer grenadier division. This was despite Kesselring, in his capacity of Commander-in-Chief South, believing that Sicily was a likely Allied objective, a view shared by General Vittorio Ambrosio the Italian Armed Forces Chief of Staff and even by Mussolini himself. Another factor, which fitted well enough with the view that the Balkans were under the greatest threat, was the reluctance of Hitler and the OKW to commit forces to Sicily and southern Italy. They would be dependent upon long and vulnerable lines of communication to the north, and in the event of an Italian collapse and defection might prove difficult or even impossible to extricate.[13]

Sicily: The Axis Defence and its Dilemmas

In July 1943, therefore, Sicily was very far from being the German-dominated fortress feared initially in Allied planning. The picture of the Axis defence obtained by various Allied intelligence sources was in general an accurate one. 'Ultra' indicated the size of the German garrison through intercepts of a signal in May detailing proposals for a supply base and the rations and fuel it would contain, and one in June from OKW to Kesselring making reference to two 'two-part striking groups' being adequate for the island's defence.[14] Precisely how these formations were likely to be used in coordination with the Italian forces on the island could not be known with certainty. In fact, the problem of how to defend against amphibious invasion was a difficult one for the Germans and Italians to solve.

Following the loss of North Africa, senior Italian and German commanders knew very well that Allied superiority at sea and in the air meant they could land where they chose in the Mediterranean. Their invasion forces at sea might be harassed by air attack, and possibly by submarines and light surface craft, but they could not be stopped. The Italian fleet was unlikely to risk a major action. Therefore the Germans and Italians were reliant upon their ground forces to defeat an invasion, and their opportunity could only come with the landings themselves. They had little experience to guide their planning of how to make the best use of this opportunity, and what they had, in some critical respects, they misinterpreted. General Fridolin von Senger und Etterlin, the German liaison officer with the Italian Sixth Army on Sicily, later recalled that German senior commanders, Kesselring among them, set too much store by the successful repulse of the Dieppe raid. They failed to appreciate the flexibility and firepower advantages that air and naval superiority gave the Allies, and consequently they underestimated the chances of a successful landing.[15]

Dieppe suggested that a landing could be destroyed at the water's edge, by maximum firepower brought to bear against the landing craft and assault troops before they were established ashore. But it was a flawed model upon which to base assumptions and planning. Dieppe was a raid, albeit in force, confined in time and space and in which the landing force had attacked a reasonably well-defended port. It had not been a full-scale invasion involving several landings in force over open beaches covering an extended area and conducted in a situation of established air and naval superiority. The 'Torch' landings indicated the hitherto unprecedented scale and increased competence of Allied amphibious capability. Its implications were apparent to those German commanders prepared to re-examine their assumptions, but too few of them were, preferring instead to attribute the Allied success in 'Torch' to the half-heartedness of the Vichy French opposition. Kesselring himself considered 'Torch' as 'virtually a peacetime exercise because it met with so little opposition.'[16] This was a disdainful view – all the more dangerous because it was not without some validity – but it too-easily discarded Allied amphibious proficiency.

To repulse a landing at the water's edge demanded an emphasis on coastal defence, with troops and their heavy weapons preferably in well-fortified fixed positions dominating the likely beaches. Supporting mechanized infantry and armour would be positioned inland within early striking distance. There were problems with this. Coastal defence could not be strong everywhere, even when the most likely invasion beaches were prioritized. To commit forces, particularly the armoured formations, in this way reduced the available reserve. This might be a fatal omission if, as was likely, there would be more than one landing to deal with and it was not immediately apparent which was the principal Allied effort. Coastal defences took time to construct. As Kesselring discovered to his consternation once Sicily became a possible invasion target, strong fixed coastal defences tended to exist, if at all, only in a few obvious locations where the Allies would not be so obliging as to land. Otherwise they were more wishful thinking than reality. He would bitterly recall that Italian assurances of the strength of Sicily's defences were 'mere eyewash' and 'all so much gingerbread'.[17] By then there was too little time to construct them.

So far Axis forces had not experienced the effects of heavy Allied seaborne and air-delivered firepower, to which not only troops defending the beaches but those positioned inland would be subject. Strong fixed defences of concrete and steel might protect those covering the beaches, but their fire might nevertheless be suppressed by a greater weight of firepower that kept them huddled in their shelters and not at their guns. Others attempting to move towards the beaches in the immediate counterattack role would be very exposed and could expect casualties and disruption. To come under concentrated and observer-directed barrages fired not just by lighter warships but by major units with heavy gun power had not, so far, been the experience of German and Italian troops. That would come with the invasion of Sicily. As Kesselring would later admit, when he witnessed such fire during the fighting at Salerno in Italy, it altered his views on coastal defence.[18]

Exposure to such firepower and a loss of flexibility and manoeuvre were drawbacks to positioning the main defensive strength at the coast. While it offered the best prospect of defeating a landing, it also staked far too much upon it. The alternative was to accept that the Allies would get ashore. This meant deploying sufficient forces on and near the coast to fight a delaying action, while holding back further inland, beyond the reach of Allied naval firepower, the bulk of the mechanized and armoured formations as a powerful counterattack force. They could be directed against the Allied beachhead identified as the principal threat. Its destruction could be expected to defeat the entire invasion, as other landings could afterwards be 'mopped up'. This method gave the Axis command more flexibility, and an opportunity to regain the initiative once the Allies had landed and shown their hand. The risks were twofold. One was that once a beachhead was identified as the principal Allied landing it might already be too strong. Delay in mounting the counterattack might be fatal, but it would prove extremely difficult for the German and Italian commanders to judge the timing of this critical opportunity. The Allies had intelligence domination, and, as they testify in their memoirs, German commanders could not be certain for days whether landings that had already occurred were the main ones. For example, von Senger recalled of Sicily that: 'it was a long time before we could know whether the landing on July 10th would be followed by further landings in other places.'[19] Allied deception operations indicating the likelihood of further landings aimed to create just this doubt, and successfully paralysed decision-making just at the time when only decisive action would serve.

The other risk with this method of defence was in positioning the counterattack force too distant from the invasion area. The greater the distance the more chance there was of disruption and delay caused by Allied air action.

Once the decision was taken to launch the counterattack time would be of the essence, and downed bridges and other similar choke- points caused by bombing would hinder the road march of the attack formations. Such delays would be cumulative, with far-reaching effects upon deployment and cohesion. In daylight, moreover, the threat of air attack upon road-bound columns attempting to reach the coast would be very great, and with Allied air superiority there was no protection other than that provided by anti-aircraft firepower, bad flying weather, or darkness. The nearer the coast, the greater in intensity these attacks were likely to be, added to which would be delaying action by Allied airborne troops. Though casualties and destruction might not be severe, the effect on morale would be great, and there would be considerable disruption and delay, so that the counter-attack force needed still more valuable time to organize before it could be committed to action. What could be certain in early 1943, and about which even the most optimistic of German and Italian commanders agreed, was that the chance to defeat an Allied sea-borne landing would be only once, and fleeting.

The coastal defences on Sicily were patchy. The designated Naval Fortress Areas covering the principal ports and anchorages of strategic importance – Messina, Augusta–Syracuse and Trapani – had heavily protected fixed positions and emplaced shore batteries with fairly modern guns and fire-control systems. It was knowledge of their existence that led the Allies to rule out direct attacks on these ports. A German-Italian dispute over the optimum location of improvised coastal batteries, the former advocating forward location to engage landing-craft approaching the shore, and the latter arguing for their placing farther back beyond the range of the main armament of Allied warships, was still unresolved when the Allies landed.[20] For the most part, beach defence relied upon pill-box positions and entrenchments of varying extent scattered along the coast, some with wire obstacles and protected by mines.[21]

These were manned by Italian Coastal Divisions, of which on Sicily there were five, along with two Coastal Brigades. Little could have been expected of these formations. Accounts unanimously acknowledge that their mainly inexperienced troops, many of them older reservists, lacked motivation, training and equipment. They were stretched thinly over extensive fronts, with few supporting heavy weapons. Without transport, they could not concentrate and had no tactical mobility. Given the prevalent Italian disaffection with the war and their own unenviable situation, it is hardly surprising that when the Allies arrived many of these reluctant soldiers gave themselves up after a token resistance or simply took to the hills. They were a significant weakness in the coastal defences, even where those defences appeared formidable.

Their intended function was to offer the initial delaying resistance to the Allied landings. They were to secure valuable time to enable the concentration against the invasion beaches of more powerful mobile formations positioned inland, before the Allies could become established ashore and link up their various individual and initially vulnerable beachheads into a continuous front. This at least was the thinking of General Alfredo Guzzoni, the commander since June 1943 of the Italian Sixth Army on Sicily. A former Assistant Chief of the General Staff, he realized the limitations of the formations at his disposal and that they would have only a brief opportunity in which to react against an invasion – 'a fleeting moment'.[22] Success would depend upon how the better-quality Italian formations on Sicily and, above all, upon the German units on the island were employed. There were some serious problems with this as well.

The four Italian field divisions on Sicily, better than the coastal defence units, still had little potential effectiveness. Three of them, the Aosta, Assietta, and Napoli Divisions, were inexperienced. The best of them, the Livorno, had been trained, ironically, as an assault landing division early in the war. All these formations had inadequate battle training. The lamentable state of the Italian Army in Sicily was the consequence of its best formations having been destroyed in North Africa, or deployed to the Soviet Union and the Balkans. None of the field divisions, each of which had some 11,000–13,000 troops, possessed sufficient motorized transport to be considered mobile, being largely reliant on horse-drawn vehicles. There were shortfalls in modern artillery, anti-tank guns, and automatic weapons.[23]

While these field divisions were concentrated inland, near the coast were specially designated mobile reserves. These were better than the coastal divisions, and the bulk of the field divisions, and attempted to combine higher levels of firepower, fighting effectiveness and tactical mobility. Typically, they consisted of a company of tanks supported by infantry and light artillery or self-propelled guns with detachments of machine-guns and motorcycle troops. Their infantry, of which there were few, were the best available on the island, being elements of the Italian Army's highly proficient Bersaglieri or Fascist 'Blackshirt' units of the type encountered in Tunisia. Despite their designation as 'Mobile Groups' or 'Tactical Groups', they had few motor vehicles. Moreover, they were seriously handicapped in the quality of their equipment and heavy weapons, for which no amount of determination or fighting spirit could compensate. Their tanks would prove no match for those of the Allies, being 1940-vintage French machines captured by the Germans and handed over by them or equally obsolescent Italian models.[24]

Much would depend upon the two German divisions on the island, the Hermann Göring Panzer Division and the 15th Panzer Grenadier Division.[25] The reconstituted Hermann Göring Division on Sicily had formidable combat power but was a far cry from its first-rate namesake lost in Tunisia. It was inexperienced and short of trained infantry – indeed its battle training only commenced in June – and there were weaknesses in the junior levels of command. It possessed two tank battalions with a combined total of 99 tanks on the eve of the Allied invasion, including thirteen Tiger tanks of fearsome reputation among Allied troops.[26] A third battalion was equipped with assault guns. The 15th Panzer Grenadier Division was a hotchpotch of reinforcement units, but well organized and led. It was not at full strength, possessing some 60 tanks (Panzers III and IV), and to augment its firepower, a rocket projector (Werfer) unit with 36 projectors. There were also about 140 German field guns on Sicily and a large number of anti-aircraft guns.

The German formations were positioned to cover the west, east and south-east of the island. Because of its tank strength, and unaware of its shortcomings, Kesselring in late June insisted that the Hermann Göring cover the east where Allied landings were expected. The terrain there was better suited to armour, but the move required redeployment of the 15th Panzer Grenadiers, with the exception of a battle group to augment the Hermann Göring's infantry, to the west. None of the senior Axis commanders on the island; Guzzoni, von Senger, nor General Rodt commanding the 15th Panzer Grenadiers wanted this, preferring the division to remain where it was. The division had been on the island longer and knew the ground in that sector well. Its coastal reconnaissance was also highly efficient.[27] However, Guzzoni knew that his operational control of the German divisions on Sicily was nominal at best, and that at what was an already delicate and sometimes tense period in the Axis relationship, there was little to be gained by jeopardizing it. Kesselring had his way, though events would prove him mistaken.

Allied Air Power and 'Husky':
The Preliminary Air Campaign

As the Allied land and sea forces prepared for 'Husky', the air forces were already heavily committed operationally with their own contribution to the invasion. Air operations to enable 'Husky' began even before the conclusion of the Tunisian campaign, and required large-scale redeployments of squadrons across North Africa and the construction of new airfields from which to operate against Sicily, mainland Italy, Sardinia and Corsica. The air campaign leading to 'Husky' was necessarily extensive in time, from mid-May to the eve of the invasion, and in space, being principally a theatre-wide battle to gain air superiority over the Axis air forces and to disrupt Axis communications and reaction capability throughout the western Mediterranean.[28] The airmen therefore had a focus quite different from that of the naval and land forces, and differing priorities. This partly explains their delay in providing firm data to the land and naval forces on the scale and nature of air support they would provide during the invasion operation, though there was as yet little functioning 'joint' command machinery. Close air support, the engagement of targets in close proximity to friendly troops and coordinated with their action, would be problematic in Sicily.

Tedder's command included the North-West African Air Forces (NAAF) under Major General Carl Spaatz, USAAF, comprising Coningham's North-West African Tactical Air Forces (NATAF) with the RAF Desert Air Force and the US XII Air Support Command, and Major General James Doolittle's Northwest African Strategic Air Forces

(NASAF). There was also Middle East Air Command (MEAC) under Air Chief Marshal Sholto Douglas, and the Malta-based squadrons under the command of Air Vice Marshal Keith Park. These represented powerful and closely integrated Allied air forces, a total of some 267 squadrons (146 American and 121 British) and, excluding maritime and transport aircraft, some 3,462 combat aircraft.[29] Equally important were the high levels of air-craft serviceability and availability of personnel, as the air campaign was by necessity prolonged and one of attrition, characterised by repeated raids on targets and high sortie rates. As he had in North Africa, Tedder wielded his formidable air weapon in a closely coordinated and phased campaign.

Its first phase, roughly from the end of the Tunisian campaign to D–7 (3 July), saw a sustained offensive against Axis air power and intensified pressure upon Italian morale, the latter intended to prepare for the maximum shock effect of 'Husky' when it occurred. Throughout this period NASAF's bombers went for the principal Axis airfields in Sicily, Sardinia and southern Italy and the major ports and naval bases for submarines and light forces – Palermo and Messina in Sicily, Naples in southern Italy and Cagliari in Sardinia. The complex web of Axis Mediter-ranean communications came under increasing weight of attack, including the all-important ferry services across the Strait of Messina between Sicily and mainland Italy. The bombers also struck at industrial targets in Naples and Bari while coordinated pressure upon Italy, and a threat to further disperse Axis air strength, came from British-based RAF Bomber Command. These raided the northern Italian cities – which indicates the geographical extent of the air offensive and the linkages between strategic and operational and even tactical effects that underpinned it. As far as possible the bombing by the Mediterranean-based forces was round-the-clock, with the USAAF heavy bombers (B-17 Fortresses and B-24 Liber-ators) and mediums (B-25 Mitchells and B-26 Marauders) bombing by day while RAF Wellingtons attacked at night. Such were the demands of this intensive air campaign that the Allied air forces were unable to meet fully the requests by 'A' Force for still wider air operations to lend greater credence to the 'Barclay' deception operation. Nevertheless, the Germans and Italians were unable to conclude from the overall attack pattern that Sicily was the Allies' invasion target.

During this phase the Allies captured Pantelleria in Operation 'Corkscrew'; this Italian fortified island contained an important long-range radar outpost, shipping observation stations and airfields. Originally conceived as an Italian equivalent to Malta, Pantelleria had a garrison of 12,000 Italian troops with well-constructed fixed defences, including some fifteen coastal gun batteries of calibres up to 120mm, and bomb-proof underground facilities all the intelligence data available indicated that to attempt to capture the island would result in heavy losses.[30] Following a gradual stepping up of air raids beginning in mid-May, the Allied air forces mounted a sustained week-long offensive against the island between 6 and 11 June in which heavy, medium and fighter-bombers dropped 5,324 tons of bombs against a target area of some eight square miles. Attacks were near continuous and involved 3,712 sorties – on occasions aircraft arriving over the island had to circle in the area to await their turn to bomb. A naval task force also bombarded the island, and on 11 June the garrison, along with 78 German Luftwaffe ground personnel, capitulated without fighting to a landing force from the British 1st Infantry Division. On the following day further air and naval bombardment forced the surrender of the smaller island of Lampedusa.

'Corkscrew' was air-forces-led and appeared as a victory for air power alone, though too much could be made of this. With 'Husky' looming, the Allies were keen to learn the extent to which defences could be subdued by bombing, and Tedder considered 'Corkscrew' a 'laboratory experiment' with the opportunity to concentrate air power against a very restricted area. The Italian garrison was not of particularly high morale, and, with the prevailing state of Italian war-weariness and disaffection with the Axis, a stubborn defence against the Allies was an unlikely contingency. While the garrison were undoubtedly dazed and their morale seriously affected by the weight and intensity of attack, the actual casualties caused by bombardment were light, and, though sources vary, it seems that at most 200, probably considerably fewer, were killed. The damage was limited, with only sixteen guns destroyed or damaged out of a total of 130. Nevertheless, the secondary-effect damage to vital equipment, such as underground cables and radar, would have been enough to seriously disrupt the effectiveness of the defence, had that been attempted.[31] 'Corkscrew'

indicated the paralyzing effect, psychological as well as physical, of concentrated air bombardment under certain conditions, and the benefit to be
gained by rapidly exploiting it. But 'Corkscrew' offered no universal
guarantees that troops well-protected and determined to fight could be
bombed into submission. In terms of what the soldiers might come to
expect of the air forces, Tedder considered Pantelleria likely to become 'a
perfect curse to us'.[32]

In the second phase of their campaign (D–7 to D-Day), the Allied air
forces closed in upon the Luftwaffe and Italian Regia Aeronautica units
best placed to oppose 'Husky', and their supporting infrastructure. Airfields and radar sites on Sicily and Sardinia came under heavier attack as
the focus of the operational lens contracted and sharpened; day and night
harassment of road, rail and sea communications intensified. To this
onslaught the German and Italian airmen had little answer. Both the Luftwaffe and the Regia Aeronautica had suffered heavily in the Tunisian
campaign, the former having lost over 2,400 aircraft and the latter over
2,000, but what was more crippling to the effectiveness of both was the
loss of irreplaceable experienced aircrew and ground personnel.[33] Indeed,
Tunisia was a blow from which the Regia Aeronautica never recovered. Its
remaining strength, little over 600 aircraft, of which over half were fighters,
was further worn down in the subsequent defensive fighting over Sicily,
southern Italy and the islands of Sardinia and Corsica.

The Luftwaffe stood little chance of contesting Allied strength or of
retaining any initiative in the air, though in view of the strategic importance
of defending southern Europe this was not for want of trying. Following
the collapse in Tunisia, the Luftwaffe was reorganized into Second Luft-
flotte (Air Fleet) covering Italy and the central Mediterranean, while in
tribute to 'Barclay' a separate Luftwaffe Command South-East was set up
covering Greece and the Balkans. Experienced and forceful commanders
were posted in from the Eastern Front. By denuding the USSR and the
West of air power, the Germans achieved an increase in operational air
strength in the Mediterranean. This was particularly so with bombers and
close-support aircraft, though the all-important fighter strength remained
constant; in Second Luftflotte from May to July this was about 290, just
over half of which were serviceable. It was not enough. There were strenuous

efforts to increase serviceability, but shortage of spare parts, difficulties in obtaining replacements, and the shattering of airfields and their facilities by the unremitting Allied bombing made this a lost battle from the start.

At the beginning of July there were about 775 Luftwaffe aircraft capable of intervening against 'Husky' and a further 63 bombers scheduled to arrive in theatre. About 289 were based on Sicily, along with 145 Italian aircraft making a total of 434, most of which were fighters or fighter-bombers. Less than half of them were serviceable. Gradually the Sicilian airfields succumbed to the weight of Allied attack. Some landing fields were deliberately spared, waiting for the Germans and Italians in desperation to fall into the trap of concentrating their fighters on them: these were then struck in further heavy raids. No better example could be found of the extent to which the Allied air forces held the initiative and were dictating the battle. On 9 July USAAF Liberators struck at the headquarters of Fliegerkorps II at Taormina and destroyed its central telephone exchange; communications went down and the entire Catania-Gerbini group of airfields ceased to function.[34]

By 10 July only Milo and Sciacca airfields were fully useable. The Axis fighters and fighter-bombers had no option but to leave the island, compelled thereafter to operate at extreme range from the Naples area or to use the Sicilian airfields only as temporary advanced landing grounds. Fighting on the defensive, its weak but initially determined bombing raids against Allied shipping and ports in North Africa gradually falling off and its reconnaissance coverage throughout the Mediterranean increasingly restricted, the outnumbered Luftwaffe fell back in retreat. Tedder's air forces had won their battle in 42,227 sorties between 16 May and 9 July, with a loss of 250 aircraft. They had accounted for some 323 German and 105 Italian machines, mostly destroyed on their airfields, and they had broken Axis air power in the Mediterranean. It was a success that in the early planning stages of 'Husky' neither Tedder nor Cunningham could have counted upon. On 9 July the air forces stood ready for the third phase of their air campaign, providing protective cover and offensive support for the seaborne invasion itself. The way for 'Husky' was clear.

4

'HUSKY':
THE BATTLE FOR SICILY

The Landings

'There was nothing we could do but pray, desperately.' — Eisenhower[1]

By then the various convoys of the invasion force were already at sea, protected by Cunningham's warships providing close escort and with strong battle forces covering against the possibility, albeit unlikely, of a sortie by the Italian fleet. To mask their destination the invasion convoys followed regular shipping patterns for as long as possible, while some movements deliberately indicated a descent on the south of France. Naval activity in the Ionian Sea also supported 'Barclay' by threatening Crete and the coast of Greece. The Germans and Italians remained in doubt until the last hours. Despite sightings by air reconnaissance on 4 and 5 July, it was only after the Allied convoys had rendezvoused for their final approach in the early afternoon of 9 July that the Luftwaffe reported concentrations of shipping, including warships destined for Sicily. At 10 p.m. Guzzoni, by then convinced that he was about to be attacked, put his garrison on full alert.

Apart from whatever awaited them in Sicily, the immediate threat to the Allied invasion forces was the weather. During 9 July this changed for the worse, raising strong winds and heavy seas, causing seasickness and misery to the troops crammed aboard their transports and assault craft. The very feasibility of the landings became doubtful, and Eisenhower at Cunningham's headquarters on Malta faced the difficult choice of cancelling 'Husky' while there was still time, or carrying it through. An anxious signal from Marshall, asking whether the invasion was on or off, did nothing to make his choice easier. 'Husky' had already gone too far to turn back easily. On the strength of weather reports indicating an easing of the wind, the decision was taken to proceed.[2]

Eisenhower and others went outside to watch the British and American airborne troops already en route to spearhead the invasion fly over

Malta. For these formations, the turn of the weather proved disastrous. Their part of 'Husky', Operation 'Ladbrooke', had already been affected by its sheer scale and hurried preparations. Unfamiliar American Waco gliders were carrying most of the British 1st Airlanding Brigade for its descent upon the Ponte Grande Bridge, but they had lacked time to train with them. For both their operation, and the American parachute drop to seize the high ground inland of the Gela beachhead, a large number of transport crews only recently drafted into the USAAF from civilian flying were employed to fly the glider tugs and the C-47 Dakotas carrying the paratroops. These pilots and navigators were inexperienced in operational radio-silence night-flying conditions, and with the onset of the severe weather many could not cope. The formations became dispersed, many of the aircrews disoriented without any idea of where they were, and they were also coming under fire not only from Axis guns on Sicily but also

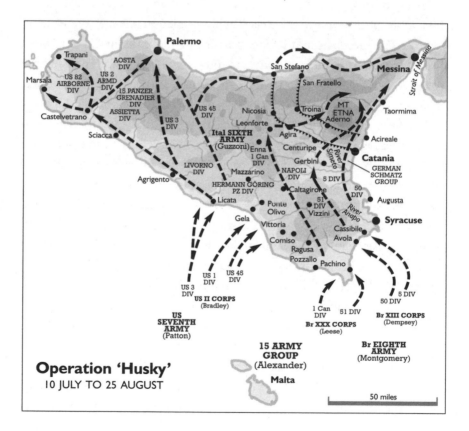

Operation 'Husky'
10 JULY TO 25 AUGUST

from the Allied ships below, because they were not on the recognized flight paths.

Some of them panicked. The tug pilots with 1st Air Landing Brigade released their gliders away from this fire but too far out; 69 of the Wacos went down into the sea and hundreds of their highly trained airborne soldiers drowned. Only two Horsa gliders reached the objective, with another 22 coming down within one mile and a further 49 dispersed over ten. Their troops converged on the bridge during the morning of 10 July and captured it, preventing its demolition and beating off Italian attacks until late in the afternoon when, with ammunition gone, they were overwhelmed. Only 15 of the 87 or so men who captured the bridge were by then unwounded. Shortly after their capture, they were rescued, and the Ponte Grande bridge recaptured, by the 2nd Royal Scots Fusiliers leading 5th Division's advance inland from the sea. The American paratroops experienced a similar fate, their drop widely dispersed all over southern Sicily between Gela and Syracuse, some landing 60 miles distant from the intended drop zone. Many were injured by landing in the high winds over broken and rocky terrain. There was no concentrated drop to protect the Seventh Army beachhead at Gela, so that by dawn on 10 July barely 200 paratroops occupied the vital high ground covering the beaches.[3]

Nevertheless, the scattered paratroops began to converge from all directions towards their objective and, wherever they encountered the enemy, they engaged them. They also created general mayhem by cutting telephone wires and ambushing unsuspecting parties of Germans and Italians. A sudden upsurge of reports of action flaring up against paratroops all over southern Sicily distorted the Axis battle picture, and caused consternation among formations, particularly the unstable Italian coastal divisions, whose rear areas seemed to be under attack. Reports were inevitably exaggerated, the strength of the airborne drop considerably overestimated, and in alarm some units withdrew several miles from their positions. The seeding throughout their areas of highly motivated and aggressive enemy soldiers, whose exact strength could only be guessed, confused German and Italian commanders and disrupted and delayed their reaction to the seaborne landings. Despite being seriously 'out of plan', the airborne part of the invasion unquestionably had its effect.

The seaborne landings in the early hours of 10 July suffered some delay and disruption because of the weather but met little serious opposition. The American beaches, most exposed to the wind and heavy seas, had their landings delayed by up to an hour. Naval gunfire by support groups of cruisers and destroyers effectively silenced those coastal batteries and artillery positions that offered resistance. Dieppe had indicated the need for greater and improved fire support to a landing force, and 'Husky' benefited from this. It was also realized that there would be a delay, at least of some hours, before the Army's own artillery could be landed and deployed for action during which vital fire support could only come from the warships standing offshore. Army artillery Forward Observation Officers and Bombardment Liaison Officers were trained to work with the Allied navies to direct this fire, while naval observers accompanied the assault troops ashore. A cruiser with 6-inch or 8-inch guns of ranges up to 29,000 yards or about 16 miles equated to a regiment of Army medium artillery, while a destroyer whose guns, mostly 4.7-inch, could lay fire out to 20,000 yards, about 11 miles, equated to two batteries of Army field artillery. Specific assault formations were assigned this formidable naval firepower, with designated destroyers and cruisers supporting their landings.[4]

The Allies also now possessed a growing range of specialized craft for direct close-in fire support of the first assault wave as they drew inshore and landed. These included landing craft equipped with rocket batteries, able in a single salvo lasting 26 seconds to drench beach defences with a weight of explosive equivalent to a bombardment by 80 cruisers or 240 destroyers in the same time.[5] It was neither a particularly accurate weapon, nor against well-fortified positions was it especially destructive. Yet it was absolutely terrifying, and it could silence coastal defence positions by the sheer weight of its fire and its shock effect, at a critical time of assault force vulnerability when naval gunfire could not be employed for fear of hitting friendly troops. Other landing craft were fitted up with older pattern naval guns, still capable of engaging and silencing enemy positions by direct fire at closer range.

In the first few hours of 'Husky' the worst enemy to the troops coming ashore was not the Germans and Italians but confusion. This, if allowed to take hold, would quickly become chaos and at the very least valuable time and cohesion could be lost. 'Torch' had indicated the problem and the solution lay in the Beach Groups, sometimes termed 'Beach Bricks' by British Middle East forces, whose first personnel ashore landed with the assault waves. They directed troops, vehicles and stores from vessels to inland assembly areas, set up a Beach Maintenance Area for vehicles and equipment, organized beachhead defence, including air defence, established communications within the beachhead and from ship to shore, and controlled the movement of casualties and of enemy prisoners of war. By the time of 'Husky' British Beach Groups were organised as permanent units, retaining unit expertise and esprit de corps, based upon an infantry battalion with additional detachments of signals, engineers, and anti-aircraft artillery. They included Royal Navy and RAF detachments under their individual service commands. For the same tasks the Americans integrated their Navy and Army units into Shore Parties, with a high proportion of engineers; USAAF personnel were also attached under command. With the improvement of Allied amphibious techniques new equipment also entered their inventory. These included the DUKW light amphibian vehicle for ship-to-shore transport, which would make a vital contribution to supplying forces over the beaches in Sicily, and vehicles and machinery for the recovery of beached assault craft, vehicles and tanks.

During 10 July the weather hampered the beach organizations, particularly in the more exposed American sector, as men struggled to unload vessels in heavy surf and high winds. Crews soon became exhausted, and work began to falter. Order and discipline started to break down, congestion threatened and situations arose that the junior naval officers, all that were available in the early stages to serve as Beachmasters, directing work on the beaches, proved in some instances unable to handle. During the afternoon more senior naval officers, released to go ashore from the support groups, arrived on the beaches. This, noted the British Combined Operations observer, soon brought a noticeable change. He subsequently reported that Naval Beachmasters must be senior officers experienced in handling tired men, and that preferably they should be bad-tempered and dictatorial by nature![6]

The Battle for the Gela Beachhead

Throughout the morning of 10 July the Axis reaction was hamstrung for want of reliable information. Little was heard from the south-east of the island. Here, positioned around Catania, a German battle group under Colonel Schmalz formed of units of both the Hermann Göring and 15th Panzer Grenadier Divisions found itself in Eighth Army's path and went into action. The Napoli Division's units in this sector seemed to have melted away and to fill the void Schmalz could do little more than offer sharp but brief delaying actions and hope for reinforcements. The lead troops of Eighth Army's XIII and XXX Corps made steady progress inland. The latter secured Pachino airfield and work began immediately to prepare it for Allied use. There was little Axis air reaction in Eighth Army's area at this time, and during the next couple of days no strong Axis forces of any defensive depth barred Eighth Army's advance towards Syracuse.

The hazy battle picture available to Guzzoni emphasized the landings around Gela and convinced him that here lay the major threat. He ordered the Italian XVI Corps to destroy it in a coordinated attack using two of the Mobile Groups, elements of the Livorno, and the Hermann Göring. The latter was out of communication with the Italian headquarters – the links between the German and Italian formations on Sicily were tenuous at best – so coordinated action was impossible. The Division Commander, General Paul Conrath, was alerted to the invasion through Kesselring's headquarters in Italy and set his Division, organised into two battle groups, moving from Caltagirone towards Gela at about 4 a.m. They had about 25 miles to cover, and would strike the advanced units of the US 1st and 45th Divisions moving inland from their beaches and also scattered groups of US paratroops. Ahead, but unknown to them, the Italian Mobile Groups and infantry of the Livorno were also moving towards the Gela area.

The American beaches and ships offshore were already under air attack. Some 370 German and 141 Italian aircraft, bombers and fighters, were active throughout 10 July, mostly in the Gela area. In sharp hit-and-run attacks they sank a destroyer, USS *Maddox*, and a minesweeper, USS *Sentinel*. The USAAF Spitfires and P-40 Warhawks flying from the islands of Gozo and Pantelleria tasked with protecting Gela worked fully stretched, their pilots having only about 30 minutes' patrol duration over their sectors. As Tedder had anticipated, there were gaps in this coverage for Axis aircraft to slip through. Overall, the USAAF and RAF fighter squadrons flying at maximum effort, some 1,092 sorties, managed to cover all of the Sicilian invasion beaches from shortly after dawn continuously for one and a half hours, after which they covered two of the beaches in any given period over the following fourteen and a half hours of daylight. It was not comprehensive, but it was air superiority nevertheless, and ship losses to air attack were considerably fewer than originally feared.[7]

Shortly before 7 a.m. several tanks of the Italian Mobile Group E broke into the town of Gela, secured in the early hours by US Rangers. It was a spirited attack, the Italians blasting at the Americans with their main armament, but it soon stalled. The tanks, ex-French R-35s, lacked manoeuvrability, were vulnerable to anti-tank weapons, and had a slow rate of fire. They were also without infantry support, and the Rangers were able to stalk them through the streets and knock them out one by one. Italian infantry arrived too late to help their tanks, but when they did the Rangers, preparing to defend from makeshift positions, were astounded to see them approaching in a compact mass formation worthy of a Napoleonic battlefield. Tactically this was little better than suicide, and under rapid fire from the Rangers' 4.2-inch mortars at about 2,000 yards range the Italian advance disintegrated, with a battalion of the Livorno all but wiped out.[8]

To the east of Gela a US Navy light observation aircraft launched by the cruiser USS *Boise* spotted about twenty tanks approaching the beachhead; these too were of Mobile Group E. The *Boise* let fire with her main armament, joined by other warships in the Gulf of Gela. The Italian soldiers must have been one of the first Axis units attempting to destroy an Allied invasion beachhead to come under such fire, to be subject to earth-moving blasts and concussive detonations of a force such as soldiers did not normally expect to experience or witness in their battles. The thunder of warship guns heard off Gela on 10 July would prove to be the crack of doom for many such attacks in future, not only in Sicily but later in Italy and in Normandy as well. It soon brought the Italian advance to a halt, and with two tanks destroyed they pulled back to the north-east. The ill-equipped, but unquestionably gallant, Mobile Group E was now practically spent.

Conrath intended his battle groups to attack early, not only to strike the beachhead while it was still vulnerable but also to avoid his men attacking into the glare of the fully risen sun. But as late as 10 a.m., no attack had occurred. This delay was caused partly by the narrow, twisting and poorly surfaced roads which the heavier German tanks, particularly the Tigers, could not easily negotiate – ironically the obsolete machines used by the Italians coped far better. The Hermann Göring troops were also unfamiliar with the ground, and no troops can move and fight over ground as effectively as those who know it well; here the 15th Panzer Grenadier Division would have done better. These were side issues to the Hermann Göring's principal weaknesses, inexperience and poor morale. The Division, pitch-forked into a battle for which its partially trained troops were unready, was not performing well and some of its officers were not competent for battle command. It was not pressing its attack. Conrath relieved his western battle group commander on the spot and took over command personally.

Even so it was about 2 p.m. before the attack was properly under way. By then valuable time had been lost and the beachhead perimeter defence had been steadily strengthened as the battalions of the US 1st and 45th Divisions' leading regiments advanced inland to link up with parties of paratroops. Naval gunfire helped break up the attack of the western German battle group, which fell back in confusion. The eastern battle group also stalled, the Tigers unable to manoeuvre off the narrow roads closed in by terraced slopes, but there was also a lack of vigour in the attack. The Division's Chief of Staff, sent by Conrath to find out what was happening because the battle group had been out of contact for several hours, set them moving again. Encountering stiff resistance from the American infantry and paratroops, and coming under naval gunfire, the attack faltered, and there were incidents of panic under fire.

There were further sporadic engagements across the as yet unconnected and tenuous front covering Gela, but the main Axis offensive effort against the beachhead on 10 July was finished. The 'fleeting moment' for the Axis had passed, and with it an opportunity. Despite the naval gunfire support and the resistance of the American paratroops and infantry, the US II Corps was as yet too weak to have withstood a coordinated attack pressed home with determination and skill. Kesselring's insistence on the redeployment of the German formations had played its part, for the 15th Panzer Grenadier Division would likely have proven a far more dangerous threat than the Hermann Göring. Nevertheless, as 10 July drew to a close the beachhead was still in great danger.

The difficulties of disembarkation on the beaches following the disruption caused by the weather resulted in few reserves being ashore even by the morning of 11 July. Landing craft were diverted to beaches clear of sandbars and mines, and congestion and delay accumulated. Vital artillery and tanks, needed to support the infantry battalions ashore, could not be landed at the intended rate. Patton recognized the threat under which the Gela beachhead stood and on the afternoon of 10 July ordered his Seventh Army floating reserve to be landed at Gela, this being a Combat Command of the 2nd Armored Division and the 1st Division's own 18th Regimental Combat Team. This would take time to have an effect. With much of II Corps artillery, armour and anti-tank units unable to land and deploy, throughout 11 July the burden of fire support would again fall upon the Navy.

Late on 10 July, Guzzoni and the Sixth Army staff and von Senger, who had seen for himself the situation at Gela, tried to take stock of the battle. It still appeared to them that they had an opportunity to destroy the Gela beachhead, and they took steps to ensure the coordination so far lacking between the various Italian and German formations. The Hermann Göring was attached to the Italian XVI Corps, and was to join the Livorno Division, the full strength of which was to be employed, along with what was left of Mobile Group E in a counterattack to go in at about 6 a.m. next day. With no opportunity for major redeployment, the plan mainly attempted to coordinate properly what had already been haphazardly attempted on 10 July. The Livorno Division's infantry regiments and tanks of Mobile Group E would attack towards Gela from the north-west while the Hermann Göring was split into three attacking columns: two would attack the beachhead head-on, while a third would attack westwards parallel to the coast to link up with them and finally eliminate and mop-up the American positions. There would be some unexpected anchors of resistance in the path of this attack. Determined to seize the initiative, the

US 1st Division advanced during the night of 10/11 July to secure some of the ground leading to its objective at Ponte Olivo airfield. By first light on 11 July battalions of the 26th and 16th Infantry Regiments had units holding a series of blocking positions; they had a few anti-tank guns and some field artillery in support.

The Hermann Göring Division renewed its attack at about 6.15 a.m. on 11 July, a tighter command grip keeping it close to schedule. In an attempt to coordinate air and ground action, Axis aircraft attacked ships in the Gulf of Gela. Throughout the day the Luftwaffe and Regia Aeronautica exerted themselves in the Gela area and made what was to all intents and purposes their 'swan song' over Sicily. The Luftwaffe managed a total of 283 sorties and the Italians 198, a scale of effort that they would not achieve again over the island as Allied air superiority tightened its grip. Allied fighter pilots, whose difficulties were much the same as they had been on the day before, achieved few interceptions. The American troops received no close air support throughout the day of desperate fighting, as the USAAF and RAF continued to prioritize fighter patrols and interdiction efforts. In the Gulf of Gela the warships and transports fought off a series of air attacks, their anti-aircraft gun crews living on their nerves all day. This would have terrible consequences later that same evening.

In the meantime, the defensive perimeter pushed out inland around Gela and the beachhead had erupted into action all along its thinly held front. As they advanced towards Gela the Italian and German tanks came under fire from mortars and the artillery units that had managed to get ashore and deploy. This fire helped to hold off the Italian infantry and tanks attacking to the west of the beachhead, but most important was the fire support provided by the Navy's ships on station in the Gulf of Gela. These were the cruisers *Boise* and *Savannah*, and several destroyers. As the Livorno's battalions approached Gela, still held by the Rangers, *Savannah*'s fire broke them up with heavy casualties. The Italian infantry were handicapped by their poor tactical ability, while their tanks had none of the potential effectiveness of the German types. Ashore for the first time in the beachhead, Patton at the Ranger command post witnessed the attempt by Italian tanks to reach Gela and directed a nearby radio-equipped Navy gunnery liaison officer to call down fire upon them. This was provided by

Boise, whose barrage turned back the Italian advance. By about midday the Italian infantry and tanks were incapable of further offensive effort. Despite the equivocal nature of Italy's commitment to the Axis at the time, the Italian soldiers of these formations had made a brave effort, and it had been costly. Little was now left of Mobile Group E, and the Livorno had suffered such casualties and disorganization as to be no longer an effective force. The best of the Italian field divisions on Sicily had been expended.

On the Italians' eastern flank the Hermann Göring's attack was initially held off by the American blocking positions. Conrath was in no mood that day to tolerate any further lack of aggressive drive in his division, however, and the attacks were renewed. Under increasing pressure, the Americans holding these advanced positions fell back. As the Hermann Göring pressed forward, the beachhead came under threat, and on the beaches themselves the unloading parties began to come under German fire. Naval support now proved decisive. The destroyer *Beatty* came in as close as she dared to the shore in order to engage the German column and disrupt its advance, her guns expending some 800 rounds of 5-inch to do it.

But by the afternoon the tanks and panzer grenadiers had overrun several of the 1st Division's units and were dangerously close to the heart of the beachhead position and the 1st Division's own command post. This was the crisis of the battle, and its outcome now depended upon the soldiers. Naval gunfire could not be called down on to American positions, and the US 1st Division was locked into a desperate battle to defend its hold on the beachhead. Patton had insisted that the tough, combat-experienced 1st Division land at Gela as an assault division. He was now vindicated, while Kesselring's insistence on assigning this sector to the Hermann Göring almost certainly cost the Axis the battle. Despite its offensive potential, the Hermann Göring Division was not up to a life-and-death grapple with the US 1st Division.

The 1st Division's anti-tank guns and artillery engaged the German tanks at close range. The infantry fought them with grenades and their own 'bazooka' rocket launchers, or took cover as they passed, to resume their fire against the German grenadiers. Later in the afternoon several M-4 Sherman tanks arrived. The prevalent soft sand had made their movement off of the beaches difficult and delayed their entry into the battle, but these were the vanguard of the 2nd Armored Division, and they were in time to engage the German Mark III and Mark IV tanks of the main German thrust. By late afternoon the Hermann Göring's offensive in the centre had reached its climax. No German tanks managed to cross Highway 115 skirting the coast, along which the 1st Division's artillery, sometimes firing over open sights, anti-tank guns, mortars and infantry held firm. And with them, so too did the beachhead. The Hermann Göring's attempt to turn the beachhead from the east came to nothing, and was held off throughout the day by a force of paratroops and infantry of the 45th Division.[9] An officer on the Hermann Göring's divisional staff later admitted that this column actually spent most of 11 July on the defensive, and its nervous troops could only be relied upon for this as long as they were not attacked.[10] These were clearly not the men to destroy a beachhead held by determined troops.

The Axis command had no clear picture of the progress of the attack on 11 July and was subject to contradictory reports, but towards evening Guzzoni was in no doubt that the chance to destroy the beachhead had passed. Aware of the state of the Italian formations, and still concerned about the possibility of further Allied landings, he ordered a halt to the Hermann Göring's attack. He directed it to move to the area south-east of Caltagirone in order to clear the area north-east of Vittoria of paratroops, indicating that the airborne scare of the previous day was still having its effect. Von Senger wanted the Hermann Göring to exploit what at the time he believed to be its success by striking east towards Comiso, a move that would cut off the northernmost Allied spearheads and facilitate the disengagement and withdrawal of the German and Italian troops to a shorter defensive line. In fact, the Hermann Göring was capable only of a withdrawal from the Plain of Gela towards Caltagirone, which it carried out, harried by naval gunfire. It reported that it had lost twelve tanks destroyed in the fighting, and a further twelve heavily battle-damaged and unfit for action, though its total of serviceable tanks was reported later that evening to be 54, including only four of the Tigers.[11] Such a rate of wastage could not be long sustained if the division were to retain its fighting power, and the switch to the defensive had not come a moment too soon. Kesselring, who at his headquarters in Rome had also been on the receiving end of a number of confusing battle reports varying from the wildly optimistic to the frankly defeatist, could only reluctantly endorse Guzzoni's decision when he arrived on Sicily the following day.

By the evening of 11 July the American units that had successfully defended their beachhead were exhausted. There were no further reinforcements lying to hand offshore, and Patton's only immediately available reserve for the Gela sector was the remainder of General Matthew Ridgeway's 82nd Airborne Division held back in North Africa. This consisted of the 504th Parachute Regimental Combat Team with its 1st and 2nd Battalions of the 504th Infantry, a battalion of parachute field artillery and a company of airborne engineers, all of which had been on stand-by to emplane since 10 July. As there was no certainty the German and Italian attack would not be resumed on the following day, Patton decided to have them flown in that evening. Although this was in line with the original Seventh Army plan, which envisaged the airborne division being brought into the beachhead as soon as possible, Patton did not take the decision lightly. The risks of an airborne fly-in to the beachhead were now very great, and of an immediacy not foreseen in the initial planning. The earlier drop had indicated the risks of confusion and disruption, but on 11 July there was real concern that the fly-in, if attempted, would go badly wrong because of the likelihood of friendly fire. Details of the flight were pre-arranged: the aircraft were to fly along a planned route the final leg of which would take them overland to the drop zone at 1,000 feet. On 6 July, Allied Force Headquarters had passed the intended pre-planned airborne route details and timings to the Naval forces, ordering that aircraft flying on the course were not to be engaged. This was followed by Seventh Army issuing its own warning instructions on the 6, 10, and 11 July. But by the latter date the realities of the beachhead battle were such that pre-arranged routes and timings could not guarantee the airborne forces immunity from fire.

Sharp German and Italian air attacks against the ships in the Gulf of Gela throughout 11 July left their gunners edgy. Patton was worried. So too was Ridgeway, who was in the beachhead. He did a round of the anti-aircraft gun emplacements to check that the gunners had been given orders concerning the airborne drop. One out of six he visited had not, and as events would prove, one was all that it would take to cause a tragedy.

Just before 10 p.m. a further Axis air attack came in, again causing the ships to take evasive action and defend themselves and at about 10.30 p.m. the approaching C-47s, the first of a total of 144, turned on the last leg of their course. They arrived over the ships off Gela only a few minutes after the Axis air attack, and although the first wave dropped their paratroops successfully, a single anti-aircraft gun, whether ashore or afloat is unclear, opened fire on the second wave as they flew in. Almost every anti-aircraft gun in the fleet and those on shore immediately took the C-47s under fire, indicating that the hitherto prevailing cease-fire had been uncertain and uneasy at best. In the inferno that followed, 23 of the C-47s were shot down – some of them were still fired on as they crashed into the sea and floundered – and 37 more were heavily damaged. Some turned back and returned to North Africa without having dropped their paratroops; others scattered them over the beachhead. Ridgeway watched from below, his thoughts not hard to imagine. Without ever having seen the enemy, 81 of his highly trained soldiers were killed and a further 132 wounded.[12] The situation on 11 July had been fraught with peril. Cunningham later robustly defended the fleet's action, and Tedder later described the airborne operation as 'fundamentally unsound', adding that the chances of all the ships and troops being adequately warned in an active battlefront where enemy aircraft were also operating were practically nil.[13] The potential for failures in communication, uncertainty and downright panic, the ever-threatening frictions of war, had been overwhelming.

The Island Campaign 12 July to 17 August 1943

With the repulse of the Axis attacks at Gela, the Allies were poised to strike farther inland against an Axis defence not yet firmed up. Alexander, on 13 July, issued orders that Eighth Army was to advance on two axes, one to capture Catania and the nearby airfield group, and the other to gain the central road network in the area Leonforte–Enna. This was in response to Montgomery's own suggestion and involved Seventh Army relinquishing the road between Vizzini and Caltagirone to Eighth Army, a move to which Patton reluctantly agreed, though it meant Seventh Army remained confined to western Sicily and covering Eighth Army's flank without exploiting its own offensive potential. Alexander was still deferring to Montgomery's interpretation of the campaign, Eighth Army remained the principal striking force and, despite the evidence of the Gela battle, he appeared still to have reservations about the US Army's capabilities. The Americans, hardly being treated as equal partners in the campaign, were feeling sore. Nevertheless Eighth Army was at this stage making good progress: Syracuse and Augusta had fallen, and Catania seemed well within its grasp.

With a clear failure to throw the Allies into the sea at Gela, the Axis command faced the question of how to conduct their campaign on the island. Were they to attempt to hold it for a prolonged period, or was Sicily to be a delaying action? Views diverged. Hitler was in no position to give his full attention to Sicily. Since the spring he had been deliberating whether to launch a major offensive on the Eastern Front to regain the initiative, an effort that would involve the commitment of Germany's carefully harboured panzer reserves in a massive attack heavily supported by the Luftwaffe, the objective of which was to destroy a large Soviet-held salient in the Kursk–Orel area to the north of Kharkov. Despite his concerns about likely events in Italy and the Mediterranean, on 18 June he decided to launch this offensive, Operation 'Citadel', in early July. He had considered, but in the end rejected, OKW advice to build up a strong strategic reserve. He needed a startling victory not only to regain the initiative but to bolster the Axis. To set 'Husky' in context with the war in the East, 'Citadel' employed 19 panzer and panzer-grenadier divisions and 14 infantry divisions, with some 2,700 tanks and assault guns and some 1,800 combat aircraft in two Luftwaffe Air Fleets. This colossal punch went in on 5 July and ran straight into strong Soviet defences. The battle was raging at its height when, five days later, Hitler was informed of the Allied invasion of Sicily.

His reaction was to order the reinforcement of the island by the 1st Parachute Division, already standing by in southern France in case of Allied descents there or against Sardinia. Kesselring, returned to mainland Italy from Sicily by 13 July, felt that the island could be held for a prolonged defence, though not indefinitely, and wanted more German troops to stiffen a line across the island. Although OKW balked at risking too many troops in the south, a view shared by both Guzzoni and von Senger because of the difficulties of a later evacuation to the mainland, Hitler inclined to Kesselring's more optimistic interpretation. It would not be the last time. Always concerned to shore up Mussolini's position, he decided to reinforce the island strongly and to bring the Allied advance to a halt. Disillusioned by reports of the collapse of Italian resistance, he ordered that the Headquarters of XIV Panzer Corps under General Hans Hube, who had commanded it on the Eastern Front and during its subsequent re-forming and training in the West, would take over the defence of the island. Units of the 29th Panzer Grenadier Division, initially held in southern Italy, were released for Sicily on 18 July.

These moves would result in a campaign different from that anticipated by the Allies. By 17 July, Hube was in Sicily and assuming tactical command of all sectors containing German troops, with Guzzoni's resigned agreement. The German grip on the Sicily command was further tightened by the appointment of Colonel Ernst-Günther Baade, a resourceful and energetic veteran of the fighting in North Africa, as commandant of the vital communications artery with the mainland, the Strait of Messina. Hube's orders, concealed from the Italians, were to eventually take complete control of all forces in Sicily and ensure the successful evacuation of as many German troops and as much of their equipment as possible. In the meantime, the intention was to make the Allies pay dearly for their advance, both in lives and in time. Three main defensive lines were envisaged, all of which made maximum use of the island's mountainous terrain and formidable natural obstacles. The main defence line ('Hauptkampflinie') ran from San Stefano on the north coast then south through Nicosia, Agira, on to Catenanuova then east to reach the coast south of Catania. Behind this the Etna Line ran from the north coast at San Fratello south through the mountain-top town of Troina then to Adrano (sometimes Aderno) to the sea at Acireale. Finally there was the Hube Line covering the north-eastern corner of the island.

Late on 13 July, Eighth Army attacked to break into the Plain of Catania from the south and soon realized that there would be no swift progress. The attack was preceded by another airborne descent, to seize the Primasole Bridge over the River Simeto in the path of the advance, this time by a parachute drop by the British 1st Parachute Brigade with supporting airborne artillery in gliders. Once again the airborne operation went awry. Despite efforts to route the C-47s away from the guns of the Allied ships, they were still taken under fire, 55 being shot at and 11 brought down, while 27 turned back to North Africa. The drop was also widely scattered. Only 12 officers and 283 men out of an intended 1,856 – barely one sixth – plus a handful of guns went into action. They managed to capture the bridge, but soon were embroiled in a stiff battle with detachments of German paratroops of the 1st Parachute Division, a battalion of which (of 4th Parachute Regiment) had arrived in more or less the same drop zone on the previous evening, their jumps timed to avoid the all-too predictable Allied fighter patrols. The bridge was lost, then finally recaptured with the arrival of the 50th Division and 4th Armoured Brigade of Eighth Army.[14] The presence of the German paratroops followed by a build-up of German strength combined with good defender's ground slowed Eighth Army's momentum and gained the Germans time to close the Plain of Catania and bar the eastern coastal route to Messina. The hammering of lines of communication by the Allied air forces had delayed and disrupted, but not prevented this strengthening of the defence.

The situation whereby Eighth Army was the Allied striking force while Seventh Army protected its flank would no longer serve. The opportunity, such as it was, to secure a rapid end to the campaign was being lost by the hour and with the arrival of each additional German soldier. Montgomery attempted to outflank the Catania position by an advance by XXX Corps through the mountains towards Enna, necessitating a change of army boundary with Seventh Army and the dislocation of the US 45th Division to free Highway 124 for XXX Corps. This caused serious inter-Allied friction as, once again, Seventh Army was apparently relegated to a sub-sidiary role, this time when one of its own formations was itself well placed to move on Enna. The belated juggling of formations cost momentum and lost whatever chance existed to break what was fast becoming a predomi-nantly German, and very formidable, defensive belt in the Sicilian moun-tains. Patton, whose frustration was now beyond reining-in, personally secured Alexander's sanction for Seventh Army to push out through western Sicily. For a coalition commander, Alexander up to this point appears to have been quite oblivious to the resentment of Patton and

American commanders at Montgomery's apparent dominating of the campaign, and at his own acquiescence to it. As Alexander did not want Seventh Army engaged in a major battle on Eighth Army's flank as it attacked northwards, Patton was to carry out a 'reconnaissance in force'. For Patton this was all he needed. In five days his troops had cleared western Sicily, captured the port of Palermo (22 July), and reached the north coast of the island. Although the main Axis strength was in the east, and the main battle had still to be fought there, Seventh Army had achieved a remarkable feat of mobility, revealing what it could do not only to its enemies but also to its ally. It had taken over 50,000 Italian prisoners, and hustled a series of German rearguards back on to their main defensive line. By the beginning of August both armies had closed up to the German Etna Line positions, Seventh Army on Eighth Army's northern flank and now its proven equal partner in the campaign.

Alexander had both armies poised for the final drive towards Messina, scheduled to begin on 1 August. For all concerned the campaign had become a hard and savage slugging match, as British, Canadian and American formations battered themselves against German defensive strongholds situated in and around mountain and hilltop towns and villages that dominated the roads and tracks below them. To drive the Germans in upon their Etna Line the cost was fearful. The 1st Canadian Division with the British 231st Infantry Brigade, attacking as part of Eighth Army's XXX Corps, captured the mountain-top town of Agira on 28 July. It had taken five days of fighting and the commitment of all three of the Canadian Division's brigades, and it had cost the Canadians 438 battle casualties and the 231st Brigade some 300. They were opposed by German troops gathered in from three Divisions; the 15th and 29th Panzer Grenadier Divisions, and the Hermann Göring Division, which had overcome its inexperience problems and was now fighting hard. The Canadians reckoned to have killed at least 325 of them, and taken another 430 prisoner along with 260 Italians of the Livorno and Aosta Divisions.[15] This was the Canadian Division's toughest battle on Sicily, but for the Allies closing in on Messina there remained plenty of strongpoints to overcome.

Eighth Army's XIII Corps was to press the Germans at Catania while the US II Corps attacked along the northern coast, Patton having brought in through Palermo the US 9th Infantry Division to reinforce his Seventh Army's striking power. The centre of the Etna Line was to be attacked by Eighth Army's XXX Corps. It had been reinforced by the 78th Infantry Division brought over from North Africa. Originally a British First Army formation, it had earned a high reputation for mountain fighting in Tunisia and was to spearhead the attack by capturing the town of Centuripe, the lynchpin of the Etna Line and the key with which to unlock the defences around Adrano and, with them, the stubborn Catania position.

Montgomery paid the 78th Division a fulsome tribute after its capture of Centuripe, giving his opinion that no other division in his army could have carried out the operation successfully.[16] The praise had been well earned. Centuripe was not only a man-made fortress but a natural one. Situated atop a razor-backed ridge, it dominated the mass of steep hills and ridges, separated one from another by rocky and boulder-strewn gorges, that lay between Catenanuova and Etna. The town of Centuripe, built on the steep edge of the final slopes of this outcrop, could only be approached, apart from over some difficult mule tracks, by a single, narrow corkscrewing road running for some two miles along the edge of a mountain ridge. Steep slopes overlooked its entire length, and slopes equally steep below the road threatened the unwary, men and mules alike, with a fall to their death. The Germans had mined the road and breached it, and their artillery covered much of its length. The slopes ascending to just below the town, some of which were at an angle sharper than 45°, were terraced for cultivation, with 'steps' of six feet separating the levels. For attacking infantry to ascend them would involve an arduous, exhausting climb. This was a daunting enough prospect whatever the enemy might be able to add; for the laden infantryman in the heat of the day it looked impossible. Extending beyond these terraces were jutting outcrops of loose, crumbling stone, or coarse and slippery grass. On the hills round about there were boundary hedges of prickly pear and cactus, with occasional plantations of olive and almond trees, and scattered around there were caves and natural pits and gullies, many of which could not be easily discerned and which provided excellent concealment for defending infantry. These troops were of high quality, the core of the defence being 1st Battalion of the German 3rd Parachute Regiment, with some additional detachments of the 2nd Battalion as well, both of the 1st Parachute Division. There was also an anti-tank troop of the Hermann Göring Division, a battery of field artillery and, it seems, some armour with the odd tank in or near the town itself.

To clear this position took all three of the 78th Division's infantry brigades fed into the attack in two days of continuous fighting between 1 and 2 August. Two of them were fought to exhaustion and its third, the 38th (Irish) Brigade which finally took the town in a feat of mountain climbing and attack stamina, very nearly so.[17] A Division's worth of infantry had been played out to overcome a defence of little more than a reinforced battalion. Yet effectiveness of the defence had been multiplied considerably by the fact that the Germans were high-quality troops, that their firepower was augmented by a heavy scale of automatic weapons, that they occupied superb well-concealed and protected positions on dominating heights, that the intense heat, forbidding terrain, and lack of supplies in the forward area eventually enervated the most determined and fittest of attacking troops, and that the configuration of the ground dictated either narrow and constricted attack frontages covered by the defenders' guns, or near-exhausting climbs before the attacking troops could approach within closing distance of their objectives. Under such conditions it had been a remarkable achievement to take the place in two days. 'Worse than Longstop', its hardest-fought battle in Tunisia, was the 78th Division's verdict on Centuripe.[18]

The End of the Sicily Campaign

'Where've you tourists been?' — American greeting to the first British
troops into Messina, 17 August 1943[19]

As the 78th Division fought to capture Centuripe, to the north the US 1st Division was fighting its hardest battle since Gela, to clear the defence zone, a maze of defended hills and ridges based upon the mountain-top town of Troina overlooking Highway 120 that skirted the north of Etna to the coast. The battle for Troina began on 31 July with the commitment into the attack of the US 39th Infantry Regiment, temporarily attached from the 9th to the 1st Division, and it finally ended on 6 August when, following the withdrawal of the 15th Panzer Grenadier Division's battered battlegroups, American troops entered the town. By then both the US 1st and 9th Divisions had been committed to the battle raging over the slopes and mountain ridges, and the regiments of the 1st Division severely reduced by casualties, their survivors worn out in the prolonged mountain fighting of attack and counterattack necessary to dislodge the Germans from excellent defender's ground. Troina, as a subsequent US Army report observed, 'was the toughest battle Americans have fought since World War I'.[20] Agira, Centuripe, Troina, it was the same pattern – each had exhausted an Allied division.

With the loss of Centuripe and Troina the Germans began their final withdrawal on Messina and their evacuation from the island across the Strait to mainland Italy. In these closing stages the Germans proved their adeptness at slipping away, successfully avoiding the short amphibious outflanking moves intended to catch them mounted by Patton along the north coast, and one by Montgomery on the east. The German evacuation had been carefully prepared, with an efficient ferry service in place by both the Germans and Italians for the separate crossings of their forces. To protect the Strait and a crossing distance of only some two and a half miles the Germans had compensated for their own lack of sea and air power by a heavy commitment of dual-purpose guns, supplemented by light automatic 'flak' anti-aircraft artillery. The total of German and Italian guns of various calibres, fixed and mobile, was formidable and may have exceeded 150; whatever the exact total, their threat proved enough to deter the Allies from risking their larger warships in the narrow waters of the Strait. Similarly, while the flak belt could not be entirely comprehensive, it was enough to deter the all-out commitment of the tactical air forces. From the end of July intercepts of German signals strongly indicated a forthcoming evacuation.[21] In any case it was an obvious contingency, and was identified as such by Alexander in early August, when he alerted both Tedder and Cunningham to its likelihood. Yet preventing the evacuation appears to have been a challenging joint problem the Allies signally failed to solve. There was no integrated plan, no closely coordinated action, no attempt to combine the effects of sea and air power as there had been to isolate the Axis in their Tunisian bridgehead.

The Germans could hardly believe their luck. Although the crossings began on 11 August it was not until three days later that the Allies realized the evacuation was actually under way. Night bombing caused some disruption and delay, but when the Germans took the risk of ferrying across in daylight under protection of their 'flak' umbrella they found it worked. The USAAF B-17 Flying Fortresses that in a few days of sustained high level daylight bombing might well have turned this smooth-running operation into a shambles, in the process also cracking open the flak belt for the tactical air forces and reducing the risk to Allied warships, were not diverted from their raids against the Italian mainland. Maintaining the coercive bombing pressure upon Italy and its government at a critical stage in the crumbling Axis relationship was of vital strategic importance; so too was maintaining a relentless attack on Axis air power to prevent its recovery. Whether in time and space these took precedence over preventing the escape of the German army on Sicily is highly questionable; historian Carlo D'Este has well described the decision not to employ the B-17s as 'the most serious of the many misjudgements made by the Allies in Sicily'.[22] Poor coordination, as much as a genuinely difficult strategic dilemma, is at the heart of this still controversial episode.

The consequence was that more than 50,000 German troops and much of their equipment including some 47 tanks, 94 guns and several thousand vehicles successfully reached the mainland. More significantly, this was far from being a rout: the German formations remained organizationally intact and, apart from losses which could be made good, they had therefore lost nothing of their potential battle effectiveness. Their continued survival would be an influencing factor in Hitler's later decision on his strategy for mainland Italy and would therefore cost the Allies dear. Some 60,000 Italian troops were also evacuated, though what the future held for them was far less certain. On the morning of 17 August the leading troops of Seventh Army entered Messina shortly before those of Eighth Army. Later that day Alexander signalled Churchill to report that 'the last German soldier was flung out of Sicily'.

'Husky' was completed and it had achieved its strategic objectives: Sicily was in Allied hands, the Mediterranean sea passage cleared. It had

††††††††††††††††††

drawn German strength south and heightened the strategic threat to Germany's southern flank. It had intensified the pressure on Italy to the extent that, on 25 July, Mussolini had been removed from power and replaced by a government under Marshal Badoglio that, outwardly professing its loyalty to the Axis, was in fact urgently seeking to extricate Italy from the war. In campaign terms, 'Husky' had frustrated the Allies. The eventual invasion plan, delayed by controversy, offered few opportunities for bold action to unhinge the Axis defence. Seventh Army's striking potential had been realized, and released, too late, reliance placed upon Eighth Army as the principal striking force for too long. This forfeited the chance, never more than brief, to clear Catania and reach Messina before the Germans formed a stiff defence across the island. This condemned the Allies to a costly battering-ram campaign that all too rapidly depleted and exhausted their attacking formations.

5

SICILY:
THE VOICE OF BATTLE EXPERIENCE

The Influence of Terrain

'The country fought over was of the roughest kind. Its chief features were high, rocky mountains and hills of volcanic origin cut by narrow and enclosed valleys and dry watercourses. Except for the limited roads, the ground communication throughout this terrain was confined to tortuous tracks and trails.'[1]

Military campaigns are shaped and the nature of their fighting influenced predominantly by the terrain over which they are fought. Sicily in 1943 presented the Allies with their mainly road-dependent mechanized armies with, at best extremely difficult, and at worst impossible, ground for manoeuvre. It gave little scope for exploiting armour. Broken by terraced slopes and foothills, by slopes and jagged crests, the ground in Sicily in 1943 presented the equipment-laden infantryman, signaller and porter with an extreme physical endurance test. Only between Syracuse and Catania on the eastern side of the island was there a belt of low-lying ground extending for some twenty miles in length and some eight wide, the flood plain of the rivers Simeto, Dittaino and Gornalunga, and known as the Plain of Catania. To the north-east of the island the ground rose through olive groves and orchards and scrub to the dominating 10,740-foot volcano, Mount Etna.

The campaign, fought in high summer, was conducted in a dry, dusty, rain-starved heat of North African temperatures, accompanied by the ever-present risk of malaria and sand-fly fever. Soldiers cannot choose their operational excursions in the manner of a tourist, but it is worth mentioning that pre-war holiday guidebooks advised against visits to the island of Sicily during the months of July and August. There were not many good all-weather roads in 1943, and there were very few parallel auxiliary or alternate routes to those that did exist. The road network such as it was contained many defiles and, frequently narrow and overlooked by

high ground, the roads were easily blocked by German and Italian demolitions. Towns and villages made natural bottlenecks, and river bridges, of
obvious importance, were all-too-easily blocked and demolished. Most
movement depended upon tortuous tracks and trails, which vehicles could
only negotiate with difficulty, if at all, and to soldiers unused to such
mountainous terrain, and certainly not rigorously trained to fight in it (a
category that included the majority of those in the Allied armies), such
ground could be very disorientating. Only time and experience taught
soldiers how to 'read' it sufficiently to know its dangers and to understand
how it might be utilized for attack and defence.[2]

This terrain compelled the Allied armies to make ad hoc adjustments in
unit organization, in methods of tactical manoeuvre and supply, in line
with the overriding imperative to maintain an offensive. The burden of
attack fell mainly upon the infantry, though the ultimate success of any
attack, examined at any level from that of division, and broken right down
through brigade or regiment down through battalion, company, platoon
and rifle section, frequently depended upon the extent of supporting fire
from the artillery or other heavy weapons and how it could be exploited.
Terrain was a factor in all of this, but there were some basic, if hard-
learned, lessons that emerged from the Sicily experience and upon which
the effective prosecution of the subsequent campaign was soon found to
depend.

One of the most important was that infantry had to withstand an excep-
tional level of physical strain when engaged in a continuous run of mountain
fighting. The US Army campaign report subsequently acknowledged that the
fighting proved the need for a previously unrealized degree of physical
conditioning and hardening, and that only training in rugged hills and mountains could provide it. Unit commanders consulted during the compilation of
the report agreed with this, adding that the usual hardening marches over
relatively flat or rolling country were simply not enough to provide troops
with the stamina required for mountain combat.[3]

The pre-campaign training given the various Allied formations had
been patchy in this respect. For one thing, there had been little time following the end of the Tunisian campaign in early May for the formations
in North Africa destined for Sicily to receive specific mountain training.

Divisions had to be withdrawn from operations at the earliest opportunity and prepared for embarkation in battle order for an amphibious operation, a complex process that in the case of a British division required some 68 days.[4] The Americans faced comparable problems. Nor had mountain fighting figured highly in the training given to the American formations that sailed direct from the United States or those similarly inexperienced British divisions and the Canadian division that came direct from the United Kingdom, though some efforts were made in the time available. For example, the commander of the 1st Canadian Division, General Guy Simonds, had an eye for what was in the offing and ensured that his 3rd Brigade, whose role in the Sicily invasion was to follow up the seaborne landings of the 1st and 2nd Brigades, attended a brief but gruelling special mountain warfare course in the Perthshire hills in Scotland. Some of the British formations that had been based for a time in the Middle East before going to Sicily were fortunate to receive some mountain hardening before the campaign – and whatever the troops might have thought of it at the time, it stood them in good stead on Sicily. A former junior officer with the British 5th Division would years later recall his battalion in Sicily marching in full equipment inland from Augusta, steadily climbing up the face of Mount Climiti along a narrow path in blistering heat and glaring light, yet able to keep up a brisk pace because they were used to such marches; the ground resembled the mountains above Damascus where they had been recently training.[5]

In Sicily it was necessary for the Allied infantry not only to be able to march and fight in mountainous country but also to pursue and maintain contact with an enemy who fought skilful rearguard delaying actions and then broke off to fall back on new positions. It was in this situation that the physical stamina and endurance required to overcome the ground and the heat needed to be combined with an aggressive initiative and resourcefulness in order to overcome the obstacles and minefields left in the enemy's wake. The US 9th Infantry Division, for example, reported the necessity of troops pushing forward immediately once contact had been lost in order to deny the withdrawing German and Italian troops the time they required for a well-organized occupation of previously prepared fall-back positions. In order to maintain advance momentum, it observed, the infantry had to be prepared to move rapidly across country, removing mines themselves and also keeping themselves supplied by mules or light vehicles. A formidable problem, as reported by the US 1st Infantry Division, was the enemy's demolition and sowing with mines of the towns and bridges forming bottlenecks on the only through-roads. This, it noted, could prolong the break in contact and delay the pursuit for considerable time.[6] The leading Allied infantry units had to keep moving if they were not to give the withdrawing enemy a respite, but this meant there was little respite for them either.

With vehicular transport often unable to get forward, the Allied infantry were reliant upon improvisation to get their supplies and, most importantly, what heavy weapons they possessed up with the leading troops. For many units this became a problem as soon as they had landed in Sicily, not only because the terrain precluded much road movement but also because the infantry lacked sufficient light transport, and also because the first battalions ashore had to move forward without waiting for all their vehicles to be unloaded from the ships. In one case, during the drive on Catania between 10 and 12 July, the British 231st Infantry Brigade (at the time under command of the 51st (Highland) Division as part of XXX Corps) provided a battalion, the 2nd Devons, for a mixed brigade group of tanks, self-propelled guns, anti-tank guns, medium machine-guns and infantry. In order to keep up with what was intended to be a mobile force, the Devons devised a system of ferrying using the few trucks available and the anti-tank gun portees, cramming the latter with troops as they towed the guns forward. The 231st Brigade as whole appropriated everything it could lay its hands on to supplement its meagre transport – Sicilian country carts, mules, horses and donkeys. 'Every little helped', recalled one of its officers, 'in the all important thing, which was to get on.'[7] Accounts suggest that every other Allied unit that had the chance did the same.

In Sicily mules became priceless assets for the infantry, and there were never enough of them for all that needed to be carried forward, so that they had to be carefully prioritized within formations and units. From its own experience, the US 9th Infantry Division subsequently warned that whatever pack mules were available it was necessary to ensure that the heavy weapons companies had enough of them so that they could keep up with the forward rifle companies, since heavy weapons were needed with the advance guard. They could not be easily transported by manhandling, especially in the mountains, and when this was attempted the heavy weapons inevitably lagged behind. It cited a case where a battalion success-fully captured a German position in an early morning surprise attack but it had advanced well ahead of its supporting weapons, which were struggling to catch up. With only two rifle companies forward to withstand the German counterattack that came in shortly afterwards, and no heavy weapons support, the position was lost.[8] In the mountains mules also played an important role in ensuring that units remained in communica-tion, as they were employed to carry the bulky wireless sets used by artillery forward observation officers and signallers in touch with rear headquarters. This worked very smoothly, as, for example, when the 3rd Canadian Infantry Brigade operating with the British 78th Division captured a bridgehead over the River Dittaino at Catenanuova in the early hours of 30 July. The attacking battalion, the West Nova Scotia, made good progress and secured its objective quickly while retaining communication through-out with brigade headquarters. Its commanding officer later observed that this was probably the first 'official' use by Canadian troops of the mules and donkeys picked up during their advance through Sicily.[9] In fact, because of the difficulty in procuring animals, the Canadians had only just by that time managed to improvise a small mule train to assist their movement, despite the fact that they had foreseen the importance of mule transport in Sicily and had taken steps to provide for it, including the provision of pack saddles and the inclusion of trained handlers in their reinforcement drafts. The British 78th Division similarly suffered through a lack of mules and pack horses. Although the Division knew from its Tunisian experience how necessary they were, it had been refused deck space, which was at a premium, for any aboard the ships transporting it from North Africa. Divi-sional staff and battalion officers therefore scoured the Sicilian countryside for them, with mixed results, for others had been before them. They obtained some ex-Italian army mules, but most of the animals they found had to be requisitioned from the local towns and villages. These, unused to carrying military equipment, proved unpredictable at best, while the civilian drivers who could handle them had no enthusiasm for working in a battle zone under fire and soon decamped. Much still had to be man-handled forward or carried up the slopes by porters.[10]

The Sicily campaign proved that something better was needed than an ad hoc organization for mules and other improvised transport. Infantry could only advance so far without daily supplies of drinking water, food and ammunition, and much time was wasted as formations made frantic efforts, sometimes searching over wide distances, to obtain yet more mules to keep the advance going. The US 3rd Infantry Division alone ultimately had 650 mules to keep it moving, and the US II Corps reckoned that a section with about 25 mules with pack saddles was a necessity for each rifle battalion. It also became apparent very quickly in the mountains that troops would have benefited greatly from some pre-operational training in handling mules. Few of them knew the proper methods of packing supplies and equipment, and units had little or no idea of how to organize mule trains efficiently. The manpower drain on units to provide packers and handlers was also considerable. There were other problems too. The advance of forward infantry units could be held up by delays in the follow-up of the mule columns, which were themselves very vulnerable and obviously important targets for German and Italian artillery and mortars, whose observers could spot their movement from the high ground. Mule casualties were often as hard to replace as those of trained infantrymen, and the disruption and sometimes scattering of mule detachments caught under bombardment, and the time taken to rally and reorganize, could deny the forward troops supply and replenishment of ammunition for hours, sometimes days.

When animals were not to hand for carrying, which was frequently the case when a unit possessed none or when those available had already been overworked and required recuperation, the situation could be far worse. The only alternative then was for the troops themselves to act as porters and carry the supplies and equipment forward. For the most part this meant climbing, frequently up steep and difficult slopes and crests in the mountainous country and, during the day, in extreme heat. This imposed immense physical strain. As infantrymen could not be expected to advance and fight as well as carry, it frequently meant that to keep one forward company supplied another company had to become porters, reducing the number of combat-available infantry. American units improvised Alaskan-type pack boards for carrying, along with various types of sling, and reported that rigid-type frames were best for soldiers to carry the heavier equipment such as mortar parts and their ammunition rounds. In one (admittedly extreme) case recorded in the US Army's campaign report, a human pack train was organized to keep frontline troops supplied, the porters having to carry 'K-rations' a distance of six miles from the ration dump to the forward positions. Each man carried two engineer sandbags filled with rations, tied together and carried front and rear over the shoulder.[11]

However inefficient and wasteful in terms of manpower, the Allied armies had no choice but to resort to such measures, and it was in these cases that the shortfalls in pre-campaign mountain hardening became apparent. Those that had both to climb and fight had, as far as possible, to be relieved of the burden of carrying, but if the attacking infantryman moved and fought better when stripped of as much as feasible of his personal equipment, it nevertheless made him more dependent – and more dependent more quickly – upon those whose job it was to climb and carry. In one example involving Canadian troops, the Hastings and Prince Edward Regiment accomplished a remarkable feat of surprise attack at night when tasked with the capture of the German-held mountaintop village of Assoro. Late on 20 July the battalion set off in single file on a march across country prior to ascending the steep eastern face of the mountain from which direction the battalion commander rightly considered the Germans would never expect an attack. The troops carried nothing but their rifles, automatic weapons, and ammunition, and, in an echo of the Grenadier Companies of an earlier age, the fittest and most active were grouped at the front to spearhead the attack. The only food each man carried was a ration of chocolate. It was a punishing climb, but it saved what otherwise might have been a hard, costly and very likely unsuccessful frontal assault along lines of approach expected by the German defenders. In the event, such was the surprise achieved by the Canadians that they took their objective by dawn without a single casualty, having first overrun a startled German observation post.

Throughout the following day, however, they were subject to counter-attacks, which they beat off with the help of well-directed artillery support. But they were nearly exhausted after the night's exertions, without food, and their ammunition began to run out. It was not until early on 22 July that they received the, by then urgently needed, food and ammunition, brought up by a hundred volunteers of the Royal Canadian Regiment who had portered it over the same distance and difficult climb.[12] Each man had carried the rations and ammunition in bandoliers and an 'Everest Pack', a specially designed carrying frame to which the Canadians had been first introduced during their brief spell of mountain training in Scotland and which, as one unit reported at that time, enabled a man to take almost the load of a mule.[13] To carry essential supplies forward in this way had been the only means of consolidating what the Hastings and Prince Edwards had gained by such audacity, and the example indicates the extent to which the limiting factors in mountain warfare were numbers of infantry-men and the extent of their physical endurance. In Sicily, the Allied armies found the terrain to be as formidable an opponent as the German soldier fighting on the defensive, and most of the time it seemed to be on the Germans' side.

The Interpretation of Battle Experience

Shortly after the fall of Messina, two army officers, one British and one American, recorded their impressions of what they had experienced during the previous weeks. The British officer, Lieutenant Colonel Lionel Wigram, was a specialist in infantry training who had been on the island as an observer to study the tactical methods employed at first hand. He had commanded various units from an infantry section through to a battalion, and he had interviewed many battle-experienced troops for their views, thereby checking his own. His verdict on the Sicily fighting was that it had been 'ideal' experience to translate into training, for it had involved situations ranging from large set-piece attacks down to company and platoon actions and the pursuit of a withdrawing enemy whose defensive fighting methods had been revealed. Wigram intended to return at the earliest opportunity in order to impart this experience from an active theatre to the Army training in the United Kingdom.[14]

The American officer would undoubtedly have endorsed Wigram's opinion. He was an infantry battalion executive officer, one of many contributing to a US Army campaign report. His experience of fighting in Sicily led him to question the preparation given his unit prior to the campaign, especially concerning battle leadership. No one in his outfit, he observed, had expected to meet the situations they encountered in Sicily. In the light of actual campaign experience, he saw that the 'field problems' they had been given during their training in the United States had been too 'cut and dried'. In Sicily the fighting, especially in the mountains and over rough terrain, demanded a high level of initiative from junior officers and NCOs, and this had proved a severe test. He called for more training in the 'ability to meet unexpected situations', and in acting on sound decisions made on individual responsibility. He also offered a sobering warning – it was time to stop belittling the fighting ability of the German soldier. He was vicious, clever and ruthless, and it would take battle leadership of the highest order to defeat him.[15]

For the British, American and Canadian formations involved, the campaign in Sicily was a comparatively short but intense period of exposure to unfamiliar battle conditions. As the American officer's comments indicated, the inexperienced formations underwent a severe baptism that revealed shortcomings in aspects of their training and preparation. Experienced divisions from North Africa were mostly made up of battle-hardened veterans, a significant advantage. Yet for them too Sicily proved a very different battleground from where their experience had been gained, most notably in the extent of the island's mountainous terrain. How this was utilized by the German and Italian defence, and its influence upon movement and fighting, was unparalleled by any previous experience in North Africa, even that gained in the Tunisian hills. The British 78th Division, for example, was regarded as mountain-warfare proficient after Tunisia and was tasked accordingly in Sicily. Yet its divisional history would later record its impressions of the Centuripe battle area thus: 'What impressed everybody was the scale of the mountainous country that had to be covered.' Clearly, nothing like it had been seen in Tunisia.[16]

So the challenge in Sicily was formidable indeed. The fighting components of the Allied armies had to adjust their basic tactical doctrine to the conditions in which they fought, irrespective of whether the unit had already been employed, and up to a point proven, in battle in North Africa, or inculcated only through training. In the latter case, the challenge was heightened by exposing inexperienced troops to the stresses and strains of battle for the first time. How successfully the Allied armies achieved this adjustment, and the lessons provided by the campaign experience, was closely examined by observation during the campaign itself and through subsequent post-battle investigation that was intended primarily to benefit their training organizations. This involved the accumulation of evidence by testimony, not only from battalion and regimental officers but also from those at corps and divisional level as well, and frequently too from the battle-hardened NCOs upon whom so much always depended in battle, and the men they commanded.

This evaluation of battle experience reflected an emphasis upon the problem of mounting and carrying through a successful attack that had, after all, been the campaign's principal challenge for Allied formations throughout. In addition there was also a need to assess the particular effectiveness of weapons and the best methods of employing them under varying circumstances. The extent to which the campaign experience validated training, and where it indicated the need for changes and improvements, was considered, and so too was how the individual soldier responded to the challenge of battle.

The Problem of Attack

Wigram believed that it had been quite easy for the Germans to defend their positions effectively by maintaining a thin screen of machine-guns, artillery and mortars sited on the reverse slope of the hills and with observation posts in the high ground, thereby enabling effective crossfire. Attacking such positions frontally, even with artillery support, played into German hands. The Germans maintained these defensive screens until the last moment, inflicting heavy casualties and then pulling back to new positions as Allied troops closed in. Attaining their objective, Allied troops invariably found the Germans had gone, leaving a small number of prisoners and only a few dead behind them. Few Allied soldiers would have argued with this assessment. Only as the campaign entered its final phase, with the Allied armies closing in upon Messina, did the Germans stand and fight, accepting higher casualties – but this was to cover their evacuation. This was the case at Agira and at Troina, where the Germans traded heavy losses among their hard-to-replace combat troops for the strategic necessity of time.

Wigram's view highlighted the problem of attacking a skilful defender in his well-chosen terrain who was adept at making the most of his limited strength in infantry and supporting firepower. In fact, Sicily gave the Allies their first real insight into how the German soldier would fight on the strategic and operational defensive. One of the most difficult challenges for the Allies was that of maintaining attack momentum once a German defence zone had been penetrated and the Germans were falling back to new positions. The closer the pursuit by Allied troops, and the quicker contact was resumed with the main German force to deny it time, the less organized and formidable those German defence positions were likely to be. But the sheer physical strain that this imposed in mountainous terrain in summer was itself a severely limiting factor for the pursuing Allied infantry, and the campaign clearly indicated the necessity of preparing troops adequately for such conditions. There was also the need to overcome the Germans' own delaying efforts, and one of the most serious encountered by the Allies was the extensive and clever German use of land mines.

The Land Mine Threat

In the Sicilian terrain, land mines proved a major problem, and under such conditions the Allies came up against the full potential of the land mine as a weapon integrated into a scheme of defence. For the Germans, land mines were not only a means of protecting their defensive positions and imposing casualties, they also offered a quick means of setting up a new defensive position. Mines also compensated to some extent for their lack of infantry to cover extended fronts. Mines were the hidden and dangerous sentries guarding approaches, and they could deny the use of valuable ground and compel attackers to follow certain routes.

Most importantly of all, the land mine was a weapon with which to secure valuable time by imposing delay. In Sicily the Allies did not encounter the extensive anti-tank minefields that the Germans had employed in the more open ground of Tunisia and earlier, but they did discover that the Germans employed mines on massive scale, and due to the terrain and the different nature of the campaign they also used them differently than previously. Several types of mine were encountered: the flat cylindrical anti-tank mines ('Tellerminen') with which Allied troops were already familiar; several variations of German and Italian anti-personnel mines; and, as the campaign neared its end, a considerable number of new types of mines with wooden casings ('Holzminen'), which were of particular concern because they defied discovery by mine-detectors. Only by carefully prodding the ground could these be located, usually with a long-bladed bayonet; the older First World War pattern bayonet was favoured by British mine-detecting teams for this reason. The Americans also reported the discovery of a mine with a plastic casing ('Topfminen'), equally hard to detect, which they considered would become more prevalent. They predicted also, and rightly, that as the Germans fell back towards their own soil the Allies would encounter more extensive use of land mines and an increased efficiency in mine weapons.[17] It was sound reasoning, for which the Sicily campaign provided plenty of evidence.

It was (and is) difficult to arrive at a reliable estimate of the casualties inflicted by German and Italian mines in Sicily, mainly because most mine casualties were fatal, and the causes of battlefield deaths were not precisely recorded. The Americans arrived at an approximate overall estimate of mines having caused 10% of their casualties in Sicily, and when in one example a field artillery battalion reported that 30% of its casualties were caused by mines this was considered an unusual case.[18] Among the infantry the majority of casualties were caused by automatic weapons, mortar fire and artillery, but the effect of land mines went far beyond killing and wounding – they also had a marked psychological effect. This was related to the nature of the specific mine types, for some German mines were particularly loathed and feared. For example, if an Allied solider had the misfortune to tread on the tiny trip hairs protruding from the ground of a 'Bouncing Betty', an anti-personnel mine was suddenly ejected out of the ground to detonate at head height, scattering lethal fragments. An extremely unpleasant variant, albeit encountered in small quantities, was one that when trodden upon immediately shot sharp, wounding objects straight upwards. If this did not kill its unfortunate victim it caused him excruciating wounds and almost certainly disposed of his virility. For obvious reasons, this type was known as a 'de-bollocker', and no doubt it was designed as much for its morale effect as its lethality.

The methods that the Germans employed also had an effect upon morale, by inducing great wariness and caution, as well as engendering a certain amount of natural fear. 'Total war' sees few niceties in the manner in which soldiers are prepared to kill the enemy, and when time permitted the German military engineers in Sicily employed ingenious and quite devilish mine-traps and booby-traps to catch unsuspecting Allied troops. In one example, wary British soldiers entered a building to find a cellar suspiciously filled with inviting whisky and gin. It was far too good to be true, and the cellar was found to be so elaborately booby-trapped that the only safe solution was for engineers and bomb-disposal teams to demolish the entire building. The dead left behind in a battle area, sometimes partially buried, were also booby-trapped to catch burial parties. The US Army campaign report quoted an infantry battalion executive officer who warned of a booby-trap danger to which troops who had just fought their first action were particularly susceptible: 'You must train men to stop souvenir hunting,' he warned. The Germans were adept at laying out likely souvenirs that often caught inexperienced troops, who after their first action set out to look for them. Many were killed or wounded as a result.[19] This was a form of psychological warfare, and it had its effect. After witnessing a few instances, Allied troops became extremely mine- and booby-trap conscious. And excessively cautious troops are not good at pursuit. The likely presence of mines and booby-traps meant a continual checking for their presence, and when discovered they had to be cleared.

Another German ploy that made this process very hazardous and pro-longed, made especially feasible with the hard-to-detect wooden mines, was multiple sowing. One mine might be discovered and removed, but another and still yet another might be buried underneath it, sometimes detonated by the removal of the first. There was no solution to this except to remove mines and check again, and again, and if necessary again, thereby increasing the time taken by mine-clearance teams. Battle accounts testify to the amount of time taken to clear routes and remove obstructions so that vital supplies could reach the forward infantry, and it was around their demolitions of communications choke-points, such as bridges and culverts, that the Germans sowed their mines most extensively, sometimes with a mix of various types requiring different methods of removal.

In time the Allied troops learned how to recognize the ground most likely to conceal mines and how to locate and remove them, but, whereas the gaining of such experience saved lives, mines invariably cost time. As the US 1st Infantry Division reported of its Sicilian experience, in the mountains the Germans proved that they could break contact by employing mines and demolitions, covering their locations with long-range artillery. It described a typical scenario in which the Germans and Italians would have withdrawn from a town through which ran just one road. The town would be found demolished, mines would be laid every five or ten feet, all bridges would be blown, nearby river beds mined, craters blown in stretches of the road, and mountain slides dropped.[20]

In terrain that was difficult if not impossible for vehicles, the comparatively few existing roads were of vital importance. So too was making maximum use of the available vehicles to get men and supplies forward, and it became common practice for Allied troops to pile aboard vehicles, even riding upon the running boards and fenders. But mines made this so hazardous that troops had to be warned against the practice. A vehicle detonating a mine might protect its driver and occupants from death if not from wounds, especially if it was sand-bagged for extra protection, but those riding on running boards and fenders were almost certain to be killed. Drivers also learned to remain on the roads. Engineers and mine clearance teams usually had little time to check and clear anything but the actual roads and many vehicles and their occupants were lost to mines simply by pulling off onto the verges, not all of which were marked as not having been cleared of mines. Little time could be spared during the advance, however, and a Gunner officer with the British 50th Division later recalled

> sitting on the bonnet of the tracked carrier looking for a disturbed surface on paths we followed, touching the driver's shoulder to stop when suspicion

arose. There was no time for "sweeping" ahead; we had to get on. One less lucky carrier had been blown up into a tree and was lodged forlornly in a leafy grave.[21]

In Sicily, as with later campaigns in mainland Europe, the Germans usually had the advantage of knowing the ground over which they were withdrawing far better than their pursuers – in any event, they certainly had the advantage of occupying it first. It was therefore obvious to them what ground their enemies would choose for concentration areas, observation posts and artillery positions, and whenever time and opportunity allowed they mined them all. This proved particularly hazardous for the Allied gunners, striving to keep up, to provide essential fire support to the infantry advance, for they had to locate and occupy new forward positions as rapidly as possible. The mountainous terrain meant that there were few really good gun positions, but whatever ground was chosen had to be swept for mines, usually beginning with the routes for the individual guns and their positions, and then gradually extending out to cover all areas of a battery's activity. The Americans reported that the provision of sufficient mine-detectors and the creation within artillery units of trained mine-clearing detachments became essential.[22] The same was true of the infantry, for in Sicily the task of detecting and clearing mines proved far too great for the engineers alone to cope with. American infantry and artillery officers were unanimous in their call for all ranks to be given some training in mine-detection and clearance.

An attempt to extend training for dealing with mines had occurred before the campaign. Several infantry regiments had sent officer and NCO cadres to the Engineer Training Center in North Africa run by the United States Fifth Army, at that time an Allied training formation, who on their return to their units conducted their own courses. Other regiments employed their own engineers to train detachments, usually of about 50 men, for use when needed. These measures, while useful, proved insufficient to meet the mine challenge in Sicily, and during the campaign infantry, artillery and armoured units detailed men from non-essential roles to the task of mine-clearance. It was not only the effect of land mines that became apparent during the Sicily campaign, but also the sheer scale of the threat that they posed.

✝✝✝✝✝✝✝✝✝✝✝✝✝✝✝✝✝✝

The Gunners' Campaign

Throughout the campaign in Sicily the Allies possessed the advantage of superior firepower, building up on the island a force of artillery that the Germans and Italians could not match. This was supplemented by naval gunfire support during the advances along the coast when actions were fought within range of warships' guns. This is not to forget the vital contribution of naval gunfire support during the initial invasion and consolidation of the beachheads when little artillery had been landed ashore.

The Allied air forces also were heavily committed to supporting the campaign, bringing under attack German and Italian defensive zones, troop and gun concentration areas, and the arteries of movement and supply. Although comparatively little of this air effort was in direct close air support of Allied troops engaged at the battlefront, German and Italian formations were given little respite in daylight from the threat of air attack throughout the depth of their sectors on the island. However, in terms of influencing the course and outcome of the fighting at the battlefront, the Allied superiority in firepower was exercised primarily by their artillery, and it was the gunners who carried the continual 24-hours-a-day responsibility of providing support to the infantry as they fought their way inland through the mountains and cleared the defended towns and villages in their path.

The gunners' greatest challenge, which they met successfully, was to keep up with the forward troops in the extremely difficult terrain. Artillery had to be used aggressively and well forward, not only to provide responsive fire support to the infantry but also as part of the pursuit, to keep the withdrawing Germans and Italians under harassing and interdicting fire, and to keep them from laying mines and demolitions. This meant that the formalized positioning of the guns, and much else in terms of pre-campaign training, went for nothing. In Sicily, guns were often positioned right in the infantry areas and sometimes even ahead of them. For example, an artillery officer with the US 45th Infantry Division recorded on two occasions in Sicily where all the Division's guns were deployed actually ahead of its front line infantry to keep the enemy under fire.[23] The pace at which the artillery had to move in order to achieve this meant continual displacement and an ongoing reconnaissance of movement routes and likely gun areas – much of this and the actual occupation of positions having to take place at night. Considerable ingenuity was employed in making the best use of whatever firing positions were available. Many of these positions in the mountainous terrain were completely unorthodox and would not have been recognized in British and American artillery manuals. 'We have had to put guns in places', recalled an American gunner officer of Sicily, 'where only a billy-goat could have gotten his hoofs.' He also pointed out that more than half the positions his batteries used in Sicily would have been considered impossible during his Division's training in the United States.[24] Sometimes guns had to be winched into such positions, and occasionally, when there was no other way, individual gun positions had to be blasted out of the rock with demolition charges. The watchwords became resourcefulness and determination, plus a refusal to accept the seemingly impossible.

Sicily amounted to a tremendous achievement for the Allied gunners, who served their infantry well throughout every stage of the campaign. As an American artillery battalion executive officer noted for the US Army's campaign report, it often appeared that an area offered no suitable gun positions, but if it seemed a case of no artillery support for the infantry because of terrain then they always found a way to get the guns in somehow.[25] He was speaking for every American, British and Canadian gunner in Sicily.

The Allied gunners coped with situations that, for the most part, their training and, in most cases, their experience had simply not prepared them. In passing on their campaign experience, American gunner officers urged the necessity of training artillery units in the selection and occupation of positions in most difficult terrain, not only to accustom them to the problems but also to inculcate the necessary degree of close cooperation and teamwork necessary between all personnel of different roles, which alone enabled the challenge to be met successfully.[26] The problem in Sicily was not just of movement and deployment in difficult ground: there was also the need to ensure a sufficient stock of ammunition in the forward area and to get it to the batteries and individual guns wherever they happened to be. This challenge was also met successfully but demanded a heavy commitment of vehicles for road movement, considerable manpower and much ingenuity and physical effort in manhandling where vehicles simply could not get far enough.

This situation was exacerbated because of the imperative to keep the Germans and Italians under near-continuous fire and the great reliance by the Allied infantry upon artillery support in both attack and defence. Ammunition was expended at a phenomenal rate. Take one example: to meet the estimated requirements of its 264 25-pounder field guns and 88 medium guns for the period 28 July to 2 August alone, the British XXX Corps had to be supplied with 142,000 rounds.[27] This was true of ammunition of all kinds, and not just for the artillery. For example, the Americans warned that it was better to have mules keep two heavy 81mm mortars of an infantry battalion's support company up with the forward troops than six. Two would keep firing for longer, whereas six would soon use up the ammunition and become useless. They also noted the high rate of ammunition expenditure of the infantry support weapons, citing a case where a heavy machine-gun had fired up to some 5,000–6,000 rounds in a single day and an 81mm mortar 800 rounds in a day. In one instance two 60mm mortars had fired off 1,000 rounds in a day. These were acknowledged to be high averages, but they make their point.[28]

In terms of gunnery technique and organizational procedure, the campaign did not see any radical changes, nor did it indicate the need for any. The basic concern of artillery battery commanders became that of identifying locations from where they could deliver the maximum support, ensure sufficient dispersion to offset the effects of enemy fire, and from where they could displace rapidly. Batteries might be positioned along a stretch of road, as were the guns of the British 78th Division during the Centuripe battle, or any on likely available ground. Once in place, the guns might be deployed according to a wide variety of firing positions depending upon what the ground permitted: staggered lines, rough 'box' positions, 'W' positions, ovals and horseshoes were all employed, though with the risk of enemy counter-battery fire or, although very infrequent, air attack, dispersion was usually emphasized. The Americans reported that they sought to ensure 75 to 100 yards between individual pieces in their 155mm batteries, and that the 105mm batteries tried for a 200-yard front whenever possible. Self-propelled batteries sometimes adopted a circle position, with 100 yards between guns.[29] Guns and positions were usually camouflaged against enemy observation, especially as the German and Italian observers possessed the advantage of occupying higher ground, from which they could look into the Allied positions to some depth. On one occasion Italian observers taken prisoner on such overlooking ground told their American captors that one of the first things they could spot was poorly arranged camouflage nets; if these were not draped properly they could easily give an artillery position away.[30] As the campaign progressed and the risk of air attack declined, camouflage discipline tended to become lax. No doubt the continual displacement that the gunners had to contend with was also a factor in this, but it was dangerous and ultimately required corrective action to ensure adherence to procedures that were often time-consuming and elaborate but nevertheless essential.

In another respect, that of issuing orders and detailed instructions, the campaign indicated that the prolonged and rigidly standard procedures emphasized in training could be, and indeed had to be, dispensed with under the pressure of time and operational realities. Field orders as outlined in training were not used in Sicily, observed an officer of the US 45th Division artillery, but fragmentary orders became the rule, and the standard practice was to get the batteries on the road, select an available position and tell the gunners to go in and shoot.[31] This was a case of valuable and necessary procedures in training proving to be a hindrance in battle, although gunners needed to become very experienced and familiar with the campaign conditions before they could thus move away from, or adapt, what they had been taught. In fact, and like so many of the Allied gunners that had gone to Sicily without previous battle experience, the 45th Division's gunners had become proficient veterans.

What Artillery Could Do

Superiority in artillery depended not only upon numbers of guns, but upon the ability to identify and locate targets and engage them quickly. Much of the fire delivered by the Allied artillery during the campaign was observed fire, directed and adjusted by forward observation officers with the leading infantry and armoured units. The Americans confidently reckoned that 90% of all observed fire was adjusted by forward observers.[32] They were invaluable, and when they became casualties or were unable to get forward with their equipment the result was often no artillery support. To take one Canadian example: when during the advance on Valguarnera on 17 July the Hastings and Prince Edward Regiment struck out across the goat paths skirting the hillsides, the tank carrying the artillery forward observer and his wireless set could not follow, and consequently the infantry were without artillery support throughout all the following day.[33]

The necessity of training and equipping infantry officers for directing artillery fire soon became apparent in Sicily. In another example, again involving Canadian troops and this time during the fighting around Cate-nanuova, the initiative of a junior infantry officer, who had taken command of his company of the West Nova Scotias after the company commander became a casualty, turned the scale against a German counterattack. Lacking a forward artillery observer, and although himself inexperienced in the role, the lieutenant directed the fire of a troop of Royal Artillery self-propelled guns by wireless, which successfully forced the Germans to retreat.[34] Throughout the campaign artillery forward observers also proved to be a means of gaining timely tactical information valuable to the leading infantry and also to the intelligence staffs of higher formations. This was acknowledged by the US 45th Infantry Division, whose staff reported the excellence of its artillery observers, who had found targets and brought down fire where it did the most good. Most of the Division's artillery fire in Sicily was directed by forward observers, it noted.[35]

The observers could not be everywhere or see everything however; they also depended upon the infantry to report likely targets to them. The Americans subsequently estimated that more than half the targets engaged by their artillery during the campaign were picked up first by the infantry and then passed to their accompanying forward observers, emphasizing the importance of good communications. The Canadian Division paid a heavy price during the campaign because of the loss of most of its communications equipment when the ship carrying it to Sicily was torpedoed by a U-boat. Following their own experience, the Americans emphasized the importance of having sufficient numbers of skilled wireless (radio) technicians to keep equipment working, and the need to train extra personnel (such as truck and jeep drivers) as operators in the basic use of such equipment. Given the terrain and the dispersion of artillery units, the functioning of artillery units also depended upon wireless or telephone and line communication. The extent of this had not been anticipated prior to the campaign and considerable improvisation was necessary. Much use was made of captured German and Italian equipment, and most artillery battalions in Sicily had small wire reels, salvaged or captured, carried on their guns.[36]

The sheer volume of fire that the Allied gunners could put down, and how quickly they could do it, was probably the severest shock experienced by the Germans and Italians during the campaign. German accounts, of which there are plenty, give voice to this. When they occupied Troina on 7 August, American troops discovered a letter from a German artilleryman: this was translated and reproduced in the US Army campaign report. It told of how the German troops were harassed from position to position by what they termed 'magic fire' (Feuerzauber), the sudden and heavy artillery barrages fired by the American guns. Experienced men considered it worse than they had been under on the Eastern Front, and there was no let up and or escape.[37] If such accounts are to be believed, and there is no reason to doubt them (in this case the letter was quoted in what was at the time a confidential US Army report), then clearly the German troops were subject to a weight of fire against which they could do little. At Troina, for example, the Americans massed twelve battalions of artillery in support of the 1st Infantry Division, whose commander subsequently reported that this enabled individual companies to be heavily supported during an attack and that the guns were able to harass the Germans day and night.[38] It was this weight of fire that frequently turned the scale against the Germans when they counterattacked precarious and thinly held American positions on the slopes.

Despite the gunners' problems of a withdrawing enemy sometimes slipping out of artillery range, and the mountainous terrain compelling high-angle fire with trajectories that prematurely burned out shells' time-fuzes, they established their ascendancy over the German and Italian guns. When engaged in counter-battery work they usually silenced German and Italian fire. In this the use of artillery observation aircraft or, in the British nomenclature, AOP (Air Observation Post) light aircraft was especially effective, made possible through the possession of air superiority. The mere presence of such aircraft over the battle area was often sufficient to silence German and Italian batteries, whose gunners knew that once spotted they would come under heavy return artillery fire or Allied air attack. In one example, cited by the US 3rd Infantry Division, when German artillery was laying heavy interdiction fire on the only road running west of Cape Orlando, along which the Division was moving, an artillery observation aircraft was sent up to try and locate the German batteries. Fire stopped as soon as the aircraft was visible to the German gunners. The Division's artillery commander then ordered a plane kept airborne all the time, and consequently not a single round was fired upon the road. This was described as universal experience throughout the campaign.[39]

It was particularly difficult to locate and engage mobile targets such as German self-propelled guns, prowling tanks employed as moving pillboxes, and (the particular bane of Allied infantrymen and gunners) the German Nebelwerfer rocket projectors. Success then depended primarily upon the forward observers and how quickly they could spot and adjust fire. The Nebelwerfer reflected the German ability to develop light-weight, simple, and cheaply produced but very potent infantry-support weapons to offset their own lack of artillery. The Nebelwerfer (literally 'smoke projector', reflecting their original purpose) was a six-barrelled weapon on a light two-wheeled carriage fitted with elevating and traversing gears. It could fire smoke or high-explosive rounds of 15cm calibre, and it had a high rate of fire, the electrically-fired barrels being released in succession over a 90-second period. The noise of the rockets led Allied troops to term the Nebelwerfer 'Moaning Minnie', and it had an unnerving effect on even experienced Allied troops. Once they had fired, Nebelwerfer crews immediately moved to other positions, making the task of Allied counter-fire particularly difficult. A Nebelwerfer emitted an immense flash on firing, but when this was seen its crew were usually already limbering up. To catch them became an art in itself – once they had gained experience, Allied forward observers could often 'second guess' the likely positions, usually about 400–500 yards from the original firing-point, to where the German crews would move and then call down fire upon them. But it was a hit-or-miss business, literally.

German infantry caught in the open, whether moving to new positions or attempting to counterattack, could be annihilated by Allied artillery fire. Recalling the brief but sharp counterattacks that German troops attempted during the Troina battle, the US 1st Infantry Division reported that they were often slaughtered by artillery before they could reach the forward American positions. On the other hand, enemy troops well dug-in were more vulnerable to the demoralizing effect of continual artillery fire that might not, in fact, inflict many casualties at all. The US 1st Infantry Division observed that the Germans were able to avoid many casualties from artillery by digging deeper than the average American soldier was willing to do, and captured German troops told how their officers had made them dig 'another two feet' when they thought they had dug enough. In some cases they dug down and 'cut under' in order to prevent casualties from air bursts. In fact, there were not many casualties when the men were in foxholes.[40] Not all the ground occupied as defensive positions in Sicily was conducive to such digging-in, and where it was not, casualties were greater.

Artillery in Support of the Infantry Attack

Reliance upon a heavy artillery concentration or upon a moving artillery barrage to get attacking infantry on to their objectives depended for success upon how quickly the infantry could follow the fire. A British observer in Sicily, impressed by the reliance upon artillery in the attack, wryly noted that if a cabbage got in the way it would likely receive a thousand tons of shell, and that a single enemy pill-box or company locality might be engaged by an entire division's artillery. He pointed out that plenty of the enemy troops would survive such a bombardment, but that 'they will still be running around in circles if your own infantry hop in quickly'.[41] There were instances in Sicily when this worked well. A concentrated weight of fire on a limited attack frontage enabled the Princess Patricia's Canadian Light Infantry to capture the 'Lion' defensive feature during the Agira battle. A German prisoner who had previously fought in

Poland, France, Russia and North Africa told his captors that he had never experienced the like before, and a captured officer reportedly asked the Canadians if he could see one of the 'automatic field guns' capable of delivering such a rate of fire.[42] Those German troops not killed or wounded were quite simply stupefied by the detonations and by the vibratory shock, being rendered incapable of resisting the attacking infantry who were following closely upon the bombardment.

In another example quoted in the US Army campaign report, a battalion commander recalled an occasion where his men could not get forward because the Germans occupied superior ground and had them pinned down with rifle and machine-gun fire. This German position then received the massed fire of nine battalions of his division's artillery, some 1,500 rounds falling in under 30 minutes. Afterwards his men emerged from cover to 'walk through' the position without loss, finding dead German soldiers scattered everywhere. Although no further details are given and the officer is quoted anonymously, his description does not suggest that his battalion was deliberately following a moving barrage like the Patricias did at Agira. Rather, their advance seems to have been blocked by a German position against which they called down fire, most probably through a forward observer, and that they resumed their advance immediately after what must have been a tremendous pounding of the enemy-occupied ground. The reference to the large number of scattered dead suggests that the Germans had not been in well-prepared defences, either because the ground was too hard or that they had not had time to dig-in properly. They had probably not expected their dominating positions to be targeted with such a saturation of fire.[43]

But, as accounts of the fighting in Sicily indicate, such instances as the Patricias' success at Agira and that cited by the American officer above were comparatively rare. In the extremely broken and mountainous ground it was usually impossible for attacking Allied infantry to move quickly enough to be able to exploit the effects of such fire. Sometimes it was a challenge even to know whether they were advancing in the right direction, especially at night – unfamiliar mountainous terrain proved very disorientating as well as being fraught with unforeseen physical obstacles. Usually those Germans who had survived the bombardment (and if they were very well dug-in it would have been most of them) had sufficient time to recover and man their weapons, knowing very well that an Allied infantry attack was in the offing. At that point, with their timed artillery support finished or with the barrage they were supposed to be following moving on too far ahead, and with their own higher headquarters at battalion level and above most likely in only intermittent contact and uncertain of their progress and exact location and of the battle situation as a whole, the attacking Allied infantry companies were quite on their own.

This was acknowledged by the British 152nd Infantry Brigade (comprising the 5th Cameron Highlanders and the 2nd and 5th Seaforth Highlanders) of the 51st (Highland) Division. In reviewing its experience, it reported that even a high standard of artillery support was not nearly as effective against dug-in troops as might be imagined and that, especially in mountainous terrain, infantry must expect to have to deal with many of the enemy with their own weapons.[44] This brings us back to Lieutenant Colonel Lionel Wigram, whose view in August 1943, after seeing battle at first hand in Sicily, was that the method of infantry attack employed was all wrong.

The Infantry Attack in Sicily:
A British Specialist's Interpretation

In Sicily, Wigram was very concerned to see how training matched up to the realities of battle. He was well qualified to comment on the tactical methods he witnessed and how they could be improved, for in England he had been the Chief Instructor at Barnards Castle in County Durham, the central battle school established to train instructors for the British Army's divisional battle schools. At these schools, students were put through a course of 'Battle Drill', a mostly practical instruction in minor tactics intended to provide the junior leaders of what was a rapidly created and militarily uninitiated 'mass citizen army' with the basic skills necessary to lead men successfully in battle.[45] Wigram had been one of the committed pioneers of 'Battle Drill', and in Sicily he had the chance to meet many of his former Barnards Castle students, by then battle-experienced officers and men, and to obtain their views and discuss his ideas with them.

Although he had begun the campaign as an observer, Wigram joined the British 78th Infantry Division when it arrived in Sicily. He understood the vital importance of assimilating and applying newly acquired battle experience to training, and he was prepared to examine critically and analyze practices that were becoming standardized and orthodox. He began by challenging the by then universally accepted assumption about the chief determining factor of the Sicily campaign – the terrain. He rejected the view, heard on all sides, that the mountainous and difficult country was ideal for defence and impossible for attack. Wigram argued that, although mountainous, the ground in Sicily was also close, covered with olive groves, plantations and crops, cut by numerous irrigation ditches and divided by walls. These were seen at the time (and have been described as such ever since in accounts of the campaign) as serious obstacles to the attack. To the method of attack employed by the Allies in Sicily they were. Wigram saw them differently, as positively advantageous to the different form of attack that he advocated – that of infiltration.

He cited German small-unit tactics from earlier in the war and, especially, how in Malaya the Japanese had used small infiltration teams to slip past British positions at night to undermine them from the rear. Operating in ones and twos and armed with light automatic weapons and machine-guns, these highly trained specialist troops had made good use of the prevailing cover to harass communications, isolate and pick off observation posts and generally to cause disorder and confusion. They had, in Wigram's view, sustained few casualties themselves but had had a disproportionate effect in relation to their numbers, for they had compelled a British withdrawal from position to position without the Japanese having to make the type of attacks the British defence was designed to meet, and which its troops expected.

With the campaign in Sicily indicating that the Germans were now fighting principally rearguard-type defensive battles and were likely to remain doing so, Wigram saw no reason why they should be permitted to exploit the terrain as they had done so well in Sicily. Instead, the attackers should themselves take advantage of it through the use of infiltration, with a tactical approach modelled on the methods previously employed by the Germans and Japanese. He advocated the organization of similar infiltration teams, suggesting that each infantry battalion could produce one or two platoons with the men trained to work in groups of three. Each group would consist of a machine-gunner equipped with the Bren light machine-gun, another with a Thompson submachine-gun and the third presumably a rifleman, though in this latter Wigram was not specific. Crucially, each team of three must be prepared to operate entirely on its own. He envisaged a scenario in which, once contact had been established with enemy positions, these teams would be sent out at dusk to be in place behind them by first light. Their action behind the enemy's forward positions, combined with the main attack threat to the enemy's front, would compel an enemy withdrawal.

The primary determinant of tactical success was the ability of the soldier. Small-team infiltration demanded a high degree of personal initiative as well as skilled fieldcraft and what might be termed 'battle-sense', the ability to 'read' a combat situation and know how to respond to it. Fieldcraft and 'battle-sense' might come with training but mostly through experience: they are the hallmark of the veteran soldier. But the required levels of initiative and aptitude for infiltration were another matter. Such attributes are personality-linked, and not every soldier possessed them. Wigram, the infantry training specialist, understood this perfectly well. He accepted that only a relatively few men could be entrusted with the infiltration role and that it was an impossible ideal to try and train the Army as a whole in it. In this he was also reflecting a reality imposed upon the British Army of the Second World War. It was handicapped by the fact that the other services, the Royal Air Force in particular, received the majority of higher-aptitude recruits. In this respect, even within the Army itself, with its own technical requirements to be met across its various arms, the infantry was the poor relation. Another factor too was the creation of the specialized volunteer fighting formations, the airborne and commando forces. Their rigorous entry requirements, toughness and, in due course, battle achievements, gave them an 'élite' status that attracted many of the brighter, individualistic, and more aggressive men away from the 'line' infantry battalions. Certainly the British and American airborne actions in Sicily indicated soldiers capable of fulfilling Wigram's requirements.

Yet Wigram was convinced that the British infantry battalions could produce men capable of infiltration fighting, and he was well placed to judge his material. To make his point, he cited an example from the latter stages of the Sicily fighting when his own battalion headquarters was being harassed by German snipers and machine-gunners concealed among the rocks and trees at the foot of Mount Etna. Wigram ordered a young platoon commander 'to deal with the matter'. At first this officer tried to employ his entire platoon but soon gave this up and instead picked just four of his men and set out with them. Throughout the rest of the day they fought what Wigram described as an infiltration battle in which they stalked the Germans with quite remarkable success. With no casualties to themselves, they killed three German snipers, took six prisoners and captured two heavy machine-guns and a large quantity of sniper equipment. Wigram recalled talking with these men on their return. They frankly admitted to having been frightened at first, but as the day wore on and they realized that the Germans were poor shots they felt a sense of superiority, and by the end were, in Wigram's soldiers' terms, 'thoroughly enjoying themselves'.

This implied that if the right men (and clearly Wigram's platoon commander knew which of his men to pick) were given the opportunity to exercise their skill and initiative under the appropriate circumstances, then their confidence and effectiveness would increase. Every platoon, he believed, could find a few such men. The fighting in Sicily indicated that the same was true of the Canadian and American infantry.

As Wigram's example indicated, the attributes necessary for infiltration work mirrored those demanded of the sniper, or of those sent to catch him. Both sides made extensive use of snipers in Sicily, and the nature of the fighting and the terrain made good snipers a valuable infantry asset. American infantry officers interviewed for the US Army's campaign study advocated a higher degree of sniper training but warned that the capable sniper had to be more than a crack marksman with a special rifle. The elements of patience, study of enemy habits and ability to operate and move with almost perfect concealment were the important attributes he needed to possess. He was, in effect, an individual. In an unconscious endorsement of Wigram, these American infantry officers went on to describe how they had dealt with German and Italian snipers in Sicily. These had been, they recalled, 'a major nuisance' when firing from well-concealed delaying positions and from the mountains. Units learned to tackle the problem in a number of ways, but the most effective method found was for infantry units to create and train special squads of 'sniper killers'. These squads would go out to locate the enemy snipers, and when they had done so part of the squad would engage the sniper's attention while the others worked around to the flanks to eliminate him.[46] No doubt the American officers and NCOs picked their men carefully for these squads, and they would have been precisely the type capable of the infiltration tactics advocated by Wigram.

Battalions from the British Commonwealth and Dominions were likely to contain proportionally a large number of men whose background and lifestyle had equipped them with the attributes necessary for such fighting. The 1st Canadian Infantry Division went to Sicily as an inexperienced formation, but as the campaign developed there were several instances of detached forces of Canadian troops successfully conducting infiltration in the mountainous terrain. One of the most notable occurred during the closing stages of the Agira battle, when the Loyal Edmonton Regiment sent out a fighting patrol of two platoons commanded, be it noted, by a Sergeant of the Battalion's Support Company, to investigate German positions north of Agira. In the hills to the north of the River Salso they surprised a force of some 200 Germans and routed them with mortar and machine-guns, killing 24 and taking nine prisoners.[47] They had clearly responded well to the opportunity to exercise their initiative and skill; Wigram would have approved.

Whether infiltration tactics would have been possible by units larger than Wigram advocated is questionable. That even battalions might achieve it was in fact suggested to him; although he did not rule out the possibility, he was extremely doubtful of its viability. The Germans, he noted, always protected their flanks by machine-gun positions and gunner observation posts, and in his opinion forces of company or even full platoon size would be unlikely to infiltrate past them successfully except on the most favourable ground. Failure would bring heavy casualties. Wigram evidently believed that to attempt infiltration with anything larger than the teams he advocated carried too much risk. Larger units might also have been unwieldy and stultified the individual initiative he considered so important. No one can discount the influence of luck, good or bad, in battle, but Wigram was seeking a surer method to unlock German defensive positions than one that left too much to chance.

There was evidence to support the fact that his infiltration tactics would work. As he himself observed, in Sicily the Germans did not withdraw from their defensive lines according to a timed schedule, nor were there any 'last ditch' stands. Instead the Germans fell back when the attack pressure was finally about to overwhelm them, usually only after they had been able to fight a prolonged defence and had inflicted considerable casualties upon their attackers, and, most importantly, when they were menaced from the rear. Indeed, it was when in danger of being outflanked and with their likely escape route threatened that the Germans finally relinquished such positions as Agira, Centuripe and the most formidable Troina, where General Rodt commanding the 15th Panzer Grenadier Division became increasingly concerned for the security of Highway 120 behind him once American infantry began to outflank his positions. It was to accelerate this process that Wigram devised his infiltration teams. Had they existed, they might very well have got forward by stealth and, by using the terrain to their advantage, disrupted the German positions that were all too often invulnerable to direct attack even when it was supported by heavy firepower. Ironically, in his own post-Sicily campaign 'experience report' General Rodt considered that Allied infantrymen were generally superior to his own men in what he termed 'Indianerkrieg', or fieldcraft, and that they had been good at small-group night-infiltration between his positions.[48]

Until such teams were formed and trained to practise their 'Indianerkrieg' against the Germans on a significant scale, however, there was no alternative for the Allies but to continue their attack methods on current lines. This Wigram accepted, though he was convinced that it was only a matter of training and that it would not take too long. Accepting that the adoption of infiltration as he advocated could not be immediate, Wigram also indicated where the method of attack as practised during the campaign fell down and could be improved. In this part of his report he provides an extremely valuable contemporary insight into the nature of the fighting in Sicily. His was a dispassionate professional assessment of a military problem and how to deal with it, prepared by an expert trainer of infantry for the Army's own use. As such, Wigram was nothing if not realistic, and he was unreservedly frank.

His viewing of battle at first hand in Sicily convinced him that 'Battle Drill' as taught was useful for training and would work in battle if applied by regular battalions who had practised it for many months. Essentially, it involved applying fire-and-movement tactics in attack and reflected the assumption that a defending enemy rifleman or light machine-gunner took a few seconds to observe a target, aim and fire. Therefore 'Battle Drill' attempted to minimize the exposure of the attacking infantry. Once coming under enemy fire, each infantry section split into three groups: two riflemen, three riflemen, and the Bren light machine-gun group of two or three men. Each group then advanced separately, sprinting for twenty yards before dropping to the ground, and then another group would get up, and so on. The Bren group moved on the flank so as to get the clearest possible field of fire when on the ground. This was the 'pepper-pot' method, and its obvious drawback was its dependence upon suitable ground and the fact that the Bren group could not be in continuous action to provide covering fire. Another, somewhat more complex, form of fire and movement, the 'lane' method, sought to solve this problem by dividing the attack into lanes for advance and Bren fire support.[49]

Sicily convinced Wigram that all this was an ideal, and that for the majority of infantry units in battle something much simpler was required. The main problem with 'Battle Drill' as he saw it was that it presupposed a platoon team in which every individual soldier knew his job and his place and that every man was brave enough and experienced enough to do as he was told. Wigram came to the conclusion in Sicily that in practice this did not happen, and that typically only about half of a platoon really understood what they were doing in battle, and that in every platoon there were a few men who would not do what was expected of them.

The actual pattern of attack in Sicily as witnessed and interpreted by Wigram was as follows. Attacks were mostly at night and invariably carefully prepared, he noted, with the troops going forward under the cover of artillery concentrations or a rolling barrage. When the barrage lifted, the surviving enemy troops opened fire with machine-guns. It was at this point, Wigram believed, that the platoon battle started and it was also then that the battle as a whole was lost or won. On very rare occasions some form of fire-and-movement was employed by company and platoon commanders, and it invariably enabled them to take the objective with few casualties. Mostly, however, there was no fire-and-movement applied at all, and the enemy positions were taken by what Wigram called 'guts and movement'. In the majority of cases, as soon as the barrage lifted and the German positions opened fire, the entire platoon went to ground in to cover, except the platoon commander and three or four 'gutful' men.

These 'gutful' men under the platoon commander would dash straight into the German position without any covering fire and take it. In some instances, Wigram pointed out, positions were taken by as few as two men, and he asserted that every battalion commander confirmed that it was always the same group of nine or ten who were there first and on whom the battle ultimately depended. Wigram had personally seen this method employed on all but one of the battles in which he took part, and it explained for him something that had hitherto puzzled him – why many experienced soldiers insisted that 'you must never allow men to lie down in a battle'. Wigram considered the method both typically British and without equal in courage, but suggestions made to him by some infantry officers that it was successful and resulted in few casualties he firmly rejected, arguing that, while this may have been true of casualties in quantity, it certainly was not true of casualties in quality. Analyzing a typical platoon as six 'gutful' men who will do anything and go anywhere, while the others would follow so long as they were well led, he pointed out that the group from which casualties could not be spared was the 'gutful' group, yet he estimated the casualties in this group often amounted to 100% per month. He warned that a more economical method of fighting had to be found.

Was he right? His assertions about infantry performance carry a good deal of conviction. After all, a typical platoon would contain a cross-section of individuals, most of whom would do their duty in battle. Though extreme circumstances tend to produce men who rise to them, often to their own and every one else's surprise, certainly not every infantryman could be expected to be a hero. Among the large number of experienced battalion officers with whom he discussed his ideas, Wigram found general agreement with only some slight divergence of views on his figures. His description of how enemy positions were captured tallies with too many descriptions in published accounts, such as official histories, regimental histories, and in contemporary battalion war diaries for Wigram to have been far wrong – of acts of heroism by individuals or by two or three men that clinched success in an attack. All too many of these men were either wounded or received posthumous awards for what they did, and the casualties in battalion and company officers and NCOs tend to speak for themselves.

This was not just a matter of courage but of experience, for as the veterans were reduced by casualties so the infantry battalions could lose effectiveness until the replacements in turn became sufficiently experienced. Attacking in Sicily was a very costly business for the infantry; Wigram was warning that it was actually far more costly than even the casualty lists indicated.

His suggested solution was for the infantry to adopt a simpler 'Battle Drill' of fire-and-movement taking account of the fact that there were only four to six men in a platoon upon whom the battle might depend. For a night attack behind artillery concentrations or a barrage which was, he noted, the commonest form of attack employed in the campaign, he advocated dividing a platoon of 22 men into three groups as follows:

- 1st Group: all the riflemen under the platoon commander.
- 2nd Group: three Bren teams (three men to each gun) under the platoon sergeant.
- 3rd Group: the 2-inch mortar team following behind the 1st Group.

The leaders of the three groups accounted for three of the most reliable men in the platoon, while the other three reliable men were to act as seconds-in-command in each group, ready to take over if the group commander became a casualty. Wigram must have been aware of the high casualties in junior officers and NCOs during the campaign, and how in battle responsibility for pressing home an attack often devolved as a result.

During an attack, Wigram envisaged the 1st (rifle) Group advancing in a fairly tight, night formation, essential in his opinion to maintain cohesion; the 2nd (Bren) Group would do the same. These groups would move side-by-side, with a gap of anything between 50 and 100 yards between them depending upon visibility, with the Bren group a little to the rear. The 3rd (mortar) Group would move behind the 1st Group, at a distance of about 50 yards.

Once the supporting artillery concentration or barrage lifted and the German positions opened fire, the rifle group would go to ground. Then the platoon sergeant, whom Wigram noted could really be relied upon to do this, would get the three Brens of his group into action at once engaging the German machine-guns. This, Wigram asserted, would invariably silence the German guns. This was an important point, and Wigram had spent some time investigating it, having checked with a large number of platoon commanders. They confirmed that German machine-guns always used tracer rounds, and always stopped firing when the Brens opened up, most probably because the German gunners did not want to draw fire and were trying to locate the Bren positions. For as long as the Brens fired the German guns stayed silent, opening up again only when the Brens had stopped. It was a noted fact that Bren fire and the fire of the German infantry MG.34 or MG.42 machine-guns was never seen or heard at the same time. Even inaccurate Bren fire would cause the German machine-guns to stop.

Wigram does not mention whether he also checked his views on this with the experience of Canadian and American infantry officers. Most likely he had no opportunity of doing so. Nevertheless, the US Army campaign report tends to bear him out. This too was quite frank, there being a general consensus among American infantry officers that their men did not shoot enough in battle, a legacy of being taught not to shoot unless a target was visible and profitable. They believed that Sicily proved this was a mistake, and they emphasized the importance of a controlled but continuous fire being directed against a locality from which the enemy was firing, whether the enemy troops were visible or not. Fire, they pointed out, reduced fire. If men halted and lay down without firing, they were invariably subjected to heavy fire, whereas if they kept moving forward and if fire were maintained upon the enemy locality, the enemy fire was immediately reduced. In their opinion, this was of such importance that it could not be over-stressed in training. Another problem they noted was that troops tended to fire at the obvious portions of the enemy position rather than straight ahead at less visible targets. Consequently the fire distribution was uneven, with stretches of the enemy position unengaged and able to concentrate their fire upon the American troops. This was seen as a deficiency in fire training in relation to fire-and-movement, the principal concern being that many troops did not yet understand that the 'fire' aspect of fire-and-movement meant suppressing the enemy position by a volume of fire to cover movement, and that it should not be a series of haphazard individual sniper duels.[50]

To continue with Wigram's suggested attack scenario: once the Brens had quietened the enemy machine-guns, the platoon commander would get to his feet, getting all the rest of the riflemen to do the same, and lead them straight into the enemy position under cover of the Bren fire. If necessary the mortar team could be ordered to put down a bomb or two, but as German machine-gunners usually did not open fire, especially at night, until the attacking troops were within 200 yards, Wigram reckoned that the enemy position should be reached in one bound. If it could not, then the attack would involve a further stage of the rifle group taking cover while the Bren and mortar groups came forward, though he considered that this would rarely be necessary.

For an attack in daylight behind an artillery concentration or barrage, Wigram advocated the same method but with the groups moving much more dispersed, and if the advance had to be made over ground likely to be covered by enemy fire then the platoon commander should tell the platoon sergeant to position the Brens before moving himself with the rifle group. For both types of attack Wigram stressed the advantage of grouping the Bren teams in the manner he suggested. Sicily indicated that in difficult mountainous terrain the Bren teams moved at a different rate from the riflemen, and too often once the riflemen came under fire there was 'a frantic scream for the Brens', who were invariably too far back. His suggested method enabled the platoon commander to watch the progress of the Bren group and to make sure that he remained in touch with them. Teamwork between the platoon commander and the platoon sergeant, he believed, was '10 times more likely to succeed' than teamwork between the platoon sections; this was another point indicated by battle experience, of which training had taken little account.

Apart from highlighting problems with the attack methods employed, the Sicily campaign also revealed some more general shortfalls in the preparation of troops for the experience and effects of battle, or 'battle inoculation', an important aspect of training common to the British, Canadian and American armies. Wigram believed that the British Army's 'Battle Schools' had not gone far enough in it and, worse, had 'missed the big point of it'. In fact, they had not really taught men the most important things, or at least they had not conditioned men enough to know what the important things to learn from their battle experiences were. Wigram lamented that troops who had been in quite a few battles were still unable to distinguish between the noise of Bren fire and the fire of German machine-guns, or between the whistle of their own shells and those of the enemy. In Sicily, he noted, men had gone to ground as soon as they heard firing, even when it was not directed at them. This, he observed, often disorganized an entire battle, especially at night. Infantry officers had to go back to find their men, who were taking cover and did not answer when called because of the noise of the fire. The problem of officers and NCOs losing 'a substantial part' of their men in this way during the confusion of night attacks was, according to Wigram, 'a very real one' and it had occurred in all the battalions he was with in Sicily. When follow-up troops also took cover for long periods on hearing firing, this meant delays in the supporting weapons and supplies getting forward.

Attacking infantry clearly had to be well 'inoculated' against the sound of firing and to know when they needed to take cover and when they did not. Wigram suggested daily exposure at the 'Battle Schools' to the sound of Bren fire, German machine-gun fire and the fire of British and German light automatic weapons. Advancing men should have fire first directed towards them and then over them so that they learned to tell the difference. Above all they had to have impressed upon them every day the importance of knowing the difference between the noise of battle and that of fire directed specifically at them. They had to learn to keep moving forward as fast as possible despite whatever noise, so long as they themselves were not the target.

Here Wigram had identified essential requirements for a successful infantry attack, coordinating effort and maintaining momentum. That the problems he identified were not restricted to British battalions is evident from the US Army campaign report. American officers admitted that some battalion commanders failed to make full use of the supporting weapons at their disposal, including the light and heavy mortars and the heavier calibre machine-guns, and advocated better training in the co-ordination of the heavy support company with that of the rifle companies. They also emphasized the importance of troops not taking cover immediately on coming under fire, especially artillery fire, and that they would be likely to suffer fewer casualties by going forward than by staying put. Troops also needed to learn to locate the position of enemy weapons from their fire and to be able to tell from which direction enemy fire was coming. Sicily indicated a 'definite need' for far more realistic 'battle inoculation' during infantry training.[51]

Most of what needed to be learned and factored into training could only become apparent with actual experience such as Sicily provided, for it had been unanticipated. An example was the need to prepare for aggressive action by foot patrols, the importance of which was stressed in the US Army's campaign report, specifically by the US 1st and 9th Infantry Divisions. In Sicily the mountain terrain often precluded vehicle reconnaissance, and long-range foot patrols by troops stripped for rapid movement and equipped with radios became very important, especially when formations were moving through lightly defended country but approaching organized centres of resistance. They were valuable not only for gaining information but for harassing the withdrawing Germans and Italians and generally maintaining contact with the enemy, giving them little respite while the main body of the Division moved up.

These patrols were small, very like the type advocated by Wigram for his infiltration tactics; to a large extent they were self-sufficient, and they were aggressive. The US 1st Division reported how its patrols would often be climbing up one side of a hill while the Germans were still retreating down the other, and how – most importantly – they could sometimes arrive in time to shoot up German demolition and mine-laying parties.[52]

In the British case, Wigram described how in Sicily the innovation was tried of equipping patrols, sent out to keep contact with the withdrawing enemy, with No.18 Wireless sets in contact with similar sets at the gunner Observation Post (OP). Wigram himself manned such an OP as one of these daylight patrols went out chasing after the retreating Germans. The gunners had registered all the likely locations where German troops might take up position. As soon as the patrol came under fire, they contacted the gunner OP, giving the locations from where the Germans were firing. The OP then contacted an entire field regiment of 25-pounders standing by, which brought down fire on the target within a few minutes. Not surprisingly, this always silenced the German opposition, and the patrol was able to move forward two miles and occupy a position well forward of the battalion and hold it for 36 hours, without casualties.

Such innovations were suggested by the particular circumstances of the campaign, and it was this experience that led to their value being recognized. Similarly, only the actual experience of battle could teach particular characteristics of the enemy, and in Sicily the Germans were able to give Allied soldiers some nasty surprises. One was that German fieldcraft and concealment was generally superior. For example, during the Agira battle, the 1st Dorsets (231st Infantry Brigade) soon learned not to send out patrols of more than two or three men because any movement brought forth heavy German artillery, mortar and machine-gun fire.[53] They could not understand how it was that, while they hardly ever glimpsed a German, every move of their own seemed to be observed and drew fire.[54]

Accounts of the fighting in Sicily refer to occasions when German troops approaching Allied positions called out in English that they were friendly units; such ruses appear to have often been employed in attack. For example, Sir David Cole evocatively describes an occasion when, holding positions along the River Simeto, his battalion was about to be attacked at night: 'We could hear with frightening clarity, amidst the stillness, equipment jingling and boots rustling through the grass: then a German voice shouting to us in strange English, "Don't fire, it's the Jocks."

Sassenach though I was, I knew that even in Glasgow nobody spoke like that.'[55] Mostly, as in this instance, the ruse was unsuccessful, though psychologically it was not without disturbing effect and could induce a dangerous uncertainty and hesitation at a critical time, particularly among less experienced troops.

The Americans also acknowledged the skill of their enemy, particularly in night patrolling. It took time for inexperienced American infantry to realize that the Germans were stealthily reconnoitring close to their positions at night, using a series of clever sound signals to pass messages. Sometimes the German infantry used a series of whistles, closely resembling bird calls, 'a sort of cheeping whistle of several sorts', reported a regimental officer of the 45th Infantry Division, 'and they can fool you very easily if you are not on to them. We were pretty generally fooled by them at first,' he admitted. By also using a sort of imitative short, yapping bark, German night patrols – for a time – were able to approach their enemies' positions and signal to each other, while the listening American soldiers believed they were hearing only the abandoned dogs from nearby deserted Sicilian houses.[56] Such errors could cost lives until soldiers came to know their enemy better, but it proved to be the sort of experience passed on in training that could save them.

The accounts of battles and the contemporary investigations such as Wigram's and that compiled by the Americans indicate that, for the Allied troops, much learning in Sicily was done the hard way, though what they learned was of immense value. Troops who had gone to Sicily completely raw to battle learned not, for example, to dig slit trenches under trees that if struck by enemy shells would shatter into vicious and often lethal fragments from which their trenches would not protect them. They learned how to move and fight in mountains, how to 'read' such terrain and recognize its dangers and possibilities. They learned to camouflage their equipment and positions thoroughly; they learned how to locate and remove mines, to recognise possible booby-traps and not to pick up battlefield souvenirs; they learned to distinguish between the yapping of abandoned Sicilian dogs and the calling of birds from the often incredibly lifelike imitative calls used by German soldiers as signals as they crept forward at night, preparing to attack. They learned how the German infantry would attack them, following upon mortar and artillery concentrations and coming in at a fast walk using marching fire or firing from the halt or from the kneeling position, probing for a weak point and a flank to turn; they learned how best to use their weapons to kill them or drive them back. Sicily proved to be a severe test, but a worse one awaited the Allied armies on the mainland of Italy, with further lessons that, once again as they encountered the largely unknown and unprepared for, would be learned the hard way.

6

PLANNING THE NEXT MOVE

The Decision to Invade Mainland Italy, June–August 1943

'Why is this poor man torturing himself in this unhappy manner?'
— Churchill, referring to Eisenhower, 2 July 1943

The task of translating the Allied strategic imperatives of removing Italy from the war and engaging German strength in the Mediterranean into realizable military objectives fell to Eisenhower as theatre Supreme Commander, and for planning purposes to his Algiers-based Allied Force Headquarters (AFHQ). Although firmly subordinate to the Allied Combined Chiefs, Eisenhower and AFHQ possessed considerable autonomy in planning theatre operations. It was also felt strongly, certainly by the American members of the Combined Chiefs, that Eisenhower should not be over-burdened with planning teams or the interference in the functioning of AFHQ that such a situation would bring. They persuaded their British counterparts of this, and a British initiative to have teams sent to Algiers from Washington and London to assist AFHQ in planning post-'Husky' operations was successfully deflected.

Allied Force Headquarters, Post-'Husky' Operations:
Planning Options, June 1943

'Buttress': Landing in the Gulf of Gioia in the 'Toe' of Italy near Reggio. Operation assigned to British X Corps Headquarters not committed to 'Husky'.

'Goblet': Landing near Crotone on east coast of Calabria (the 'Ball' of the Italian 'Foot'). Operation assigned to British V Corps Headquarters not committed to 'Husky'.

'Musket': Landing at Taranto in Apulia in the 'Heel' of Italy. Operation assigned to Headquarters United States Fifth Army not committed to 'Husky'.

'Gangway', 'Mustang', 'Barracuda',: Plans to land forces at Naples in conjunction with rapid overland advance from the south of Italy, in the event of weak Axis resistance and the intact capture of Naples port.

'Brimstone': Invasion of Sardinia by United States (Fifth Army) forces and British (X Corps) forces, alterative to invasion of mainland Italy.

'Firebrand': Invasion of Corsica by French forces.

†††††††††††††††††††

In early June 1943 in the run up to 'Husky' the AFHQ planners had faced the question of whether, after the capture of Sicily, the Allies should invade the Italian mainland. When Churchill with Brooke and Marshall had visited AFHQ in the wake of the 'Trident' Conference to discuss this question with Eisenhower and his senior theatre commanders, there had been a good deal of optimism in the air. Churchill had pushed for a decision to continue the war to Italy after 'Husky', and Eisenhower and his commanders had generally favoured the concept providing that 'Husky' went well and that the Axis situation rendered rapid follow-up landings in Italy feasible. Only Marshall had interjected a note of caution and advocated a 'wait and see' policy, which was sound enough, as everything depended upon the progress and outcome of 'Husky'. With this Churchill had to rest content, and Eisenhower was authorized to set up two planning staffs, one to examine the option of landings in mainland Italy and the other to examine the principal alternative, an operation to capture the island of Sardinia.

The problem that bedevilled AFHQ was that of uncertainty. No one could be sure how 'Husky' would go or whether it would bring an Italian collapse – or if it did not, what subsequent operation or combination of operations would achieve it. How hard the Italians would fight in the defence of their homeland territory was uncertain, especially as there was increasing evidence of Italian disillusion with Mussolini and the war, and with the alliance with Hitler. Were the Allies to expect a stiffening of Italian resolve to defend their country from Allied invasion, or would the opposite be the case, as the approach of the Allies offered Italians an opportunity to break away from Hitler and the Axis? The German reaction to 'Husky' and to Allied operations that might follow it was even more difficult to gauge; so too was the military strength Hitler might deploy to the Mediterranean and where, and how, he might use it. Only 'Husky' and its aftermath could provide the answers to these questions, and in the meantime AFHQ had only one certainty to influence its planning appreciations. In accordance with the strategic priorities agreed during 'Trident', whatever operations in the Mediterranean theatre followed 'Husky' would have to be carried out with significantly fewer forces and considerably less assault shipping. Little wonder, therefore, that AFHQ took an extremely cautious line.

Eisenhower had reported his assessment of the post-'Husky' options to the Combined Chiefs on 30 June. 'Husky' was then only ten days away. Quite clearly, as this major operation, of a type and scale never previously attempted, loomed closer it cast its shadow on what might follow. Eisenhower was steeling himself for a hard and costly battle on Sicily – he certainly could not discount its possibility. In his appreciation he stressed the slenderness of the resources he would have in theatre following the capture of Sicily and the despatch to Britain of seven of his best divisions and much of his assault shipping. He had tempered his earlier enthusiasm for landings on the Italian mainland. While he outlined several possible operations in southern Italy, he warned that they required a minimum of six divisions. The possibility of an opportunistic jump to the mainland from Sicily following a rapidly successful campaign on the island was not discounted, but neither could it be anticipated. The post-'Husky' options could not depend upon the availity of forces commited to 'Husky'. Eisenhower also pointed out that, while a rapid and successful 'Husky' would lead him to favour landings in the 'toe' of Italy, if the six British divisions earmarked for the task looked insufficient to ensure the subsequent capture of Apulia (the 'heel') or to advance to Naples, where they could be reinforced by divisions sent direct to the captured port, then it would be better to land instead in Sardinia. He was disinclined to landings in Apulia. They would take until November to prepare, by which time the weather would preclude long periods of supply over beaches, while the reductions in assault shipping ruled out landings in sufficient strength. They would also be beyond the cover of fighters based on airfields captured in Sicily. If 'Husky' indicated the likelihood of such strong Axis resistance on the mainland as to make landings unfeasible, he recommended a full-scale operation to capture Sardinia, though the time needed for organization and preparation meant this itself could not occur before 1 October.

'Why', an exasperated Churchill demanded of the British Chiefs of Staff on 2 July following receipt of Eisenhower's report, 'is this poor man torturing himself in this unhappy manner?'[1] For Churchill, the situation appeared far simpler than to the Allied Supreme Commander, who seemed beset by difficulties and obstacles at every turn. If 'Husky' went well, then the next step was obvious; the Allies should land in Italy. If 'Husky' failed, then the problem of 'where next?' did not arise. It seemed to Churchill that Eisenhower and AFHQ were 'wrapped up in their staff work', and their apparent inclination towards the capture of Sardinia instead of carrying the war to the Italian mainland indicated a weakening in resolve. Eisenhower's report lacked the bold spirit to battle that so appealed to Churchill and which he so seldom detected in senior commanders charged with great responsibility. Moreover, as once before during the planning of 'Husky', AFHQ had become so 'wrapped up in its staff work' as to produce such a pessimistic assessment that it came unacceptably close to counselling against the operation it was charged to prepare and that had been already agreed at the highest political and military level.

The result then had been a sharp reminder to AFHQ delivered through the Allied Combined Chiefs that 'Husky' was not a matter for debate, but was definitely 'on'. In the case of post-'Husky' operations, however – and despite Churchill's own determination to see a campaign in mainland Italy – such top-level Allied agreement was as yet lacking; it was therefore appropriate for Eisenhower to point out the likely risks and avoid committing himself when Allied strategy was itself not yet firm.

The British view was nevertheless hardening, and even within Eisenhower's command the equivocal approach was by no means unanimous. Tedder for one believed that occupying ground on mainland Italy would shake the already wavering Italian morale far more than a landing on Sardinia and would contain more German forces. Landings in Italy would also be easier to support from the air, while the difficulties of capturing Sardinia were in his opinion being 'skated over', as he had informed Air Marshal Sir Charles Portal, the British Chief of the Air Staff in a telegram of 1 July.[2] Two days later, another senior Allied airman, General 'Hap' Arnold of the USAAF, and a member of the Combined Chiefs, queried whether air considerations could influence the post-'Husky' decision. He observed that an advance from southern into central Italy would secure airfields from which Allied bombers could strike at vital strategic targets that were as yet beyond their range.[3] Although there was no immediate response, this was a weighty argument, for the importance of the Combined Bomber Offensive in weakening Germany in preparation for 'Overlord' was by then firmly acknowledged. On the same day, 3 July, the British Chiefs of Staff signalled to the Combined Chiefs their conviction that 'Husky' would be best exploited by offensive action on the mainland of Italy to remove Italy from the war. This would also contain greater German forces than an invasion of Sardinia, and should be the primary consideration.

The American Joint Chiefs remained unconvinced, wary of a mainland campaign that could all too easily escalate beyond their control to the detriment of 'Overlord', and they balked also at Eisenhower's request, made in his appreciation, that some assault shipping intended to leave the theatre be retained to give his forces the necessary sea-borne lift. The Combined Planning Staff recommended allotting him some 90 cargo ships and a further convoy in August, though the latter could only be at the expense of the build-up in Britain. That was as far as its American members were willing to go. Its British members held that opportunities in the Mediterranean after 'Husky' should not be forfeited by denying Eisenhower the necessary landing craft and were looking to find the flexibility in the 'Trident' resource allocation that, as far as the Americans were concerned, did not exist. Even they recommended that the Combined Chiefs should not face this dilemma until whatever shipping losses occurred in 'Husky' were known. Churchill and the British Chiefs of Staff had gained some ground in advocating a campaign in Italy, but whether their hopes could be realized depended upon the progress and outcome of 'Husky'.

With 'Husky' under way came an increase in confidence about pursuing operations on mainland Italy. On 13 July, Churchill instructed British planning staffs in London to examine the concept of a descent on the Italian west coast directed to seize the port of Naples and to follow this with a rapid advance on Rome. Impatient with excessively cautious plans focusing upon landings well to the south on the toe and heel of the peninsula, Churchill pithily asked Brooke and the Chiefs of Staff: 'Why should we crawl up the leg like a harvest bug, from the ankle upwards?'[4] Three days later Marshall advised that the Allied Combined Chiefs should inform Eisenhower of their interest in this concept in preference to an invasion of Sardinia. Marshall's backing for this operation surprised the British, but he had not become a late convert to the Mediterranean strategy – it was more that events seemed to offer an opportunity to get the whole Italian business cleared up, freeing resources at last for 'Overlord.'[5] Two days after that (18 July) Eisenhower, with the backing of his senior commanders, jumped off the fence and reported to the Combined Chiefs his recommendation that, providing the Germans did not deploy substantial reinforcements, the war should be carried to the Italian mainland. Lieutenant General Mark W. Clark, commanding the, as yet non-operational, US Fifth Army in Morocco, was ordered to prepare plans for the Naples landing, now codenamed 'Avalanche'.

The fall of Mussolini on 25 July hastened matters and induced greater boldness. Eisenhower, conferring with Alexander, Tedder and Cunningham on the following day, were in tune with Churchill in so far as they felt the situation now warranted a high-risk operation against the mainland. The Combined Chiefs ordered Eisenhower to mount 'Avalanche' at the earliest date. Eisenhower's own planners pointed out that lack of assault shipping meant that this would be the second week in September, and that it would be several weeks before there was enough to allow a crossing of the Strait of Messina. As always, shipping was the constraint; Clark was ordered to prepare to conduct 'Avalanche' accordingly. On 16 August, as the last of the German and Italian garrison of Sicily were preparing to escape across the Strait, Eisenhower reported that 'Avalanche' would go in on 9 September. It would be preceded between 1 and 4 September by a landing near Reggio in Calabria to secure the Strait, a task given to Eighth Army and codenamed 'Baytown'. These operations were sanctioned by Churchill and Roosevelt and the Combined Chiefs, by then at the 'Quadrant' Conference at Quebec held between 14 and 24 August.

'Quadrant' occurred at a time when the Mediterranean strategy at last promised decisive results. Italy was in crisis. Mussolini had been deposed, the Sicily campaign was on the point of being successfully concluded by the Allies, and the Italians were in contact with the Allies to secure the best deal that they could get. As far as Churchill and the British Chiefs of Staff were concerned, this was the time to exploit fully the situation in the Mediterranean. But this view collided with an equally determined American view that 'Overlord' must have absolute priority in resources – there could be no going back on the establishment of this priority and the agreement on post-'Husky' Mediterranean force levels to which the British had acquiesced, reluctantly and with serious reservations, during the 'Trident' conference in May.

The British case, argued once again forcefully by Brooke, was that the pursuance of opportunities in the Mediterranean was vital in order to create the necessary conditions for 'Overlord'. There was some strength in this argument. COSSAC (Chief of Staff to the Supreme Allied Commander), the British Lieutenant General F. E. Morgan and his Anglo-American staff set up in Britain to prepare plans for 'Overlord' had identified two criteria that had to be met. These were the reduction of German fighter strength in the West, and the reduction of German forces in France and the Low Countries before the invasion, as well as the restriction of their rate of reinforcement for two months after the landings. Brooke argued that it was by tying down German forces in Italy and by seizing the Italian airfields that these criteria could be met; therefore more flexibility was needed in allocation of forces to the Mediterranean. This was the contentious issue, for Marshall was adamant that there could be no change in the build-up schedule for 'Overlord'. The Americans were concerned that, as before, Mediterranean operations would escalate beyond control, and this could only be at the expense of 'Overlord'. Morgan was already voicing concerns that the cross-Channel invasion was likely to be inadequately resourced. There was considerable British frustration at what appeared to be American strategic short-sightedness and willingness to let priceless opportunities in the Mediterranean slip by for want of flexibility. There was also some resentment that, as the constraining factor seemed always to be assault shipping, American landing craft production, under King's hand, continued to favour the Pacific theatre. This was matched by American suspicion that the British had their hearts in a cross-Channel operation no more than they had in 1942; they did not altogether trust the British linking of Italian operations with 'Overlord'. Italy and – despite Churchill's disavowal of any intention to place armies there – the Balkans, must not be allowed to become the Second Front by default.

As with the previous conferences, the final report agreed by the Combined Chiefs on 24 August reflected a compromise, though again what the British ultimately walked away with was substantial. Operations in mainland Italy were now agreed in a more focused and phased campaign. In the first phase, Italy was to be eliminated as a belligerent, and the Allies were to establish airfields in the Rome area and if possible farther north. Churchill's desire to secure the first Axis capital, Rome, looked set to be realized and the armies that would be established shortly on the mainland given measurable goals. The second phase involved the capture of Sardinia and Corsica, which would provide further airfields and offer bases from which to strike at southern France. In the third phase, 'unremitting pressure' would be applied on German forces in northern Italy to create the conditions for 'Overlord' and for an invasion of southern France also to support 'Overlord', involving the bulk of the re-equipped French Army and Air Force. 'Unremitting pressure' meant an offensive, and though there would be little flexibility in the allocation of forces, the link between an Italian campaign and 'Overlord' had been firmly acknowledged.[6] In the meantime, 'Baytown' and 'Avalanche' had to get the armies into mainland Italy.

'Avalanche' had a strategic logic to justify its risks, but 'Baytown' was a questionable operation, disliked intensely by Montgomery and his staff. They were unclear as to precisely what it was intended to achieve. Alexander's instructions issued on 20 August were to secure a bridgehead on the mainland to secure the Strait for naval forces, to follow up German rearguards in the event of a German withdrawal and to engage as many German forces as possible to assist 'Avalanche'.[7] The view within Eighth Army was that to assist 'Avalanche' effectively by pinning German forces 'Baytown' should be simultaneous. But this was ruled out on grounds of available naval and air support. It therefore appeared to make more military sense to have Eighth Army reinforce the 'Avalanche' bridgehead, once secured, thereby cutting off German forces in the south rather than having to pursue their rearguards laboriously up the peninsula in difficult terrain. The challenge to this would have been one of supplying two armies. De Guingand, Montgomery's Chief of Staff, was to regret that an attempt was not made to establish Eighth Army in Italy through the ports of Taranto,

Brindisi and Bari, saving considerable administrative difficulties later.[8] 'Baytown' was ordered, however, and as Montgomery's biographer, Nigel Hamilton observes, Allied planning was once again characterized by dispersed landings.[9]

By this time political factors linked to the possibility of an imminent Italian surrender and change of sides, combined with hopes of Italian military assistance, were influencing planning and generating considerable optimism in the Allied camp. 'Baytown' seems to have been as much a calculated coercive lever on Italian decision-making as a military operation (though the two do not always sit well together). The two commanders most unaffected by the prevailing atmosphere of expectant optimism were those about to land their armies on mainland Europe – Clark and Montgomery. Neither was happy, and both had good cause to be frustrated with the situation in which they had been placed. Clark's 'Avalanche' landing was extremely high-risk, a limited-strength venture into uncertainty. Montgomery's 'Baytown' carried less risk but did not seem the best option. Montgomery made no secret of his belief that the notion of the Italian Army having any chance to fight the Germans was 'utter nonsense'. With little firm data on the likely opposition to 'Baytown' coming back from advance landing parties inserted across the Strait, Montgomery decided that his two divisions, all that shipping would allow in the assault, would at least go in under a thoroughly prepared operation that would ensure their lodgement. It was his insurance against uncertainty, and his own conviction that nothing worthwhile would come out of the Italian surrender.

7

THE SURRENDER OF ITALY,
AUGUST–SEPTEMBER 1943

The Italian Situation

On 25 July, when the campaign in Sicily was at its height, the Fascist dictator of Italy, Benito Mussolini, was removed from power on the orders of the King of Italy and placed under secure arrest. The new government formed by Marshal Pietro Badoglio, a former Chief of Staff of the Italian armed forces, immediately affirmed its loyalty to the German-Italian Axis and its determination to continue the war at Germany's side, but in fact this was no more than a ploy intended to ease German suspicions and to forestall German military action to reinstate Mussolini. Hitler, furious at the news of his fellow dictator's fate, had indeed contemplated such a course and had only been dissuaded from it in favour of a 'wait and see' policy with some difficulty.[1] Mussolini's fall from power had been provoked by the situation of Italy in the summer of 1943, which had become one of desperation. Since Mussolini's decision to enter the war in June 1940, Italy's military unpreparedness and a consequent series of defeats in Greece, North Africa and East Africa had brought humiliation and an increasing dependence upon German military and matériel support. By 1943, Italian strategic independence was no more than a face-saving sham; Italy was completely tied into and subservient to Hitler's strategic designs and looked very likely to be first to pay the grim penalty for their failure.

Neither the German alliance nor the war had ever been universally popular among Italians, and Hitler had long recognized that the reliability of Italy as an ally depended upon Mussolini alone. After the final Axis defeat in North Africa in May 1943, the Anglo-American Allies were well placed to take the war to the Italian homeland. Allied bombing of communications and industrial centres in mainland Italy intensified, not only to create the necessary conditions for their invasion of Sicily and, later, the mainland but also to keep the Italian regime and people under pressure. War-weariness in Italy and opposition to continuing the war increased, heightened by an awareness of Italy's vulnerability. The best Italian army units were in no position to defend the country. They had either marched into Allied captivity in North Africa or were fighting alongside the Germans on the Eastern Front, where they were slowly but surely being bled to death. Other formations were helping the Germans to hold down Yugoslavia and the Balkans or were providing garrisons in the Aegean islands, southern France, Corsica and Sardinia. The Allied invasion of Sicily soon exposed the shortcomings in training and equipment of the Italian formations on the island, and the strength and duration of the defence became dependent upon the German troops.

As Sicily turned into a devastated battleground in which the Axis were gradually losing ground, and with a similar threat to mainland Italy drawing closer with every yard the Allied armies advanced, the political situation within Italy reached crisis. On 24 July the convened Fascist Grand Council in Rome passed a motion introduced by Count Dino Grandi, President of the Fascist Chamber, this called for the reform of national government and the return of power to the Chamber, Council of Ministers, and the Grand Council and the assumption of constitutional power by the Crown.[2] This effectively called for the end of Mussolini's personal hold on power and his lamentable direction of Italy's war effort. For a considerable period of time he had been incapable of effective decision-making or of asserting Italy's position and interests within the Axis.

This had been proven beyond doubt on 19 July during a conference between the Germans and Italians at Feltre in the Dolomite mountains. Hitler had called this conference in urgent response to the increasingly uncertain political situation in Italy and the likelihood of Allied action against the Italian mainland, and with a view to once again boosting Mussolini. At Feltre, Mussolini appeared a broken man, silent and listless and apparently stupefied during Hitler's two-hour haranguing of the Italians, during which he demanded greater Italian commitment to the war and further military effort, particularly the reinforcement of Italian forces in southern Italy. For his part, Mussolini had completely failed to argue the case of Italy's exhaustion. During the meeting, Mussolini received the news that for the first time Allied bombers had struck targets near Rome – for Italy, time was running out.

On 25 July, following the Grand Council's vote of censure and a brief audience with King Victor Emmanuel III, an extremely shocked Mussolini – who seems to have been completely unsuspecting – was arrested and spirited away to the first of several places of incarceration thought to be safe from likely German rescue attempts.

His successors faced the knife-edge dilemma of securing the best means of extricating their country from impending disaster. To court the Allies might just save Italy from becoming a wasted battleground. It might secure the best possible deal for the country through negotiation while the Italians still held something with which to bargain – their armed forces and a willingness to change sides and fight alongside the Allies against the Germans. There were considerable problems with this, however. One was that they had somehow to circumvent the stated Allied policy of accepting nothing but the unconditional surrender of their enemies, announced during a press conference at the end of the Allied 'Symbol' Conference in January 1943. Both Roosevelt and Churchill had initial reservations at Casablanca about including Italy in 'Unconditional Surrender', and the events of August 1943 suggested they had been right: 'Unconditional Surrender' had effectively slammed a door in the face of Italian attempts to defect from the Axis. The Badoglio regime would not easily prise it open.

Moreover, the Italians could not be certain whether the Allies, even if receptive to their peace overtures and readiness to change sides, were in any position to provide timely assistance against the Germans. Allied intentions could only be guessed at without intelligence that they were unlikely to provide, initially at least, to Italian emissaries. Yet if the Italian military were to make a stand against the Germans and cooperate effectively with the Allies, some indication of forthcoming Allied operations was essential. Without such information, the Badoglio government was unable to provide its military with contingency instructions. None of this would be of much help to those Italian formations outside Italy, on the Eastern Front and the Balkans, whose fate in the event of an open breach with Germany remained perilous.

By far the most serious difficulty confronting the Italians was the fact that the Germans already had sizeable forces in their country, and more were on the way, ostensibly to help defend Italy from the Allies. In stark contrast to the Allies, the Germans were on the spot, posing a significant threat by being well placed to take over the country and its military installations. To resist such a move successfully the Italian military required firm instructions, planning, timely warning and Allied assistance. The Badoglio government could ensure none of these. It had to step very warily indeed in order not to provoke German military action; for as long as possible, the fiction of the Axis had to be maintained – there was no feasible alternative. There could be no question of simply dissolving the Axis and aligning with the Allies; nor would the Germans simply accept Italian neutrality and go away, leaving the country to be occupied by the Allies. The problem with buying time to secure a deal with the Allies behind the Axis façade was that it left little or no room for manoeuvre in terms of refusing the entry into Italy of further German formations.

There were some tense moments at times along the Brenner Pass as German commanders encountered reluctance and obstructionism on the part of their Italian counterparts in allowing them to cross into Italy.[3] As they crossed, these German commanders did not fail to notice the Italian soldiers busily restoring the border defences that faced north – they were obviously working to instructions, but it could hardly have been the British and Americans that they expected to come from that direction.

During August 1943 the mask of Axis unity began to wear very thin, but for the moment at least it was in the interests of both the Badoglio government and Hitler and the OKW to hide behind it. Hitler could dissemble as well as the Italians; indeed he had already been doing so for a considerable time.

Italy: The German Perspective

The Germans had been aware of the growing anti-war and anti-German feelings among Italians from before the loss of North Africa. General Enno von Rintelen, the OKW's Liaison Officer to the Comando Supremo (Italian Armed Forces High Command) and German Military Attaché in Rome, had warned in March 1943 that Italians, including the military, considered the North African situation to be hopeless and that they felt increasing doubt as to Germany's ability to win the war. The view was being openly voiced that it would be better for Italy to have the Anglo-

American Allies arrive than Bolshevism from the USSR.[4] From Hitler's perspective, such reports indicated a failure in firm leadership: increasingly he had to accept that Mussolini's hold on power might well be tenuous. Equally, he had no trust for any other potential Italian leader and tried to bolster Mussolini's position including, in April 1943, the offer of heavy equipment, including tanks, with which to arm a new Italian formation, the 'M. Division' forming near Rome. Recruited from Fascist 'Blackshirt' militia, Hitler saw this as analogous to his own SS divisions, whose loyalty was primarily to him and the Nazi ideology. It was starting to look as if Mussolini might be soon in need of a similar well-armed body with which to crush treachery in his own camp.

Following the loss of North Africa, German concerns about Italian reliability gained further ground. By the end of May the OKW, on Hitler's direction, had prepared secret plans under the codename 'Alarich' for the takeover of Italy in the event of Mussolini being deposed and an attempted Italian defection. There was no question at that time of simply abandoning Italy; Italian soil would be held and defended because southern Europe and the Balkans were of vital importance as a bastion of security for Germany. Plans were also in place for the takeover of Italian-controlled areas of the Balkans. Hitler was always sensitive to threats to this region, and so was the OKW, not only because of its role as an outer bastion but also because it was a source of raw materials and fuel without which the German war effort could not be sustained. Because of this Hitler was always ready to believe in the likelihood of an Allied descent on Greece, or in Allied landings in Yugoslavia to open a front there in conjunction with the partisans. To him, and to the OKW, such operations would make a great deal of strategic sense. Therein lay the seeds of the success of the Allied deception operations 'Barclay' and 'Mincemeat'.

The Italian occupation forces in Greece and Yugoslavia were therefore performing a vital role, and it was realized in the spring of 1943 that if Italy were to collapse they would have to be replaced. In the event of Italy actually changing sides, they would also have to be neutralized and at least disarmed before the Italian troops passed their weapons over to the resistance or joined them. Plans for the takeover of Italian responsibilities in the Balkans went under the codename 'Konstantin'. The problem for the

OKW in the late spring of 1943 was to find the necessary additional. troops for 'Alarich' and 'Konstantin' should these operations become necessary. The Eastern Front was a continual drain on manpower, and divisions committed there could not easily be extricated; nor was it easy to find replacements for their combat losses. There were also troops holding down the occupied countries, with divisions of varying strength, equipment and states of training and quality deployed throughout occupied Western Europe from Norway to the Spanish border. There were very few reserves and no uncommitted strategic reserve at all that could be called upon. In the event, it was proposed to employ up to seven divisions that would have to be withdrawn from the Eastern Front and six from occupied France for 'Alarich', in addition to those German formations already in Italy. The operation, Hitler decided, would be entrusted to Field Marshal Erwin Rommel, who was then recovering from the breakdown in health he had suffered in North Africa.

In the meantime, Hitler and the OKW continued to try and pin Mussolini and the Comando Supremo firmly down to providing a greater war effort, and to tie the Italians even closer in to German-controlled operations. The Comando Supremo was nominally the principal Axis headquarters in the Central and Western Mediterranean, this being acknowledged as an Italian-dominated theatre; theoretically at least, German troops in theatre were under its direction. German representations to this headquarters were conducted by von Rintelen, but very often also through Field Marshal Albert Kesselring, the Luftwaffe officer who since October 1941 had held the post of Commander-in-Chief South ('OB Süd') of German forces in the Mediterranean.

Kesselring's command included the Luftwaffe in theatre, Second Luft-flotte (Air Fleet), until June 1943, when this passed to Field Marshal Wolfram, Baron von Richthofen for operational command. Kesselring's role by then was becoming more and more one of higher theatre command rather than high-level liaison. This was because increasingly the Germans required an alternative independent national command structure in Italy, able to function outside the Comando Supremo, which they did not trust. To an extent this had always happened, in that German formations in practice remained under German control, but in the spring of 1943 events in the Mediterranean and in Italy in particular provided the Germans with an imperative to increase the functional capability of their forces and their ability to operate in the face of Italian hostility.

In June 1943, Mussolini, after some vacillation, accepted a German offer of troop reinforcements for Italy, largely through the influence of von Rintelen and Kesselring and their pressure upon the Chief of the Italian General Staff, General Ambrosio. The suspicions of OKW were then aroused towards the end of June when the Italians began to request war matériel on a colossal scale. Their demands included 2,000 aircraft and equipment for seventeen tank battalions, eighteen anti-tank or assault-gun battalions and guns for seventy field and anti-aircraft artillery batteries. There was no question of German industry being able to meet these demands in addition to keeping the German armies supplied, and the suspicion was that the Italians knew it – and that the inevitable German refusal would be Italy's excuse for seeking to make peace.[5] It would not have been the first time that the Italians had employed such tactics. Mussolini himself had set the precedent in September 1939, when he had presented a similar impossible request to Hitler as the condition for Italy honouring her alliance obligation to go to war at Germany's side. German inability to meet the demand then had provided Mussolini with his excuse to remain neutral, and only the German victories in Poland, Scandinavia, the Low Countries and France had induced him to enter the war in June 1940 to claim some of the spoils before it was too late.

Now, however, in the early summer of 1943, Mussolini was in far too deep to extricate himself by such means. There was no early reply to the Italian request, only a series of fruitless and frustrating discussions. Both sides were playing for time. Mussolini was increasingly a broken reed as leader, wavering from hopeless pessimism to flights of impossible fancy and optimism but providing no consistent firm lead to save Italy. Prominent military and political figures within the Fascist Party were now plotting to have him removed from power, and indications of their machinations were reaching Hitler, though not it seems the senior German representatives in Italy.

Kesselring would state in his memoirs that he had been surprised by Mussolini's arrest. He had met Mussolini on 24 July shortly after the latter had been in conference with Grandi. Mussolini told Kesselring how much he and Grandi were in accord and how loyal Grandi was to him, yet later that day it was Grandi who introduced the reform motion in the Fascist Grand Council. 'I had to ask myself', recalled Kesselring later, 'which was the more astonishing: Mussolini's credulity or Grandi's wiliness.'[6]

The German ambassador, von Mackensen, had also apparently told Kesselring on 24 July that he had positive information that Mussolini was in no danger, that he was still master of the situation. However, days before this, shortly after his meeting with Mussolini at Feltre, Hitler was reading a report compiled by SS intelligence predicting an Italian coup against Mussolini and his replacement by Badoglio, and that Badoglio would attempt to make peace with the Allies once the Allies had captured Sicily.

Clearly Hitler had determined not to take his senior commanders in Italy into his confidence; indeed he was scornful of their evident lack of insight into political affairs in Rome, and at his briefing conferences in far-away East Prussia he tended to ridicule their reports, almost as if they were a joke. With information in his hands, of which they were completely unaware (provided by Himmler's SS operatives in Rome), he could well afford to. He believed Kesselring far too credulous and trusting of the Italians. Details of contingency planning, and Rommel's intended role of taking control in Italy, he kept from him.

Nevertheless, events in Italy were moving quicker than even Hitler had anticipated, despite his political acumen and the intelligence available to him. News of Mussolini's arrest came as a shock. Partly at least, this was because of the focus in attention accorded the Eastern Front, where on 5 July Operation 'Citadel' had been launched. The attack was made against a salient held by the Red Army in the area of Kursk–Orel. 'Citadel' had been Hitler's brainchild, and it proved to be a major strategic error. It was 'blown' long before it began, and the Soviets were waiting with extensive anti-tank defences and their own armoured forces poised to strike. A week of heavy fighting and severe losses brought no significant gains but wasted Germany's panzer reserves and, with them, Germany's future ability to take the strategic offensive. Then, in the wake of 'Citadel', the German forces had to brace themselves for defence against the expected Soviet counteroffensive. In the meantime, the Anglo-American Allies had landed in Sicily and brought the situation in Italy to the fore. The problem for the OKW, however, was that 'Citadel' had consumed the Eastern Front forces earmarked for the 'Alarich' and 'Konstantin' operations that now looked to be necessary rather sooner than anticipated.

Despite possessing fewer forces, and the critical situation in the Soviet Union, Hitler's initial reaction to the news of Mussolini's fall was to prepare a military response and seize Rome. The leading German airborne force commander, General Kurt Student, who had planned and directed the invasion of the island of Crete in 1941, was alerted for an operation to seize the Italian capital and round up the Italian government and royal family. A list of leading Italian politicians, military officers and members of the royal family known to be hostile to Germany was demanded from von Mackensen on 26 July. Von Mackensen referred the military objects of Hitler's intended revenge to von Rintelen, but this the latter courageously refused to provide, having no wish to be responsible for what would have been a massacre of many who were innocent; he instead reported that there was no evidence that individual leading Italian soldiers were definite enemies of Germany.[7] This attitude almost certainly cost von Rintelen his job; he had been in post as Attaché since 1938 and representative with the Italian military since 1940. He was an officer and gentleman of the type Hitler both despised and distrusted, and like Kesselring he was thought to have become far too close and sympathetic to the Italians to discern their intentions. He was replaced at the beginning of September. Hitler's pathological prejudices apart, in believing that these men were too easily duped, he may well have been right. In any case, Hitler for once listened to wiser counsels that cautioned against precipitate action; these included not only a seriously alarmed Kesselring in the south but also Rommel, whom Hitler had hastily recalled from an inspection of German forces in Greece; Grand Admiral Karl Dönitz the Commander-in-Chief of the German Navy; and General Alfred Jodl, the OKW's Head of Operations.

It was essential from the German point of view that the machinery of state, law and order, and the functioning of communications within Italy continued, and for the moment this was best ensured by the Badoglio regime. Open hostilities with the Italians would risk Italian forces closing the Brenner Pass and the vital routes to Austria and southern Germany,

isolating the German forces in Italy. Moreover, there were German formations engaged in fighting a delaying action against the Allies in Sicily –
their line of evacuation across the Strait of Messina and withdrawal
through Italy had to be kept secure. There was also the Italian Fleet to
consider, and the prevention of its defection to the Allies. All this required
time in which to deploy forces for a takeover when Badoglio finally
revealed his hand. In the weeks following Mussolini's fall, Italy became a
chessboard upon which the Germans and Italians tried to outmanoeuvre
each other. In this the Germans gained the upper hand through their
increasing military presence; the Italians could protest but could do
nothing short of armed resistance – the final step they dared not take.

Rommel was established at Munich in a newly-activated Army Group
B headquarters, which would later be moved to Canossa in North Italy,
with troops covering the passes into Italy. His responsibility covered all of
Northern Italy from the French border in the west to the Yugoslav
(Croatia) border in the east, and extending southward the length of the
Italian peninsula to a line running east–west from Pisa through Arezzo to
Ancona on the Adriatic coast. By mid-August eight German divisions
drawn from France, Denmark and Holland, and including the SS Panzer
Division Liebstandarte Adolf Hitler pulled out of the Eastern Front, had
crossed into the north of Italy or were poised at the frontier. Kesselring
retained command of German forces south of this line as 'OB Süd', but
such was his exclusion from Hitler's plans that he was as surprised as the
Italians when the German 2nd Parachute Division suddenly arrived from
France to land on the airfields near Rome, though he was pleased enough
to see them.[8] This was part of Hitler's design to tighten a secure ring
around the Italian capital, upon which the 3rd Panzer Grenadier Division
was also closing in from Tuscany. Such moves were conducted as un-
obtrusively as possible under the fiction of military redeployments and the
need to create a mobile reserve against Allied invasion. But their real
reason was quite clear to the Italians.

At the end of July the Chief of Staff to the Comando Supremo, General
Ambrosio, had given secret verbal orders to defend Rome against a
German takeover attempt and deployed five divisions near the capital
Others were deployed to cover the passes into Italy and the naval base at

General Sir Harold Alexander, Allied 15th Army Group Commander, Lieutenant General Mark W Clark, Fifth Army Commander, and Lieutenant General Sir Richard McCreery commanding the British X Corps of Fifth Army, photographed during Alexander's visit to the Salerno beachhead on 15 September 1943. On this day General Alexander firmly ruled out any thought of an evacuation, and in fact the crisis of the desperate battle for the beachhead was drawing to a close. (IWM NA 68222)

Experience in North Africa indicated the need for artillery to have increased mobility and armoured protection, and in the British case an early development was the Bishop, mounting a 25-pounder gun on the chassis of a Valentine tank. Artillery support proved of vital importance to the Allied infantry in Sicily and Italy, and its firepower proved decisive on many occasions both in attack and in defence. This photograph, taken near Cava in Italy in September 1943, shows the crew of a Bishop inside their fighting compartment with ammunition to hand. (IWM NA 7260)

Before relinquishing Naples, the Germans conducted a systematic demolition of its port facilities to deny them to the Allies. In the foreground of this photograph can be seen some of the wrecked harbour installations. The first Allied troops, the King's Dragoon Guards of Fifth Army's X Corps, entered Naples on 1 October 1943. Within three weeks, and despite the German destruction, specialist Allied repair teams had the port handling 5,000 tons of supplies daily. Here the first Allied convoy to arrive at Naples can be seen entering the harbour. (IWM NA 7414)

Opposite page, top: In Italy the Allied armies had to conduct many opposed river crossings, under fire from German mortars and artillery and hampered by extensive minefields. The terrain all too often also favoured the Germans, as this photograph indicates. Taken during the crossing of the River Volturno as the Allies advanced towards the Gustav Line, the photograph shows troops of the Cheshire Regiment man-handling ammunition up the steep bank of the river. Their light portable assault boats can be seen in the background. The battalions of the Cheshire Regiment provided the heavy machine-gun support troops in British divisions, and their presence would have been urgently required across the river to support the infantry. (IWM NA 7719)

Opposite page, bottom: Once the infantry had carved out a bridgehead across the river, it was imperative to get tanks and supporting weapons such as anti-tank guns across to them, in order to enable the bridgehead to withstand the inevitable and fierce German counterattack. Here a Sherman tank of the 4th County of London Yeomanry fords the Volturno at Grazzanise on 17 October 1943. The infantry already across the river would have been pleased to see it. (IWM NA 7859)

Above: During the crossing of the River Volturno between 12 and 16 October 1943, gaps had to be cut through both banks of the river to enable armour and other vehicles to get forward to support the assault troops. Here a Bren Gun Carrier passes through a gap in the steep north bank of the river, cut by 272 Field Company, Royal Engineers, under heavy German fire. (IWM NA 7761)

The Monte Camino massif was an important and strongly defended feature within the German Bernhardt Line and was attacked in early December 1943 by the British 46th and 56th Divisions of Fifth Army's X Corps. This photograph shows British infantry of the 1st London Scottish (56th Division) negotiating the difficult steep slope of loose stones, boulders and tufted grass. Despite colossal artillery support, attacking Monte Camino between 1 and 8 December cost X Corps 941 casualties, much of the fighting occurring in cold and heavy rain. Before being forced to withdraw, the German 15th Panzer Grenadier Division's dogged defence that cost it 974 casualties. (IWM NA 9630)

Coldstream Guards shortly after they had been withdrawn from Monte Camino following the unsuccessful first assault on the feature. Their exhaustion is plain to see. By this stage the demands made by mountain fighting in winter upon the stamina and physical endurance of troops was becoming all-too evident. (IWM NA 8722)

The difficulty of evacuating casualties in mountainous terrain in winter is exemplified in this photograph, showing stretcher-bearers carefully bringing down a casualty from Monte Camino in heavy rain. The fatigue is evident in their faces. (IWM NA 9367)

††††††††††††††††††††

La Spezia, while by mid-August Italian formations had been alerted, also by verbal orders, to guard military, logistic and transportation installations against a surprise attack. No provocative offensive steps were to be initiated unless the Germans began unequivocal collective action.

The final Axis conferences between the Germans and Italians, held at Tarvisio and Bologna on 6 and 15 August respectively, were quite tense. Hitler did not attend either of them, but his hand was evident. The Italians were faced at Tarvisio with the direct question of whether they were in negotiation with the Allies, which they denied. Italian protests against German troop movements, about which they had not been consulted and to which they had not agreed, availed nought. The Bologna conference achieved nothing for the Axis, the continuing pretence of which was becoming hard to sustain, though the Italians managed to secure agreement on the move of some of their troops from France and the Balkans, which now suited the Germans well enough. The Germans openly announced the existence of Army Group B under Rommel's command. An obtrusive presence at the conference was the large number of heavily armed SS troops – the menace and import of which were so obvious that not only the Italians but also von Rintelen objected strongly.

Both he and Kesselring were increasingly out of step with Hitler's policy towards the Italians, about which they were being deliberately kept in the dark. Kesselring, on learning of the Bologna conference, to which he had not been summoned and to which Rommel would go to represent Hitler, offered his resignation, but this Hitler would not accept. Nevertheless, Hitler had determined by then that it would be Rommel who would command all the German forces in Northern Italy and that Kesselring would ultimately be subordinate to him as well as to OKW. This dovetailed with the prevailing longer-term strategic concept that, in so far as Hitler and the OKW had yet decided the matter, lay behind their planning for Italy. While the Germans were determined to seize vital communications, transport routes and military installations throughout Italy when the Italians defected, there was at this stage no intention of attempting a prolonged defence of southern Italy in the event of Allied landings on the mainland. Instead it was assumed that there would be a delaying action fought by the formations in the south, which would withdraw steadily northwards to come eventually under Rommel's Army Group B. In the north the Germans would hold – though where precisely was still undecided – and there Hitler intended that a puppet Fascist regime would be established. The obvious leader for this would be Mussolini, and Hitler was sparing no pains to have him found and rescued. This mission had been entrusted to a tough and audacious SS Special Forces officer called Otto Skorzeny.

In the meantime, on 22 August, an Army Headquarters was formed to command the German formations in southern Italy, which by then included those that had been evacuated from Sicily. This was the Tenth Army. Its command was given to General Heinrich von Vietinghoff, an experienced panzer general who had commanded LXXVI Panzer Corps and later Ninth Army in the Soviet Union in 1942 and subsequently Fifteenth Army in occupied France. Tenth Army would remain under Kesselring's overall direction while it was operating in the territory of OB Süd. As the end of August approached, the Germans put the specific details and other finishing touches to the 'Alarich' and 'Konstantin' plans, both now coordinated under the ironic codename 'Achse' ('Axis'). Not only in Italy, but throughout the Balkans, the Aegean and southern France, German army, naval, and Luftwaffe units stood ready to take over the key installations and equipment of their Italian counterparts and to disarm their garrisons. The Germans now dominated the chessboard and awaited only the final order to declare 'checkmate'.

Italy: The Allied Reaction and Intelligence Picture

Although hardly well placed to intervene, the British and Americans were closely monitoring much of the German activity in Italy, and indeed throughout southern Europe. The interception and decoding of German 'Enigma' signals through 'Ultra' provided a reasonably accurate and for the most part up-to-date intelligence picture, and was also the means of verifying the information being provided by the Italians themselves. The fall of Mussolini presented the Allies with a strategic dilemma, evident at various levels of decision-making and planning, and despite the inform-ation at their disposal there remained considerable uncertainty.

The first Italian attempts to open negotiation with the Allies had occurred well before the removal of Mussolini. In the middle of February

1943, decrypts of Italian diplomatic signals indicated that the Italian Cabinet had considered sending an emissary to Lisbon to make contact with the Allies, at a time when Mussolini was incapacitated by illness. There were also Italian approaches made to representatives of the British Special Operations Executive (SOE), the organization created to gather intelligence, conduct sabotage and help equip and train the underground resistance forces in occupied Europe. These were made in neutral Switzerland and involved the suggestion that an Italian general should come to Cyrenaica in North Africa for discussions.

The British Cabinet was prepared to countenance this on the understanding that the Italian emissary could offer constitutional credibility and that no Allied commitments could be made to him without high authority. Nothing further came of this, indicating that the Italians were merely taking soundings and that possibly the initiative had been made by disaffected elements without the necessary full authority.

There was quite clearly a significant and potentially influential body within the Italian Fascist regime that was wavering in its support of the Axis, but by the spring of 1943 suggestions from within the Allied camp that this should be exploited and approaches made to such Italians came up against the immovable obstacle of the 'Unconditional Surrender' policy. As Churchill and others had well appreciated from early in the war, Italian support for Mussolini's military adventurism and for the alliance with Nazi Germany had never been more than luke-warm. Now, in the spring of 1943, economic hardship within Italy and widespread concern at the consequences of the war indicated that such Allied overtures would likely have significant effects. In April a suggestion emanated from Eisenhower's Allied Force Headquarters (AFHQ) that a high-ranking Italian prisoner-of-war could be employed to approach the commanders of Italian island garrisons in the Mediterranean to induce their surrender, though this was not taken up. By the late spring, AFHQ, the British Joint Commanders-in-Chief in the Middle East and SOE were all urging that Allied propaganda towards Italy should be moderated in tone, with a move away from insisting upon 'Unconditional Surrender' towards emphasizing the advantages of seeking Allied protection and the safeguarding of Italy's future.[9] The problem was that this was considerably more straightforward

to advise than it was to implement. It was one thing for senior Allied commanders in the Mediterranean to discern that Italy was wavering, and on
the basis of it proffer sound advice that would potentially increase the
effectiveness and success of their future military operations. It was quite
another problem for the Anglo-American political leadership to act on
such advice.

Churchill, Roosevelt and their advisors were always conscious of the
sensitive alliance with the Soviet Union and their continual need to allay
Stalin's suspicions concerning Anglo-American willingness to come to full
grips with the Axis in Europe, as his constant calling for the opening of a
major Second Front indicated. Considerable effort had been made by the
Anglo-Americans to convince Stalin that their operations in the Mediterranean during 1942–3 would be of significance and would constitute a
major effort. In this atmosphere of not quite trust, if not outright distrust,
to compromise on the binding and mutually reassuring commitment that
'Unconditional Surrender' imposed upon the Allies was no light matter
and was potentially dangerous.

The possibility of a separate peace being made by an ally may never have
been considered a strong one, neither with regard to Anglo-American
concerns that Stalin would make such a deal with Hitler, nor with regard to
Stalin having similar concerns about the Anglo-Americans. For all that,
however, until Nazi Germany was clearly doomed it was a spectre that
would never completely go away. Even within the very close Anglo-
American alliance, reassurances of commitment were required. Churchill,
for example, felt it necessary to unequivocally dispel a lingering American
concern that once Hitler had been defeated in Europe, Britain would wane
in her commitment to prosecute the war against Japan in the Far East and
Pacific fully. Adherence to 'Unconditional Surrender' played an important
part in demonstrating such resolve and maintaining an alliance unity that
could not therefore be easily broken nor called into question.

On the other hand, it seems that in the Mediterranean in the spring of
1943 the 'Unconditional Surrender' policy also helped to enforce a unity
within the Axis. This is not to suggest that it lost the Allies an opportunity,
for even if the 'Unconditional Surrender' policy had not existed, the
Italians were in no position to break away from the Axis, and if they had

tried the Allies were in no position to take advantage of it. Indeed, they were hardly better placed to react when far more serious Italian overtures resumed with urgency after the fall of Mussolini.

The likelihood of an Italian attempt to make a separate peace had led the Allies to consider the terms they should offer, an inevitably long and complicated process of investigation and debate that began early in 1943, following work initiated by the British Foreign Office Ministerial Committee on Reconstruction Problems. Progress was hampered by differing British and American views, the former advocating that an Italian government be left in place to administer the country under Allied direction, the latter believing an Allied military government should be established following an unconditional surrender and the suspension of Italian government machinery. At the heart of this debate were differing perceptions on precisely what 'Unconditional Surrender' should entail for Italy. It had not been resolved when the whole process was overtaken by events on Mussolini's removal from power.[10]

News of this meant that renewed Italian approaches could only be a matter of time. For Eisenhower, whose Allied Force Headquarters was actively planning and preparing the further operations in the Mediterranean primarily directed against Italy that had been agreed by Churchill and Roosevelt and the Combined Chiefs of Staff, the events in Italy provided an opportunity demanding immediate action. The forthcoming landings on the Italian mainland, which would follow the still ongoing campaign in Sicily, would gain immeasurable benefit from active Italian military support. This was particularly so in the case of the intended 'Avalanche' landing near Naples, which on 26 July, following the news of Mussolini's fall, the Allied Combined Chiefs ordered Eisenhower to carry out as soon as feasible.

Eisenhower urged that the Allies should broadcast at once to the Italian people an assurance – the gist of which was that Italy would be granted a fair and beneficent peace should she request it and cease all collaboration with the Germans. This was intended to place irresistible pressure upon the new Italian government from within Italy. He had also drawn up a set of conditions to which the Italians would have to agree. The phrase 'Unconditional Surrender' was not used, but his terms included demands for the Italians to cease all hostilities against the Allies, to surrender their fleet, hand over all their prisoners-of-war and compel the Germans to evacuate Italian territory and the island of Corsica, which would be made available for Allied operational use. Eisenhower's right to establish military government and effect changes in personnel would have to be acknowledged.

In practice, this amounted to a demand for the Italians to take military action against the Germans, for in no other way could such terms be met. Eisenhower needed something workable for dealing with the Italians, and he needed it at once. He also wanted his terms, which became known as the 'Short Terms' in contrast to the 'Long Terms' still being formulated by the Allies, to be broadcast to the Italian people. His military imperative was obviously to create the most favourable conditions for his intended landings in Italy.

However, although sympathetic to this, Churchill and the British War Cabinet, and behind them the British Foreign Office, were against both broadcasting the 'Short Terms' to the Italian people and empowering Eisenhower as a military commander (though a very senior one) to personally negotiate them. For one thing, the Italians had not yet asked for any terms at all. The British view also reflected concern that the comprehensive longer-term resolution of complex political and reconstruction issues following an Italian surrender would be jeopardized in favour of short-term military advantage. The fear was one of storing up trouble for the future. On the one hand it was an example of Eisenhower, as the senior military commander in theatre trying to hold the threads together at the none-too-easily discernible point at which, in war, the political and military lines of responsibility must cease to be blurred and become distinctly separate – a situation exacerbated at the time by the Allied political line having been caught unprepared by events. On the other hand was the view that unless the full Allied political machinery handled the surrender negotiations, the Italians might secure undue advantages that would later cause the Allies difficulties within Italy and wider embarrassment. After all, to treat with Fascism in any form was contrary to 'Unconditional Surrender' and therefore remained an unacceptable option. Although Eisenhower's 'Short Terms' were couched in such a way as to reduce its prominence and to an extent save Italian face and smooth their decision-making in favour of the Allies, 'Unconditional Surrender' was most certainly still there. It afforded no compromise, and ultimately the Italian government would have to bow to it.

Eisenhower did receive sanction for a general broadcast to the Italian people. This was made on 29 July and, given their circumstances and fears, it had a noticeable effect. The 'Short Terms' were not broadcast. Eisenhower, acutely aware of the pressing military timetable, urgently requested on the same date that if the Italians made an approach he should be allowed to use his discretion and negotiate on the basis of the 'Short Terms' rather than lose an opportunity to gain significant military advantage. In this he had Roosevelt's backing, and Churchill, who was in any case determined to lose no opportunities in Italy, agreed.

As Churchill suspected they would, however, the Italian overtures to the Allies that Badoglio and the King of Italy decided on 28 July to initiate came through traditional diplomatic channels and not in the first instance to Eisenhower. On 4 August, the Marchese d'Aieta, Italian Foreign Office representative to the Vatican, made the first contact at the British embassy in Lisbon, where he had an interview with the British ambassador to Portugal, Sir Ronald Campbell. Two days later, on 6 August, a further Italian Foreign Office emissary, Signor Berio, made the second contact at the British embassy in Tangier. The tenor of the approaches by d'Aieta and Berio were similar, though whereas d'Aieta's mission was to inform the Allies that Italy wanted peace and that only Allied military intervention would enable her to break free from the Germans, Berio was empowered to negotiate with representatives of the British government or those of General Eisenhower.

Both d'Aieta and Berio stressed that Badoglio had no choice but to maintain an outward show of loyalty to the Axis in view of the increasing German military presence in Italy, and to prove this point and demonstrate good faith d'Aieta had brought details of the present and intended German order of battle in Italy. This, as yet, the Allies were unable to check through 'Ultra', but in any case Berio's was taken the more seriously of the two approaches. Not surprisingly, both Berio and d'Aieta stressed the need for the Allies to support the Badoglio government as the only means of ensuring law and order and as a bulwark against Communism, and both entreated the Allies to stop the bombing of Italian cities. By this time Churchill and the British Chiefs of Staff were at sea, en route to the 'Quadrant' Conference to be held with Roosevelt at Quebec. Once coordinated between Churchill and Roosevelt, Washington, and the British War Cabinet in London, the Allied response was cautious.

Churchill's view was that Badoglio by his own admission was out to double-cross someone and, under the circumstances, it was most likely to be Hitler. He was right, though, as Churchill himself probably suspected, Hitler was quite aware of the possibility. No one, as Badoglio was about to discover, is prepared to trust a turncoat. While Badoglio could hardly have seen his own duty to his country, or Italy's predicament in such terms, neither could he have realistically expected the Allies to welcome him unreservedly.

On 12 August, Berio was informed that there could be no negotiation, only 'Unconditional Surrender' and that the Italian government would have to place itself in the hands of the Allies, who would state their terms.[11] The bombing of Italian industrial and transportation centres was to continue; apart from the fact that the Germans were making use of these facilities, the Allies were in no mood to let up on a pressure that was clearly having a strong effect upon Italian willingness to remain within the Axis. All this amounted to the Italians having to throw themselves on the mercy of the British and Americans, although Berio was reminded of the Allied commitment to an honourable capitulation by Italy and the restitution of her place in the 'new Europe'. 'It is curious', the British official historian has pertinently observed, 'that in these instructions the repeated statements by the unfortunate Italians, that they were in no position to surrender whether unconditionally or otherwise, should have been so completely ignored.'[12] Italian protestations of helplessness made no impression at all.

Throughout the spring of 1943 the British Joint Intelligence Committee (JIC) had been forecasting that vigorous Allied action against Italy, including an invasion of Sicily coupled with an intensive air campaign and landings on the Italian mainland, would bring about an Italian collapse and a request for an armistice. By the beginning of August events had vindicated this view, but the JIC had also argued that if Italy collapsed the

Germans would not have the forces to be able to hold all the country. They would withdraw to the north, reported the JIC in April 1943, and would not be able to prevent the establishment of an Italian government that would be willing and able to make a separate peace with the Allies. In May an intercept of a Japanese diplomatic signal indicated that the Japanese at least were of the same opinion, that Germany would try and hold northern Italy and it was reasonable to suppose that they had good grounds.[13] Throughout the Allied invasion of Sicily, the fall of Mussolini, and the first Italian peace-feelers, though there may have been an increase in uncertainty, there was still no concrete intelligence to counter the view that the Germans would extricate their forces from southern Italy and hold a line in the north – hardly surprising, as at the time this was precisely what Hitler and the OKW did intend.

On 3 August the JIC reported their opinion to the British Chiefs of Staff, about to leave for Quebec. When Italy collapsed the Germans would be unable to spare more than four divisions to add to the three in the south and what could be salvaged from Sicily. Consequently, while they might try to hold a temporary position across the country along a line running west–east from Pisa to Rimini, or along the line of the river Po, they were more likely to hold the mountains in the extreme north, the Maritime Alps in the west and Venezia and the Tyrol in the east. This was not necessarily what an Allied campaign on mainland Italy was intended to achieve. Nor did it square with the case argued by the British to overcome American scepticism: that landings in Italy would support 'Overlord' and the Soviets, by compelling Hitler to send significant forces into Italy as well as the Balkans.

In fact, there seems to have been more than a degree of contradiction within British thinking about Italy. There was the intention to exploit an Italian collapse and surrender by securing airfields, ports and the capital, Rome, very likely with active Italian military assistance and in the wake of a German strategic withdrawal to the north. Such exploitation was feasible even with the limited Allied forces that would be left in the Mediterranean once the 'Overlord' priority came into effect, as the Allied formations in Italy would not be expected to be fighting their way northwards up the length of the peninsula. Moreover, in these circumstances, with the

Germans withdrawing in the face of Allied landings, much could reasonably be expected of the Italian forces. They could both hasten and disrupt the withdrawal, and help to secure ports and airfields of strategic importance, while the Germans would lack both the strength and time for prolonged operations against them and for Nazi-style vengeance against the Italian people. But this scenario might not achieve the stated aim of drawing German forces into Italy. A German withdrawal to the far north, and certainly one into a mountain bastion, would enable the Germans to conserve forces, not expend them. If Hitler was indeed induced to pour troops into Italy, thereby weakening his forces in France and on the Eastern Front, this would inevitably affect the nature of the campaign faced by the Allied formations landed in the south of Italy. They could face a very hard and costly battle, and one that would stretch their resources to the limit. It would also affect the Italian position – what their forces could achieve and the extent to which the Allied formations would be well placed to assist them. En route to Quebec, the British Chiefs of Staff decided to urge operations that would remove Italy from the war and compel the Germans to send reinforcements into the country and into the Balkans as a means of assisting 'Overlord' and the Soviets. That was still the British position on an Italian campaign.

A very real problem facing the Allies in early August was that while German intentions remained uncertain, so did everything else concerning Italy. Nor were there as yet indications of Hitler's build-up of strength in Italy and on its borders. The first reports of this came with the third emissary from the Badoglio government to make contact. General Giuseppe Castellano, Ambrosio's Chief of Staff with the Comando Supremo, arrived at the British embassy in Madrid on 15 August. His tracks covered by travelling with an accredited party of Italian officials en route to Lisbon, Castellano's mission was primarily to address the military aspects of Badoglio's potential defection from the Axis. The professional diplomats of the Italian Foreign Office had not welcomed this move, but supported it nevertheless. Like Eisenhower, the Italians were now feeling the urgency of firm arrangements.

They did not know Eisenhower's pressing timetable, but they had one of their own because every day brought more German troops into their country – and with them a reduction of the chance of successful Italian military resistance. Nor, when Castellano left Rome, had anything been heard from the earlier emissaries, itself a cause of concern. Castellano was well placed to provide the Allies with an insight into the military situation within Italy, and the British ambassador, Sir Samuel Hoare, was convinced that his mission was genuine. Castellano stated that he was authorized by Badoglio to inform the Allies of Italy's situation: that German troops were entering the country in strength, that the Italian Army and Air Force lacked equipment, and that the Italian government was unable to act unless the Allies landed in mainland Italy. If and when they did, Italy was ready to join the Allies and fight the Germans, and Italian forces in the Balkans would also cooperate with the guerrillas in Yugoslavia (though significantly he referred to the right-wing 'Cetniks' of General Draza Mihailovic rather than the Communist Partisans of Joseph Broz Tito).

Castellano came equipped with details of the German dispositions in Italy and the news that there were now thirteen German divisions in the country. He saw his role as that of coordinating Italian military action with that of the Allies, and for this he requested a meeting with one of Eisenhower's staff when he reached Lisbon. According to Castellano, Badoglio was urging immediate concerted planning. It was not part of Castellano's mission to entreat for surrender terms, nor to negotiate them. In this Badoglio and the Allies were at cross-purposes. The root of the matter remained 'Unconditional Surrender', but that was not the only problem. Not only was Badoglio apparently underestimating the influence of this policy upon the Anglo-American response to his overtures, his expectations of the Allies also indicate an assumption that an Allied invasion of mainland Italy would occur in far greater strength than Allied strategy and the forces at Eisenhower's disposal would actually permit. In Castellano's approach may be discerned the same belief, along with the imperative to pin the Allies down to what they were going to do, where, and when.

The Allied political and military leadership were now caught in a dilemma. Insistence on 'Unconditional Surrender' along with its full details and ramifications now being put together in the 'Long Terms' might well lose an opportunity to gain maximum advantage from the avowed Italian willingness to fight the Germans. Hoare had warned after meeting

Castellano that, unless the Italian government were assured of Allied landings and the opportunity to fight the Germans alongside the Allies, they
would not have the courage to change sides but would just drift into chaos.
Eisenhower's timetable for the 'Baytown' and 'Avalanche' landings was
ever pressing, and it was now even more important to secure Italian military assistance. Castellano's news of German strength in Italy was sobering, as Allied intercepts of German signals had not so far provided this full
picture. Doubts about the chances of 'Avalanche', considered something
of a gamble from its inception, were starting to grow at AFHQ. If the
Italians really would fight, it might make a lot of difference – in fact it
might make all the difference.

In practical terms, effective Italian military cooperation and concerted
action meant that the Italians would have to be provided with some details
of the Allied plans, and in enough time for the Comando Supremo to
conduct its own preparations and issue the necessary secret instructions to
Italian forces. This was what Castellano was after. But from the Allied
perspective, to entrust the Italians with such details, to place in their hands
the likely success of Allied operations and the lives of thousands of Allied
soldiers, was unthinkable. Even if Badoglio could be trusted, and of this
the Allies could hardly be sure, this did not mean all those who were in his
confidence could be. There was also the possibility that once cognisant of
Allied intentions, and particularly the strength of the Allied invasion, the
Badoglio government might decide that it was not after all in Italy's interest to change sides and that a better chance lay in remaining loyal to the
Axis. The irrevocable step had not yet been taken: the Italians could still
draw back, possibly use the information they had gained to secure a better
position within the Axis or, if Hitler struck first, use it to avert his
vengeance. For the Allies, all these were uncertainties around a risk that
simply could not be taken.

News of Castellano's arrival and request was transmitted to Churchill
and Roosevelt at Quebec, who faced the problem of reconciling the need
for Italian assistance and the need for Allied operational security. The
British Foreign Secretary, Anthony Eden, expressed the view of the professional diplomats of the Foreign Office, very likely anticipated by their
Italian counterparts, who had not been at all keen on the Castellano initiative.

††††††††††††††††††††

His advice amounted to having no part of Castellano, or his mission. To take the Italians into Allied confidence on military matters was out of the question. In any case, once Allied troops were ashore in Italy the Italians would have to cooperate, and the imposition of 'Unconditional Surrender' would not change that. So far as the Balkans was concerned, an Italian change of sides would be of little benefit but would very likely become a liability. For the Allies to negotiate with an Axis power that had been responsible for brutal repression in what was a vicious and often merciless struggle would send the wrong message to the resistance in Yugoslavia, who would be discouraged[14]. Moreover, British Intelligence had been aware for some time of the Italian link with Mihailovic, considerable data having been gained through intercepts of German signals traffic. These told of much German frustration and suspicion because their own anti-guerrilla operations in the Balkans, which consumed large numbers of troops, were hamstrung by the Italians deliberately not acting against the Cetniks and in their areas of responsibility even protecting them.

By this time the British and Americans were disillusioned with Mihailovic. He had forfeited their support through his collaboration with the Italians and through his reluctance to engage in serious action against the Axis. The complicating factor in Yugoslavia was that, in addition to an ongoing war against Axis occupation, there was a latent civil war between right and left that had already partially broken out, exacerbated by factional fighting within these polarized groups. Rather than fight the Axis, Mihailovic tended to conserve his forces and engage more often than not in action against Tito's partisans. As far as the Allies were concerned Tito, who unlike Mihailovic was fighting a determined war against the Axis, was the man to support. So Badoglio's offer, relayed by Castellano, for the Italians to support Mihailovic in the Balkans struck a hollow and altogether discordant note. It also threatened to complicate matters with the Soviets. Eden and the Foreign Office were particularly concerned that for the British and Americans to negotiate with Italy and compromise on 'Unconditional Surrender' would heighten Stalin's already deep suspicions of the Western powers.

All this was sound thinking, and might have been adopted had it not been for the now urgent concerns about the chances of the forthcoming

Allied landings in Italy. Castellano's information about German strength in Italy, added to the knowledge of the successful German evacuation of their divisions from Sicily across the Strait of Messina to the mainland, altered the odds considerably against 'Avalanche'. The military imperative that had concerned Eisenhower for so long now began to override other longer-term considerations at the highest political level. Churchill and the Chiefs of Staff at Quebec decided against the Foreign Office advice. Churchill in particular believed that the Italians could achieve a great deal against the Germans in Italy, especially in the sabotaging of communications and transport upon which German forces relied. Roosevelt and the American Joint Chiefs of Staff agreed and endorsed a British suggestion that attempted to provide Badoglio with a palatable imposition of 'Unconditional Surrender' while ensuring Italian military assistance and the preservation of Allied operational security.

Eisenhower was authorized to send two of his staff, one British and one American, to Lisbon where they were to present Castellano with the 'Short Terms' for an armistice, with the added *douceur* that the extent to which Allied terms might be modified would depend upon the extent of Italian support to the Allies. Once agreed, Eisenhower would notify the Italians of the date and hour of the armistice, which would be announced a few hours before the Allied landings on the mainland. Badoglio must agree to announce the armistice simultaneously with the Allies, and order the Italian forces and people to assist the Allies and resist the Germans. Italian naval and merchant shipping and aircraft must proceed to Allied ports and airfields or else be destroyed to prevent their use by the Germans, and Allied prisoners-of-war must be released. Their forces in the Balkans should be evacuated. In the meantime, before the armistice was openly announced, the Italians should conduct passive resistance and minor sabotage, and protect their Allied prisoners from the Germans.

Brigadier Kenneth Strong, Eisenhower's British chief of intelligence, and his American Chief of Staff, Major General Walter Bedell Smith, met Castellano in Lisbon late on 19 August for what turned out to be an all-night session. Castellano, whose mission had been primarily one of military coordination, now found himself confronted by the Allied armistice terms. Once this situation had been clarified, Castellano agreed to return to Italy with the 'Short Terms'. He also opened up further with information, including the disquieting fact that several thousand German SS troops had been drafted into Rome, and that the German 2nd Parachute and 3rd Panzer Grenadier Divisions were in place to threaten the capital. By 23 August this information had reached the Quebec conference, and by this time 'Ultra' signals intelligence had also provided confirmation of Castellano's German order of battle in Italy.

His picture of the Italian military situation was not an encouraging one; lack of fuel limited the movement of ships and aircraft, the Germans controlled most airfields, the Italians could do little to prevent the Germans moving Allied prisoners-of-war, and their formations in the Balkans could not be withdrawn to the coast. Castellano was told that the Italians must do what they could. Voicing concerns about German reprisals against the Italian people, including a possible use of gas, once the armistice was announced, he was assured that the Allies would counter this with retaliation. It was also suggested to him that it was better for Italy to endure a few days of German vindictiveness than to become a battleground of prolonged attrition.

This attitude reflected the belief that the Germans would withdraw rapidly northwards once the Allied forces were ashore, and indeed Castellano had reinforced this thinking. His own information was that the Germans would attempt to hold a line from Genoa in the west to Ravenna in the east, and if that proved untenable, then a line along the River Po. Early on 20 August, Castellano left to begin his return journey to Rome. His request to be told where and when the Allied invasion would occur was refused, and he was promised only that Eisenhower would make his announcement some five or six hours before the landings. This effectively ruled out concerted action. Badoglio was to inform the Allies by 30 August of his acceptance, and in that event Castellano would fly to Sicily on the following day to meet again with Allied representatives. He was also provided with a wireless transmitter (W/T) set and code plan by SOE for the Italians to use to make contact, along with the information that the Italians held as a prisoner-of-war in Milan an experienced British operator.

With Castellano en route to Rome (where he would not arrive until 27 August) to give his government just three days to consider the Allied 'Short

Terms', the Allies finally agreed on the 'Long Terms', their detailed and comprehensive surrender conditions. While requiring 'Unconditional Surrender', these allowed for an Italian government to continue to function under Allied auspices. But the introduction at this stage of these terms, with their 43 clauses, brought unwelcome complications. The Italians were now to be informed that these rather than the 'Short Terms' represented the Allied conditions for Italy's surrender. This problem was passed down to the Allied Supreme Commander in theatre, and the reaction of Eisenhower and his AFHQ staff, not surprisingly, was one of consternation.

Their plans for 'Baytown' and 'Avalanche' had just been given final approval at Quebec on 24 August, but in the light of intelligence data the realization was dawning at AFHQ that the German forces already in southern Italy belonging to Tenth Army might prove sufficient to defeat 'Avalanche' – even without reinforcement by German divisions brought down from the north. Consequently, any Italian action that might disrupt and delay the German reaction to Clark's landing was increasingly seen not just as a bonus but as a prerequisite. Now all that seemed to have been achieved to secure this assistance looked to be jeopardized by presenting the Italian emissaries, who had taken the 'Short Terms' in good faith and who were expected to return having agreed to them, with a longer and far more complex set of conditions. These the Italians would have to examine carefully clause by clause – there would be queries, objections, negotiations, procrastinations and, above all, delay.

On 28 August, Eisenhower appealed to the Allied Combined Chiefs of Staff that, for the sake of 'Avalanche', when Castellano arrived in Sicily in three days' time, most likely with acceptance of the 'Short Terms', the matter be allowed to stand. It was a powerful and irrefutable argument. In fact, AFHQ had that day acted quickly and decisively, though unconventionally, to prevent the surrender process being derailed by an initiative from which they had been hitherto excluded.

A further Italian emissary, this time sent by General Mario Roatta, the Italian Army Chief of Staff, had turned up at the British embassy in Lisbon on 26 August. This was General Giacomo Zanussi, an officer on Roatta's staff, but his only credential was that he had with him a distinguished British senior officer, Lieutenant General Sir Adrian Carton de Wiart, who had been captured by the Italians near Bardia, in the Western Desert campaign, in 1941. Zanussi's mission had been agreed to by Badoglio and Ambrosio out of a sense of urgency and because nothing had been heard from Castellano; they had not informed the Italian Foreign Ministry. Little could be made of Zanussi or his mission at Lisbon, but he was given a copy of the 'Long Terms' that had come through by Foreign Office telegram. Although he voiced reservations about 'Unconditional Surrender' and the likely German action if the Italian surrender were to be announced publicly, Zanussi agreed to return to Italy with the terms.

On hearing of this potentially dangerous move, however, Eisenhower's team at AFHQ stepped in. They were inclined to trust neither Roatta nor, by extension, Zanussi. Either deliberately or inadvertently, this latest Italian move could negate the efforts made with Castellano. They had Zanussi intercepted at Gibraltar and brought to them at Algiers, where Strong, Bedell Smith and the British political representative at Eisenhower's headquarters, Harold Macmillan, interviewed him. Zanussi satisfied them of his genuineness, and he was allowed to contact Rome to urge agreement to the 'Short Terms', but he was not permitted to transmit the 'Long Terms' for the delaying effect this might have on Italian decision-making. Both Churchill and Roosevelt subsequently condoned AFHQ's action, and on 30 August Eisenhower received authorization to secure Castellano's signature to the 'Short Terms' before the Italians were to be given the 'Long Terms.' Churchill's sharp retort on 1 September to the British War Cabinet's demur at this method – 'All this would be blown sky high if we lost the battle and were driven back into the sea' – expressed the now overriding concern for 'Avalanche'. In just eight days Clark and his Fifth Army would be going ashore at Salerno.[15]

On 30 August, AFHQ received confirmation from Rome by the W/T link that Castellano would come to Sicily on the following day. The negotiators from AFHQ, Zanussi with them, were waiting. This meeting, held at General Alexander's headquarters at Cassibile, was to disappoint them. Castellano had not come to sign anything. Instead, he brought the news that, with the Germans occupying the country in strength, the Italian government was virtually helpless, and that to announce the armistice before the Allies were in a position to protect Rome, where the King and government would remain, would bring disaster. Badoglio's own view was that the Allies should land to the north of Rome with at least fifteen divisions. This was a clear indication of his expectations of Allied strength, and one good reason for the Allies to keep from him both the actual scale of their invasion and where it would take place. In effect, Badoglio was not ready to commit himself until certain of the military situation, whereas the Allies wanted to be certain of the Italian surrender and military assistance to ensure the success of 'Avalanche'.

Castellano's requests, now more urgent and seconded by Zanussi, for details of the Allied invasion were stonily refused. By this time it was really too late for concerted action – Badoglio and the Comando Supremo were completely in the dark, unable to provide specific instructions to Italian formations. This was the necessary price of Allied distrust of Badoglio, and of the need to maintain operational security. Instead, the Allies were banking upon the general disruption and confusion that would be caused to the Germans by the Italian surrender and change of sides, but in this they were reckoning without the German contingency plans, of which their intelligence had so far provided only the sketchiest information.

Castellano, accompanied by Zanussi, returned to Rome, having been warned that the Allies were about to drive the Germans out of Italy whatever happened and that their country was about to become a battleground. The duration of that battle, however, would be shortened if the Italian government agreed to the Allied terms. Castellano's parting shot was to request that the Allies at least land an armoured division at Ostia and an airborne division near Rome to help the Italians to defend their capital. This struck home. Although the sea-borne landing of an armoured division was impossible – no such division or the shipping for it could be spared, and in any case the suggestion made no military sense – the airborne plan was taken up. Although it would be a tremendous risk, it was nevertheless only one more risk among many about to be taken in Italy by the Allies and it might bring great dividends by ensuring Italian support and creating havoc and confusion for the Germans when 'Avalanche' went in. Moreover, the US 82nd Airborne Division, under Major General Matthew Ridgway, was available in theatre though earmarked as part of Clark's 'Avalanche' force.

Alexander was prepared to countenance the risk and recommended the proposal. Eisenhower accepted his recommendation, and both Churchill and Roosevelt gave their approval. Eisenhower broke to Clark the unwelcome news that his already dangerously limited force was to be further reduced and explained why it was necessary. It gave Clark small comfort. The scheme was desperate. As a military proposition it might well be called hare-brained, especially as the Allies, via their signals intelligence and Castellano, had a reasonably accurate picture of the German strength in and near Rome. Its only justification was that both politically and militarily the Allies were about to gamble for high stakes in Italy, that they anticipated significant Italian military assistance and that their intelligence indicated a German withdrawal and not a prolonged battle.

On 1 September Badoglio and Ambrosio heard Castellano and Zanussi's report. It cannot have made pleasant listening. After weeks of making contact, the Italians had received no firm assurances of the Allied military assistance that alone made defection from the Axis feasible. No details of intended Allied operations had been forthcoming to make concerted action possible, and there was reason to fear that the forthcoming Allied landings would not offer protection to Rome, the government and the monarchy. Their own intelligence sources and the Italian Admiralty warned that the Allied landings were likely to occur too far to the south, the area between Naples and Salerno being a strong possibility. Similar appreciations came from German intelligence sources and aerial reconnaissance reports.

Badoglio and the Italian government had failed to induce the Allies to treat them as a prospective ally. The only certainties they faced were negatives: the increasing German strength in their country; the predictable ferocity of Hitler's reaction once they showed their hand; the imminence of their country becoming a battleground; the likelihood of much of it remaining under a hostile German occupation; and their own inability to control or even influence events. In the end, the only hope seemed to be that of acceding to the Allied terms, a course approved by the King. Through the W/T link they informed AFHQ that the terms were accepted and confirmed Castellano's return to Sicily on the following day.

They remained at cross-purposes with the Allies, however, for Castellano was given no authority to sign on their behalf but only, once again, to try and coordinate military plans. When this became apparent at Cassibile, the AFHQ reaction was one of dismay at what appeared to be Badoglio's prevarication. Alexander himself, as the senior Allied officer available, was called in by the AFHQ negotiators to overawe the Italians with a show of anger. This he did in great style. He and some of his staff turned up in parade order, booted and spurred, Alexander affecting a desire to meet Castellano and feigning the assumption that the Italians had signed the surrender. When informed they had not he displayed considerable indignation, left them in no doubt that it was time they made up their minds, and warned them of the likely consequences of breaking faith. Just as impressively Alexander and his officers then left, and the Italians hurriedly returned to their own tent to confer. To learn the result of his inspired piece of theatre, Alexander then crept around the outside wall of an orchard to avoid being seen, rejoining the AFHQ team by climbing over the wall.[16]

Castellano relayed these developments to Rome. He received authority to sign only on the afternoon of the following day, 3 September, by which time Montgomery's Eighth Army had already begun to cross from Sicily to the mainland in the 'Baytown' operation. With Eisenhower present, Castellano signed agreement to what were the 'Short Terms'. Only afterwards was he given the Allies' 'Long Terms'. These were a shock to him, as was their reference to 'Unconditional Surrender', at which he expressed reservations on his government's behalf.

Both sides were still clinging to unrealistic expectations of the other, and on this, in the last days and hours before 'Avalanche', the Italian surrender process broke down. For his part, Castellano appears to have over-played his hand in committing the Italians to providing the necessary military assistance to the Rome operation, codenamed 'Giant II' by the Allies. Either his own picture of the Italian forces near the capital and what they could do was hopelessly optimistic or he was attempting to draw from the Allied team greater confidences as to their own strengths and intentions. During the planning conducted on Sicily during 3–4 September, attended by Ridgway of the 82nd Airborne, it was agreed that the Italians would secure four airfields in the Rome area and defend them to enable the landing of the American airborne troops, who were to arrive several hours before the Allied sea-borne invasion in the south. Ridgway was understandably sceptical about the chances of 'Giant II' and wanted one of his officers to assess the situation on the spot and coordinate the operation with the Italians.

This task fell to the 82nd's divisional artillery commander, Brigadier General Maxwell Taylor. It seems odd that despite Castellano's own knowledge of German strength around Rome, known also to the Allies through their intelligence, this operation was viewed so sanguinely at AFHQ. Italian pleadings of military helplessness throughout the previous weeks had been either disbelieved or disregarded, and Castellano's turn around in attitude – from one of emphasising Italian inability to act without strong Allied assistance to one of assuring significant help to 'Giant II' – was not seriously questioned. There was no possibility of 'Giant II' offering significant assistance to the Italians – at most, a division of highly trained and motivated but inevitably lightly armed airborne soldiers. And, as Maxwell Taylor later recalled, there was no question of the 82nd arriving in Rome as a full division because the available airlift was sufficient for little more than a regiment.[17] The Allied senior commanders were grasping at straws.

It was also arranged that Eisenhower and Badoglio should make simultaneous broadcasts, announcing the Allied granting of an armistice to Italy and the cessation of hostilities between them, at 6.30 p.m. on the evening before the Allied landings. Despite all his efforts Castellano was still denied the date of these landings and consequently any firm timetable for 'Giant II'. He was told only that the landings would occur within two weeks. For the Allies, operational security for 'Avalanche', and their bluff as to the actual strength of their invasion, remained paramount. The effect was to mislead the Italians, and by so doing increase the risks for Ridgeway's men. For the Rome operation to stand any chance of success required the three Italian divisions near the capital to play a full and active role, and for this it was necessary to alert and brief their commanders and staffs in sufficient time to ensure that the necessary preparations were in place. Instead, Castellano fell back on deduction from what he had been told, and not told, and concluded that the Allied landings would likely occur on 12 September. He reported thus to Rome, where Badoglio, Ambrosio and Roatta wrongly assumed that there was more time in hand than was actually the case. Clark was preparing to land at Salerno early on 9 September.

Although serious enough, this misinterpretation was only part of the critical dissonance between AFHQ and the Italians. On 5 September the plans agreed between Castellano and AFHQ were received in Rome with surprise and consternation, because they were considered to have no foundation in reality. This was made forcibly clear to Taylor who, after being smuggled into Rome on 7 September, brought the news to the completely unprepared and horrified Italian leaders that the airborne division would be landing within 24 hours. For General Giacomo Carboni, commander of the Italian motorized corps in the Rome area, the operation was an impossibility: the Germans controlled the stocks of fuel and ammunition, neither of which his troops had enough for a major battle; nor did the Italians wish to see their capital become a battleground. Badoglio agreed, and also refused outright to comply with the terms agreed by Castellano, arguing that an immediate armistice was impossible. Taylor, like Castellano before him, now faced a political situation quite beyond his brief, but he did manage to insist upon Badoglio sending a message to Eisenhower direct. He also got a message through on the following morning, 8 September, cancelling 'Giant II'. This was received in North Africa and reached the airfields on Sicily only just in time to halt the loading of the 82nd's transport aircraft, some of which had just taken off and had to be flagged down.

Also on 8 September, Eisenhower received Badoglio's urgent request for a postponement of the surrender announcement. With 'Avalanche' now only a few hours away, there could be no question of allowing Badoglio to play for time, and Eisenhower determined to force his hand. Churchill and Roosevelt were agreed that the announcement of the Italian surrender should be made without consideration of any embarrassment to the Italian government. The Italian request was firmly refused, with warnings added of the consequences for Badoglio and the Italian government of failure to honour their signed agreement, including the threat to 'publish to the world the full record of this affair'. This effectively removed any other option from Badoglio. The only hope now for his government was to accede. No volte-face, though it was briefly considered, could possibly avert German reaction. It was too late. An hour after it had been scheduled, at 7.45 p.m., and following Eisenhower's 6.30 p.m. broadcast, Badoglio made his own announcement from the radio station in Rome. In the following hours, as German units closed in upon the city, he and the senior political and military leaders and the royal family left the capital for the port of Pescara, where they boarded an Italian Navy corvette for Brindisi in the south, arriving there on 10 September.

Behind them was chaos and confusion. Shortly after Badoglio's own announcement, Hitler ordered the activation of Plan 'Axis'. Throughout the country German units moved swiftly to disarm Italian garrisons and take over their installations and equipment. There were some instances of fighting when Italian officers and their men put up a resistance, but these were overcome and ruthlessly dealt with. In fact no Italian resistance with any chance of being effective could have been organized in time, since no firm instructions for this contingency had been given to Italian formation commanders. The timing of the surrender announcement took most of them completely by surprise. For this the Allies, as well as the Badoglio regime, were responsible. It was also in these circumstances that a significant factor emerged that the AFHQ planners had too little considered in their hopes of Italian military assistance – the extreme war-weariness within the Italian Army. As the Germans set about their takeover of the country, many Italian formations simply melted away, their soldiers abandoning their equipment and very often their uniforms to disappear into the civilian population, glad that for them the war was over.

Early on 9 September the Italian fleet put to sea from La Spezia and Genoa to rendezvous with ships of the Royal Navy that were to escort them to Malta. In the afternoon, one of three formations of German Dornier Do 217 bombers despatched from their airfield in southern France to intercept and attack the Italian ships sighted their quarry. These aircraft were armed with radio-controlled bombs, which had only recently entered the Luftwaffe's inventory, and one struck the magazine of the Italian flagship, the battleship *Roma*, which exploded and sank with great loss of life. It marked a bitter end to the Axis alliance. By then the leading elements of Clark's Fifth Army were ashore at Salerno and encountering a

German reaction that would increase in strength sufficiently to threaten the survival of the beachhead. There was no assistance from the Italians, whose formations in southern Italy had been dispersed, and their equipment and positions taken over by von Vietinghoff's German Tenth Army.

Was this inevitable, or did the Allies lose a valuable opportunity through their handling of the Italian surrender? It is questionable whether any such opportunity ever existed. Hitler and the OKW were well aware of the potential of an Italian defection. The Germans possessed the advantage of a sizeable military presence in Italy that they were able to increase; against it the Italians could do nothing but protest, while still endeavouring to preserve the façade of the Axis. Without Allied military help the Italians were genuinely helpless, and whatever they could do against the Germans could only be effective in the context of an Allied invasion into the initial operations of which their contribution had been integrated in planning and execution. This was never a possibility. The 'Unconditional Surrender' policy meant that the British and Americans could not in a short space of time regard the Italian government that replaced Mussolini as an ally, only as an enemy suing for peace on Allied terms. Nor would it have been justified, in terms of operational security alone, for so recent an enemy, still formally at least in alliance with the Germans, to be taken fully into Allied military confidence. The concerted planning that alone would have enabled coordinated action at the time of the Allied landings was therefore ruled out. It is doubtful too whether the Italian Army, whose best units were no longer in Italy, having been destroyed in North Africa or sent to the Soviet Union and the Balkans, would have been able to perform effectively against the Germans even if given the opportunity by the Allies and by its own government. As the 'Giant II' concept indicated, there was a considerable degree of wishful thinking in AFHQ's expectations of Italian military capability, unrelated to what intelligence reported of the actual situation in Italy.

All these were factors generated by the Allied situation regarding Italy in the summer of 1943. Events in Italy caught them unprepared, and they were attempting to pull off an elaborate bluff in regard to the strength of their invasion. Although their strategic planning endorsed further operations to knock Italy out of the war following the capture of Sicily, they could only be conducted with the forces agreed for the Mediterranean theatre. The fall of Mussolini and the first serious peace overtures from his successors caught the Allied political and military leadership without a coherent policy. They were caught in the dilemma – how to secure the maximum advantage of the situation compatible with the 'Unconditional Surrender' policy and before the German hold on the country became too strong. This meant masking 'Unconditional Surrender' behind the 'Short Terms' and bluffing the Italians into an armistice announcement and into fighting the Germans in expectation of a strong Allied invasion that offered them their best, indeed their only, option for their country. The reality was somewhat different. Italian action was desired to facilitate an Allied invasion that was well known at AFHQ to be weak, indeed dangerously so, and something of a gamble. Operational security aside, the actual strength of the Allied invasion and the location of the landings that would follow 'Baytown' simply had to be kept from Badoglio. Too little security was offered to the Italians to offset the risks they were expected to take. To reveal to Badoglio the extent of Allied dependence upon Italian military support would either rule out the surrender and compel the Italians to seek the best possible terms from Hitler within the Axis, or else it would present Badoglio with a bargaining position vis-à-vis the Allies completely incommensurate with 'Unconditional Surrender'.

In the event the Allies failed in their bluff. To an extent they were victims of it. They forced Badoglio's hand, but he and the Comando Supremo had been kept in the dark too long, denied the information and time upon which worthwhile Italian military action depended. The German strength in Italy had also by then become too great and their contingency plans too well prepared. The surrender of their country and the swiftness of the German reaction caught the Italian formations unprepared. They had little choice other than to disband themselves and could offer no assistance to the Allies who were committed to a campaign in mainland Italy on a shoestring of resources. It would indeed prove a hard way to make a war.[18]

8

ASHORE IN ITALY

'Baytown'

'This advance up Italy was a veritable Calvary. Our speed was determined
by the capacity of the sappers to repair bridges and other demolitions.'[1]

The crossing of the Strait of Messina by the British Eighth Army saw a
heavy punch thrown, which in the event struck very little. Although units
of the German 29th Panzer Grenadier Division and the 26th Panzer
Division were known to be covering Calabria, only a single German regiment (15th Panzer Grenadier Regiment) of the former had two battalions
deployed near the invasion sector, mostly guarding the principal roads.
The Italian Seventh Army in southern Italy had four Coastal Divisions in
Calabria, but they were in the same dire condition as their counterparts
had been on Sicily. The 211th Coastal Division, widely and thinly spread,
covered the invasion sector to the north of Reggio.

They were very much on their own when the Germans pulled away
farther inland as the massive artillery bombardment from Eighth Army's
guns came down across the Strait – to which the heavy guns of the US
Seventh Army also contributed, supplemented by a naval bombardment of
Reggio and heavy air attacks.

The 1st Canadian and 5th Divisions of Eighth Army's XIII Corps
landed mostly unopposed. The Canadians found empty beaches, lacking
even the expected wire and mines, and reported their stiffest resistance to
be from a puma, escaped from the Reggio zoo. The 5th Division reported
that a battalion officer was slightly injured by a brick thrown at him by an
Italian artilleryman, whose commanding officer was found weeping in his
dugout. His battery of coastal guns still had their muzzle covers fitted.[2]
Most Italian soldiers encountered on or near the beaches willingly helped
unload the landing craft. Only light casualties were caused by some
desultory long-range German shelling from the hills and later in the day

by some hit-and-run air attacks. These too were few, for in the days leading to 'Baytown' the Allied air forces had pulverized the airfields around Foggia; in any case the Regia Aeronautica was incapable of much offensive effort and the Luftwaffe was concentrated in the Naples area.

Eighth Army's worst enemy by far was the wild mountainous country of Calabria, with steep terraced mountain slopes descending to small coastal bays. Roads were few, threading their way through the mountains with twists and turns, and with many bridges over rivers, culverts and tunnels. There could be no movement off the roads, except by steep and narrow mountain cart tracks. It was not necessary for the Germans to deploy many infantry to delay Eighth Army in this countryside – just a few, with engineers and, above all, explosives. Every bridge, culvert, gully and viaduct in Eighth Army's path was blown. Mines were sown with the usual ingenuity. Sometimes the Germans petrol-soaked the hillside scrub, into which their rearguards would fire a few incendiary rounds to ignite it on spotting the arrival of the British infantry.[3] Great quantities of Bailey bridging material was used by Eighth Army to enable progress, but it needed to be brought forward for each task. Such construction and even rudimentary repair of demolitions all took time. As in Sicily, the Germans were proving masters of delaying tactics and, once again, the terrain was their ally.

An attempt was made to get forward by sea, and on 8 September a sharp action was fought at Pizzo as units of the 231st Brigade landed opposed by troops of the 29th Panzer Grenadier Division, whose withdrawal along the coastal route they had interrupted.[4] There was little naval support, and only the deliberate beaching under fire of a damaged LST from which self-propelled artillery blasted its way out to engage the Germans turned the scale: after a day of fighting the Germans broke off under the cover of darkness. By 10 September, the Eighth Army advance had covered about a hundred miles to reach Catanzaro and Nicastro, the 'neck' of Italy's 'toe', but momentum was now slowing down as the advance was still dependent upon lines of communication and supply stretching all the way back to the Strait of Messina and across to Sicily, and there was plenty of scope for congestion and delay. By this time Clark's Fifth Army was ashore and fighting for its life at Salerno. There could be no early link up.

Avalanche: An Opposed Landing

'Not until months later, when I had occasion to fly low over the German positions at Salerno, did I wholly realize how well the enemy had been able to observe our movements and thus shift his strength and artillery to oppose our thrusts. In this respect the German advantage was nothing less than appalling.'
— General Mark Clark[5]

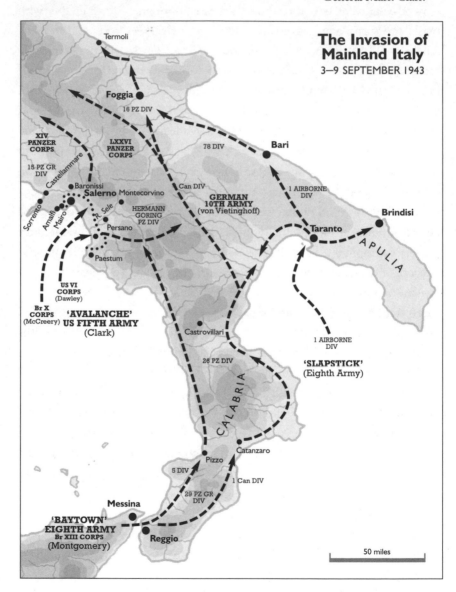

The Invasion of
Mainland Italy
3–9 SEPTEMBER 1943

Military planners must sometimes through necessity accept, not the best option, but the 'least worst', and this was the case with 'Avalanche'. While the concept of an amphibious strike at Naples was sound, translating it into practical reality ran into some insurmountable difficulties, leading to a very high acceptance of risk. The first problem was where to land. The most obvious landing zone was the Bay of Naples itself, and this was the first one ruled out because of its defences. Extensive minefields guarded the sea approaches, and while the Allied navies might have swept them clear there were still formidable coastal gun defences. The Allies were in no mood to let the Germans deal them another Dieppe. That left beaches to the north of Naples in the Gulf of Gaeta, or to the south in the Gulf of Salerno.

Clark strongly favoured Gaeta, and had no liking at all for Salerno. The Gaeta beaches had no overlooking mountains and led straight into the Campania Plain. This was highly favourable to armour and offered the chance for a successful landing and rapid exploitation inland to cut off German forces to the south and compel their hasty abandonment of Naples, before they had time to systematically destroy its port facilities. Airborne troops could land to the north, to hold the line of the River Volturno against German interference from that direction while the beachhead and advance inland took firm hold. Yet there were some drawbacks to Gaeta. The beaches were not good for a landing, with sloping gradients and offshore sandbars awkward for the run-in of landing craft. They also looked to be fairly well defended, with pill-boxes and gun positions protected by minefields and wire, indicating that the Germans and Italians had appreciated their likely attraction to the Allies. But while the nature of the beaches and their defences might have been overcome, the deciding factor was air power. Gaeta was well beyond the range of Allied single-engined fighters, which would have to fly from airfields on Sicily. Although the Luftwaffe could not match the Allies in the air, the handicap of Allied fighter range would allow it to offer a threat to the landings, and on this question Tedder was adamant. Clark was never wholly convinced of the primacy of this air argument and would later recall that, in any case, American and British airmen differed on the question. Tedder's was the deciding air voice, however, and it clinched the matter. Clark's memoirs, perhaps influenced by hindsight, suggest a lingering regret that Gaeta was not selected for 'Avalanche'.[6] He did not oppose the plan as Montgomery had opposed the initial 'Husky' plan. But Clark, about to fight his first battle as an Army commander, was not Montgomery.

So, against his own inclination, by 12 August Clark knew he was going to Salerno, where the beaches themselves were not merely suitable but ideal. The offshore waters did not shoal, there were fine inshore approaches for larger vessels, and the beach gradients were good for landing craft. The beaches were wide enough for the landing of troops and equipment and had good exits leading inland to the main coastal road, Highway 18, running north to Naples and on to Rome. Salerno had a small port, and just to the west was the little harbour at Amalfi, both of which would be useful for the landing of supplies. About three miles inland and within early reach of the landing force was the airfield at Montecorvino, capable of handling four fighter squadrons. Its capture would enable the fly-in of Allied squadrons to solve the air support problem – Salerno was within range of Allied single-engined fighters, but only just. RAF Spitfire VBs flying from Sicily and fitted with long-range tanks would still have only some 25 minutes over Salerno, their pilots keeping a watchful eye on their fuel gauges. USAAF twin-engined and twin-boom P-38 Lightnings fitted with extra tanks could stay an hour, but despite their formidable firepower the Lightnings lacked the manoeuvra-

---

Luftwaffe Strength, Italy, Sardinia, and Southern France, 31 August 1943.[7]

Fighters/Fighter-bombers: 223 Southern Italy (117 serviceable); 26 Sardinia (15 serviceable)

Ground Attack: 28 Sardinia (10 serviceable)

Bombers: 104 Northern and Central Italy (37 serviceable); 72 Southern Italy (37 serviceable); 100 Southern France (36 serviceable)

Reconnaissance: 29 Southern Italy (18 serviceable); 10 Sardinia (4 serviceable); 20 Southern France (6 serviceable).

Note the wide discrepancy between numbers of aircraft available and those actually serviceable for operations. Serviceability states varied daily, but by August 1943 the Luftwaffe was suffering maintenance difficulties as a result of Allied air attacks upon its airfields and infrastructure throughout the Mediterranean, as well as a severe shortage of spare parts. This inevitably affected the attainable rate of effort. The Allied strategic bombing of Germany was also having its effect, particularly in draining Luftwaffe strength away from the Mediterranean in order to reinforce the Reich's own air defences.

bility for dogfighting the German Fw 190s and later-type Bf 109s. There were eleven Axis airfields at just over 100 miles distance from Salerno, and while Tedder's bomber squadrons were set to hammer them, their complete neutralization could not be guaranteed. Even at Salerno, air cover for the landing force and shipping would be problematic.

The real problem with Salerno, however, and why Clark did not want to go there, was the terrain just inland of those ideal landing beaches. The Bay of Salerno was ringed by mountainous high ground giving excellent observation over the Bay and its beaches, and affording a defender ideal fire positions. For an invader from the sea it would be like landing into an overlooked amphitheatre. There was no need of fixed defences, for nature had endowed a defender with a formidable position from which to contain a beachhead or from which to sally forth to destroy it. From the high ground, a rocky spur Monte Paito descended to the sea, cutting off the Bay from the Gulf of Naples except for two narrow gorges – potential sally ports for the defender. The American campaign historian observes that there was no solution to this terrain problem, so the planners did not dwell upon it.[8] Their hands were tied. Salerno offered an ideal landing site for an unopposed descent on the Italian coast and for a rapid seizure of Naples, facilitated by the Italian surrender (possibly even direct Italian assistance) and a German withdrawal. But it was no place for a landing force to have to fight a beachhead battle.

In August during the run up to the landings, the Allies could not be sure which of these contingencies they would face. Intelligence sources, including the interception of German signals traffic and data provided by the Italians, indicated the reinforcement of the German presence in Italy. There were some 16 German divisions in the country, including those extricated from Sicily, but more were on the way and a new Army Group B had been activated to control those in the north. Yet this had to balance against indications, again also confirmed by the Italians, that in the event of Allied landings the Germans would withdraw to the north, possibly to hold a defensive line across the country from Pisa to Rimini or, if that were untenable, the line of the River Po. If this was to be the case, then the landings stood in no serious danger. In fact, the increase in German strength reflected Hitler's precautions against an Italian defection, and his intention at this stage was that the German forces in the south under Kesselring would pull back to the north to come eventually under Rommel's Army Group B command.

As August drew to a close, the conviction that Kesselring's forces in southern Italy would withdraw to the north began to wear very thin at Eisenhower's AFHQ. Something akin to panic seemed to take hold as the planners, only too aware of what the post-'Husky' shipping constraints implied for Clark's landing strength and rate of build-up, began to worry, not about the Germans in the north of Italy, but about the strength Kessel-ring already possessed in the south within early striking distance of Salerno. At the Quebec Conference, Eisenhower's Deputy Chief of Staff reported to the Allied Combined Chiefs that Montgomery's 'Baytown' landings in Calabria were not expected to encounter very strong German opposition, but he admitted to anxiety over 'Avalanche'. Clark was likely to be confronted by German forces of strength comparable to his own within a few hours of landing, and once the Germans detected the weak-ness of his force they might move reinforcements 'to the sound of the guns', so that he could be faced eventually by up to six divisions. Also the terrain just inland from the beaches would favour any such German response by helping to pen Clark in his beachhead. At the end of August, AFHQ spelled out their concerns in more detail. Their assessment reflected the German forces already in southern Italy, but for this reason it was considered unrealistic by the Military Intelligence Branch of the British War Office (MI 14) in that it did not allow for the likelihood of the Germans releasing formations from the north of Italy. Their own estimate allowed for this contingency and increased Clark's likely trouble to a total of seven-and-a-half German divisions, three of them armoured, by D+10.

Allied Force Headquarters (Mediterranean): Assessments of Possible Rate of German Concentration at Salerno, submitted 31 August 1943[9]

D-Day: 1 panzer division and up to 3 battalions of parachute infantry in place to confront landing.

D+5: German strength increased to 2? panzer divisions (1? weak) and 1? panzer grenadier divisions (equivalent to a full panzer division).

D+10: German strength increased by a further panzer division and a further weak panzer grenadier division.

They also predicted that the Germans would have a margin of force superiority of at least one-and-one-third divisions by D+17. This was a rate of build-up with which the Allies, given their shipping limitations, would be very hard put to compete.

The Allied picture of German army dispositions in southern Italy was accurate. By late August they knew of the activation of the new German Tenth Army to command LXXVI Panzer Corps in Calabria and XIV Panzer Corps in the general area of Naples, along with the identity and location of its principal formations. Tenth Army had been created on to relieve Kesselring's headquarters of tactical responsibilities in the event of fighting. The Allies could only guess how General Heinrich von Vietinghoff and his Tenth Army would react to 'Avalanche'. His orders in fact covered two eventualities. If the Allies landed in southern Italy he was to withdraw northwards towards Rome, the principal German concern at that time being to extricate their forces. If the Italians defected first, he was to disarm them. If the Allies landed and Italy remained firm, he was to act with the Italians against the landings, much as had occurred in Sicily. Timing therefore was all, for if an Allied landing threatened to cut off his northward withdrawal, Vietinghoff would have little option but to fight.

German Tenth Army (General Heinrich von Vietinghoff), Southern Italy, 31 August 1943[10]

XIV Panzer Corps (Lieutenant General Hans Valentin Hube)
(Lieutenant General Hermann Balck from 2 September)
Naples Area.

16th Panzer Division (Major-General Rudolf Sieckenius)
Gulf of Salerno to Agropoli
Strength (approx): 15,000 troops.

15th Panzer Grenadier Division (Major-General Eberhardt Rodt)
Gulf of Gaeta, from Terracina to mouth of river Volturno
Strength (approx) 12,300 troops.

Hermann Göring Panzer Division (Major General Paul Conrath)
Sorrento Peninsula, from river Volturno to Castellammare
Strength (approx): 15,700 troops.

LXXVI Panzer Corps (Lieutenant General Traugott Herr) was deployed in Calabria with the 29th Panzer Grenadier Division and the 26th Panzer Division, a combined strength of some 30,000 troops.

Tenth Army also controlled the 1st Parachute Division, stationed in the Foggia area, with some 17,000 troops.

The Germans could not be sure of precisely what the Italian Government would do, or when, or whether it would order Italian formations to help the Allies. Nor could the Germans, any more than the Allies, be sure how the commanders of individual Italian formations would respond to political events. Some of them, such as the commander of the Italian Seventh Army in southern Italy, had formed a solid and sympathetic relationship with their German opposite numbers.

As August turned into early September, German uncertainty as to Allied intentions, though it could not be entirely dispelled, gradually became certainty. Through their intercepts and decryptions of German signals, the Allies were able to monitor this process. On 1 September they were reading an appreciation by the German naval authorities dated 28 August. This astutely identified that the Allied shipping and forces assembled in the Mediterranean was more than would be required for attacks on Sardinia and Corsica and, while a descent on southern France could not be ruled out, the Allies' objective was most likely southern Italy, and that they were coming soon. Once Montgomery had landed in Calabria on 3 September, there could be little doubt. The importance of Naples and its nearby airfields to an Allied invasion of mainland Italy were obvious, and the Germans were as capable as the Allies of assessing the likely landing places.

In the first week of September, German reconnaissance aircraft reported convoy sightings, and added to the picture built up by Allied air raids in southern Italy, a landing near Naples was considered imminent. On the afternoon of 8 September, German naval units were alerted for a landing, and the Luftwaffe reported that for 9 September its effort would be directed against a landing near Salerno. By the early hours of 9 September both the 16th Panzer Division in its positions around Salerno and the Hermann Göring Division just to the north were on maximum alert. Clark had no chance at all of achieving surprise. That the Italian political situation reached crisis point also worked against him. The Allies at last forced the hand of the Badoglio Government and, as the 'Avalanche' convoys approached the coast on the evening of 8 September, Italy's capitulation and armistice with the Allies was publicly announced. Most Italian military formations were caught completely at a loss and unprepared, having received no warning or instructions because of the elaborate secrecy, and vacillation, of their government. This ruled out organized Italian military opposition to a German takeover and dashed Allied hopes of any worthwhile Italian military assistance to their operations.

The German 'Axis' contingency plans were activated at once. Throughout the country, Italian commanders, many of them surprised and bewildered by the announcement, found themselves confronted by German officers incensed by a feeling of betrayal delivering ultimatums for them to hand over their positions, weapons, and supplies. There was no chance of successful resistance. In southern Italy, the Italian Seventh Army handed over its fuel stocks and equipment to the German Tenth Army without trouble. Italy's defection does not appear to have affected the morale of the Germans other than to have imbued them with a grim determination typified by the laconic announcement issued by the German naval command in Italy and quoted, with evident if grudging respect, in subsequent British and American accounts: 'Italian armistice does not apply to us. The fight continues.'[11]

It was in this spirit that von Vietinghoff's troops set about manning the vacated Italian positions along the western coastline. Hitherto the Germans had not occupied such coastal defences. They had been left to the Italians on the assumption that, as in Sicily, the Allies were bound to land but that the Germans in support of the Italians would provide the main counterattack force against their beachhead. The timing of the Italian surrender and the lack of organized Italian resistance to the German takeover brought German troops into this coastal defence role, and for the Allies this would prove a bad bargain. Despite the German strategic intention to withdraw to the north, when 'Avalanche' occurred German units would be at once engaged in a beachhead battle, and both von Vietinghoff and Kesselring would have operational and tactical flexibility in how they responded to it. Neither would pass up what looked to them to be a fair chance to destroy an Allied landing. The odds against 'Avalanche' noticeably increased.

Approaching the coast near Salerno, Clark and his soldiers aboard their ships had listened to the announcement of the Italian surrender, broadcast over loudspeakers. There was great jubilation at the news of the first Axis power to fall, and a general easing of pre-battle tension. According to one witness this had its drawbacks, the Commanding Officer of the British 201st Guards Brigade observed: 'From the point of view of the soldier who had to do the landing the time chosen was an unfortunate one. It aroused in the troops a quite unjustified hope that the landing itself would be a pleasant picnic, to be followed by a speedy and easy advance on Naples.'[12] There were some aboard the ships not so much cheered by the news as disquieted by what it could mean. They would have much preferred to meet Italian soldiers on or near the beaches.

Clark's own planning had suffered from a variety of last-minute changes, the available shipping and the extent of the 'lift' of men and equipment remaining in doubt as late as 5 September (with D-Day 9 September). This uncertainty tested Clark and his corps and divisional commanders to the very limit of their patience. There were also disputes to solve between the army, determined to get as much combat strength on the beaches as soon as possible, and the Navy over the type and extent of ships' loadings, and with the air forces who needed personnel and equipment landed to get newly captured airfields working. That priority had to be given to the combat troops and equipment that in the first place might have to seize the beachhead, hold it and then push inland to secure the airfields was by no means obvious to some. Clark's main concern was that there was not even enough shipping to ensure this with a margin of safety. In the American sector of his beachhead there was only enough lift for an assault landing by a reinforced division, instead of the two divisions with which he originally intended to land. He received a further heavy blow on

---

'Avalanche': Allied Assault Landing Force, Order of Battle[13]
United States Fifth Army (Lieutenant General Mark W. Clark)

US VI Corps (Major General E. J. Dawley)	**British X Corps** (Lieutenant General R. L. McCreery)
US 36th Infantry Division	British 46th Infantry Division
US 45th Infantry Division	British 56th Infantry Division
Corps Reserve: US 3rd Infantry Division US 34th Infantry Division	Corps Reserve: British 7th Armoured Division British 23rd Armoured Brigade
US Rangers: 1st, 3rd, and 4th Ranger Battalions	British Special Service Brigade: No. 2 (Army) Commando No. 41 (Royal Marines) Commando

3 September when the 82nd Airborne Division was taken from him for 'Giant II'. He had counted upon it for additional infantry. When 'Giant II' was aborted and the 82nd once again made available to Fifth Army, it was too late to influence the initial landing operation.

There was one brighter note, provided by the Royal Navy. Mindful of the Sicily experience and the likely air threat to the landings, the British Chiefs of Staff determined to send what fighter cover they could. Four escort aircraft carriers normally engaged on convoy duty were despatched to the Mediterranean, so that the naval commander for 'Avalanche', Vice Admiral Henry Kent Hewitt, USN, would have as part of his force the Royal Navy's Force V under Rear Admiral Sir Philip Vian, consisting of one light fleet carrier and these four escort carriers. Between them they had eleven Fleet Air Arm squadrons with a total of 108 Seafire fighters (naval Spitfires). These would prove invaluable.

In outline the Fifth Army plan was for the British X Corps to land on the left in the northern part of Salerno Bay on a two-division front. The 46th Division would take Salerno itself and secure the stretch of Highway 18. The 56th Division would capture Montecorvino airfield and the important road and rail centre six miles inland of the coast at Battipaglia, and link up with the Americans at Ponte Sele over the River Sele, which constituted the corps boundary. US VI Corps would land on the Fifth Army right with a single division, the 36th, which would land at the site of the ancient city of Paestum and advance inland to secure the high ground between the southern point of the Bay at Agropoli and Altavilla, thereby covering the approaches to the beachhead from the south and east. This was a lot for a single division, but the 36th was an American 'triangular' division with three infantry regiments, each being the near-equivalent of a British brigade, having three infantry battalions. Additional supporting arms and attached artillery and armour units brought each regiment up to a 'Regimental Combat Team' (RCT) for battle. For the assault landing, the 36th Division's regiments were also increased to 20% above strength, each having some 9,000 men. Each assault landing RCT also had 1,350 vehicles and 2,000 tons of supplies, with a seven-day supply reserve plus 20% safety margin. Standard ammunition stocks were increased in each unit to enable three days of intense battle.[14] Following an initiative by the Division's commander, Major General Fred L. Walker, the 36th Division's Engineers had further increased firepower by modifying 48 DUKW amphibious vehicles to carry 105mm howitzers ashore.

To secure the high mountainous ground to the north of the Bay was the task of US Rangers and British Commandos. Three Ranger battalions would land at Maiori and move inland uphill to secure the Nocera Pass, while two Commandos would land at Vietri to secure the Cava Gap through which ran Highway 18 to Naples. The Rangers and Commandos were very high-quality troops, and much could be asked of them. But they were lightly equipped and could not be expected to hold their positions for

---

German 16th Panzer Division:
Strength and Dispositions, Salerno Area, 9 September 1943.[15]

The 16th Panzer Division was a reconstituted 'Stalingrad' division, so-called because the original formation had been destroyed in that battle in January 1943. The division was rebuilt around a leavening of the original division (about 4,000 men) in France during March and moved to Italy in May. At the time of Salerno it was the only fully equipped panzer division in southern Italy. It had 4,074 vehicles, 455 of which were armoured. Its organization and principal fighting units were approximately as follows. In the immediate wake of the Italian surrender on 8 September 1943 it also secured Italian weapons and equipment.

2nd Panzer Regiment: 2nd Battalion with staff and panzer companies: total of 87 Panzer IV tanks (with long-barrelled 75mm guns); 3rd Battalion with staff and panzer companies: total of 37 'Sturmgeschütz' assault guns (75mm guns). There were also seven Panzer III tanks, some of which were flamethrowers, and twelve Panzer 38T (Czech) or possibly Panzer IIs. The 1st Battalion was in Germany re-equipping with Panzer V 'Panther' tanks.

64th Panzer Grenadier Regiment of two infantry battalions, the 1st mounted in half-tracks and the 2nd in lorries and available vehicles. Well-equipped with heavy weapons (anti-tank guns and infantry support guns).

79th Panzer Grenadier Regiment with two motorized battalions each of three rifle companies and a support company. Also well equipped with heavy infantry support weapons.

16th Reconnaissance Battalion with one armoured car company, two infantry companies in half-tracks, and one heavy reconnaissance company.

16th Panzer Artillery Regiment: the 1st Battalion had two batteries each of six SdKfz 124 'Wespe' SP 105mm light field howitzers, and one battery of six SdKfz 165 'Hummel' SP 150mm heavy howitzers; the 2nd Battalion had three batteries each with three 105mm light field howitzers; the 3rd Battalion had two batteries each of three 150mm heavy field howitzers, and one battery with three 100mm K-18 guns.

Flak: two motorized heavy batteries each of four 88mm guns and three 20mm guns, and one light battery with nine 20mm guns and two SP quad 20mm guns.

16th Panzer Pioneer Battalion with one half-track and two motorized companies, well-equipped with heavy support weapons. In the German Army, pioneers were combat troops specializing in, and equipped for, the assault role.

German 16th Panzer DivisionDispositions: Salerno Area[15]

The division was configured for mobile anti-invasion defence into four battle groups. These were positioned inland from the coast at distances from three to six miles, while approximately six miles separated the battle groups from each other. Names followed the battle-group commander.

Battle Group (Major) Dörnemann
(OC 16th Panzer Reconnaissance Battalion)
16th Panzer Reconnaissance Battalion

One assault gun company of
3rd Battalion, 2nd Panzer Regiment
Detachments of SP artillery
One pioneer company
Area Salerno–Baronissi (approx 4–5 miles
north and inland of Salerno)
Landing zone of US Rangers,
British Commandos and 46 Division

Battle Group (Colonel) Stempel
(OC 64th Panzer Grenadier Regiment).
64th Panzer Grenadier Regiment
(two battalions)
3rd Bn, 2nd Panzer Regiment,
(less one company with Dörnemann)
one artillery battery
One pioneer company
Area (rough triangle) Pontecagnano–
Montecorvino–Battipaglia
Landing zone of British 46 and
56 Divisions

Battle Group (Colonel) von Holtey
(OC 2nd Panzer Regiment)
2nd Battalion, 2nd Panzer Regiment
(less two companies with von Doering)

One artillery battery
One pioneer platoon
Area Persano (Division reserve)

Battle Group (Colonel) von Doering
(OC 79th Panzer Grenadier Regiment)
79th Panzer Grenadier Regiment (two
battalions)
Two companies 2nd Battalion,
2nd Panzer Regiment
One artillery battery
Reconnaissance and pioneer detachments
Area Albanella–Ogliastro–Rutino
Landing zone of US 36 Division

The battle groups were for mobile reaction to an Allied landing. Heavy anti-aircraft artillery was sited at Salerno port and in the area Montecorvino–Battipaglia. The Division's battle HQ was near Battipaglia. The Division's fuel and ammunition stocks were sufficient for five days of fighting. The first line of defence was along the shore of the Bay of Salerno where the Division manned a series of positions and strongpoints. Shore defence was not a panzer division role, and it took up valuable infantry. Most of the 16th Panzer Division's coastal positions were of platoon strength, with machine-guns and some 20mm anti-aircraft guns in a ground/anti-landing-craft role. For example, the 1st Battalion of the 79th Panzer Grenadier Regt had a strongpoint at the mouth of the River Sele manned by 40 grenadiers with six machine-guns and a 75mm gun. Some coastal positions taken over from the Italians were quite formidable, and of these there were eight. In the US 36 Division sector there was one at Paestum (with a company of grenadiers with mortars, anti-aircraft guns in a ground/anti-landing-craft role, and some field guns) and one at Agropoli on the southern shore of the Bay. In the British X Corps sector there were five strongpoints. Most were wired and mined, though the Division laid comparatively few mines on its extended coastal front, some 2,400 of anti-tank (Tellerminen) and 1,500 of anti-personnel. Teller mines were laid randomly ten-to-fifteen yards from the water's edge in belts 60–100 yards inland. Barbed-wire obstacles covered some machine-gun positions, and some trees had been felled and wired. No underwater obstacles or booby-traps had been laid. Artillery was inland of the beaches and in the overlooking high ground.

long against German infantry supported by heavy weapons and armour – they would need the earliest possible relief by the main landing force. Neither of Clark's two British assault divisions was particularly experienced, while the US 36th, while highly trained and keen, had never been in action. This too was risky. Only two months earlier at Gela the US 1st Division had shown the value of having an experienced formation in the beachhead. Few Army commanders have ever knowingly entered a hazardous operation as handicapped as Clark at Salerno.

The convoys sailed at staggered intervals from Oran, Tripoli and Bizerta in North Africa carrying the main assault divisions, and from Palermo in Sicily carrying the Commandos and Rangers. They successfully brought the 'Avalanche' assault forces to their rendezvous off the Gulf of Salerno late on 8 September. There had been a few air attacks following Luftwaffe sightings, and a Landing Craft (Tank) was sunk and an Landing Craft (Infantry) damaged, both of them in a 46th Division convoy. No attempt was made to interfere with the convoys by naval action. With the Italian fleet on the point of surrendering to the Allies and the Germans lacking the necessary forces in the Mediterranean, there was little probability of this, though that risk was insured against by the Royal Navy providing a formidable outer covering force. This was Force H, which included four battleships, two fleet carriers and eighteen destroyers. Its presence helped to confuse the German air reconnaissance picture of likely landing zones, and it drew some of their air attacks away from the transport convoys. Considerable naval firepower was also on hand to provide close support to the landings. As part of the invasion armada under Admiral Hewitt's overall command were six cruisers, two anti-aircraft cruisers, and 39 destroyers. In addition there were gun-armed (LCG) and rocket-armed (LCR) landing craft.

In the last few minutes of 8 September the warships and transports of the assault convoys, 450 of them in all, lay about ten miles off of their assigned beaches, formed into three lines of transports and three lines of landing ships. They were showing no lights and observing a strict radio silence. In the Southern Attack Force (US VI Corps) zone the transport ships reached their positions for lowering landing craft at 1 a.m., followed fifteen minutes later by those of the Northern Attack Force (British X

Corps). The shore-to-shore landing vessels carrying the 46th Division moved closer towards the coast, and the convoy carrying the Commandos and Rangers reached the lowering position at 1.47 a.m. According to plan, the naval minesweepers that had already been busily clearing lanes for the convoys and transports swept ahead to clear the final approach routes. Throughout the convoys the assault troops began to descend the ladders and scramble-nets slung from the ships' sides to the landing craft waiting for them below. When loaded, the landing craft pulled away, their crews making for the rendezvous points, about four miles offshore, from where guide boats were to take them in to their landing beaches. This tranship-ping and rendezvous process took about three hours and was nerve-wracking for soldiers facing the imminent prospect of battle. Although the sea was calm, there was plenty of sea-sickness among the troops, and as the moon had set (just before 1 a.m. at 0057) it was very dark.

At 1.58 a.m. one of the 16th Panzer Division's coastal observation posts reported sighting ships offshore, and at about 2 a.m. the Northern Attack Force began to come under shell fire from the land, the protecting war-ships returning fire. At 3.7 a.m. shore positions of the 16th Panzer Divi-sion reported the approach of landing craft, there being no doubt by then that they were right in the path of an Allied sea-borne invasion. Eight minutes later, those holding positions along the coast in the sector allocated to the British X Corps started to come under an intensive fifteen-minute bombardment from naval guns; to the south their comrades holding positions in the American VI Corps zone were spared this. Fifth Army was about to make the only large-scale opposed amphibious landing of the Italian campaign, and one of the hardest of the entire war.

The US Rangers landed at the small fishing and seaside resort town of Maiori, the destroyer HMS *Ledbury* guiding in the small LCAs as near as possible to the beach. There was no opposition, and the first Rangers ashore (4th Battalion) soon established a beachhead and took up blocking positions covering the roads in the hills above the town. The Rangers, moving swiftly uphill and carrying only their weapons, ammunition and light rations, disposed of some small groups of Germans that they sur-prised on the roads. These were engineer mine-laying teams, and to this extent the Rangers' landing had caught any intended defence unprepared.

The 1st and 3rd Ranger Battalions landed in turn to ascend the six miles up to the Chiunzi Pass atop the Sorrento Peninsula. Flanking teams carefully searched the wooded, ravine-cut mountainsides for Germans but encountered none. During the morning the Rangers reached their objective overlooking the Plain of Naples and covering the Nocera Pass and Highway 18. Their commander, Colonel Darby, reported his Rangers' success and their intention to hold their positions to Clark aboard his command ship USS *Ancon*, and his men dug-in for what they hoped would be a short-term defence and an early relief by the main landing force. The Rangers had enough ammunition for about three days; apart from a few 'bazooka' hand-held rocket launchers, their only heavy weapons were their 4.2-inch mortars. Heavier firepower could only come from the Navy, and for this they had two British forward observers with them in contact with the ships.

Companies moved along the coast westwards to secure Amalfi and to the east to secure their flanks, and patrols were sent out to make contact with the British Commandos. In the afternoon the Rangers ambushed an unsuspecting reconnaissance patrol of three German armoured cars, one of which escaped. Their crews had no idea the Rangers were there. These belonged to the Hermann Göring Division, the formation that had the Sorrento Peninsula as part of its defensive responsibility. Thereafter, as the day wore on, small parties of German troops began to probe the Ranger positions. The Rangers found these Germans extremely hard to spot amid the rocks and foliage, as they wore highly effective camouflage, most probably 'appropriated' from Italian stocks. They were only the advance guard, testing the strength of the Allied landing in that sector.

With a minesweeper, a gun-armed landing craft (LCG) and the destroyer HMS *Blackmore* leading, the LCAs carrying Lieutenant Colonel Jack Churchill's No. 2 (Army) Commando headed inshore towards the Marina beach at Vietri shortly before 3.30 a.m. Ten minutes before the landing craft touched down, *Blackmore* and the LCG began firing at the shore, aiming for the buildings on the seafront and a coastal battery built into the cliffs above. There was no return fire, though the battery released a display of coloured flares, presumably as an alarm. The Commandos landed unopposed and quickly set about securing the beach. Mortars were rapidly set up to provide covering fire as the main body clambered up through the stepped vineyards to take the battery position from the north-east. Only a handful of German gunners were found there, and these immediately surrendered. Like the Rangers, the Commandos had achieved surprise, and the first Germans they encountered seemed to be dazed. A headquarters was found, recently abandoned in haste.

The Army Commandos were followed ashore by No. 41 Royal Marine Commando. By the time they landed along with Brigadier Robert Laycock and his headquarters, the German response was stiffening, with some mortars in the hills above Vietri firing upon the landing beach. Small parties of German troops, still seeming bewildered, were also encountered and dealt with between Vietri and the sea. While No. 2 Commando sent two of its troops, each of some 66 men, to cover the western exit from Salerno, with the rest forming a brigade reserve, the Marines cleared Vietri itself. They overcame some sporadic resistance and destroyed a medium gun and its crew positioned in the town square. They also moved up into the hills to clear the villages of Cava and Dragonea, and then, as planned, dug themselves in to defensive positions on each side of the La Molina Pass.

Casualties so far had been light, but the battle had been a confused one with teams of Commandos bumping into parties of Germans in the darkness. There were some sharp fire-fights, and at least on one occasion German troops reached close enough to the beach to take landing craft and unloading parties under smallarms fire, causing panic and disruption. Some crews closed ramps and pulled away from the beach; others in some follow-up landing craft bringing in supplies, seeing the beach under mortar and smallarms fire and figures running about, and then coming under fire themselves, turned about in order to return to their ships, shouting warnings to other incoming craft. Possibly the crews were insufficiently experienced to recognize what was actually going on; in any event, back at their ships they reported that the Germans had overrun the Commando beachhead! This caused considerable alarm and it took several hours before the confusion was properly sorted out. It caused a break in the Commando supplies; indeed, the Commandos never received much of their personal kit and some of their equipment. General Hawksworth, by then ashore in the main landing area with the forward units of his 46th

Division, had also been told that the Commandos had been driven out of Vietri. He urgently signalled Laycock to get it back 'at all costs', only to receive Laycock's indignant reply that this was impossible as he had never lost it in the first place.[16]

The Commandos were cheered when a Ranger patrol arrived from Darby's force to make contact with them. Apart from that, however, the news had been disquieting, with indications that things were not going at all to plan at the main landing beaches. First there were reports that the leading brigades of the 46th Division were ashore but were being held up east of Salerno. Later a signal came in from Hawksworth's headquarters to warn Laycock that there could be no firm link-up before late afternoon. Although a couple of armoured cars from the 46th Division's reconnaissance regiment eventually appeared along the road from Salerno and passed the forward Commando positions near Cava, they soon came back and returned the same way which did not look good.

Already the Commandos holding some of the blocking positions were under pressure as German units of increasing strength attempted to fight their way back towards Vietri. Particularly worrying was the presence of German tanks. Several Panzer IVs were encountered during the day and fought off with PIAT shoulder-launched anti-tank projectiles and some of the light 6-pounder anti-tank guns that had followed the Commandos ashore. These tanks had additional armour plating fitted to protect their suspension and turrets, and the latter especially gave the Mark IV a superficial resemblance to the massive turret of the fearsome Tiger. Possibly this accounted for some reports of Tigers being encountered, though none were in fact present in the Salerno sector. The Commandos knocked out at least two of the tanks in the fighting, but their own casualties began to mount steadily. Like the Rangers, they were only lightly equipped. As yet, the Germans, caught off-guard, were unsure of what they were up against and were reacting in a piecemeal and largely uncoordinated way. This state of affairs could not last. Although the Commandos and Rangers had successfully gained vital positions protecting the northern flank of the Salerno beachhead, theirs was a tenuous hold.

X Corps had landed under considerable German fire. Even as the LSTs were lowering the smaller assault craft just after 1 a.m., they had been engaged by the 16th Panzer's 88mm batteries positioned in the hills. Destroyers immediately took station about a mile offshore to engage them, but the German guns were not easily silenced and were mobile, changing positions frequently. Throughout the day destroyers kept them under fire, expending about 60% of their ammunition stocks and receiving some hits in return, but they could not prevent the ships, beaches and the roads leading from them coming under German fire. Accompanying the smaller landing craft to the beaches were some LCGs, whose gun crews prepared to provide direct close-in fire support against the German shore positions. There were also some of the LCRs, rocket-firing landing craft equipped to discharge up to a thousand 5-inch rockets electronically in salvoes over a period of five minutes. This weight of fire could completely saturate a restricted area. In the 46th Division landing, these were employed to blast away suspected minefields on the beaches, and the craft carrying the assault battalions were ordered to follow these rocket barrages. Because of this two battalions were landed on the wrong beaches, those assigned to 56th Division, which caused congestion and also separated the misplaced assault infantry from their brigade area and supporting weapons and vehicles.

Stubborn German positions caused delays and inflicted casualties on the beaches, but the 16th Panzer Division's battle groups also made some sharp jabbing counterattacks against the 46th Division's units as they moved inland. In one of them, assault guns and half-tracks of Battle Group Stempel caught a company of the 5th Hampshire Regiment (128th Brigade) in an enclosed lane and practically wiped it out: the Hampshires were unable to escape, and most of them were shot down by machine-gun fire or crushed under the German tracks.[17] Gradually some supporting M-4 Sherman tanks and self-propelled artillery were landed and moved inland, helping to clear German strongpoints and fending off counter-attacks, but this took up most of daylight – by late morning it was clear that there would be no early entry into Salerno. The 56th Division experience was similar, with the assault troops encountering heavy machine-gun fire and mines, causing casualties and delay. Inland of the beaches the infantry found the going difficult – low-lying ground that had been flooded, dykes, fields, hedgerows and high-grown tobacco plants, amongst which German snipers and small machine-gun teams could hold up an advance. It was disorientating ground, ideal for ambush. Small groups of the 16th Panzer's tanks, some of them flamethrowers, lay in wait to pounce on the advancing infantry, who, until supporting Shermans were landed and moved up, had only their PIATs with which to fend them off. Although limited in strength, the German battle groups were fighting aggressively, imposing checks and then moving off to do the same elsewhere. This ensured that at the end of the day most of the British units had advanced little more than three miles inland. Troops of the Queen's Brigade succeeded in reaching Montecorvino airfield, surprising some Luftwaffe personnel and shooting-up aircraft there, but a strong counterattack by one of the 16th Panzer's Pioneer companies prevented them securing a hold, and the airfield remained in German hands. A tank and infantry counterattack also ejected the British troops who had reached Battipaglia.

Gains were limited, but X Corps had established its beachhead. Brigade and divisional headquarters were ashore and functioning, artillery and armour gradually coming into action and the follow-up battalions landing and moving up to increase the vital infantry strength. The accumulation and flow of supplies was steady, and at the water's edge the Beach Groups had largely sorted out the initial confusion. The first personnel and vehicles of the RAF and Army air support units and the airfield construction companies were ashore. But the cost of gaining the initial lodgement was high. The casualty clearing stations set up on the beaches and the other medical units worked feverishly, as they invariably did, throughout that day. They were subsequently reckoned to have treated 449 battle casualties, a figure that presumably discounts those who were beyond all help.[18] A few miles inland the battle was intensifying, removing any doubts that the struggle for the beachhead was only beginning.

To the south the US 36th Division, with the 142nd RCT on the left and the 141st RCT on the right, had landed into an inferno. In this sector the 16th Panzer Division deployed two strong companies to defend the beaches from a series of strongpoints near the shore. Machine-guns and mortars had good fields of fire, and the medieval tower at Paestum offered a good observation post from which to direct artillery fire by guns sited in the foothills inland. Trees had been felled by the Division's Pioneers to improve fields of fire and reduce cover for an attacking force; likely beach exits were covered by machine-guns and mortars, and barbed-wire and booby-traps had been laid.

The odds were weighted further in favour of the defence because, in contrast to X Corps to the north and contrary to Admiral Hewitt's advice, Walker decided not to land his Division under the cover of a naval bombardment. This was mainly in the interest of achieving surprise. It was thought that such a bombardment might alert an unsuspecting defence, especially as German attention at the critical time would likely be focused on the X Corps landing to the north. It was thought that there was a chance his Division could land unmolested and make swift progress inland – an unnecessary preliminary naval bombardment would lose them this chance. In any case, Walker was not convinced that there were suitable targets for such a bombardment, or that it could be properly coordinated with his landing in darkness. He was confident that in the period immediately following the landing his tanks and artillery would be able to provide the necessary fire support, in addition to naval gunfire support on call once the assault troops were ashore. This meant that as the landing craft carrying his leading assault waves approached the uncannily silent shore, the Germans preparing to defend were not under fire.

But as soon as the landing craft beached and the infantry emerged they came under a hail of machine-gun fire and were blasted by mortars and artillery. Some of the landing craft offshore were hit and began to burn, and some of those in the following waves began to divert course to avoid the fire, while others milled about. Confusion began to take hold. On the beaches the soldiers of the 36th Division faced the severest test, and one for which no amount of battle simulation could have adequately prepared them. They soon became veterans. Fortunately, a good deal of the German machine-gun fire fixed to sweep the beaches had been set too high (this was the case on the British beaches as well) and the first wave pressed inland. It was the following waves that became disrupted by an increasing volume of German fire, and two of the four beaches were closed down for several hours, delaying the landing of heavy support weapons and tanks, and causing great congestion on the remaining beaches. By about 5.30 a.m. some of the DUKWs carrying field guns were landed, but it was several hours before some tanks could get ashore under the protective covering fire of a destroyer.

Naval fire support was at first problematic as a result of communications breakdowns, and in the first hours of the landing the American infantry fought largely alone, and with their own weapons, to overcome German strongpoints and ward off the German armoured counterattacks. By late morning USS *Savannah* was in action, her guns directed by her shore party and laying out her fire as she had done off Gela to silence a German railway gun and break up a German tank counterattack, one of several made during the morning and afternoon. She was joined by the cruiser *Philadelphia* and several destroyers. On the beaches and just inland there were many instances of personal gallantry that turned the scale of the fighting and enabled, by the end of the day, the 36th Division to have carved out a beachhead around Paestum. It had taken some 500 casualties in its landing, about 100 of whom were killed.[19]

The landing on 9 September was not seriously molested by the Luftwaffe, though German fighters and fighter-bombers made 108 sorties, and bombers 150 sorties. The protective screen provided by the Seafires (265 sorties) in the early morning and late evening, and by the Sicily-based fighters (about 700 sorties) at maximum range during the day was comprehensive enough to prevent the Luftwaffe achieving a breakthrough, and its bombers increasingly turned to night raids.

9

'AVALANCHE':
THE LANDING BATTLE EXPERIENCE

'The landing operations at Salerno and adjacent beaches were the first
in this theatre to involve serious enemy resistance, and for this reason the
general tactical lessons are of special interest and importance.'[1]

D-Day at Salerno saw the Allies carve out an invasion beachhead in the
teeth of German opposition. In the light of Allied strategy, especially
'Overlord' projected for 1944, it was important to extract as many lessons
as possible from the experience. It was significant that, although the
German opposition on D-Day was tough, it was still only provided by a
single, over-stretched, German formation. The 16th Panzer Division had
been insufficient to defeat the landing and had not really been configured
to do so: its shore positions and its battle groups were intended to impose
delay and disruption, gaining time for reinforcements to arrive, and in this
respect it had been largely successful. It had dealt severe and costly checks
while retaining its own flexibility. General Walker of the 36th Division
acknowledged that, 'The German troops encountered, although relatively
small in numbers, were employed with great skill and showed stamina,
initiative, and a determination to fight.'[2]

The fact that the 16th Panzer's armoured battle groups were deployed
close to the beaches enabled them to strike at the landing forces when they
were still disorganized following the resistance on the beaches and the
confusion it caused. What saved the situation for the Allies was the lack of
concentrated German strength; each of the battle groups covered a wide
area, and none of them could afford to become inextricably embroiled. All
the counterattacks were made with small numbers of tanks and armoured
vehicles, and local successes could not be followed through. As an
example, the Pioneer company that checked the Queens at Montecorvino
airfield had no sooner done so than they were ordered to break off at once
and rush to Battipaglia to check a British advance there. This dismayed the
German troops, who were all set to press home their attack on the Queens

and achieve what they thought, and not without reason, would be a decisive success.[3]

One of the points to emerge from post-battle assessment of the landings was that of timing. The timings of the landings on 9 September had, it was subsequently reckoned, not allowed sufficient darkness for the landing of the assault troops and their supporting weapons: the onset of daylight before this had been completed materially assisted the Germans and allowed a comparatively small defending force to identify weak points and stage its counterattacks. The daylight also enabled the Germans to exploit their superior observation and direct artillery fire on to the still-ongoing unloading of the assault troops and their equipment. Counterattack by tanks was identified as the most serious threat to a landing following daylight, and it was essential that anti-tank weapons were ashore and ready for action with the assault infantry by that time. 'The enemy employed tanks in groups of from five to twelve,' reported the 36th Division, 'In some cases, but not all, infantry accompanied the tanks. In other cases infantry resisting the advance of the landing troops was supported by tanks. The enemy tanks moved slowly under concealment searching for our infantry …'[4] The assault infantry, it was stressed, had to have all possible weapons for dealing with tanks. This had not been the case on some of the beaches in both VI and X Corps sectors, and the infantry paid a high price for it.

By far the greatest lesson, stressed in both British and American assessments of the 9 September landings, was that of coping with the unforeseen and with disorganization and chaos. This was above all a challenge for unit commanders at all levels to ensure that control did not break down under the stress of battle. Both the VI Corps and X Corps landings saw instances of troops being landed on the wrong beaches and separated from their parent formations and headquarters. 'Officers of all echelons', warned the 36th Division, 'must not lose sight of their primary planned objective, and regardless of temporary disruption must act quickly to carry out their missions and reorganize their troops to resume the general plan of attack.' The 36th Division performed well on 9 September, but the US Army report acknowledged that, 'our training has not yet produced disciplined officers and disciplined men. Throughout the operation there was ample proof that control which is so essential to infantry operations and is so difficult to obtain and maintain was not achieved in an adequate degree.'[5] Problems identified were that troops tended to bunch up and become bogged down on the beaches under fire – officers had to urge them to keep going – and that positions inland were selected by some unit commanders more with cover and concealment in mind than their suitability for delivering effective fire on the enemy. Some units, on moving and taking position inland, failed to dispose themselves adequately for defence. This was no doubt caused by a combination of inexperience, post-beach landing reaction and tiredness, and they suffered accordingly from the attentions of the 16th Panzer Division.

In both sectors the terrain itself imposed some unforeseen difficulties: brigade, division, battalion and company commanders all had to cope when the battle they found themselves in was going very far from plan. It was one thing, for example, to land a follow-up brigade on the beaches, every man knowing they had to proceed to a pre-designated assembly area inland, where they would be reunited with their vehicles and equipment and sort themselves out before taking up their pre-planned role in the battle order. It was quite another for that brigade to land and find that their intended assembly area was still a battleground, and to be fed into that ongoing battle on an ad hoc basis. Strain and fatigue were evident, and officers had to be able to combat its effect on their men. 'Officers of all ranks', warned one subsequent British report, 'must be prepared and physically fit for long periods on their feet and short periods of rest.'[6]

10

THE SALERNO BEACHHEAD BATTLE, 10–16 SEPTEMBER

'They lay like two Christian captives in either corner
of a great Roman amphitheatre ... '[1]

This is how a leading military historian has graphically described the tactical position of X and VI Corps on the morning of 10 September. Clark had to break his Fifth Army out of the 'amphitheatre' or see it destroyed there. He was under a severe disadvantage because the Allied shipping, as had been feared, could not build up his force at a rate likely to compete with a German concentration against his beachhead. Kesselring and Vietinghoff accepted the challenge and set their formations towards the sound of the guns. LXXVI Panzer Corps in the south was ordered to delay Eighth Army with rearguards but to rush the bulk of its 26th Panzer Division and 29th Panzer Grenadier Division northwards to Salerno; XIV Panzer Corps sent its 15th Panzer Grenadier and Hermann Göring Divisions to pressurize the 'Avalanche' beachhead from the north and prevent a break-out towards Naples.

None of these German formations was particularly strong. The 15th Panzer Grenadier and Hermann Göring Divisions were still recovering from the Sicily fighting and had only about 70 tanks and assault guns between them, while the Hermann Göring was short of infantry, though had two paratrooper battalions (1st Parachute Division) attached. Kesselring and Vietinghoff needed not just a holding force but a force strong enough to destroy the beachhead. A battle group of the 3rd Panzer Grenadier Division would be on its way from Rome, but Kesselring needed more, and here Hitler and the OKW worked in the Allies' favour – they refused Kesselring's request for the two panzer divisions held in northern Italy under Rommel's command to be released to him. They were still determined to implement a withdrawal to the north and had no intention of risking valuable forces in southern Italy that might be cut off by further Allied landings. It was as well that they did not know of the shipping constraints under which the Allies were now pursuing their Italian campaign. As it was, however, the Germans were able to concentrate strong elements of six divisions against Clark, who had little more than his assault divisions in the beachhead.

Eisenhower and Alexander were well aware that at Salerno they now had a major battle – and very likely a crisis – on their hands. But there was little that could be done immediately: Clark was on his own, and he would have to fight with what little he had. On 10 September Alexander signalled Montgomery, exhorting him to maintain the maximum pressure on the Germans on his front so that they could not divert forces away to Salerno. The terrain through which Eighth Army's XIII Corps was struggling hardly allowed for this; the Germans could gauge Eighth Army's likely rate of advance and, to a great extent, dictate it. Nor was there the transport to sustain an advance by full strength formations; only light forces could get forward. Eighth Army's logistics were a nightmare and would remain so until the southern ports were secured and working to capacity. What the Germans could not do was prevent Eighth Army's advance altogether, so that Vietinghoff and Kesselring knew they had a limited time window in which to destroy the besieged Salerno beachhead before Eighth Army arrived to relieve it.

For two days, 10 and 11 September, X and VI Corps tried to consolidate their gains and secure more of the high ground, while the Germans fought to contain them until they could launch their decisive counter-attack. On 10 September the Rangers and Commandos came under increasing attack, the latter observing German infantry working their way forward in the undergrowth while more German troops were seen arriving in vehicles at Cava. These were from the Hermann Göring and 15th Panzer Grenadier Divisions, and they were only held off with difficulty. The German troops and their fire positions were difficult to spot in the dense undergrowth, and they were up to their usual tactical ingenuity. In one instance a Commando position was approached by what appeared to be a burly 'Tommy' in British battledress dragging a wounded German by the collar and swearing at him in 'fluent Billingsgate', but as soon as they were close the 'Tommy' and his 'prisoner' suddenly hurled stick grenades at the Commandos and opened fire with concealed machine-pistols. Other

German troops had been creeping forward under the cover of this diver-sion, and a fierce close-quarter fight ensued. It was with some satisfaction that the Commandos later recorded that both the bogus 'Tommy' and his 'prisoner' were among the dead.[2]

The 46th Division secured Salerno, and a Navy team moved in to get the port working, but it proved impossible to use the harbour yet because the Germans kept it under heavy artillery fire. The 56th Division could make no gain at Montecorvino airfield, and fighting around Battipaglia was intense. The Germans had shifted their main weight against X Corps, rightly identifying this as the intended Allied strike force for Naples, and they intended to keep it locked into its shallow beachhead. This gave VI Corps a reprieve. The 141st RCT, which had taken heavy punishment during the landings, was able to reorganize and move inland to cover the southern part of the beachhead. The floating reserve, two RCTs of the US 45th Division, came ashore on both sides of the River Sele (which flows into the bay and divided the two corps). In attempting to extend the VI Corps beachhead and close the gap with X Corps at Ponte Sele, they ran into a counterattack by the 29th Panzer Grenadier Division, just arrived from Calabria, and were forced back. Similarly a battle group of the 26th Panzer Division fought its way into Battipaglia, going straight into action from its line of march from Calabria. It captured the town and took prisoner 450 Royal Fusiliers who had been cut off by its attack. To the north around Vietri the Commandos and some battalions of the 46th Division who had moved up to support them were by then in action against units of the 3rd Panzer Grenadier Division. The Germans were winning the battle of the build up.

The air battle had also intensified since 10 September, with the Luft-waffe achieving about 100 fighter-bomber sorties in close support, some of the Bf 109s equipped with awesome firepower – underwing 21cm 'Nebelwerfer' rockets for ground attack. This concentrated effort against the Salerno beachhead meant that Eighth Army was unmolested from the air, but over Salerno the overall Allied air shield remained strong, with over 1,200 sorties flown by land-based fighters and 400 by the Seafires, though the carrier group was then reaching the limit of the operational 'surge' demanded of it – the Seafire pilots flying without much let up were becoming seriously fatigued, ten Seafires had been lost and 32 damaged, mostly in deck-landing accidents. Allied bombers attacked road movement and communications choke-points, but, with fighters mainly committed to the long-range air patrols and with their bases still too distant from the battle-fronts, it was possible for the Germans to move their divisions up from Calabria against the beachhead without serious interference from the air.

On 12 and 13 September the beachhead endured its greatest threat as German attacks became more coordinated and powerful. Both X and VI Corps were hard pressed and held on to their main positions only because of the weight and quality of the naval gunfire support and that of the artillery by then ashore. Every available infantryman was committed, and Clark had no reserves to hand. On 13 September an attack spearheaded by armour of the 16th Panzer Division well supported by infantry broke through between the River Sele and Paestum, penetrating to within two miles of the beaches. It was fought off by two battalions of American artillery and a scratch force of infantry, the gunners engaging the Germans over open sights and using up 4,000 rounds in an hour of desperate fighting before the Germans finally wavered and withdrew.

This was the turning-point in the battle, though no commander on either side seems to have known it at the time. Indeed, on 14 September, Clark and his staff initiated tentative contingency planning with Admiral Hewitt for a re-embarkation of either VI or X Corps, though most likely the former, and using its troops to reinforce the other. This drew strong protest from Commodore Oliver, the naval commander of the northern attack force, and General McCreery the X Corps commander, who both believed that it could not be done under German fire and would be suicidal if tried. The scheme seems more to have been one of worst-case insurance and last resort rather than one of serious intent. It was the doctrine of the US Command and General Staff College to always have such a contingency plan for an amphibious operation – but that Clark should have it weighing on his mind revealed just how grave he felt his situation to be. On the following day, Alexander, visiting the beachhead, heard of this planning and firmly put a stop to it, well aware that even the slightest rumour of a move implying evacuation would be fatal to morale. 'This is one of the times when I saw General Alexander show his steel,' recalled his American Chief of Staff, General Lyman Lemnitzer. It was a command decision of courage and conviction, for as his biographer observes, had disaster struck the beachhead the blame for having no emergency plan organized to rescue its troops would have been laid squarely on Alexander.[3]

Now was not the time for evacuations, and Alexander was more qualified than most to know the difference between an operation that could be saved by the Allied armies fighting hard with their backs to the sea and one that could not. Not for nothing had he carried the heavy responsibility of commanding the British Expeditionary Force throughout its final days in France, three years before on the beaches of Dunkirk.

Moves were already under way to offset the local German superiority. Eisenhower had obtained the Combined Chiefs' sanction for Tedder to divert his heavy bomber forces temporarily away from strategic targets and call them directly into the land battle against the Germans around Salerno. Alexander himself had secured the use of eighteen LSTs, under orders to leave the Mediterranean for the Far East, to rush reinforcements to the beachhead instead. Accepting the risk to two of his capital ships that the Allied navies could ill afford to lose, Cunningham despatched the battleships *Warspite* and *Valiant* at full speed from Malta to add their 15-inch gun power to help save the beachhead. Clark, aware that the 82nd Airborne Division was again at his disposal, requested an urgent reinforcement drop, and a regimental combat team parachuted into the VI Corps sector on the night of 13/14 September. In contrast to the Gela reinforcement disaster, the Allied ships observed a strict no-fire discipline despite a Luftwaffe raid, and the drop was a complete success. An operation on the following night to drop a regimental combat team well behind the German battlefront at Avellino was widely scattered and achieved little. It did not repeat the panic and disruption caused to the Germans and Italians on Sicily; this time the Germans were of different steel and the paratroops had to go to earth, small parties hiding out in the hills until the Allied advance caught up with them. The first tanks of the British 7th Armoured Division landed in the beachhead on 14 September, and in the VI Corps sector the remainder of the US 45th Division. The US 3rd Infantry Division was en route from Sicily. The balance of forces at Salerno was turning in favour of the Allies.

Superior Allied firepower meant that whatever chance the Germans had of destroying the beachhead had now passed. Hard fighting continued, but naval gunfire on an unprecedented scale ensured that the German attacks were broken up and also made a lasting impression on German commanders, Vietinghoff and Kesselring among them. They had no answer to it and called urgently and repeatedly upon the Luftwaffe to attack the warships. The Luftwaffe did indeed have an answer, and a potentially serious threat to the Allied naval forces. It deployed its special guided-missile unit, III/KG 100, equipped with Dornier Do 217K bombers armed with the new glider and rocket bombs that were released and then visually guided by radio control to their targets, a small flare in the tail assisting the bomb-aimer's direction of the weapon. There were two bomb versions. The armour-piercing unpowered Fritz-X 1400 could be released from 18,000 feet, beyond the interception ceiling of Allied fighters except the P-38 Lightning. It had a steep trajectory and such a terminal velocity (800 feet per second) that it could neither be shot down nor avoided. The rocket-powered Hs. 293 bomb could be released from greater distance and, like a miniature aircraft, had wings and conventional ailerons. Fritz-X was used against the Allied shipping concentrated off Salerno and there was no shortage of good targets for them. USS *Savannah* and the British cruiser *Uganda* were both hit and damaged. So too was *Warspite*, hit by a salvo of three Fritz-X and seriously damaged, shipping some 5,000 tons of water. Like *Uganda*, she had to be towed back to Malta, lucky not to have been sunk, and would not appear again in action until off the Normandy beaches the following June. USS *Philadelphia* survived a very near miss that sent shock waves throughout the warship, and a hospital ship was struck and sunk. It was a harbinger of a new age of aerial warfare, but the Luftwaffe possessed the weapon on too limited a scale to overturn the course of the beachhead battle; nor did it have the equipment, and crew training had yet to be perfected. On average, the bomber crews obtained one hit per 15 sorties.[4]

Once committed to the battle by Tedder, the Allied strategic forces subjected the German positions around Salerno to saturation bombing, at a density sometimes reaching some 760 tons of bombs per square mile. Whatever damage and casualties this caused, soldiers subjected to it could not fight effectively and certainly could not attack under it. The Allied tactical air forces were by now operating from airfields in southern Italy which had been secured by Eighth Army's advance, and also from rough but serviceable airstrips rapidly constructed within the beachhead. The weight of Allied fighter-bomber attack increased, and the range limitation initially exploited by the Luftwaffe was eroded.

On 16 September came the first link up between advance patrols of Eighth Army, from the 5th Division pushing hard and side stepping the 26th Panzer Division's rearguards, and the light screen of American troops pushed out towards the south from the beachhead by VI Corps. On the same day Kesselring and Vietinghoff resignedly accepted that their effort at Salerno must be ended and the battle broken off. Tenth Army needed time to redeploy in the face of Eighth Army's threat, and also to prepare for the now inevitable emergence of Fifth Army from its beachhead, which had so nearly become its graveyard. The Allied armies were set to pose a continuous advancing front across Italy. On the day that Clark had landed at Salerno, troops of the British 1st Airborne Division crammed aboard the warships of the 12th Cruiser Squadron, which Cunningham had made available at short notice, entered Taranto harbour in the wake of the Italian surrender. There was no opposition, though the fast minelayer *Abdiel*, packed with troops, struck a mine and sank quickly with the loss of 150 men. But an important port and naval base had been gained, and its possession would ease Eighth Army's supply difficulties during its advance along the Adriatic coast of Italy.

On 17 September, Vietinghoff attacked once more at Salerno, with a thrust from the north and another from the east, both directed against X Corps. Both ran into heavy defensive fire and could make no progress. Their main purpose was now to cover the German disengagement, for Vietinghoff was under orders to withdraw steadily and stubbornly northwards, destroying everything of military value in his wake, forming as he did so a continuous defensive front across Italy. He was to hold the Allies off from Naples as long as he could, to give the German demolition teams arriving in the port with their equipment sufficient time to make a thorough job of wrecking its facilities. Then he was to fall back to the Rivers Volturno and Bifurno (the Viktor Line), where he was to buy valuable time – he was directed to hold it until 15 October at least – while to his rear were prepared two further very strong defensive lines across Italy.

At Salerno the beachhead had been saved by the stubborn fighting of its defenders, by the approaching threat of Eighth Army, which caused German commanders to keep anxiously 'looking over their shoulders' in the latter stages of the beachhead fighting, and above all by the weight of air and naval firepower thrown into the battle as an emergency measure to stave off disaster. It was to the latter that the German commanders attributed their failure. For the Allies the Salerno beachhead battle was a defensive success, but it fell short of victory. There had not been, and would now not be, a rapid seizure of Naples – the original 'Avalanche' gamble had not come off. The German soldiers pulling out of the mountains that overlooked the bay did not consider themselves beaten, though they had been thwarted of a success that their senior commanders had, with good reason, believed to be within their grasp. They had dealt some very hard knocks. 'The Germans may claim with some justification to have won if not a victory at least an important success over us,' was Alexander's even-handed verdict on 'Avalanche'.[5] The Germans left behind 840 of their comrades who had been killed, while another 630 were missing and over 2,000 had been wounded. Upon X and VI Corps they had inflicted some 8,659 battle casualties.[6]

At Salerno the Allied Command had stuck Clark's neck out a long way, and he had only narrowly escaped disaster. Churchill, who had been very anxious throughout the Salerno battle and at whose shoulders had gathered the unquiet shades of Gallipoli, realized this only too well. 'I hope you are watching above all the Battle of "Avalanche" which dominates everything,' he had signalled Alexander on 14 September, reminding him that, 'None of the commanders engaged has fought a large-scale battle before,' and reminding him too that General Sir Ian Hamilton had been too remote to save the situation at Suvla Bay at Gallipoli in 1915, whereas had he been on the spot he could have done so.[7] The implication of this was clear. But Alexander had found himself confident in Clark when he had visited the beachhead and intervened only when he felt it absolutely necessary. He and Eisenhower, who had tried to move heaven and earth to get reinforcements and firepower to the beachhead in time, had both known very well how precarious Clark's situation had been. The commander who had known it most of all was, of course, Clark himself, and he would remember it.

11
AUTUMN FRUSTRATION

As the German Tenth Army withdrew, the Allies could take stock of what confronted them in Italy. Although Salerno had been a close call, the possibility of Clark having to fight such a battle for his beachhead had been anticipated in AFHQ assessments, albeit not with much equanimity. Nothing had occurred to alter the view that the Germans would withdraw to the north of the country, where they would probably try to hold a line stretching from Pisa to Rimini. It would be there that the Allies would face the problem of how to achieve the task set Eisenhower following 'Quadrant' – that of maintaining 'unremitting pressure' on the Germans in support of 'Overlord'. On 21 September, Alexander wrote to his two Army commanders, Clark and Montgomery, from his 15th Army Group headquarters and gave them his envisaged four-phase development of the campaign. First, Eighth and Fifth Armies must establish a line from Salerno to Bari; then capture Naples and the Foggia airfields. This should be followed by the capture of Rome and its airfields; and the fourth phase would be the capture of the port of Leghorn and the communications centres of Florence and Arezzo.

The timescale thought probable was the capture of Naples by 7 October, Rome by 7 November, and the gaining of the line Lucca (north of Livorno) to Ravenna by the end of November.[1] Although shipping would be limited because of the primacy of 'Overlord', there should be sufficient for the Allies to land 'small but hard-hitting' mobile forces of brigade-group size to cut off German units and hasten the German withdrawal. Alexander had to cut his amphibious 'coat' to his limited 'cloth' of shipping, but Allied command of the sea and the vulnerability of German positions to coastal outflanking were advantages that the Allies could hardly afford to waste. Much might be achieved by exploiting them even on a small scale. Nevertheless, only an assured and ongoing German retreat would have induced Alexander to contemplate risking 'penny-packet' landings of the kind he and Montgomery had deplored in the initial planning for 'Husky'.

Intelligence, including intercepts of German signals, supported the assessment of a German withdrawal to the north and that it was well under way. Only decisive success against an Allied landing, as had been attempted at Salerno, was considered likely to have deflected the Germans from this course, whereas failure would almost certainly confirm them in it. The interception and decryption of a report by the Japanese Ambassador in Berlin, who had been assured that the Germans had no intention of fighting in central or southern Italy, confirmed the view.[2] Another indicator of northward withdrawal was seen in the German evacuation of Sardinia and Corsica under the direction of General von Senger und Etterlin. Had the Germans been working to an elaborate deception scheme they could not have better misled the Allies and set them up for a complete and unexpected overturning of their strategic hopes in Italy. In fact, Hitler's decision to alter his strategy of northward withdrawal was about to change the nature of the Italian campaign.

Hitler had thought Kesselring too credulous in his dealings with the Italians, but increasingly he was coming to respect his capabilities as a theatre commander. Moreover, Kesselring was an optimist himself – he did not need to come under Hitler's personal spell in order to have faith in achieving military success – and he was a determined fighter. Rommel had returned from Africa embittered, his counsels tainted by his experience of fighting against overwhelming Allied superiority. His view that only in the north could Germany hope to retain a firm hold on Italy, and that Allied sea and air power would render it impossible to defend the peninsula, had a sound logic. It also fitted with the very real concern shared by Hitler and the OKW during August and most of September that their divisions in southern Italy would be lucky indeed if they escaped being cut off by the Allies. But Rommel's view had a taint of defeatism. When weighed in Hitler's mind against a more positive alternative, also founded in strategic logic, it was unlikely to prevail. At Salerno, Kesselring had shown his willingness to give battle and his ability to check the Allied advance. Tenth Army had been successfully extricated from what could have been a trap; the threat posed by the Italian defection had been dealt with; and under

Kesselring's direction and von Vietinghoff's command it was demonstrating its ability to make good defensive use of the terrain in the south. A
precipitate withdrawal to the north might not after all be necessary, and
the first glimmering of light began to dawn that the Allies could not, after
all, be so well off in shipping for amphibious operations as first assumed.
In any case, if strong defences could be held until the onset of winter
weather, Allied ability to mount such operations would be further reduced.
Hitler's inclination was always to hold ground, never willingly to relinquish
it. Usually he had to impose such a policy upon recalcitrant Army generals
who came up with plenty of good reasons for retreating; he was unlikely
to resist a commander, and a senior Luftwaffe officer at that, who could
give him good reasons to stand fast and a promise of holding ground when
he had already resigned himself to the necessity of retreat. All it needed
was a strong strategic argument and an assertion of military feasibility to
swing him round to a stand-fast strategy in southern Italy. Kesselring
provided them.

As Kesselring reported to the OKW in mid-September, it seemed to
him unlikely that the Allies would advance farther into Italy once they had
gained the Foggia airfields. They were far more likely to strike at the
Balkans. This squared with military logic, for there seemed little for the
Allies to gain by fighting their way northwards in Italy, 'against the grain'
of the country, when the Balkans, so vital to Germany, would be vulnerable. To Hitler, always sensitive about the strategically vital Balkans, this
made sense. It was ironic that Kesselring was expecting the Allies to do the
one thing that the Americans would never have stood for, placing sizeable
forces in the Balkans. His argument was that to relinquish central and
much of northern Italy to the Allies would facilitate their descent on the
Balkans. It would require fewer troops to hold them in the south of Italy
than in the north. And by holding them in the south they could be denied
the airfields from which their bombers could strike at industrial targets in
southern Germany and Austria.[3] In effect, he could better protect the
Balkans and the Reich by imposing a campaign upon the Allies in Italy in
which they would have to fight south of Rome. They would not then dare
to weaken their armies in Italy of forces for the Balkans, as then they would
be vulnerable to a counterattack that he would be well placed to launch to

regain the Foggia airfields – even the threat of this would pin them down in Italy. Kesselring was confident of the defensive lines that he had identified and planned, that they would hold if the Allies were rash enough to wear themselves out by trying to dislodge him from them by head-on attack. The amphibious outflanking threat remained the principal risk, but it had lost a good deal of its earlier force and did not outweigh the advantages of standing fast in the south. It was a risk worth taking.

Hitler had laughed at Kesselring's trusting reports on Italian loyalty to the Axis, but he did not laugh at his military appreciation. Instead, as September turned to October, he became more and more inclined to back him. Otto Skorzeny had fulfilled the task entrusted to him and had found out where the Italians had hidden Mussolini, in a remote mountain skiing resort at Gran Sasso in the Apennines. Skorzeny had plucked Mussolini away in an audacious airborne commando raid on 12 September and brought him back to Germany. Now Mussolini was to head a puppet Fascist regime established at the end of September under German protection in northern Italy, the Social Republic, or Salò Republic, after its place of residence on the shores of Lake Garda. To increase its credibility was a further reason for retaining as much Italian territory as possible. Nor did Hitler see why he should hand the Allies the Italian capital, Rome, on a plate; let them get past Kesselring first, if they could.

On 1 October, Hitler crossed the strategic Rubicon, sanctioning Kesselring to plan on holding the Allies south of Rome. Three days later he ordered Rommel, whose Army Group B in the north had thus far been conserved, to despatch two divisions and artillery south to reinforce Kesselring. A month later, on 6 November, he formally appointed Kesselring Commander-in-Chief South-West and head of Army Group C, with command authority over the Italian theatre including the forces in the north which became Fourteenth Army. Rommel was given the task of inspecting the Atlantic Wall in the north-west, where his name and reputation would indicate to friend and foe alike German determination and ability to defend 'Fortress Europe'. But the fighting command he had entrusted to Kesselring.

The Allies were aware of the change in German strategy in Italy by 8 October, intercepted signals revealing Hitler's instructions to Kesselring, while those between Luftwaffe liaison officers provided details of the defensive lines being prepared.[4] The knowledge caused considerable dismay. There was, as Eisenhower reported, a 'drastic change' in the situation facing the Allies in Italy – 'We have always trusted this kind of evidence,' Churchill cabled to Roosevelt on 10 October, 'and I therefore agree that we must now look forward to very heavy fighting before Rome is reached instead of merely pushing back rearguards.'[5] Hitler's decision effectively put paid to Churchill's particular hope of mounting an invasion of German-occupied Rhodes and of clearing the Aegean of German forces as a strong lever to induce Turkey to enter the war. Instead, Eisenhower and Alexander now required all the available resources that Allied strategy had allocated to the Mediterranean theatre for the battle they faced in Italy. It began to look very much as if the Italian campaign upon which the Allies had embarked was likely to serve German strategic interests rather better than their own.

As Fifth Army along the Tyrrhenian coast and Eighth Army along the Adriatic gathered themselves for their northward advance, the full implications of what confronted them became apparent. The Apennine mountain range running the length of the peninsula faced the Allies with narrow plains along the Tyrrhenian and Adriatic coasts, cut with rivers, rock-strewn valleys and gullies. Roads able to support the advance and logistic tail of a mechanized army were very few; only the State roads could do so. In the west these were Highway 7, running along the Tyrrhenian coast to Rome, and Highway 6, leading to Rome through Cassino and the Liri Valley. In the east Highway 16 ran along the Adriatic coast with Highway 17 inland of it skirting the Apennines. East-to-west the principal lateral roads were Highway 87 from Termoli to Naples, Highway 86 from Vasto to Mignano, and Highway 5 from Pescara to Rome. The advance of primarily mechanized and road-bound armies dependent upon such a limited road network in difficult terrain could therefore be predicted, and even to a large extent channelled by a resolute and skilled defender.

In its move up from Salerno, Fifth Army was delayed by stubborn rearguard actions, but on 1 October the first Allied troops, the King's Dragoon Guards of X Corps, entered Naples. The port was in ruins and the city's electrical and water systems wrecked and polluted. Delayed-action mines and booby-traps had been laid in public and administrative buildings. This had been anticipated, and specialist Allied repair teams had the port handling 5,000 tons of cargo daily within three weeks. What the Allies could do nothing about was the weather. The autumn rains had started, turning unsurfaced roads and tracks into quagmires. The advance, particularly in the mountains through which Fifth Army was struggling, began to stall in mud. The good flying weather would soon be gone until the following spring, and, despite the superiority of their air forces during the intervening months, air support would be a bonus for the Allied armies rather than a certainty. Ever since the first Allied landings in Sicily the terrain had been the German soldier's ally; now so too was the weather.

On 24 October at a commanders' conference convened by Eisenhower, Alexander reviewed the Allied situation in Italy. It was sobering and gave little cause for optimism. Eisenhower fully endorsed Alexander's report, and forwarded it to both Roosevelt and Churchill. Alexander had not minced his words. The balance of forces in Italy favoured the Germans: the Allies had eleven divisions in the south facing nine German, but there were fifteen more German divisions in the north, making a total of 24. The Allied rate of build-up had been slowed by shipping shortages to the extent that by the end of January 1944 there would still be only seventeen Allied divisions. In November, moreover, seven veteran divisions would leave the theatre for Britain to prepare for their task of spearheading 'Overlord'. Reductions in landing craft ruled out outflanking moves of any size, while the German demolitions of roads, bridges, railways and port facilities meant that many of the landing craft available in theatre were in continual use running supplies along the coast for the armies. There were no other vessels for this task, so clearly the landing craft could not easily be withdrawn from it; in the meantime, wear and tear and maintenance problems for these precious craft increased.

Alexander also observed that the priority in shipping accorded the strategic air forces to get them established on the Foggia bases reduced the build up of Fifth and Eighth Armies, a situation likely to continue until December. This was a clear instance of how Hitler's decision had derailed Allied strategy. While the Allied armies were likely to be chasing German rearguards, their build-up could reasonably take second place to intensifying the Allied strategic air offensive against Germany by bringing the Mediterranean strategic air forces into action as soon as possible against industrial targets beyond the range of British-based bombers. But once the Allied armies in Italy faced the immediate prospect of heavy fighting, in which they would have to take the offensive, this priority was all wrong. Yet it could not be quickly changed.

The Allied armies could not afford to stand still south of Rome – this would merely surrender the initiative to the Germans. Also, as Alexander acknowledged, the Italian capital had 'a significance far greater than its strategic location'. Not only that: the Allies had to keep attacking to secure sufficient depth to protect Naples and the Foggia airfields from the threat of a German counteroffensive. 'It would therefore appear that we are committed to a long and costly advance to Rome,' warned Alexander, 'a "slogging match" with our present slight superiority in formations on the battlefront offset by the enemy opportunity for relief; for without sufficient resources in craft no out-flanking amphibious operation of a size sufficient to speed up our rate of advance is possible.'[6] The Allies had become the prisoners of their own strategy, their options reduced to one, that of keeping the German army engaged in the months before 'Overlord' by attacking in Italy, their only land theatre, but under the most unfavourable circumstances of terrain and weather.

Since the first landings on the mainland, the predominantly mechanized Allied armies struggled to get forward in adverse terrain, but their experience thus far had not prepared them for what was yet to come. They had encountered stubborn rearguards that, added to the ideal terrain, imposed delays. At Salerno the mountains hemming them into their beachhead had been an obstacle, but it had been the Germans who had done most of the attacking during the battle. The Allied armies had yet to launch themselves against extensive natural mountain strongholds that had been turned into fortresses by skilled German military engineering and in which German formations were determined to maintain not rearguards but a prolonged defence. Cunningly laid minefields, well-sited artillery, mortars and machine-guns dominating the restricted lines of approach, and narrow attack frontages into which Allied troops would be deliberately channelled, plus a lavish use of concrete and steel to protect defence positions – all were being prepared in the mountains. Below them in the lower-lying ground, each river line would be a defensive obstacle requiring assault crossings and extensive bridging operations. In Italy the Allies were set to lose men and time.

12

THE MAINLAND CAMPAIGN
TO THE WINTER LINE

Closing to the Winter Line

Despite their difficulties of weather and terrain, the Allied armies made contact with the first strong German line in their path, that following the River Volturno in the west opposite Fifth Army and the River Bifurno in the path of Eighth Army. Amphibious outflanking moves had now to be made with limited forces and shipping. A bold attempt to loosen the resistance in the path of the British XIII Corps by a landing behind the German front to seize Termoli was made by only about 1,000 Commando and Special Raiding Squadron troops. The bulk of them were transported in four Landing Craft (Infantry), without naval escort. They achieved a surprise landing on the night of 2/3 October and secured the town and port intact, but they fought a fierce battle with the German garrison, about 400 troops of the 1st Parachute Division. The advance units of the British 78th Division arrived during the following day, some through the port, and a crossing was gained over the Biferno.

The Germans had been caught with their guard down by the Termoli landing – an indication of what might have been achieved had more amphibious assets been available. But for this reason and because of the threat posed by this first breach in the line Tenth Army had been ordered to hold until 15 October, the Germans hit back, very quick and very hard. Kesselring ordered the 16th Panzer Division, already under orders to reinforce LXXVI Panzer Corps on the Adriatic, to counterattack immediately. The Division was depleted and tired, like most of the German formations that had been in the line continuously, but it was still full of fight and dangerous. After a difficult lateral road march through the mountains, by 4 October its first tank and infantry battle groups were attacking the Termoli bridgehead, which was soon in desperate straits because engineers had not been able to finish a vehicle crossing over the Biferno and only a few tanks had managed to cross in support. A solid eighteen hours of pouring rain had not helped the engineers in their task. The British infantry battalions suffered heavily for having little armour and too few anti-tank weapons with them in the bridgehead and one of them, the 8th Argyll and Sutherland Highlanders, suffered 162 casualties. It took the urgent completion of the tank crossing and the arrival of Canadian tanks after a forced march, plus the landing in the port of a further brigade of the 78th Division, heavy artillery support and the arrival of two destroyers off the coast to provide further gun power to help turn the scale. There was also an intensive close air-support effort by fighter-bombers, for which the US XII Air Support Command, usually supporting Fifth Army, also swung its effort to the Adriatic sector to assist the RAF Desert Air Force. Between them their pilots flew more than 800 sorties in two days in the Termoli battle zone. By 7 October, the 16th Panzer Division was pulling back to the River Trigno. Once again the Allies had experienced a close call because of their difficulties in adequately reinforcing a landing force in sufficient time to ward off a German counterattack, and once again it had been a superior weight of firepower that had averted disaster.

The main river crossing battle was yet to be fought, on the Volturno on Clark's Fifth Army front. XIV Panzer Corps, now under the command of von Senger, deployed its formations along the river line with, beginning at the coastal reaches of the river, the 15th Panzer Grenadier Division, then the Hermann Göring Division, while the 3rd Panzer Grenadier Division covered the upper reaches and maintained contact with the 26th Panzer Division, the right-flanking formation of LXXVI Panzer Corps. None of these formations was particularly suited to the role, and they were far from fresh, but Tenth Army was still handicapped by the policy, only beginning to change, of holding forces back in the north. If a strong defence were to be held in southern Italy, particularly in the mountains, then what Kesselring and von Vietinghoff needed was infantry – and three infantry divisions were under orders to move south.

Nor were Clark's formations fresh. None of them had previously conducted an opposed river crossing, which was the only option as the delaying effect of weather and terrain prevented any chance of rushing the river before the German defences were in place. Therefore there was no 'corporate knowledge' of how to approach what was a complicated and hazardous form of attack. The campaign was now presenting largely unanticipated demands for which the Allied armies were ill-prepared and ill-equipped: for example, supplies of essential bridging material, upon which the campaign in Italy was increasingly looking to depend, were quite inadequate. For X Corps about to tackle the Volturno, some 200–300 feet wide, there was only just sufficient for one 30-ton tank bridge and one 9-ton vehicle bridge. Clark's plan was to attack the river line with both his British X Corps and US VI Corps on the night of 12/13 October, the British near the coast and the Americans inland on the higher ground. While an extended attack frontage offered the chance to exploit success, it allowed little to be held back in reserve. But time, and the need to gain ground before the weather worsened and the campaign stalled, was a strong imperative.

In the British X Corps sector the 46th Division made the main attack at the coast, with the Navy providing fire support and also covering the landing by LCTs of supporting tanks on the far bank once the assault infantry had carved out their crossing. Inland the 7th Armoured and 56th Divisions fixed the German line, looking to get across if they could, but found that the obvious crossing site at Capua, where Highway 7 crossed the river, was thoroughly bolted and barred by the Hermann Göring Division. Their attacks were supported by an artillery bombardment, and this probably focused German attention. The Germans were by this stage perhaps over-confident that they could depend upon the predictability of their opponents. Little progress was made. But nearer the coast the 46th Division crossed silently without a barrage and was successful, two brigades establishing a bridgehead into which five battalions had crossed by dawn on 13 October. The Navy covered the disembarking of supporting tanks and guns on the northern bank of the river mouth, but then came a hitch as this ground was found to be thickly sown with mines. The Sappers could not quickly clear them as they were of the wooden and newer plastic types, which defied detection; out came the bayonets for a laborious and time-consuming search by prodding. The tanks could not get forward to assist the bridgehead until the following day, and in the meantime – as at Termoli – the infantry bore the brunt of the German reaction, the 15th Panzer Grenadier Division striking back with tank and infantry battle groups. The ferrying across of anti-tank guns by raft and the timely arrival of tanks secured the bridgehead, but the Germans put up a stubborn defence to delay its expansion.

In the VI Corps sector the American infantry of the 3rd, 34th, and 45th Divisions made good use of the orchard- and vineyard-scattered terrain of the river's upper reaches where, in contrast to the waterlogged and open lower levels, there was better cover for an approach. The river in this sector was also fordable, and the 3rd and 34th Divisions crossed success-fully, their main problem being well-directed German artillery and machine-gun fire from the overlooking high ground. It was in this sector that the German grip on the Volturno was shaken, and Clark exploited this by adjusting the boundary between his corps to get the British 56th Division over the river where the US 3rd Division had constructed a 30-ton bridge near Triflisco, to the north-east of Capua. This unhinged the strong German position at Capua and for the Germans the Volturno became untenable. By 19 October, Fifth Army was established across the river line in strength. The German Tenth Army had fulfilled Kesselring's order to hold the line until 15 October. It then fell back grudgingly, with the usual delaying tactics, to a line from which it would not be so easily dislodged.

In the Eighth Army sector the patrols of the 78th Division pursuing the 16th Panzer Division to the Trigno found the road bridge intact, but as soon as the main body of the leading brigade came into view the watching German engineers detonated their charges, leaving a 200 foot gap. The river was fordable, however, and the 78th Division pushed across to run up against the first serious opposition at the little town of San Salvo and its ridge. In a night attack on 27/28 October by the 38th (Irish) Brigade, the Royal Irish Fusiliers attacking over the rain-sodden ground were cruelly hit by German artillery and mortar fire; the battalion commander and the two leading company commanders were killed, and all the platoon commanders killed or wounded.[1] Not surprisingly, the attack stalled. It was a week before the Division was gathered up for a full-scale attack, supported by the Navy with two destroyers bombarding the town of Vasto behind the German front and a flotilla of torpedo-boats simulating an amphibious descent. Thirty DUKW amphibians sailing from Termoli were to bring up extra artillery and tank-gun ammunition to ease dependence on the roads and fords, and this time the 78th Division Commander, General Evelegh, determined that there would be no attack at all until his tanks and anti-tank guns were already across the Trigno in the bridgehead – the Allied formations were learning. The attack met stiff resistance and the 16th Panzer Division had the best of the first tank-versus-tank battles amid the olive groves, the Shermans being at a disadvantage against the lower-built Panzer IVs which, stalking through the groves, were hard to spot. Then, rather to the surprise of the 78th Division, but under an increasing weight of attack, the Germans pulled back, leaving well-prepared positions in haste. They fell back to high ground beyond the River Sangro.

The Winter Line

'Prisoners told us that this was the winter line and that the
orders were that there was to be no withdrawal from it.'[2]

As they pushed north from the Volturno on the Fifth Army front and over the Trigno on that of Eighth Army, the Allies had cleared a series of delaying positions known as the Barbara Line. By early November they faced the barrier Kesselring had placed in their path to hold them south of Rome.

Before Clark's Fifth Army stood the Bernhardt Line, sometimes referred to by the Germans as the Reinhard Line. This was a belt of strongpoints constructed and manned by XIV Panzer Corps in a narrow valley known as the Mignano Gap, through which passed Highway 6 on its way northwards to Cassino and the Liri Valley. Ringed by mountains, the Mignano Gap offered a superb defensive zone of dominating high ground and depth. To the north of the Gap were the heights of Monte Cesima, Monte Sammucro, Monte Lungo and Monte Rotondo, while to the south were Monte Maggiore, Monte La Difensa and Monte Camino. Yet the Bernhardt Line constituted only an outpost position, a forward glacis in the XIV Panzer Corps sector, to the main defensive line across Italy that Kesselring had selected and that he intended to be so strong 'that the British and Americans would break their teeth on it.'[3] This was the Gustav Line.

The Gustav Line followed the length of rivers, though it was not primarily a river defensive line. From the Tyrrhenian coast in the west to the Adriatic in the east, it followed the line of the River Garigliano, then that of its tributaries, the Gari and Rapido, as far as Cassino, and upwards into the high mountains of the central Apennines to the Maiella range eventually to follow the line of the River Sangro to the Adriatic. The rivers were covered by positions well forward but thinly manned, typically by small parties of infantry with machine-guns and often protected by extensive mine-belts. Supporting them were artillery and mortars situated in the overlooking high ground with excellent observation, and it was in the mountains that the most formidable defence positions were constructed, mutually supporting and immensely strong, in some cases blasted out of the rock with explosives, and difficult to spot. They covered the likely approaches with interlocking fire, and, where feasible, these were augmented with deliberate flooding and minefields to channel attackers into fire-dominated 'killing zones'. On the Adriatic side of the Apennines, the higher ground upon which LXXVI Panzer Corps based its main defence positions stood back some three miles from the line of the River Sangro, which was wide, gravelly but generally shallow amid low-lying and, in winter, waterlogged ground. Highly defensible ridges and deep gullies were the principal obstacles to the attacker in this sector.

The high mountain bastions and the full and deep rivers were in the XIV Panzer Corps sector opposite Fifth Army, and the strongest point of the Gustav Line was at Cassino, where Monte Cassino topped by the famous Benedictine monastery overlooked the Rapido and dominated Highway 6 and the entrance to the Liri Valley. This was the gateway to Rome, through which an advancing mechanized army would need to pass along Highway 6 to exploit the room to manoeuvre afforded by the Liri Valley beyond. The alternative routes to Rome would be along Highway 7, skirting the west coast but too easily blocked from the overlooking mountains and flooded from the Pontine Marshes; or from the Adriatic side, but this would require dependence upon the limited road network for the daunting task of attacking laterally east-to-west across the Apennine range. From Kesselring's perspective, the Allied options could be discerned and countered. He could be confident that between them the Bernhardt and

Gustav Lines would hold the Allies through the winter, and in Allied accounts they are sometimes referred to generally as the Winter Line position.

At the beginning of November, Fifth Army drew up to the southern foothills of the Bernhardt Line and, at the coast, reached the Garigliano to find the bridges all blown and wide mine-belts covering the banks and flood plains. Some of the hardest mountain fighting of the entire campaign was about to take place as, in appalling conditions of wet and the increasing cold of the oncoming Italian winter, Fifth Army set out to storm the mountain positions of the Bernhardt Line. To the armchair strategist it seems sheer madness. Fifth Army's divisions had been in action continuously since they came ashore at Salerno. They were now battle-hardened, certainly, but they were also tired, and what they confronted now would tax the freshest and fittest of men. Yet there could be no let up in the offensive pressure. The Allies were aware that the Germans were working systematically to strengthen the positions beyond the Bernhardt Line and that to delay would only give them the chance to make them stronger. The general scheme at this stage was for Clark to fight his way towards Rome through Highway 6 while Montgomery broke through to Pescara and then swung west to move on Rome from the east along Highway 5. The Allied Combined Chiefs had agreed to Eisenhower's request to retain assault shipping destined for 'Overlord' in the Mediterranean until 15 December, giving the opportunity for two modest amphibious strikes, one on each coast, to loosen the German hold – providing the Allied armies had managed to advance far enough to make them effective. On the west coast to support Fifth Army a landing by a single division was thought possible on suitable beaches near the small port of Anzio to the south-west of Rome. Planning for this went under the codename 'Shingle', though it was considered that Fifth Army would have to get as far as Frosinone, beyond Cassino and the Gustav Line, before it was feasible. Time was all.

On 5 November the British 56th and US 3rd Divisions attacked into the high ground at Monte Camino, the southern anchor of the Bernhardt Line held by the 15th Panzer Grenadier Division. The US 45th and 34th Divisions attacked farther north around Venafro into ground held by the 3rd Panzer Grenadier Division and one of the infantry divisions recently arrived from the north, the 305th. In Sicily the Allies had experienced mountain fighting in summer; now Fifth Army was tackling higher ground in winter conditions. To attack meant hours of exhausting climbing. Despite efforts to improvise mule trains, there were insufficient animals to hand because the need for mountain fighting of this intensity had neither been anticipated nor prepared for. The infantry began to penetrate into ground well beyond vehicle access and in which only human porters could bring up supplies. Entire battalions had to be employed in the role to keep a barely adequate flow of supplies to the forward companies strung out on the mountain slopes.

The German defensive fire was effective, and it was difficult to provide accurate artillery support and, even when the weather allowed, air strikes against their well-protected and difficult-to-locate positions. Guns could not get forward to deploy, high trajectories were needed, more often than not the Germans had the better visibility and observation. One mountain ridge looked too much like another, especially from a fighter-bomber pilot's cockpit when the visibility was poor. General bombardments, though employed, could not be counted upon to neutralize the German posts, while the terrain made it near-impossible for infantry to follow-up such fire quickly and so take advantage of its effects. Clark's infantry casualties mounted sharply. It took hours to hand-carry wounded back down to the aid stations, and positions gained on the precarious slopes and outcrops left men exposed to the effects of weather as well as German fire.

For all that, in a truly remarkable effort, Fifth Army gained footholds on Monte Camino, Monte La Difensa, and Monte Rotondo, and the penetrations near Venafro caused the Germans such alarm that they pulled infantry elements of the 26th Panzer Division from LXXVI Panzer Corps on the Adriatic to replace the shaken 305th Infantry Division, and called the 29th Panzer Grenadier Division out of Tenth Army reserve to replace the equally shaken 3rd Panzer Grenadier Division. The tenacity of the Fifth Army attack and the intensity of the fighting was a shock to the German command and stretched their own forces. Panzer divisions, however good, possessed too few infantry for mountain warfare; nor was it a sound policy to waste hard-to-replace panzer grenadiers, trained to work with armour, in such fighting. The Bernhardt Line fighting showed that attrition was draining both sides. Though the Germans might be brought close to breaking-point, the Allied infantry were always too exhausted and depleted by casualties to be able to make the final effort necessary to push their enemies to the point of collapse. It was the weather and the supply problem that defeated Fifth Army. Clark was forced to pull his forward units off the mountain slopes because of the impossibility of supplying them, and many of their troops were suffering the effects of cold and wet – there were many frostbite cases. On 15 November, recognizing that Fifth Army was for the present 'fought-out', Alexander called off the attack.

Meanwhile Eighth Army had closed up to the Sangro, with patrols of the leading formations probing the German defences. Montgomery's attack across the river began on 20 November but was immediately hampered by the onset of heavy rain and flooding. A bridgehead was established, but the bridges thrown across the river by Sappers could not withstand the floodwaters rushing down from the mountains, and supplies and reinforcements then had to be ferried across. There were no heavy German counterattacks, but the weather had given Kesselring time to reinforce the static 65th Infantry Division holding the Sangro with some mobile battle groups of Tenth Army's workhorses, the 16th and 26th Panzer Divisions, while the first arrivals of the 90th Panzer Grenadier Division brought down from the north also began to strengthen the line. The weather abated, and, on 29 November, Montgomery resumed the attack in his typical Eighth Army style, employing an initial pulverizing heavy artillery bombardment. The Desert Air Force also provided full-scale support, adopting the 'cab-rank' system whereby its fighter-bomber squadrons maintained flights of aircraft over the battle area in radio contact with a controller with the forward troops able to call them down at once on to specific points of German resistance. The 65th Division was shattered beyond recovery by this overwhelming firepower, Eighth Army troops taking many prisoners including the German divisional commander. Counterattacks by the German mobile formations made no impression against the weight of Eighth Army's attack, and the broken 65th Division's positions were lost for good. However, a new defensive line following the next river, the River Moro, was soon established and against this Eighth

Army for the moment could make no headway. Momentum had slowed over the difficult ground, and there was as yet no flood-resistant bridge constructed over the Sangro to sustain a further offensive bound. Once again a pause was needed.

Strategic Stock-Taking

With the Allied armies in Italy battering their way into the Winter Line, there could be few illusions about what the Italian campaign was going to involve. In terms of Allied strategy, however, the only alternative to maintaining the attack in Italy would result in giving the Germans a reprieve, whereby forces could be used on the Eastern Front or to strengthen the West before 'Overlord'. The Italian campaign therefore survived the 'Sextant' and 'Eureka' conferences that set Allied strategy for 1944. 'Sextant' was a meeting between Churchill, Roosevelt and the Combined Chiefs of Staff, attended also by Generalissimo Chiang Kai-shek of China, and ran from 22 to 26 November. It was then broken by 'Eureka' in Teheran between 28 November and 1 December, attended by Churchill, Roosevelt, the Combined Chiefs, with Stalin and his Foreign Minister, Molotov, and senior military representative, Marshal Voroshilov. The British and Americans then resumed 'Sextant' in Cairo between 3 and 7 December.

Churchill and the British Chiefs of Staff were disappointed in their hope for some flexibility in the 'Overlord' timetable. They had hoped to be able to gain the maximum benefit from weakening the Germans by operations in Italy and threatening their position in the Balkans. But Stalin unequivocally threw his weight behind 'Overlord', insisting upon the Allies mounting the cross-Channel invasion in the spring of 1944. He also supported an operation tabled by the Americans for a landing in southern France, a concept codenamed 'Anvil', to support it. Though it was as yet uncertain whether an invasion of southern France would precede or follow 'Overlord', it threatened to remove Allied divisions from Italy and with them any chance of exploiting into southern Europe and hastening a German collapse in the Balkans.

Neither the Americans nor the Soviets were convinced by British arguments that a vigorous pursuit of the Italian campaign would assist 'Overlord' and the Soviets by pulling German forces away from the West and the East. With the experience thus far in Italy they had little reason to be. The Soviets knew that since the beginning of October the Germans had released divisions from France, the Balkans and Italy for the Eastern Front. Before 'Sextant–Eureka', British Intelligence knew very well through 'Ultra' that the Germans were transferring divisions from Italy to the East. By mid-November these were the 24th Panzer Division, 76th Infantry Division, and the SS Panzer Division Liebstandarte Adolf Hitler. By 18 November it was also known to the British that Kesselring had been ordered to part with the 16th Panzer Division as well, that his plea to retain part of it was granted, and that the 2nd Parachute Division near Rome was also on its way to the Eastern Front.[4] Only a serious reverse in Italy and the likely collapse of their front would compel the Germans to reverse this trend and draw heavily upon other theatres. The Allies agreed to continue their advance in Italy to the Pisa–Rimini line, but their ability to inflict such a defeat on the Germans in Italy seemed increasingly unlikely as the campaign would remain on a shoestring of resources. Contrary to British hopes, the strategic timetable had become more inflexible, and battering away head-on at positions like the Winter Line without the means of amphibious outflanking moves would not shake the Germans or get the Allies very far. Unless something could be done, opportunities were going to be lost.

The overriding consideration remained the availability of assault shipping, a situation in which the Allies were seriously embarrassed because they found themselves committed to four significant amphibious operations within the following six months which they now realised were well beyond their means. These were an imminent 'Shingle' on the Italian west coast to support Fifth Army's advance; an invasion of the Andaman Islands codenamed 'Buccaneer' to support a Chinese offensive in northern Burma against the Japanese, which was proposed for March 1944; plus 'Overlord' and now 'Anvil' as well – both by the end of May 1944. It did not help that Roosevelt had unilaterally promised 'Buccaneer' to Chiang Kai-Shek as a means of encouraging the Chinese war effort, while Admiral King's proposed allocation of all American assault shipping production scheduled for March 1944 (25 LST and 66 landing craft) to the

European theatre could not cover the additional vessels needed for a two-division assault landing for 'Anvil' and a follow-up of eight divisions. 'Overlord' itself was still predicated on only a three-division initial assault landing – less than had been mounted for 'Husky' – and this was a cause of increasing concern to its planners.

Faced with this reality, and also the fact that 'Buccaneer', in its demands for additional troops and aircraft carriers, was escalating alarmingly in its requirements (as military operations once in the hands of their planners are apt to do), Roosevelt took the initiative and informed Chiang that 'Buccaneer' could not be mounted. The Pacific therefore remained the principal theatre against Japan, but a window was opened for the retention of assault shipping (68 LSTs) in the Mediterranean until 15 January 1944, enabling slightly more flexibility for an amphibious outflanking move in Italy.

Clearing the Bernhardt Line

In the meantime the Bernhardt Line had still to be tackled. Fifth Army at the beginning of December was stronger but for intensive mountain fighting would still have few reserves. It had received the US II Corps from Sicily with the US 1st Armored Division, and both the US 36th and 34th Divisions were assigned to the corps. The 2nd Moroccan Division arrived from French North Africa – particularly important as the Moroccans, with French officers and NCOs, were expert mountain fighters. The American-Canadian 1st Special Service Force, comprising six battalions of well-equipped Commando/Ranger-style troops highly trained for mountain warfare, was also a valuable addition, and the 1st Italian Motorized Group, the first Italian formation to take the field against its erstwhile ally, was attached to Fifth Army. The deficit was that two experienced formations, the British 7th Armoured and US 82nd Airborne Divisions, had left for 'Overlord', but clearly an effort had been made to compensate with formations better suited to the requirements of the campaign. Rather than wait until Alexander's suggested 12 December, Clark urged him to allow Fifth Army to renew the attack ten days earlier, on 2 December. Alexander agreed but warned Clark that he would be coming up against a stiff defence and counselled him to avoid heavy casualties. Clark was confident and his army ready – the earlier the better to ensure the likelihood of 'Shingle' before the assault shipping deadline. 'Don't worry,' he told Alexander, 'I'll get through the Winter Line all right and push the Germans out.'[5] Fifth Army was, after all, less than ten miles from the entrance to the Liri Valley.

The Fifth Army plan was for a three-phase attack. In the first, all-too aptly codenamed 'Raincoat', would come the capture of Monte Camino and the heights to the south of Highway 6. In the second, Monte Lungo and Monte Sammucro to the north would be taken; and in the third would come an advance into the Liri Valley with the 1st Armored Division ready to exploit. There was greater sophistication in this attack plan, and considerable effort was made to maximize Fifth Army's chances of achieving a breakthrough. The assembling of shipping in Naples and appropriate naval activity and bombing raids was aimed at unnerving the Germans and pinning their reserves by convincing them of an imminent amphibious landing behind their positions in the Gulf of Gaeta, north of the River Garigliano. Colossal firepower was laid on to support the infantry who would have to storm the heights. But Fifth Army was still up against a formidable combination; a stubborn and determined German defence, near-inaccessible, high mountain terrain and the effects of bitter cold and very heavy rain. Between 2 and 4 December rain fell so heavily that even mules could not use some of the mountain trails. It was not only German fire that would cause casualties to Fifth Army's attack battalions but also terrain-related injuries, the debilitating physical effects of wet and cold, and sheer exhaustion.

Beginning on 2 December, and preceded by an abortive but costly diversionary attack by the British 46th Division, the British 56th Division attacked Monte Camino. There followed a savage round of attack and counterattack against the 15th Panzer Grenadier Division's companies. By 6 December the highest point of Monte Camino, where there was also a monastery, was in British hands. Four days later the remaining slopes were secure; some of the defending German units had left their withdrawal too late and, when the river rose under the flooding and washed away their light bridges they could only escape by swimming, leaving their equipment behind. Between them the British Divisions in X Corps had suffered more than 1,000 casualties in taking Monte Camino and the adjoining slopes. The US II Corps attack on the Monte La Difensa–Monte Maggiore high ground began on the afternoon of 2 December under a bombardment by 925 guns, including 24 of the newly introduced 8-inch howitzers. Thereafter the gunners worked hard to provide fire support when needed, despite their guns often tipping into muddy quagmires and having to be winched out, inadequate range tables and limited observation, and the problem of securing enough elevation to bombard very high ground.

The German positions proved resilient to bombardment, though the weight of fire the Allied gunners could put down cut off German positions from reinforcement and supply, and made tactical movement impossible. In a bold night ascent over ground that could only be described as perilous, the 1st Special Service Force reached the peak of Monte La Difensa by dawn on 3 December. They had achieved surprise and had brushed aside small – and no doubt startled – German posts. The danger of slipping off the narrow ledges into the deep ravines below had been as much, if not a greater, threat to the men than German fire. But it did not take the Germans long to react, and the battle to retain the high ground lasted until 8 December, during which time the Special Service Force could not be relieved on the slopes. By then they had been exposed without shelter to cold, unceasing rain, fog and icy wind as well as German fire. They had no hot food. They had beaten off German counterattacks and also taken the nearby Monte la Remetanea. The cost was high: 511 casualties, including 73 dead, 9 missing, 313 wounded or injured and 116 cases of exhaustion. The Special Service Force commander, Colonel Robert T. Frederick, reported that his men, who must have ranked among the fittest in any of the armies fighting in Italy, needed a minimum of three days' rest after coming down from La Difensa before they could be reassigned to battle.[6]

Similarly exploiting surprise and following in the wake of the Special Service Force ascent on La Difensa, two battalions of the US 36th Division's 142nd Infantry secured the ridge surmounting Monte Maggiore. Mules could not climb the steep slopes, so the assault infantry had to carry their own ammunition and light rations, while a third battalion of the 142nd and two companies of the 141st Infantry were assigned as porters to keep them supplied. These had three miles to climb to reach the forward positions, sometimes along steep muddy trails over which they could only crawl, using ropes to drag packs behind them. A round supply trip took twelve hours. Attempts to use fighter-bombers to air drop supplies between 5 and 7 December were unsuccessful; the pilots were hampered by poor visibility, the ridged and broken terrain offered no dropping points accessible to the infantry from where they could recover the supplies, and German positions were far too close. The German defenders of the 15th Panzer Grenadier Division were in no better situation, battered by artillery and with little relief, and they were unable to dislodge the American infantry from their hold. In the first phase of its attack, Fifth Army had fought its way into the Bernhardt Line.

In the next phase Clark hoped to open the mile-wide valley between Monte Sammucro and Monte Lungo through which ran Highway 6. Here, situated a little to the north of the Highway was the village of San Pietro Infine. Its sturdy stone buildings with thick walls and terraced levels ascending the slope of Monte Sammucro offered an immensely strong and inaccessible defensive position. The 29th Panzer Grenadier Division held this sector with a regiment deployed on Monte Sammucro and another on Monte Lungo. A battalion was positioned in San Pietro and turned it into a minor fortress, with weapons emplacements amid the buildings and terraces, possessing good observation over Highway 6 and Monte Lungo. Only cart tracks and trails over Monte Sammucro offered a means of breaking into the village. The defence of San Pietro was insisted upon by the OKW and by Hitler himself, overruling Kesselring's inclination to spare Tenth Army's infantry. Like Alexander, Kesselring was only too aware of the need to conserve hard-to-replace troops for future battles.

II Corps could obtain little firm data on the defences at San Pietro despite active patrolling. The plan was for an attack using two battalions of the 36th Division's 143rd Infantry to secure Monte Sammucro and take San Pietro from the rear. The attached 3rd Ranger Battalion would attack to clear high ground to the east of Monte Sammucro and keep in touch with the VI Corps, which was pressing forward into the high ground still farther north to draw German reserves away from the II Corps front. The Italian 1st Motorized Group were to take Monte Lungo, and II Corps went to considerable trouble to ensure that the first Italian attack against the Germans would be successful: they laid on heavy fire support.

Late on 7 December three battalions of the 143rd Infantry and the Rangers struck at the Monte Sammucro heights in a two-pronged attack. On the northern slopes good progress was made, and by the following morning the crest was in American hands. This was only the start of hard fighting, however, as the German 71st Grenadier Regiment counter-attacked vigorously over the next four days. On the southern slopes of Sammucro and against San Pietro, no progress could be made at all. The 2nd Battalion of the 143rd Infantry made only 400 yards before running into a hail of German artillery, mortar and machine-gun fire. Allied guns pounded San Pietro into rubble, and further attacks were made, all to no avail; the village was impregnable.

The Italian attack on Monte Lungo on 7 December may have been 'blown' the night before it was launched by some of its soldiers with old scores to settle crawling out towards German positions to taunt their occupants with threats of what was in store for them. Be that as it may, and despite its fire support from the American guns, the Italian attack ran into concentrated German machine-gun and mortar fire and was shattered. Just like the Livorno Division at Gela in Sicily, the Italians attacked in a compact mass formation and suffered accordingly – 376 casualties. Their cohesion shattered, after several more unsuccessful attempts to get forward, the Italians fell back in the afternoon upon the American positions.

Monte Sammucro and San Pietro began to take an unacceptably heavy toll of the American infantry, and by 10 December the 1st Battalion of the 143rd Infantry was down to 340 men, or half strength. Clark had few reserves but attached to II Corps the 504th Parachute Infantry. He also wanted tanks employed to assist the infantry in cracking the San Pietro position: although the terrain was known to be far from suitable for armour, the rising infantry casualties made it worth the attempt. On 15 December an attack went in supported by sixteen Shermans, with a British Valentine bridge-laying tank obtained from X Corps to help them negoti-ate the ground. There followed two more days of fighting, and this time the American infantry broke into San Pietro and cleared some strongpoints with bayonet and grenade, though were driven out again by counterattack. Tank officers and engineers had worked hard to devise various, and in some cases ingenious, methods for the tanks to negotiate the terraces in order to support the infantry with their fire, but much of their effort proved in vain. It was a gallant try, but the terrain triumphed in the end. The single narrow road was mined, and the surrounding ground was either too sodden or too steeply terraced and enclosed for the tanks to manoeuvre, and they had little or no visibility. Vulnerable to German anti-tank weapons, twelve of the Shermans were destroyed or disabled.

The German hold on San Pietro was only loosened when on 16 December Monte Lungo fell to a surprise pincer attack from Monte Maggiore, and its loss threatened the battalion holding San Pietro with isolation. The American infantry were showing an increasing skill in the use of mountainous terrain learnt through hard experience, levering open defences that were impervious to direct attack. To the north the US VI Corps had dented the positions held by the German 44th Infantry Division, brought down to replace the 26th Panzer Division's units sent to the Sangro, and farther north still the 2nd Moroccan Division threatened the positions of the German 305th Infantry Division between Monte La Rocca and Monte Pantano. The Moroccans were proving skilled mountain fighters, and the rate at which they could move through the high terrain was proving a surprise to their Allies as well as to the Germans. They were well placed to turn the north flank of XIV Panzer Corps. With Hitler's grudging sanction, Kesselring allowed Tenth Army to pull back the 29th Panzer Grenadier and 44th Infantry Divisions.

On 17 December, American patrols found San Pietro suspiciously and uncannily silent. The Germans had gone. The fighting at San Pietro had cost the 36th Division 1,200 casualties, including about 150 killed, over 800 wounded and some 250 missing. The 504th Parachute Infantry had taken 277 casualties, including 50 killed.[7] It was the hardest battle for a strongpoint in mountain terrain experienced since the 1st Division's battle at Troina in Sicily, and the Allied armies could not afford many like it. San Pietro, like Troina, held a key position within a defence zone, but there were many such potential strongpoints ahead where the Germans might, with an investment of little more than a battalion, draw the teeth of an

Allied brigade or even a division, especially if attacked directly. As both Troina and San Pietro indicated, such positions could be outflanked and pinched out, and certainly Allied troops were becoming more mountain-adept and capable of such methods, but they still involved hard fighting in arduous terrain. Battles such as Fifth Army had fought along its front, in which infantry companies were drained away to achieve gains that could be measured in yards, and in which a colossal expenditure of artillery ammunition was needed for them to be able to do it, had not been experienced since the First World War. They cost men, they cost time, and the Allied armies could spare neither.

On 18 December, a bitterly disappointed Clark signalled Alexander, to reluctantly recommend the cancellation of 'Shingle'; there was not the least chance of his Fifth Army being in a position to support the amphibious outflanking move before the assault shipping deadline of 15 January. Three days later Alexander concurred. Fifth Army had pushed the Germans out of the Bernhardt Line, but in so doing had exhausted itself. There was no possibility of an immediate break in to the Liri Valley. In between stood the Gustav Line, to which the Bernhardt Line had been only the outer bastion, and to which the XIV Panzer Corps was falling back.

On the Adriatic flank Montgomery had replaced the tired 78th Division as the spearhead in his drive along the coast with the 1st Canadian Division. While the 8th Indian Division and the 2nd New Zealand Division battered against stubborn German positions inland of the coast at the hilltop village of Orsogna and along the River Riccio, the Canadians made an assault crossing of the River Moro on 8 December. Clearing the line of the Moro and the lateral road held by the 90th Panzer Grenadier Division, rushed down from the Florence area to stop them, took twelve days of intensive fighting, through ground cut by gullies and ridges. The Canadians kept up the offensive pressure throughout, despite the rain and mud and a spirited German defence in which the 90th Panzer Grenadier Division spent itself in heavy counterattacks. For both sides casualties were heavy. By 20 December the Canadians had broken the 90th Panzer Grenadier Division to the extent that units of the 1st Parachute Division had to be brought in to stiffen the German line. Canadian patrols reached the port town of Ortona, and here the nature of the battle changed.

Instead of falling back to the next river line as expected, the Germans decided to stand and fight in Ortona, entrusting its defence to the 3rd Parachute Regiment and, specifically in the town itself, its 2nd Battalion. For the first time Allied troops were to come up against an urban area deliberately turned into a defensive zone in which to fight a prolonged battle. In the USSR the Germans had become proficient at such fighting, and the paratroops and engineers turned Ortona into a hornets' nest of mutually-supporting strongpoints with good fields of fire. Buildings were demolished to block streets, the rubble strewn with mines and booby-traps; other buildings were turned into strong defensive positions from which machine-guns and anti-tank guns covered all approaches, and some buildings were rigged with explosives ready to be detonated once they were occupied by the attackers. A labyrinth of tunnels and concealed holes deliberately made in the interconnecting walls of buildings through which men could crawl enabled the paratroops to conduct a form of tactical movement in the battle and to effect reliefs and keep their strongpoints supplied.

By the time the 2nd Canadian Infantry Brigade had fought its way through Ortona to the northern outskirts of the town on 28 December its troops were the Allied Armies' street fighting experts. They had learned very fast and had cleared the paratroops out in a week of hard fighting that cost them 275 casualties, including 104 killed. They had cleared Ortona building by building with the help of supporting tanks and anti-tank guns and, in the close-quarter fighting, efficient use of their own infantry weapons. They had developed the necessary tactical methods to clear an urban area. The German paratroops pulled back to the River Riccio some two miles north of the town, but they left the bodies of at least 100 of their comrades in the rubble of Ortona for the Canadians to find.[8]

The battle for Ortona marked the end of Eighth Army's offensive, as winter weather now compelled a halt. Montgomery himself felt that enough was enough: to attempt to continue the offensive would use up resources that would be better conserved for the following spring, when the weather would change sides and start to favour the Allies. Montgomery had never been a believer in the Italian Campaign, and he deplored the situation in which the Allied armies now found themselves. Nor was he prepared to waste lives; there was no chance of an imminent breakthrough to Rome from the Adriatic flank and he told Alexander so. Alexander realized this well enough but still could not allow a relaxing of pressure along the entire front. The situation had changed, and there was a new urgency in the imperative to attack. He instructed Eighth Army to do as much as it could short of a major offensive to keep LXXVI Panzer Corps sufficiently under pressure to prevent it shifting forces to Clark's front.

It would do so with a new commander, for Montgomery, appointed as land forces commander for 'Overlord', prepared to leave for England. At the end of December he made his farewell to the Army with which his name would always be associated. General Oliver Leese succeeded him. Eisenhower, too, was preparing to leave the Mediterranean to become the Supreme Commander for the cross-Channel operation he had championed so strongly in 1942. General Sir Henry Maitland Wilson would succeed him as Allied Supreme Commander in the Mediterranean. To Alexander was left the Italian Campaign. As its Commander-in-Chief, he faced the hard tasks of achieving in Italy whatever victory could be obtained there with the resources likely to be made available to him, and of providing the maximum possible assistance to the operation that would firmly relegate his theatre to second place: 'Overlord'. For just a few months more his would still be the only Anglo-American land theatre against the Germans. And, largely through Churchill's intervention, there was a chance, albeit a slender one, that the Allies might unlock the Gustav Line and open the door to Rome before 'Overlord' occurred.

13

THE GUSTAV LINE

Breaking the Gustav Line

'The hard fighting of recent months had convinced me that the Allies' reckless expenditure of troops must conceal some ulterior objective.' — Kesselring.[1]

The German Tenth Army's holding of the Gustav Line south of Rome was contingent upon there being no Allied seaborne landing to unhinge it from the rear. Kesselring had accepted this risk, and had induced Hitler to accept it too, but he could never disregard it. While his subordinate commanders could permit themselves to become focused on their immediate battlefronts, Kesselring, figuratively speaking, had always to keep glancing over his shoulder and make some provision to counter the amphibious threat. There was little firm intelligence available to him. The Luftwaffe's air reconnaissance effort had tailed off and interpretations offered to him by the Abwehr were contradictory. On the one hand an Allied landing was considered unlikely; but on the other there were reports of Allied shipping concentrations in southern Italian ports that certainly indicated a landing to be a feasible option. As 1943 turned into 1944, Kesselring tried to view the situation in Italy as Alexander must see it. As he did so, he became increasingly convinced that Alexander could not allow his armies to edge forward by battering away at the German defences in head-on attacks for much longer. He would have to put an end to this by attempting a landing behind the Gustav Line. The landing would almost certainly occur within striking distance of Rome, and would be coordinated with an offensive from the south.

Kesselring's nervousness, his 'invasion-phobia' as he called it, was militarily well-founded. But Alexander's hands were tied and his options limited by the Allied lack of assault shipping and by the predominance of 'Overlord' and its timetable. These were as decisive for Kesselring's ability to hold the Gustav Line as the bravery of his soldiers, the terrain and the weather – perhaps even more so. As Kesselring's conviction grew that the Allies were about to spring at him from the sea, Alexander was indeed preparing such an operation. But it was far short of what he would have liked – his amphibious outflanking move, upon which the fate of his campaign would depend, was to be mounted on the by now usual shoestring of resources.

Churchill had visited Eisenhower in Carthage on return from 'Sextant' and had fallen seriously ill with pneumonia, his condition aggravated by overwork and exhaustion. While recovering in Carthage he gave thought to the unsatisfactory situation in Italy; the armies unable to get forward and the real possibility that 'Overlord' and 'Anvil' would eventually deprive Alexander of the forces he needed to gain Rome and inflict a major defeat upon the Germans. Churchill had fought too long and too hard for the Italian campaign to accept this state of affairs lightly. 'In no case can we sacrifice Rome for the Riviera,' he telegraphed the British Chiefs of Staff on 23 December, 'We must have both.'[2] On Christmas Day he attended a conference of Allied Mediterranean Commanders-in-Chief: Eisenhower, Maitland Wilson; Alexander, Tedder and Admiral Sir John Cunningham (who had succeeded his cousin Sir Andrew Cunningham as Naval Commander-in-Chief in October on the latter's appointment as First Sea Lord). It was by way of being a 'hand-over' conference (with Eisenhower soon to depart to England) but the purpose was also to discuss the 'Shingle' concept and the possibility of increasing its landing force from a single division to a corps operation, with an initial landing by two divisions. All were agreed on the desirability of loosening the deadlock and dealing the Germans a blow in Italy. Churchill was particularly keen on the idea, as he put it, of hurling a 'wild-cat' on to the shore behind the German defensive line that would thrash about and cause havoc and alarm across their lines of communication and induce a withdrawal from the Gustav Line.

Eisenhower, while in favour, had reservations about the size of the landing force, believing that it would have to be of 'several strong divisions' if it were to achieve anything. Alexander too was concerned on this score, but in general there was a good deal of optimism that a landing operation appropriately timed with an offensive from the south against the Gustav Line would succeed in shaking the Germans out of their otherwise near-impregnable positions. The problem remained landing craft, particularly the larger LSTs. A two-division lift required 88 vessels, and, while there were 104 in the Mediterranean, 68 of these were due to leave in the middle of January for Britain. More assault craft were beginning their journey from the Indian Ocean to Europe and would arrive in the Mediterranean with time to assist in the support of a landing, but the timeframe was narrow.

Churchill put the case to Roosevelt, requesting his agreement to a three-week extension of the time that assault craft could remain in the theatre, to enable a landing on or about 20 January. Various measures, such as reductions in English Channel training for their crews and necessary refitting being carried out in Mediterranean rather than in British yards, would make up the three weeks. As Churchill suspected, there was usually some slack in administrative schedules that, with vigour and will, could be tightened. 'If this opportunity is not grasped,' Churchill told Roosevelt, 'we may expect the ruin of the Mediterranean campaign of 1944.' Churchill's case was a strong one, and it was in no one's interest, except Hitler's, to see the Italian campaign drag on in its present state in the months before 'Overlord', or for the Allies to begin their major operations in France while, as Churchill put it, 'leaving a vast half finished job' behind them. On 28 December, Churchill received Roosevelt's reply agreeing to the extension providing that the 'Overlord' timetable was unaffected. Churchill was to comment with some bitterness that had he asked for a three-division lift he would have got nothing at all.[3]

The planning of military operations can sometimes be imbued with pessimism and over-insured against perceived risks to the point of stultification, as Churchill had feared was happening to the planning of 'Husky' in the previous April. On the other hand they can also be under-insured, conceived on a high of optimism when a proposed operation appears to provide the answer to an otherwise insoluble strategic and operational impasse – consequently its risks may be too little regarded in a pervading atmosphere of renewed hope and relief that few are prepared to challenge seriously and against which dissenting voices can make no impression. There was much that was altogether wrong about the landing scheme the Allies now embraced for the campaign in Italy, a sense of grasping at straws. It seems that the commanders involved were suppressing considerable reservations at the time.

They must have been, for even with the shipping extension 'Shingle' would land just two divisions well beyond the German front, with enough shipping to sustain them for only eight days in the confident expectation that by then it would have shaken the Germans out of the Gustav Line and linked up with the main body of Fifth Army. Yet the Salerno experience of the previous September ought to have suggested something about German reaction capability against an amphibious landing, especially one of limited strength, and they had the evidence of the Bernhardt Line battles to indicate Fifth Army's likely rate of advance against the Gustav Line. To say that they were optimistic is an understatement. It was unfortunate, perhaps even tragic, that the one commander who needed to have been at that Carthage conference was not present – Clark, the Army Commander who had held on to the Salerno beachhead 'by his fingernails' in September, whose Army had just been pushed to the limits and beyond in overcoming the mountain strongholds of the Bernhardt Line, and to whom would be entrusted both the landing operation behind the Gustav Line and the simultaneous frontal attack upon it. Had Clark been at Carthage, his must have been the most authoritative voice on the feasibility of what was proposed for his Army, and he above all was the commander who needed to hear at first hand from Churchill the strategic level view of precisely what the operation was intended to achieve.

Churchill deplored the necessary haste and so did every other senior Allied commander, but none of them could do anything about it. The Allies had to move very fast even within the new shipping timeframe. This affected planning, and General Sir William Jackson has set this challenge in the wider context of the experience of Mediterranean amphibious operations thus far: 'Husky planning had taken five months, Avalanche six weeks, and now the enlarged Shingle had to be completed in three weeks.'[4] This was not enough. One consequence, and a fatal one, was that there were too many misconceptions about the operation. At Carthage on Christmas Day the idea was mooted of a landing to the north of the Tiber, in fact of an operation involving more than one landing, but Alexander left the conference convinced that this had been completely ruled out and that what had been agreed was an enlarged 'Shingle', which meant a landing concentrated – if a two-division landing could be called that – at Anzio and

Nettuno. Yet, on 4 January, Churchill, who by then had moved to Marrakech to recuperate, signalled Alexander to query why planning was going ahead for what he saw as 'a much less ambitious movement' and 'certainly a different one' from what he had expected. He was still thinking of landings to the north and south of the Tiber.[5]

Alexander's reply emphasized the importance of the landing threatening XIV Panzer Corps' lines of communication at the same time as it was attacked frontally by Fifth Army. The best objective was therefore the Alban Hills (Colli Laziali) to the south-east of Rome and situated between Highways 6 and 7 running up from Naples to the capital, and which the landing force could threaten to cut. The best beaches leading to a good road inland to this objective were at Anzio–Nettuno. The landing threat had to be close enough to threaten XIV Panzer Corps, and close enough for an early link up with Fifth Army. Alexander had no intention of weakening his already meagre 'Shingle' force by further dispersing its strength by another landing north of the Tiber, which would also complicate his shipping and maintenance problems.

In early January concern grew at the weakness of the 'Shingle' force being just two divisions, though two more, including the US 1st Armored Division, were earmarked to follow-up, and, more realistically, it was acknowledged that shipping would have to be available to sustain the landing force for a period likely to be longer than eight days. The weakness of the force led to a dilemma that no Allied commander could easily solve, and to still greater divergence between concept and reality. In his concept of a 'wild cat' Churchill envisaged the landing force behaving very aggressively, to 'tear out the bowels of the Boche' as he would put it. As a concept this made sense, because for a weak landing force to alarm the Germans out of the Gustav Line would require considerable bluff, and for that to succeed the landing force would have to raise as much havoc as possible both to mask its own weakness and to cause exaggerated reports of its strength and intentions to reach the German command. It would have to do this quickly, as the initial shock and surprise effect of the landings upon the Germans would have to be maintained. A momentum would need to be built up from which they could not recover their balance. Only in this way could the Allied command hope to panic Kesselring into believing that the one eventuality he had reason to fear above all others was upon him, thereby inducing him to order a withdrawal from the Gustav Line to avoid the entrapment of XIV Panzer Corps. The 'wild cat' concept therefore implied that the landing force must go 'all-or-nothing' and operate in a calculatedly reckless manner. It implied the deliberate acceptance of immense risk, gambling with the possible destruction of the landing force in the event of the 'bluff' not succeeding, even to the point of what could have been viewed in normal circumstances as military irresponsibility. The landing force could not afford, if the 'wild cat' concept were to succeed, to spend priceless time in consolidation and securing its beachhead before striking inland.

Kesselring's later assertion in his memoirs that the Allies 'had missed a uniquely favourable chance of capturing Rome and of opening the door on the Garigliano front' suggests his own acknowledgement that he might have been bluffed by Churchill's 'wild cat'.[6] Whether this was a candid admission based on a professional military assessment of his own situation and likely reaction at the time, or whether he was retrospectively criticizing the Allies' military performance while doing less than justice to his own qualities as a commander, we cannot know. Churchill's 'wild cat' might have worked. But to do so it would have required every commander involved from Alexander and Clark downwards to sign up to, and be prepared to implement, irrespective of the risk, what amounted to a 'death or glory' operation. It is unlikely that unequivocally presented with this reality they would have been prepared to hazard their soldiers in such a way. The Rangers and Commandos, airborne troops and special raiding forces, were trained for bold and exceptionally hazardous operations, and were attuned to high levels of risk, but to convince Kesselring that a major full-scale invasion had occurred behind the Gustav Line would have been beyond their scope. Far more than an amphibious raiding feint was needed; the task required conventional infantry and armoured formations in what must obviously be a fully prepared and large-scale landing. And to constitute a 'wild cat' once ashore these formations would have to be used in anything but a conventional manner.

This in itself meant that there was little chance of Churchill's 'wild cat' ever being implemented. Instead what Alexander and Clark prepared to implement in January 1944 was 'Shingle', and they wrestled with its principal dilemma in the context of an orthodox amphibious landing operation: how an insufficiently strong landing force could balance the need to establish a secure beachhead against the risk of German counterattack, with the need to strike inland aggressively. In fact, it could not be balanced at all. Approached in this way, there was no solution except either the complete negation of the 'wild cat' concept or the complete disregard of sound amphibious landing experience and procedures. The latter appears never to have been seriously considered. Alexander imagined 'Shingle' in terms of a compromise, probably the best possible under the circumstances: the consolidation of the beachhead by the two assault divisions and the creation of a reserve for contingencies. This would be followed by an advance from the beachhead spearheaded by a 'mobile hard-hitting force' consisting of one or two Regimental Combat Teams supported by tanks and self-propelled artillery stripped for maximum mobility. But he did not envisage this force even being loaded for the beachhead until D+3.[7] The initial landing would be by two infantry divisions, which needed to carve out and establish the beachhead, the necessary priority for such an operation – but no 'wild cat'.

On 12 January Alexander issued his Operational Instruction, outlining the object of the landing as 'cutting the enemy lines of communication and threatening the rear of the German XIV Corps'. He did not, however, forcibly impress upon Clark a requirement for the landing force to strike out aggressively from its beachhead as an urgent priority. The fact of the landing and the creation of a beachhead had to suffice as the immediate threat to the rear of the Gustav Line until the landing force was ready to strike out from a secure beachhead. This risked loss of momentum, the dissipation of shock and surprise – and giving the German command time to take stock of the threat and react to it. Clark followed this with his own instruction, which was for the landing force to 'seize and secure a beachhead in the vicinity of Anzio'. From there it was to advance to the Alban Hills, but the term 'secure' firmly fixed its priorities. At Salerno, Clark had landed initially with three divisions on a two-corps front, and it had very nearly been not enough. Eighth Army had arrived to threaten the Germans but could never have reached Salerno in time to save the beachhead, and it had not had to fight its way through anything like the Gustav Line.

Looked at in this light, 'Shingle' was far more hazardous. Ironically, their awareness of German reaction capability gained through the Salerno experience ensured that Alexander and Clark, in emphasizing the need to secure the Anzio beachhead, would allow the Germans sufficient time and opportunity to react to 'Shingle' in much the same way. They could try to ensure their beachhead but could do so only at the likely cost of not achieving the immediate purpose of the operation with which they had been entrusted.

The Allies had an accurate intelligence picture of German dispositions in Italy and could gauge in what strength and in what time they could react. It was reckoned that a composite force of various units including some tanks, but equivalent to at most two divisions, could be in action against the landing force by D+3. There was every chance of the initial landing achieving surprise and meeting little opposition.[8] The longer-term German reaction, their ability to bring forces from northern Italy against the beachhead, had received little detailed study. There was hardly time for it, but in any case this eventuality was not intended to arise. The collapse of the Gustav Line and an early link-up with Fifth Army would make it irrelevant. But here too was an uncomfortable dilemma. An aggressive landing force stood more chance of shaking the Gustav Line and, as intended, enabling the breakthrough of Fifth Army and an early link up. It would also disrupt and confuse any German attempt to concentrate against the beachhead. The problem was that it stood more chance of being destroyed itself. On the other hand, an inert landing force which spent the first critical days consolidating its beachhead, might not shake the Gustav Line at all, thereby ensuring and prolonging its own isolation from Fifth Army. In this case the Germans might well have the time and opportunity to concentrate considerable strength against it. The problem was a self-fulfilling dilemma; in trying to insure against a strong German reaction to the beachhead, the Allies were actually increasing the likelihood of the Germans being able to make such a reaction.

'Shingle' was scheduled for 22 January 1944, and the task was assigned to the US VI Corps under General John P. Lucas. Lucas had replaced General Dawley as the corps commander after the latter had shown signs of breaking down under the strain of the Salerno battle.

In the face of Allied air sieperiority, the Germans in Italy fought without the benefit of much air support. Nevertheless, the terrain and winter weather did much to offset this disadvantage by providing the Germans with strong defensive positions difficult to locate and attack from the air, and by denying the Allies good flying weather and visibility. The Germans also invested heavily in anti-aircraft firepower to protect their ground formations and positions from air attack. Taken in November 1943, this photograph shows a multiple 20mm anti-aircraft gun, capable of a high rate of fire, positioned in the snow-covered hills near Monte Camino in the Bernhardt Line. These weapons were also frequently used to engage ground targets in support of German infantry. In this instance, and despite the winter weather conditions, the crew are clearly keeping a sharp watch for approaching Allied aircraft. (IWM MH 6320)

Above: A conference of Allied commanders aboard the Headquarters Ship HMS *Bulolo* during Operation 'Shingle', the Allied landings at Anzio. On the left is Rear Admiral Thomas Troubridge, the Naval Task Force Commander, and on the right is Major General W. R. C. Penney, commanding the British 1st Infantry Division. In the centre is one of military history's most unfortunate commanders, Major General John P. Lucas, commanding VI Corps and to whom 'Shingle' had been entrusted. As this photograph suggests, Lucas was feeling the strain of both having commanded his corps through the hard Bernhardt Line fighting and his concerns over 'Shingle'. Fifty-four years old in 1944, he looks older. (IWM NA 11049)

Opposite page: This photograph was taken at Carthage after Prime Minister Winston Churchill, recuperating from a bout of pneumonia, had given Christmas Day lunch to a distinguished party of visitors, 25 December 1943. The Prime Minister appears to be wearing his padded silk dressing gown decorated with blue and gold Chinese dragons. In the front are General Eisenhower, soon to leave the Mediterranean to become the Allied Supreme Commander for 'Overlord', Churchill, and General Sir Henry Maitland Wilson, soon to replace Eisenhower as Allied Commander-in-Chief in the Mediterranean. Among those in the background can be seen Air Chief Marshal Sir Arthur Tedder (second from left), Admiral Sir John Cunningham (behind Eisenhower's right shoulder), General Sir Harold Alexander (between Eisenhower and Churchill) and, at far right, Eisenhower's Chief of Staff General Walter Beddell Smith. At a conference held that morning, Churchill had argued forcibly for Operation 'Shingle', an amphibious landing behind the German Gustav Line at Anzio, to unlock the stalemate in Italy. (IWM NA 10075)

Above: One of the most famous war photographs – the ruined shell of the monastery at Monte Cassino following the controversial Allied bombing in February 1944. The photograph indicates the immensely strong construction of the monastery, and the extent to which its ruins provided the German defenders with a fortress following the Allied bombing. (IWM NA 15141)

Opposite page, top: This photograph shows Field Marshal Albert Kesselring (second from right), the highly capable German Commander-in-Chief in Italy. Kesselring's optimism and his conviction that the Allies could be successfully held south of Rome influenced Hitler's decision to alter his planned strategy in Italy of withdrawal to the north, and Hitler entrusted the campaign in Italy to his command. Kesselring conducted a model defensive campaign in Italy; his command grip was firm throughout, and the Allies could never panic him. On the right of the photograph is Field Marshal Wolfram von Richthofen, the commander of the Luftwaffe's 2nd Air Fleet (Luftflotte 2). The photograph was taken at a forward command post during the fighting at Anzio-Nettuno. (IWM HU 55161)

Opposite page, bottom: A photograph from the Anzio beachhead. British soldiers take cover in a shallow trench from German shelling during the breakout. The photograph indicates typical beachhead terrain. (IWM NA 153060

Above: Mud was a formidable enemy to Allied soldiers in Italy once winter arrived, bogging down vehicles and equipment and making unsurfaced roads and tracks unusable. Movement and supply suffered accordingly. Here the unfortunate crew of a jeep try to dig their vehicle out of the mud, a photograph taken in the Anzio beachhead in January 1944. (IWM NA 11314)

Opposite page, top: A fine depiction of the Gothic Line terrain in a photograph taken near Mondaino on 6 September 1944. A Priest 105mm self-propelled gun negotiates an awkward hairpin bend on a mountain road. The dust thrown up by its movement might well have attracted the attention of a German artillery observer in the hills and drawn fire. Priest was the British name for the US M-7 Howitzer Motor Carriage, the principal artillery equipment of US Armored Divisions and which were also widely used by British formations where they replaced the Bishop. (IWM NA 18392)

Right: Winter conditions in Italy are depicted in this photograph of a British 5.5-inch gun of the 178th Medium Regiment, in action on Christmas Eve, 24 December 1944. (IWM NA 21006)

The end in Italy: Lieutenant General von Senger und Etterlin, the commander of the German XIV Panzer Corps, is received by General Mark Clark, commanding the Allied armies in Italy, ieutenant General Richard McCreery, commanding British Eighth Army, and Lieutenant General Lucian K. Truscott, commanding the US Fifth Army, at 15th Army Group Headquarters. He was there to receive instructions regarding the unconditional surrender of German forces in Italy and West Austria. (IWM NA 24791)

Subsequently Lucas had taken the corps through the advance from Salerno and the Bernhardt Line battles, and it was not relieved in the Fifth Army line until 9 January, less than a fortnight before it was due to land at Anzio. There was a further complication. Churchill and Alexander had been concerned at the prospect of an American force carrying the risk of 'Shingle' alone, and it was decided that one British and one American division should form the landing force. Apart from the time factor, this was administratively awkward and a potential obstacle to a smooth-functioning operation in which time was critical. Eisenhower had realized this and, before leaving the Mediterranean, had done his best to reassure Alexander that the operation and its requirements must come before all other considerations. He signalled him that he need not allow political concerns to stand in the way of his military judgement, whether the concern was that of an all-American corps being hazarded by a British Commander-in-Chief, or whether selection of an all-British corps might be viewed by some as a British attempt to ensure that their troops were the first to enter Rome. He must feel able to use the troops best fitted for the task, unburdened by such worries.[9] For evidence of Eisenhower's stature as an Allied Supreme Commander one need look no further than this signal. In the event, however, Alexander decided that the risks must be shared. The US 3rd and British 1st Infantry Divisions, the latter from Eighth Army, would constitute the initial landing force.

Alexander and Clark between them had translated Churchill's 'wild cat' into 'Shingle', and an orthodox and, perhaps more feasible and more realistic, amphibious landing operation. But, in relying upon the initial fact of a landing followed by a delayed offensive action to have an effect on the German command, they had also made the purpose of the operation far more questionable, especially to those charged with carrying it out. Uncertainty about 'Shingle' was felt strongly at VI Corps. 'If this is to be a "forlorn hope" or a "suicide sashay" then all I want to know is that fact,' wrote Major General Lucian Truscott, commanding the US 3rd Division, to the Fifth Army Chief of Staff Major General Alfred M. Gruenther as late as 18 January, adding, 'If so, I'm positive that there is no outfit in the world that can do it better than me – even though I reserve [the] right (personally) to believe we might deserve a better fate.'[10]

The corps commander, Lucas, was incapable of addressing such concerns or of enthusing and motivating his command. He was by no means a dynamic leader, nor was he fresh after the Bernhardt Line battles, but there was a deeper problem to entrusting 'Shingle' to him: he had no enthusiasm or motivation to impart. If ever a commander embarked upon an operation in which he had absolutely no faith at all it was Lucas. He was sunk in gloom and deeply pessimistic about the enterprise, and he had little confidence in the Allied command team that had foisted 'Shingle' upon him. To him, 'Shingle' was too much like Gallipoli with, he noted, 'the same amateur ... still on the coach's bench'. Encouragement from Alexander and Clark left him unmoved, 'They will end up by putting me ashore with inadequate forces and get me in a serious jam. Then, who will take the blame?' he confided to his diary on 14 January.[11] Four days later he was still further depressed when the one amphibious rehearsal that time allowed him, held off Naples, proved a complete shambles. Most troops turned up on the wrong beaches. Release errors by the naval forces, caused partly by the haste with which everything was being put together and exacerbated by worsening weather, resulted in a considerable amount of the 3rd Division's vital equipment including 43 DUKWs and nineteen 105mm guns ending up at the bottom of the sea. Shortfalls had to be made up from Fifth Army's formations.

Having just fought through the Bernhardt Line, Lucas had good reason to doubt assurances that Fifth Army would get through the Gustav Line quickly to reach his beachhead, and the optimism of his senior commanders baffled him. Suspecting they might have access to intelligence on the German situation and intentions that he did not, he was still at a loss to understand why, if the Germans really were about to crack, there was not a greater investment in his force. Convinced he was too weak to achieve anything whatever the circumstances, he determined to take no chances. Had Alexander and Clark intended to act according to Churchill's 'wildcat' concept they could never have left Lucas in command of the landing force. Almost certainly they would not have done so. They would have had to have given very serious thought indeed to the commander of such an operation. On the other hand, as a highly competent and steady corps commander who could be relied upon to establish his force ashore, Lucas was sound, and there would have appeared no prior necessity to remove him from his corps. Nevertheless, and despite their own emphasis upon a secure beachhead, both Alexander and Clark still expected their corps commander to attack out from the beachhead when the time was opportune. In this Lucas would disappoint them.

In what he referred to as the 'Battle for Rome', Alexander intended Fifth Army to attack the Gustav Line several days before 'Shingle' went in, to draw Kesselring's reserves south and away from the Anzio area. Once fully committed there, 'Shingle' would then threaten the rear of the Gustav Line. Thus the main body of Fifth Army would attack to facilitate 'Shingle', which would in turn enable the breaking of the Gustav Line. On the Fifth Army front fighting had continued, as the 'Shingle' timetable permitted no pause or redeployment from the Bernhardt Line offensive – Fifth Army had to keep attacking. Clark intended to pin XIV Panzer Corps and draw in its reserves by pressure all along its front. VI Corps had been replaced by the French Expeditionary Corps under General Alphonse Juin, with the 2nd Moroccan Division and now also the 3rd Tunisian Division. They were to turn XIV Panzer Corps' northern flank by pushing towards Atina to the north of Cassino and constituted the most serious mountain-fighting threat to the German defences.

The British X Corps would make an assault crossing of the Garigliano with the 5th Division at the coast, brought over from Eighth Army to replace the 'Overlord'-bound 7th Armoured, and the 56th Division. These were to turn XIV Panzer Corps' southern flank. With the German line fully stretched and with reserves pulled in to hold its flanks, the main Fifth Army punch would go in against the centre of the German line. The British 46th Division would cross the Rapido near the village of San Ambroglio to cover the left flank of the principal attack force, the US II Corps, which would make an assault crossing of the River Rapido near the village of San Angelo. This task fell to the US 36th Division; once they had broken the German line there, Clark intended to exploit to the Liri Valley with the US 1st Armored Division to turn the German defences in the Cassino area from the south-west. The US 34th Division would support by putting pressure on the Germans in the area of Cassino town. Fifth Army's attack on the Gustav Line was scheduled for 17 January.

Whenever the weather allowed, the Mediterranean Allied Air Forces, now under the command of General Ira C. Eaker following Tedder's departure to serve as Eisenhower's Deputy for 'Overlord', were out in strength to prepare for and support the Fifth Army effort. Bombers, including those of the strategic air forces, struck at German communications feeding Tenth Army and the arteries of movement upon which a German reaction against the beachhead would depend. Marshalling yards and rail lines as well as road choke-points were targeted. The US XII Air Support Command attacked targets in the battle area, and its fighter-bombers conducted offensive sweeps beyond. In the six days leading to the opening of the Fifth Army attack the Allied bombers made some 1,500 sorties against which the Luftwaffe, its airfields also heavily under pressure, could answer with only some 200 sorties. On 20 January 1944 it had less than 300 operational aircraft, compared with the 2,700 or so operational combat aircraft under Eaker's command. While the Allied air onslaught disrupted German movement across central and much of northern Italy, the time of year, with shorter hours of daylight and the likelihood of poor flying weather, meant that the Allied air forces could give no assurances of stopping German movement at critical periods or preventing a build-up against the 'Shingle' beachhead. Moreover, the effect of air attack against well constructed and concealed German positions in the mountains of the Gustav Line was also limited. Air power could support, but could not decide, the forthcoming battle.

The battle that was about to start would be fought – for the most part – by tired armies, Allied and German alike. For both Fifth Army and XIV Panzer Corps there would be little margin in that most critical of assets: infantry. Divisions on both sides were not at full strength following weeks of heavy fighting. Kesselring, von Vietinghoff and, at XIV Panzer Corps itself, von Senger, all faced the threat of an Allied attack stretching the German defence to the point at which it would break. There was not much elasticity and few reserves. Kesselring had thirteen divisions in central Italy under Tenth Army, and eight in the north, three of which were still forming. As Kesselring was increasingly aware, a number of divisions had to be kept in the north always to secure communications against the increasing Italian anti-Fascist resistance and partisan activity. Indeed, in the north a separate, vicious and quite distinct struggle was under way that would affect German ability to wage the campaign in central Italy against the Allies. Behind the XIV Panzer Corps sector to the south of Rome, Kesselring held back just two divisions as his insurance against the Allied amphibious landing he felt sure must soon occur. These were the veteran 29th Panzer Grenadier Division and the 90th Panzer Grenadier Division, recovering and rebuilding after its mauling along the Moro by Eighth Army's Canadians. They were under the headquarters of I Parachute Corps near Rome. Two divisions were not much insurance, but if used quickly enough against a landing they might be enough to contain it, as the 16th Panzer Division had at Salerno.

Alexander had some twenty divisions in Italy, twelve of them confronting the Gustav Line and three earmarked for 'Shingle'. He and Clark faced the risk that, in the mountains of the Gustav Line, Fifth Army's divisions would become so weakened by losses that they would be incapable of exploiting their gains and turning break-in into break-*through*. The generation of commanders like Alexander, who as young men had experienced 1914–18, were haunted by a familiar nightmare – wholesale waste of life for insignificant territorial gain. But however determined they were to avoid its repetition, attacking strong mountain positions threatened to wear out divisions quickly through casualties and sheer exhaustion, and without adequate reserves to reinforce success stalemate was far more likely than rapid progress. On the Adriatic front, Eighth Army could do little to help. Not only had Leese parted with the 1st Division for 'Shingle', but also the 5th Division for Fifth Army, and Alexander had taken the 2nd New Zealand Division as his 15th Army Group reserve for the hoped-for exploitation into the Liri Valley. Leese had nothing with which to attack and needed all his strength to maintain his front; at least General Traugott Herr's LXXVI Panzer Corps opposing him was no better off. The Battle for Rome would be decided on the western flank of the Apennines, where a great deal depended upon 'Shingle' and Lucas.

The northern flank of XIV Panzer Corps was causing von Senger and the German command some alarm, for Juin's North African hillsmen were proving hard to stop. The 44th Infantry Division could not hold them, and nor could the 5th Mountain Division, fed piecemeal into the battle without the opportunity to acclimatize itself to the terrain and winter conditions in the Italian mountains. Kesselring had high hopes of this division and was trying to get other German mountain formations released for Italy. But he had forgotten how armies the world over go about their business: the 5th Mountain Division had been sent to the Leningrad sector in Russia and had not seen a mountain for a long time. Despite its title, the 5th Mountain Division was no more suited to mountain warfare than a standard infantry division and it faltered under the cruel weather and the ferocity of the French colonial troops' attack. Casualties mounted, some battalions reduced to less than 200 effectives, and morale began to crack. On 13 January, the Division's commander, General Julius Ringel, reported that with losses in some units amounting to 80 per cent, his division was being destroyed.[12] Tenth Army had no choice but to sanction its partial withdrawal. Juin's troops now overlooked the valley of the Rapido and menaced Cassino from the north. But they too were exhausted and depleted, with nothing further to commit, and this as much as XIV Panzer Corps throwing in its reserves had forced a halt. As von Senger acknowledged, the battle at times had 'seemed to hang by a thread'.[13]

The Garigliano front then erupted, as on the evening of 17 January, X Corps crossed the river in a surprise offensive, the preparations of which had been successfully concealed. The 5th Division mounted an amphibious assault to support its crossing at the coast. One battalion in DUKWs was to land on the far bank of the river mouth behind the German lines. This came to pieces through poor coordination and bad luck, many of the DUKWs becoming lost and actually landing behind their own lines instead. Those troops who landed correctly found themselves in a large German minefield and under fire. The German 94th Infantry Division held an extended front along the river, with its main positions pulled back from the banks. It had compensated for its lack of strength by a liberal and quite concentrated sowing of anti-personnel mines covering the banks and approaches. There were so many mines that the 5th Division reported its area as a 'mine marsh', and its battalions, along with those of the 56th Division, suffered heavy casualties and delay because of them. Bridging was difficult under German artillery fire, well directed from the high ground beyond the river, and most supplies and supporting tanks and anti-tank guns had to be ferried across. But a bridgehead was established that the 94th Division was incapable of destroying. On 18 January, von Senger at the 94th Division's command post realized that his southern flank was in serious danger and that without some armour support it would not hold. If it collapsed his corps would be rolled up from the south, meaning the end of the Gustav Line. Having no more reserves, he contacted Kesselring to request the release of the 29th and 90th Panzer Grenadier Divisions to his corps, confident that if he had them in time he could counterattack and restore his front.

This was Kesselring's first moment of truth in the battle. If he allowed the XIV Panzer Corps front at the Garigliano to collapse for want of reserves, it would then be too late to restore it, and the Gustav Line would be turned. To prevent this he had to act fast and decisively – 'half-measures were useless,' he recalled. But it meant the commitment to the Gustav Line of his insurance against an Allied landing. Kesselring must have felt that he had no choice and ordered I Parachute Corps to restore the situation at the Garigliano, but it was a decision made with deep misgivings. In his own memoirs von Senger stated that had he been in Kesselring's place he probably would not have done it, which is rather odd given the situation he presented to him at the time.[14] High command is a thankless business.

Kesselring was reacting just as Alexander intended, leaving the way open for 'Shingle', though the soldiers of X Corps at the Garigliano had little enough cause to be pleased. The arrival of the German formations meant they were subject to heavy counterattacks, and hard fighting as their bridgehead over the river came under threat of destruction from German troops who meant serious business. Ground changed hands several times, and once again it was superior artillery support that enabled the British battalions to hold on. By the end of the month they had suffered over 4,000 battle casualties; although they were across the river to stay, they were firmly on the defensive.

With XIV Panzer Corps battered on its northern flank and fighting desperately to hold on in the south at the Garigliano, and with all reserves committed, the US II Corps attacked in the centre. The US 36th Division was to cross the Rapido to the north and south of San Angelo, a village overlooking the river but which was itself dominated by Monte Cassino. The winding Rapido, some 30 feet wide, fast-flowing, unfordable and flanked by flood banks, was a formidable crossing task in itself, but it was made far more hazardous by the extent of the German defences in this sector. Held by the 15th Panzer Grenadier Division, the San Angelo area had been turned into a fortress. Whereas in the Bernhardt Line strong-points had been largely improvised, the Germans had made good use of time to exercise their defensive ingenuity in the Gustav Line, and the San Angelo sector was one of its strongest points. Set back on the high ground covering the river and its approaches was an in-depth defence zone con-sisting of well-camouflaged concrete and steel pill-boxes, dug-in tank turrets, machine-gun and mortar positions. These enfiladed the bends in the river and had interlocking and mutually supporting fields of fire. Mines and wire obstacles, and some carefully prepared booby-traps also lay in wait for attackers. In San Angelo itself, much of which was deliber-ately demolished, well-concealed strongpoints had been constructed inside buildings and protected by rubble. They were hard to spot and even harder to destroy with artillery or bombing. Another San Pietro had been created. The river and its approaches were well covered by German artillery and mortars, while nothing could escape the view of German observers and gunners on the slopes of Monte Cassino.

On the evening of 19 January the British 46th Division attempted to cross the Rapido, but the current, increased by the Germans opening the sluices of an irrigation dam to the north, was too strong for the assault boats, and few men managed to get across. Surprise was lost, and the 15th Panzer Grenadier Division's troops holding the river began to react: artillery fire came down and the attempt was called off. The 46th Division subsequently became drawn in to support the hard-pressed 56th Division fighting to hold the Garigliano bridgehead, but its apparent failure to make a full-scale effort to cross the Rapido caused dismay and bitterness at US II Corps, especially as high ground near San Ambroglio covering the 36th Division's crossing would remain in German hands. There was an extremely uncomfortable feeling, felt within X Corps as well as US II Corps that the Americans had been let down. The problem seems to have been that the X Corps effort was primarily at the Garigliano, where it soon had a major battle on its hands that required all its infantry. If the 46th Division's crossing was so vital to the 36th Division's attack, then a full-scale assault crossing would have been necessary – the 46th Division appears to have been equipped to put a brigade across at most. To cross both the Garigliano and the Rapido in strength seems to have been beyond the realistic capability of X Corps.

Two American commanders went into Fifth Army's offensive deeply unhappy and full of foreboding about the task assigned them. One was Lucas of VI Corps; the other was Walker of the 36th Division. He was aware that his Division was to attempt a river crossing in the face of the German main line of resistance with its flanks exposed and overlooked by dominating high ground. His attack had to be mounted in haste, and his Division had not recovered from the fighting in the Bernhardt Line, in which its regiments had each lost about a 1,000 men. Replacements had by no means made up these losses, and those that had arrived were inexperienced and were given no time to become properly assimilated into their units. Normally a period of rest, reorganization and training would follow a major action to enable this process, so that the infantry sections and platoons would go into their next action as teams. The time imperative denied this to the 36th Division and also prevented proper rehearsals and coordination between infantry and engineers. 'We might succeed,' Walker confided to his diary shortly before his Division went into the attack late on 20 January, 'but I do not see how we can.'[15]

Walker tried to maximize surprise and cover for the assault by attacking in darkness, albeit at the risk of increasing the difficulty of the troops negotiating largely unfamiliar ground. Throughout the day in 124 sorties P-40 Kittyhawk and A-20 aircraft of the XII Air Support Command sought out strongpoints and gun posts in and around San Angelo and Cassino, but the German positions were largely invulnerable to their bombing and strafing; they also caught German vehicles trying to move, which were not. Sixteen battalions of field artillery stood by to hammer the German positions for 30 minutes before the crossing, afterwards to provide observed fire support during the attack. The 141st Infantry to the north of San Angelo prepared to cross with its 1st Battalion in assault boats, the 3rd to follow in boats and on engineer footbridges. South of San Angelo the

143rd Infantry would cross its 1st and 3rd Battalions simultaneously, the first wave in assault boats. With the onset of daylight, smoke generators were to mask the crossing sites from German observation.

At 7.30 p.m. the American guns began to fire their preparation, and the assault battalions began to move forward, bayonets fixed and most troops carrying extra belts of ammunition. There was dense fog. Things began to go wrong from the first, as accurate German return artillery and mortar fire at once came down on the approaches to the river, destroying and damaging many of the previously dumped assault boats and causing heavy casualties to the troops struggling to carry other boats and bridging material forward over the long trek to the river bank. Under this fire and in the fog, men strayed into minefields, causing further casualties and disruption. Boats were dropped and abandoned, and the 141st Infantry had a quarter of the engineers' equipment needed for its crossing destroyed. Engineers managed to erect four floating-duckboard foot-bridges, but all were soon damaged, with only one left over which troops had to pick their way carefully one at a time. By dawn on 21 January no more than 100 troops were on the far bank, but as all radios had been lost or damaged in the crossing they were out of touch with the main body on the eastern bank. A runner got across to them with orders to dig in and await reinforcement, as further crossings had been suspended in daylight as too hazardous. The 143rd Infantry experienced much the same, though had more troops across by dawn. They had no chance of advancing from the river bank in the face of the German defences and remained pinned under heavy fire. With daylight revealing their every move to German observers up on Monte Cassino, they had little chance, and, when German tanks began to close in, their situation became desperate – there were no anti-tank weapons across to support them. Most troops were pulled back across the river.

Further crossings were made by the 143rd and 141st but could make no progress against the German positions. The gunners supported as best they could but with communications cut with the assault troops, and few pre-registered targets, their fire could not be directed where it was needed. With casualties mounting and German counterattack pressure building up on 22 January the 143rd pulled its troops back across the river. Those of the 141st were trapped, their footbridges blown by German fire. They were eventually overwhelmed, with only a few men managing to swim back. This was the end of the 36th Division's crossing of the Rapido, and this time Walker's Division had lost 1,681 casualties: 143 killed, 663 wounded and 875 missing.[16] General Eberhardt Rodt of the 15th Panzer Grenadier Division reported to XIV Panzer Corps his successful repulse of an assault crossing at the Rapido without drawing upon reserves, his own losses being 64 killed and 179 wounded. Only later when the number of American dead and prisoners, some 500, became known did the German command appreciate the extent of their defensive success. Such was the strength of feeling engendered by the 36th Division's repulse at the Rapido that after the war it was the subject of a Congressional Enquiry, which, in reviewing the evidence and circumstances under which the attack was made, exonerated Clark.

14

ANZIO AND ROME

'My God! It looks like another Salerno.' [1]

Supported by over 300 warships and assault craft Lucas' VI Corps landed at Anzio before dawn on 22 January. Only two companies of the 29th Panzer Grenadier Division were resting in and around Anzio and they were not at alert; much surprised, they offered little opposition. They were the only German soldiers within some 25 miles of Anzio. It was the Luftwaffe that reacted initially, its first raids coming in during the morning. These were small hit-and-run affairs, the day's total amounting to at most 50 sorties. A strong Allied fighter shield protected the landing while bombers and fighter-bombers struck at German airfields and communications. By the end of the day Lucas had 36,000 troops and some 3,000 vehicles in a widening beachhead covering Anzio and the surrounding low-level and mostly open ground. The beachhead would have a 25-mile frontage by the end of the following day.

The German reaction was initially one of consternation. The first reports reaching Kesselring during the early hours of the morning indicated a full-scale landing and, knowing the extent to which his guard was down, he immediately began to fear for the Gustav Line. With the door to the Alban Hills and Rome wide open, he knew time was likely to be against him. It was now Kesselring's second moment of truth, and the point at which he vindicated Hitler's confidence in him. He remained calm and put in motion the earliest possible reaction of which his forces in Italy were capable, while alerting OKW to the landing. German units near Rome, including reinforcement drafts for the Hermann Göring Division and some Flak units, whose 88mm guns would be invaluable, were ordered to get to the beachhead fast and block the routes to the Alban Hills. Fourteenth Army in northern Italy was alerted and ordered to send what formations it could, and by evening the bulk of two infantry divisions and a newly formed SS Panzer Grenadier Division were on the move to the south.

By 8.30 a.m. Kesselring was on the telephone to a worried von Vieting-hoff ordering him to release whatever he could from the Gustav Line. The headquarters of I Parachute Corps was recalled from the Garigliano, and so were parts of the 3rd Panzer Grenadier and Hermann Göring Divisions and the 71st Infantry Division. British X Corps would be glad to see them go. From the Adriatic front the 26th Panzer Division and elements of the 1st Parachute Division were ordered to Anzio. This process was to an extent eased by an existing coastal defence alarm procedure set up in Italy, in that the issuing of a pre-designated codeword – in this case 'Richard' – set machinery in motion to enable the rapid move of forces to a specific coastal region. The OKW, whose perspective on the landing was not merely Italy-focused but seen in terms of an assault on 'Fortress Europe', immediately alerted formations to move to Italy from other theatres: the 715th Motorized Infantry Division from southern France, the 114th Jäger Division from the Balkans and several training and forming infantry and panzer-grenadier regiments from Germany. Luftwaffe bomber groups equipped with Junkers Ju 88s prepared to move at once to Italy from Greece and Crete, Germany, and France, some of the crews having bombed London only the night before. About 50 Dornier Do 217s and Heinkel He 177s with radio-controlled glider bombs flew in to reinforce anti-shipping units based in southern France, from where they could operate against the beachhead.

German reaction capability was always phenomenal, but time remained the chief factor, and the critical period could really be measured in hours. By darkness on the day of the landing an ad hoc and precariously thin defensive screen comprising a few battalions of some extremely apprehensive German soldiers had been thrown around Lucas's beachhead. Their observers and patrols had peered carefully at the Allied troops setting about their tasks on and just inland of the beaches, and by evening their reports told Kesselring what he badly needed to know. The Allied formations were throwing out patrols and recce teams but they were making no move to advance on the Alban Hills, and there were no signs of an impending large-scale attack from their beachhead. Kesselring began to relax; whatever the Allies were up to it was not as he had initially feared, and time might be on his side after all. When Vietinghoff, who understand-

ably enough was panicking, rang Kesselring that evening to suggest that
his forces should withdraw from the Gustav Line at once and come up to
destroy the beachhead, no doubt thinking of Salerno and the need to strike
quickly, much to his surprise, Kesselring ordered him to stand fast: there
would be no abandonment of the Gustav Line.

This reaction by von Vietinghoff goes some way to vindicating the original 'wild cat' concept, and Kesselring's later assertion that the Allies
missed their chance. A number of senior Allied soldiers have subsequently
given well-founded professional assessments of 'Shingle', arguing that had
Lucas behaved differently and struck out for the Alban Hills straight away,
as he might, the landing force would have been overextended with exposed
lines of communication and destroyed by the German reaction.[2] No doubt
they are right, and their opinions focus on the fate of the 'Shingle' force –

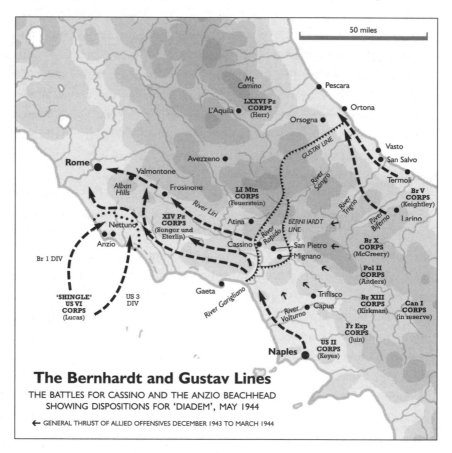

The Bernhardt and Gustav Lines

THE BATTLES FOR CASSINO AND THE ANZIO BEACHHEAD
SHOWING DISPOSITIONS FOR 'DIADEM', MAY 1944

← GENERAL THRUST OF ALLIED OFFENSIVES DECEMBER 1943 TO MARCH 1944

but what about the Gustav Line? The lingering question is not so much whether the Germans could have achieved the destruction of VI Corps while still holding the Gustav Line, but whether in the event of an aggressive 'wild cat' they would have had enough confidence to believe that they could do so. Had they not had the confidence, once they abandoned the Gustav Line, leaving only rearguards and delaying forces behind, would they still have had enough time to destroy Lucas before the main body of Fifth Army broke through? In the harsh reckoning of war, would the likely loss of VI Corps have been an acceptable cost to clear the Gustav Line and reach Rome? Probably not, for apart from the question of accepting such a near-deliberate sacrificing of their soldiers, could the Allies afford to allow the Germans the propaganda triumph of destroying an Allied seaborne invasion only some six months before 'Overlord' was launched? Neither Alexander nor Clark as the responsible senior commanders could have viewed such a risk with equanimity.

Alexander and Clark were in the beachhead with Lucas on D-Day and were satisfied with the landing and its progress. They were a lot less satisfied – in fact they were seriously worried – when in the following days Lucas showed too little aggression. They knew that the German response was building up and wanted the securing at least of Cisterna and Campoleone on roads leading out of the beachhead to Valmontone and Albano. The beachhead was gaining strength, but it was 30 January before Lucas, with the US 45th Division and units of the 1st Armored Division (less a Combat Command on the Cassino front) ashore, felt confident enough to attack. But by then it was too late: the German strength around the beachhead was too strong. The attack was held and fighting raged until 2 February, when the beachhead went over to the defensive in anticipation of having to fight for its existence. Fourteenth Army, under General Eberhard von Mackensen, now controlled the German force containing and preparing to destroy the beachhead.

In the meantime, Fifth Army continued to batter at the Gustav Line with little success. The 36th Division's repulse at the Rapido was followed by the 34th Division crossing to the north of Cassino and penetrating into the high ground to break into the Liri Valley some four miles beyond; the town would also be attacked from the north. General Alphonse Juin's

French Corps was to press to the south-west to threaten XIV Panzer Corps' communications. Despite appalling weather conditions, the Americans maintained their attack against what must rank as one of the most formidable mountain defence zones ever encountered. By 11 February the 34th Division had fought its way across the slopes and ridges to reach about 1,500 yards from the monastery atop Monte Cassino, and they had broken into the northern outskirts of the town itself, which had been turned into a fortress. They were less than a mile from Highway 6 in the Liri Valley. But by then its rifle companies had been reduced by casualties

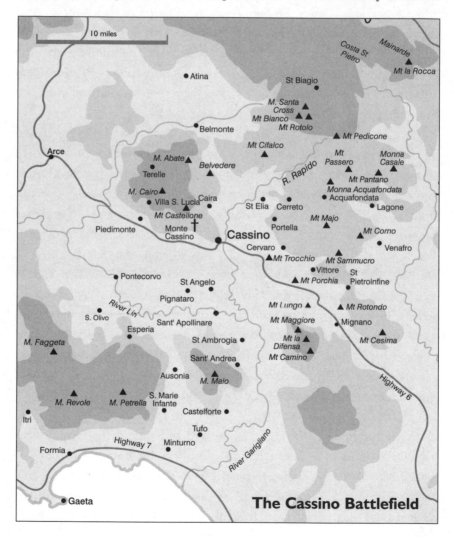

The Cassino Battlefield

to handfuls of men clinging to precarious positions and suffering from the effects of extreme cold and wet. It had taken the terrain, the weather and the feeding into the battle by the Germans of the 90th Panzer Grenadier Division stiffened by battalions of the 1st Parachute Division brought over from the Adriatic to defeat the 34th Division, but it had been fought into the ground. Signals intelligence in early February had told the Allies that the German defence was straining every nerve to hold the American attack and that their situation was desperate. But fresh troops were needed to exploit the gains won at such cost by the Americans.

Alexander had created II New Zealand Corps, bringing over the 4th Indian Division and the 78th Division from Eighth Army to join 2nd New Zealand Division and placing them under the command of Lieutenant General Sir Bernard Freyberg. Originally intended as the exploitation force for the Liri Valley, II New Zealand Corps had to take over from the exhausted Americans and keep up the attack pressure, not only to give the German defence no respite and maintain momentum but also now to maintain pressure on the Gustav Line and keep German strength away from the threatened Anzio beachhead. The Indians and New Zealanders, both battle-hardened formations with distinguished fighting records, gained an idea of what they were in for as they relieved the Americans, some of whom were so weak and frost-bitten that they had to be lifted out of their positions and carried back down the slopes on stretchers. Relief was a difficult task: the tracks and trails were under German shell-fire, there were not enough mules (there never were), and some of the mules carrying forward ammunition and grenades were caught by German fire and killed, leaving the forward units short.

The battleground taken over from the American infantry was the worst possible for an attacker, its nature and characteristics not easy to discern from a distance through field glasses and certainly not from a map. The rock-strewn slopes held unsuspected clefts, hollows and areas of thorn and scrub through which it was impossible to move. In places the only possible attack frontages were narrow, with only a platoon or handful of men able to get forward at a time; these were obvious to the Germans and well covered with fire and obstacles. Extensive minefields, belts of barbed-wire and deliberate flooding of the lower ground all helped channel attacks into the defenders' guns. The defensive zone extended into the Liri Valley, with villages and farm buildings turned into well-protected strongpoints. Tank turrets were dug-in, camouflaged, their guns covering approaches. Trees were cleared for fields of fire, their stumps left as anti-tank obstacles, and wide anti-tank ditches were dug. Steel shelters for troops to survive bombardment and armoured pill-boxes had been provided by the OKW – Cassino had been designated a 'Fortress' area. The town held many bunkers and even tanks concealed in its buildings, their cellars and ground floors strengthened to resist bombardment. On the slopes of Monte Cassino and the surrounding heights, gun positions and shelters for the crews and observers had been blasted out of the rock by engineers. The monastery on Monte Cassino overlooked all, and Allied soldiers felt themselves under its watchful eyes. It is now generally accepted that the monastery was not itself occupied by the Germans, but in the early weeks of 1944 there was not an Allied soldier in the valleys below who would have believed it. In any case, it was perched on top of a fortress and to that extent the Germans had made it hostage to the fortunes of war.

This battleground defied Alexander until May. The New Zealand Corps made two major attacks, in February and in March. In the first, which began on 15 February, the monastery was shattered into ruins by heavy bombing and artillery fire. General Francis Tuker, commanding the 4th Indian Division and whose troops were expected to continue the attack across the slopes from the positions so hard won by the US 34th Division, believed the monastery would be used by the Germans as a strongpoint against his men. He would have preferred to attempt an out-flanking move to isolate Monte Cassino rather than a direct attack, but if the latter were ordered he requested that the monastery should be bombed to prevent the Germans making use of its formidable construction as a defence against his men. The final difficult decision was Alexander's, who realized that with Allied lives at stake the request could not be refused, and there was the morale of the Allied troops and their perception of the monastery's role in the German defence to consider.

In the event, poor coordination removed any chance of the bombing assisting the 4th Indian's attack. Taking advantage of a brief period of good flying weather, the raid was mounted on 15 February by USAAF heavy and medium bombers without alerting the forward troops, who were aware only that the raid was scheduled for the following day. They were unprepared to follow up the bombing immediately, and by the time they were able to attack it was too late – the Germans had quickly moved in to occupy the still very substantial ruins and turn it into a major strongpoint. Tuker had been thwarted on two counts, both of which were fatal to his Division's chances. The bombing had not been properly coordinated for his troops to immediately exploit its effects, which would have been the only worthwhile method, and it had not been of a type sufficient to flatten the monastery beyond effective defensive use. Tuker, aware of the RAF's special 'Blockbuster' anti-masonry bombs, had envisaged and requested that the air forces employ large-calibre bombs for the blasting of large buildings, but such weapons were not in theatre.[3] Despite many bombs and shells finding their target, too much of the monastery was left standing. The 4th Indian Division pressed its attack gallantly but suffered heavily for no appreciable gains. The New Zealand Division had no better luck trying to break into Cassino. The German defence was hard-pressed and increasingly reliant upon the paratroops of the 1st Parachute Division, who took over the defence of the monastery and Cassino and staked their already formidable reputation on holding it.

While II New Zealand Corps broke its teeth on the Cassino position, von Mackensen attacked at Anzio. Hitler was determined to destroy the beach-head, knowing full well that sooner or later (and probably sooner) the Allies would be launching a cross-Channel invasion. If his armies could prove that amphibious invasions were not a viable proposition, the cross-Channel invasion would almost certainly be delayed and might not be made at all. It was far more than the Allied landing forces that he hoped to destroy on the Anzio beaches. From long distance he immersed himself in the planning of the attack, interfering in tactical matters in a way that Kesselring and von Mackensen had no choice but to accept. Although von Mackensen had numerical superiority, the equivalent of ten divisions against the equivalent of five Allied, he could not match Allied firepower. The Salerno battle scenario was repeated in that for four days the beachhead was in a critical position, but superior Allied firepower – artillery and naval gunfire – and the diversion of the major Allied air effort to support the beachhead, broke the German attack. Casualties on both sides were heavy, and in terms of combat troops neither could easily replace their losses. Kesselring now found himself in a trap similar to the one he had imposed upon Alexander since October, compelled to take the offensive in Italy and mortgage his future ability to wage his campaign by what amounted to the 'reckless expenditure' of his own troops. 'Shingle' had not shaken the Gustav Line, but it had imposed another battlefront upon the Germans in Italy that was draining their forces. With the defeat of the German attack, the unhappy Lucas was relieved of command of VI Corps and replaced by Truscott. Lucas may well deserve the credit for the beachhead being established enough to withstand the German onslaught, but he had long forfeited the confidence of Clark and Alexander, and he had shown himself not to be the man to lead the eventual breakout offensive from the beachhead that was forming part of Alexander's longer-term plan.

With the Germans having shot their offensive bolt at Anzio, there still remained the Gustav Line. On 15 March, the New Zealand Corps again tried to break the Cassino position, this time by making the main offensive effort through the town itself. Once again there was reliance upon air power, and it proved to be excessive and misplaced. Allied airmen were keen to help the Allied armies forward and to demonstrate what they could do, and there was a degree of overconfidence that a heavy bombing of the German defences at Cassino would obliterate them and allow the soldiers a walk-over. This was not shared by the senior Allied air commander, Eaker, whose own experience of employing strategic bombing gave him a sharper insight than his tactical air commanders into what it meant in practical terms. He suspected that heavy bombing of the town would generate so much rubble and cratering that the soldiers would be lucky to walk over anything. It would prove counterproductive and obstruct their advance. He agreed to do all he could to support the soldiers, however, and stifled his own doubts about Freyberg's confident intention of using bulldozers to clear routes for his tanks and infantry.

On 15 March more than 400 Allied heavy and medium bombers delivered just over a thousand tons of bombs on Cassino, about half of the bombs falling within a mile of the town centre. Some 900 pieces of artillery added their fire in a prolonged barrage. The town was pulverized, and to observers it seemed that very little could have survived. For the first time Allied troops were to attack an urban strongpoint given such treatment. In fact, rubble was being piled on top of rubble, and carefully constructed bunkers and shelters, while buried under it, were not necessarily destroyed. Their occupants, while shaken, were not necessarily killed or wounded, though they might well have to dig themselves out, or be dug out by others. There were some 300 German paratroops occupying positions in the town, and about half of them became casualties or were buried under the rubble. The remainder, being above-average soldiers, emerged from cover and prepared to defend. The New Zealand tanks and infantry confronted a nightmare of craters and rubble they simply could not negotiate, and the onset of heavy rain turned craters into small lakes, some of which needed bridging equipment to cross. Bulldozers were held off by German fire and in any case could make little impression on the masses of rubble; nor could frantic ramming by tanks. The infantry went forward, as always, but it was no 'walk-over'. The battle in the town and the supporting attack by the 4th Indian Division on the Cassino heights lasted until 25 March and did not crack the defence. While the New Zealanders firmly established themselves in Cassino, they could not eject the paratroops from it.

With the onset of spring, Kesselring began to lose the weather advantage, and the Allied air forces were out in force to compel his withdrawal in an intensive air offensive against lines of communication. Operation 'Strangle' aimed to starve the German armies by interdicting their supplies by systematic air attack on, primarily, the road and rail network upon which they depended, but ports and river communications were also targeted. Some 50,000 sorties were flown by heavy, medium and fighter-bombers, putting immense strain upon the German armies. Thousands of vehicles were destroyed, daylight movement was severely disrupted, and supply stocks fell, but not such as to impose a withdrawal by air action alone. That would require concerted action with a ground offensive, and Alexander was preparing one that would finally break the Gustav Line. Originally conceived by General John Harding, Alexander's Chief of Staff, the plan for the spring offensive was to bring over the bulk of the Eighth Army from the Adriatic to make a concentrated attack in the

Cassino sector to reach the Liri Valley. Fifth Army would take over the coastal sector and attack along the axis of Highway 7. Combined with an appropriately timed breakout from the Anzio beachhead, the operation was intended not only to break the Gustav Line but to encircle and destroy Kesselring's forces south of Rome, thereby fulfilling the campaign's aim of assisting 'Overlord' by the destruction of German forces in Italy, which Hitler would have no choice but to replace.

The offensive was codenamed 'Diadem' and was meticulously prepared. Once approved by the Allied Combined Chiefs (and in this Eisenhower's support was crucial), Alexander received the necessary reinforcements to bring his strength up to 25 Divisions. Kesselring's forces were overstretched between containing the Anzio beachhead and holding the Gustav Line, and his own awareness of his vulnerability to a further amphibious landing was adroitly exploited against him by an elaborate deception operation. He was determined not to repeat his mistake of the Garigliano, and was induced to keep his guard in place against a nonexistent amphibious threat.

On 11 May, 'Diadem' was launched with a heavy artillery pounding of the German positions. Complete surprise had been achieved. Hard fighting faced the British XIII Corps crossing the Rapido where the US 36th Division had tried in January, but by 13 May a secure crossing was established and by 17 May the Liri Valley was opened. On the following day the Polish Corps of Eighth Army, after bitter fighting against the German paratroops and suffering heavy casualties, occupied the monastery on Monte Cassino; the surviving paratroops had slipped away to avoid entrapment. Juin's Corps had unlocked the Aurunci Mountains on the Fifth Army front, and the Gustav Line was breaking apart. Kesselring, realizing that this time he had held his reserves back for too long, could not sustain the fall-back position – the Hitler Line – which Canadian armour and infantry forced by the end of 22 May.

By 25 May Truscott's forces were breaking out of the Anzio beachhead; the weakened German forces could no longer contain them, and the road to Valmontone on Highway 6 was open to a determined thrust. Alexander intended that Truscott should get there before whatever reserves Kesselring could muster, trapping the Germans now falling back from the

Gustav and Hitler Line positions. This was Truscott's understanding too. Then, in one of the most controversial decisions of the war, Clark intervened unilaterally to redirect a surprised and initially reluctant Truscott away from Valmontone to make the main thrust along Highway 7 and the Alban Hills towards Rome, leaving the task of closing the door at Valmontone to the US II Corps moving up towards the beachhead along the coast. Clark appears not to have taken his Army Group Commander into his full confidence, and by the time Alexander was informed of what was happening it was too late for him to order a reversal. It would probably have led to chaos in any case, without achieving the intended objective – Alexander was far too professional a soldier to risk that and too good a coalition commander to raise an Anglo-American controversy by trying it. Clark had opened the stable door, and Truscott's horse was already too far bolted into the Alban Hills to call back.

A complex balance of personal and professional motives lay behind Clark's decision, and if it is not possible to dismiss the charge that he was motivated by the lure of Rome and the conviction that his Fifth Army had earned the right to enter the Italian capital first, neither is it possible to deny that there were sound military reasons for what he did. Eighth Army's advance through the Liri Valley was becoming a traffic jam in an attempt to get the mechanized and armoured divisions through, German rearguards were fighting as stubbornly as ever, and under such circumstances there would be no guarantees that the force holding the door at Valmontone would have been strong enough to bar it. To make Truscott's main thrust upon Valmontone would also have left his flanks open to the Germans holding the Alban Hills. Whatever the motivation, the consequence was that the Germans did manage to prevent the Valmontone door closing upon them completely, and Tenth Army squeezed through the gap to fight another day. What Churchill called the 'cop' in his anxious signals to Alexander, urging him to entrap and destroy as much of the German forces as possible, was quite substantial, albeit short of what Alexander had originally hoped; to Alexander it was, as he signalled to Brooke on 4 June, 'a fair cop'. It had cost his armies some 42,000 casualties.

The shattered Tenth and Fourteenth Armies fell back over the Tiber and through Rome, behind rearguards provided by the paratroops who were always called upon in the direst circumstances to hold the line. On the Adriatic, the German forces fell back to conform. Tenth and Fourteenth Armies left behind some 20,000 of their troops to become prisoners of war and had suffered about 10,000 battle casualties.[4] Losses in vehicles had been severe due to the frequent daylight attacks by the Allied tactical air forces whose fighter-bombers, ranging over the battlefront and beyond, harried the German troops relentlessly. Much heavy equipment and most of their tank strength had also been lost. Four Infantry divisions had been destroyed, and three more had been so shattered that they had to be withdrawn for rebuilding and re-equipping, while a fourth was broken up to provide reinforcements. To enable Kesselring to restore the front in Italy, Hitler and the OKW had no choice but to send him four replacement divisions, and reinforcements on a scale equivalent to three more. Here at last was vindication of the Italian campaign drawing significant German strength.

Just over two months later a similar scene would be re-enacted with the remains of a defeated German Army escaping across the river Seine in France, leaving most of its equipment and thousands of its unburied dead, in the charnel house of the 'Falaise Pocket' in Normandy. Alexander's 'Diadem' achievement had, as intended, helped to make that later victory possible. On 5 June, Clark entered Rome, and on the following day the Allies landed in Normandy. 'Overlord' had begun, overshadowing the Italian campaign. The time of greatest strategic opportunity for the Italian campaign may have passed, but its contribution went on. Plenty of fighting lay ahead for the Allied armies in Italy, more mountain strongholds to overcome, more rivers to cross as they maintained their offensive pressure to keep the Germans engaged and to draw their strength. There was still a very long way to go.

15

TO THE GOTHIC LINE AND BEYOND

Pursuit North of Rome

In the autumn of 1943 the Allied armies struggling northward in mainland Italy had been drawing closer towards another major German defensive line. In June 1944, in the immediate wake of 'Diadem''s success, history was starting to repeat itself. A major German defensive line still awaited the Allies pursuing Tenth and Fourteenth Armies and upon which they were falling back, a line begun under Rommel's direction in northern Italy almost a year before. This was the projected Pisa–Rimini line, renamed the Gothic Line in April 1944. In an attempt to divorce it from undue significance in the perceptions of friend and foe alike, after the fall of Rome it was again renamed: on 16 June it became the Green Line. But to the Allies it was always known by its more dramatic designation, the Gothic Line.

Whereas the Bernhardt Line and even the Gustav Line were looked upon by the Germans as delaying positions, albeit in the latter case of a formidable and prolonged nature, the Gothic Line was originally conceived as a bastion to hold Italy. A legacy of Hitler's original intention to defend the country along the northern Apennines, it had become a victim of his subsequent change of mind to stand and fight south of Rome. Work and construction materials had been diverted south to strengthen the Gustav Line instead, so that in the wake of 'Diadem' as Tenth and Fourteenth Armies sought to escape entrapment and destruction, the Gothic Line remained unfinished. Faced with the critical situation in Italy, Hitler and the OKW immediately ordered the resumption of work on an intensive scale. In the meantime Hitler made it quite clear to Kesselring in a series of sharp signals that he expected him to stop retreating and stand and fight before the Gothic Line. This stung Kesselring, who might with justification have felt that he had already proven his willingness and ability to do just that in Italy.

His immediate problem was one of avoiding total collapse. His principal concern was Fourteenth Army, which was effectively shattered and now

vulnerable in the open terrain to the west of the River Tiber – ground that
for the first time in Italy favoured the British and American mechanized
armies, who were exploiting it well. He replaced von Mackensen, who had
failed to hold against the Anzio breakout, with General Joachim Lemelsen
in a move to give Fourteenth Army more confidence and reinforced it with

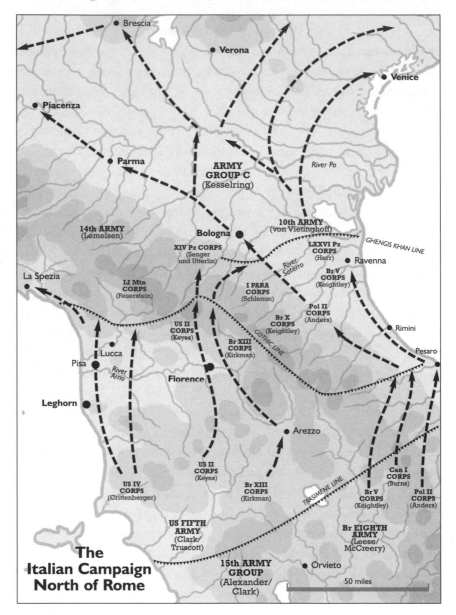

The
Italian Campaign
North of Rome

three new, but inexperienced infantry divisions hastily sent to Italy, one of them from as far as Denmark. More importantly, he moved those old battle hands the 29th and 90th Panzer Grenadier Divisions and the 26th Panzer Division into the Fourteenth Army sector under I Parachute Corps, while LXXVI Panzer Corps shifted to cover Tenth Army's right. Tenth Army was far less vulnerable east of the Tiber and in more difficult ground closer to the Apennines; von Vietinghoff could be depended upon to make good use of it. But there could be no minimizing the danger Kesselring's forces were in, when divisions could muster no more than 2,500 men at most and stand-bys like the 1st Parachute Division and the Hermann Göring Division numbered barely 1,000 all ranks. Constant air attacks were disrupting their movement and cohesion. Bombing caused innumerable railway cuts and vehicle columns on the roads were regularly shot-up by roving Allied fighter-bombers whose pilots rarely saw such concentrated targets. Nevertheless Kesselring insisted upon his troops holding a series of delaying positions for as long as possible and was firm in quashing any sign of a 'retreat momentum' taking hold of his senior commanders – Lemelsen received a severe 'tongue-lashing' on 15 June for allowing his troops to fall back twenty kilometres in a single day and did not enjoy it, but as far as Kesselring was concerned his armies simply could not afford to give ground at such a rate.[1]

Kesselring was determined to allow a fall-back only in order to hold for as long as possible a line extending over better defensive ground to the west and east of Lake Trasimene. By 20 June, Clark's Fifth Army and Leese's Eighth Army were running into stiffer opposition – an exhilarating time of armoured spearheads advancing more than 30 miles in a day had not lasted long and was now past. The Allies would have to fight through the Trasimene Line, while Kesselring gained pause for breath and took stock. He determined to use it in his own way. Still under criticism from Hitler and the OKW for the ground given up, and prodded to hold unsatisfactory and only partially viable ad hoc defensive positions that were more likely to see his own men end up in PoW cages than to seriously delay the Allied advance, Kesselring flew to Hitler's headquarters on 3 July to argue for a free hand. There he was subjected to a lecture on why he should adopt a defensive approach on the model fought on the Eastern

Front, to which Kesselring bluntly responded by asking Hitler whether after Stalingrad and Tunisia he could afford to lose two more armies. On the other hand, if allowed to fight his battle in his own way, Kesselring guaranteed to significantly delay the Allied advance, at least in the Apennines, and bar the southern route into Germany so that the war could continue into 1945. Hitler had heard such assurances before from Kesselring and had no cause so far to regret backing him; once again he listened to him.[2]

Whereas Hitler adopted the strategy advocated by his Commander-in-Chief in Italy, the Allies did not adopt that advocated by theirs. By early June there was little chance of catching the German armies before they reformed along a coherent line – whatever chance had existed of that had gone. They remained just one jump ahead of Alexander's armies, whose logistic tails were struggling to support their spearheads. Nevertheless, 'Diadem' boosted Alexander's confidence in what might be achieved by his armies, and he now submitted a plan to the theatre commander, Wilson. In this he argued for the retention intact of his armies in Italy for a further major offensive that would crack the Gothic Line and compel Hitler to send a further eight to ten divisions into Italy to prevent a collapse – the best way in his view of assisting the campaign now under way in Normandy. Underpinning his case was evidence available through signals intelligence of the parlous state of Kesselring's armies and of the German intention to hold along the Gothic Line. This, Alexander was convinced, they would be unable to do unless strongly reinforced from either the western or the eastern fronts. Apart from the fact that Alexander had no wish to see his armies robbed of experienced divisions for 'Anvil', he seems to have been genuinely certain of their capability to attack and exploit successfully in difficult terrain – neither the Apennines nor even the Alps could now defy them, he reported to Wilson. He advocated a single, concentrated punch (for logistics and terrain would afford no other) against the Gothic Line as soon as possible. He believed that his armies could reach Florence before the end of July and would be in a position to attack the Gothic Line in mid-August. Once through the Apennines, he could strike west towards France or east, which he favoured, towards Ljubjana and ultimately Vienna.[3]

To accept Alexander's concept meant the cancellation of 'Anvil', an operation already agreed between the Americans and British (albeit reluctantly in the latter case) and, most importantly, with Stalin. No army commander wants to see the break up of his force, especially just as it has achieved success, and Clark, who was set to lose Truscott and his experienced VI Corps as well as the French Corps to 'Anvil', backed Alexander fully. So too did the senior naval and air commanders, who were equally unhappy at splitting their forces between Italy and a new campaign in southern France. Wilson, in the awkward position of already having reported to the Combined Chiefs that 'Anvil' should rapidly follow 'Diadem', also supported Alexander as best he could. Churchill, not surprisingly, strongly favoured the concept. Not only did he believe in its soundness as a military proposition, it also promised to transform the Italian campaign, to which he had always been committed, from a subsidiary theatre to one ranking in significance beside the campaign in the west, vindicating the resources and cost invested in it.

Brooke and the British Chiefs of Staff were not so easily convinced. Even in view of the intelligence picture available on Kesselring's situation, no sober military assessment of Alexander's concept could easily accept the apparent optimism with which he viewed an attack through some of the most challenging terrain imaginable for any army, especially after the Bernhardt and Gustav Line experiences. Brooke looked askance at a winter campaign through the Alps, which an ongoing offensive following a breakthrough of the Apennines in the early autumn must involve. This, he pointed out to Churchill, would mean that not only the Germans but also the terrain and weather would be the enemy.[4]

On the other hand, Alexander's argument, that his armies were now proficient in fighting in Italy and were confident, was not one to discount. They had gained valuable, if costly, experience since the autumn of 1943 and knew their enemy, the ground and how to use it better than ever before. Experienced formations had now attained a strong 'corporate knowledge' of the nature of their particular war in Italy, and Alexander's concept looked to exploit this proficiency and confidence when it was at its height. There was also the fact that in Italy an opportunity existed to deal the Germans a further heavy blow in the near term, whereas in southern France it did not. Brooke and the British Chiefs of Staff set aside their initial misgivings and supported Alexander because they concluded that to keep his armies intact and exploit the situation in Italy in the shorter term would harm the Germans far more than 'Anvil'.

Nevertheless, and despite Churchill taking up Alexander's cause with all his vigour, the Americans would not be moved. The debate swung to and fro until 2 July, when the Combined Chiefs of Staff finally instructed Wilson to go ahead with 'Anvil'. It was to have priority over the campaign in Italy and was to be mounted on 15 August. The debate had been the sharpest disagreement between the British and Americans over the Italian campaign, and its outcome decided once and for all the campaign's subsidiary place in wider allied strategy. The American arguments were strong, militarily and politically. Apart from the fact that 'Anvil' had already been agreed at the highest level, Roosevelt was under a political imperative to ensure that the American formations waiting to enter the European war, more than 40 divisions, did so in France, now widely perceived to be where the decisive battle would be fought. Consequently their deployment to a less vital theatre could hardly be justified; nor would Roosevelt's own position be secure if reverses were suffered in France for the want of troops sent elsewhere. Such factors could not be ignored in the higher direction of the war. On military grounds Marshall, not unlike Brooke, believed that the Alps would enable the Germans to conserve forces and send troops to France while still holding Alexander in the mountains. He might well have felt that his worst fears over fighting in Italy had been justified over the previous months, even despite 'Diadem', and that in Italy, 'enough' was now 'enough'. Brooke's own initial unenthusiastic response to the concept indicates a similar feeling. Alexander could well argue that his armies were highly skilled and motivated, and should exploit the opportunity open to them. But, however justified, this was an Army Group Commander's view of his own tempered fighting machines and the battle in which they were involved, and to an extent it was blinkered. The euphoria of 'Diadem' was felt most strongly in the Mediterranean theatre among those who had brought it about. Beyond the theatre it could not altogether dispel the memory of that long and fruitless battering against the Gustav Line and the

Anzio beachhead stalemate. Now that the campaign in North-West Europe was actually under way, the Allies could not afford a repetition of that experience, and they certainly could not countenance two stalemates, one in France and the other in Italy. With the notable exception of Churchill, and despite the support accorded Alexander by Wilson, Brooke and the British Chiefs of Staff, at the higher levels of command confidence seems to have lapsed about the longer term possibilities in Italy. They were backing Alexander mainly because they liked 'Anvil' even less.

Eisenhower's was the decisive voice. He had supported Alexander over 'Diadem' but, faced with the difficult battle confronting Montgomery in Normandy and the threat there of the Allied offensive momentum breaking down, he needed those extra divisions and the ports for their entry in France. He argued for 'Anvil'. There was also the political question of employing French forces for the liberation of France. The French formations in Italy under Juin, understandably enough, felt this very strongly. Their heart went out of the battle in Italy when what was to them a far more important battle called them, and for which they knew they were already under orders. It was Alexander's further misfortune that they constituted his most mountain-adept troops.

Once the die was cast, Alexander had to revise his planning in the knowledge that he would lose seven divisions, much of the logistic organization that supported his armies and enabled their forward movement and supply – such as highly skilled railway repair companies – and that he would have a greatly reduced scale of air support. Clark's Fifth Army was hard hit by 'Anvil', reduced to four infantry and one armoured division and denuded of a third of its corps artillery battalions. Yet Alexander's instructions from the Combined Chiefs remained to cross the Apennines and close to the River Po, exploiting beyond should the situation allow. Clearly the view was that his remaining forces would be sufficient for this and that a major offensive in Italy was unnecessary.

In the meantime, the Germans were urgently working on the Gothic Line defences. There was little chance of them making good the time lost earlier in the year when the Gustav Line received priority. Nevertheless, by August Kesselring knew that he had a belt of defences extending over 200 miles from the River Magra below La Spezia inland to block the Apennines, concentrating strongpoints to cover particularly the Futa Pass on the route northward from Florence to Bologna, and running along the River Foglia to the lower ground of the Adriatic coastline near Pesaro. The extent of the work was patchy, relying mostly upon field-type positions that could be rapidly constructed: machine-gun and mortar positions, anti-tank ditches, minefields and cave positions blasted out of rock. Heavier defences such as dug-in tank turrets and concrete and steel shelters were few. Kesselring also received a further four divisions to bolster his strength. These were not of high quality nor experienced, and Kesselring too had to part with some of his better mobile formations – the Hermann Göring Division to the Eastern Front and the 15th Panzer Grenadier Division and 3rd Panzer Grenadier Divisions to the West. Yet he retained sufficient strength to impose delay upon the now depleted and extended Fifth and Eighth Armies.

It took hard fighting to prise the Germans out of the Trasimene positions by the end of June. Along a series of minor defensive delaying lines the familiar battle pattern reappeared of utilizing terrain to impose a halt with small teams of tanks and infantry that would pull back after two or three days, having compelled their pursuers to probe around them, and then deploy for a concentrated attack on yet another mountain feature, ridge line or hilltop village. For some particularly defensible positions they made a longer fight of it – a six-day battle for the mountain-top town of Rosignano for the American 45th Division, and the town of Arezzo, nestling amid mountains and which had to be unlocked in concerted attacks over a week between 9 and 15 July by units of the New Zealand Division, 4th Indian Division and 6th Armoured Division. The fact that Alexander's armies possessed good tactical intelligence about the strength of the German formations and their dispositions did little to alleviate this type of problem. Once again the Germans were securing time, and for Alexander the summer was slipping away. On 4 August the Germans fell back across the River Arno into the final delaying position, some 15 miles in front of the Gothic Line itself, extending across the Apennines from Pisa to the River Metauro. In their wake, the advanced guard of their pursuers closed up to the demolished bridges over the Arno.

The Gothic Line

Alexander had originally intended to break through the Gothic Line on a central axis, concentrating his striking power on the communications centre of Florence and directing his main attack over the Apennines towards Bologna. Although it was the most mountainous sector, with some heights exceeding those of the Gustav Line, the configuration of the ground was such that an attack could conform to it by moving through valleys rather than across them and along the courses of rivers as opposed to having to cross them. The intention had been to employ the mountain troops, the French Corps in particular, to unlock the heights to enable the main weight of assault to drive through the valleys, the adjacent wings of Fifth and Eighth Armies together constituting the central punch. In effect, the plan this time was to make deliberate use of the successful tactics that had emerged from the Bernhardt and Gustav Line fighting. Some fourteen divisions, in four corps, would have made the central punch, while on the flanks other formations would have pinned German strength to prevent the shifting of reserves to the breakthrough sector. Concentrated air power would have paralyzed German movement behind the Gothic Line and assisted the break-in attack and, as in 'Diadem', would have cleared the path for Allied spearheads once through the main defence zone. They would also have disrupted German attempts to reform into a cohesive line. A deception scheme had already begun, intended to suggest that the main assault would occur in the Adriatic coastal sector towards Rimini directed upon the Romagna and the valley of the River Po – a convincing enough possibility – to draw German strength away from the centre to where the ground was more level and an attack more likely. The plan was intended to apply the experience thus far gained in Italy. If it had been fully backed with resources and mounted early enough in the wake of 'Diadem', it might well have worked.

But once 'Anvil' was firm, Alexander simply did not have the resources for this plan, though he still hoped for a central punch in which Eighth Army would have to carry the main burden of attack due to Fifth Army's reduced strength. It was at this point that one of his Army commanders, Leese of Eighth Army, lost confidence in the plan. It depended upon mountain troops, of which he had none, and his formations were neither

†††††††††††††††††††

experienced nor equipped for mountain fighting. Their commanders were only too aware of this fact. If his Eighth Army was now to be the main effort, then he much preferred to make it in the Adriatic coastal sector better suited to his armour and artillery and to his Army's set-piece approach to battle. His former Army commander, Montgomery, might almost have been at his shoulder as he presented his case to Alexander, Wilson and Harding on 4 August, sheltering from the sun under the wing of a Dakota transport aircraft during an impromptu meeting on Orvieto airfield.

Leese unquestionably had a case. Whether it outweighed the advantages of the existing plan or carried greater risk Alexander had at once to decide. He did not like the proposed change, for to carry out the necessary redeployment would lose some three weeks of a summer already passing too rapidly away; in September would come the autumn rains, reducing the tracks and roads to mud. The deception plan, already focusing Kesselring's attention where Leese now wanted to attack, would have to be reversed; such double-bluffs are doubly chancy. Nor did the Eighth Army staff like the proposed change. Whatever problems awaited them in the mountains, the alternative that Leese proposed confronted his army with a series of rivers to cross, each potentially defensible and each requiring a crossing operation. Attack momentum was likely to quickly break down. It was not a pleasing prospect, yet Alexander bowed to it. His own confidence about relying upon a central attack may well have been sapped now that his mountain troops were lost to him and the balance of his armies altered. He chose not to impose his will upon a doubting subordinate who would have to fight the battle. Leese made it clear that, whatever plan Alexander decided upon, he would go all-out to make it work. But once again Alexander was too experienced a soldier and commander-in-chief not to know that a subordinate Army commander, upon whom much will depend, needs a plan in which he believes. Leese's plan was adopted, and codenamed 'Olive'.[5] To break the Gothic Line, Alexander now depended upon Leese's attack to make progress and draw Kesselring's strength, while Clark's Fifth Army, bolstered by Eighth Army formations, took advantage of any German weakening in the centre. It was reminiscent of the earlier two-handed approach to battles in Italy, which faltered through lack of concentration and sufficient strength to exploit gains. It would take some fine juggling, and it had to be successful in barely a month.

On 15 August the landings in southern France took place, an operation renamed 'Dragoon'. It encountered little opposition; nor did the subsequent advance through the valley of the River Rhône. Ten days later, 'Olive' began, Leese attacking with three corps abreast. At first Eighth Army achieved tactical surprise and broke into the Gothic Line – the Germans had not detected Eighth Army's redeployment to concentrate in the coastal sector, and they were slow in interpreting the weight and import of the attack when it began. When they did realize, it caused Kesselring and von Vietinghoff considerable consternation as they struggled to find the troops necessary to stop Eighth Army's momentum. At the Coriano Ridge, the final high ground blocking Leese from the Romagna, they managed to hold, feeding in the 26th Panzer Division and the 29th and 90th Panzer Grenadier Divisions to support the infantry. Savage and intensive fighting, with tank and infantry losses heavy in Eighth Army's attacking formations, continued well into September. The RAF Desert Air Force, carrying the burden of air support in Italy since 'Dragoon', made a maximum effort at the Fifth and Eighth Army battlefronts to help the troops forward, flying hundreds of fighter-bomber and medium bomber sorties daily against German strongpoints and communications choke-points. By the time the German formations, all of them heavily battered, relinquished Rimini on 21 September, the rain had begun. Meanwhile, Clark's Fifth Army, attacking in the mountains, broke through the Futa and Il Giogo Passes on the central axis but suffered from the same problem it had experienced on the Bernhardt and Gustav Lines – too few reserves to exploit what had been gained by what were by then exhausted formations.

Unremitting pressure prised the Germans out of the Gothic positions, but there were to be no significant victories in Italy before the end of the year, only a steady, monotonous and costly edging forward over river-lines and hills, drawing heavily upon ammunition stocks that dwindled fast as commanders tried to expend shells rather than lives. In mid-December offensive operations in Italy came to a halt, with the Allies still short of Bologna. They could only resume in the following spring. Winter had triumphed again, imposing another bleak endurance test for the soldiers in the mountains and again enabling the Germans to hold on. Events in other theatres also took their toll of the Allied campaign in Italy. The shock of the German offensive in the Ardennes, which began on 16 December, and the likelihood of a prolonged western campaign focused Allied priorities to the extent that in January 1945 even Churchill supported the removal of divisions (three) from Italy to the West to strengthen Eisenhower's offensive. The German withdrawal from Greece meanwhile left a Communist uprising in its wake and the threat of civil war, so two British divisions were rapidly sent from Italy to restore order while a settlement was negotiated. And at the request of the Canadian government, to concentrate its forces in North-West Europe, the three divisions of I Canadian Corps left Eighth Army to join the First Canadian Army in the Low Countries.

In the meantime, following the death of Sir John Dill of the British staff mission in Washington, Wilson had left to take his place. Alexander became Supreme Commander of the Mediterranean theatre on 12 December, and Clark in turn replaced him as Army Group Commander. Truscott returned to Italy to take over Fifth Army. Leese had already left in October to take command of Fourteenth Army in Burma, the X Corps commander, General McCreery, replacing him at Eighth Army. Then, at the end of January, Alexander received a directive from the Combined Chiefs to the effect that the armies in Italy were to contain the Germans and prevent their withdrawal to the other battlefronts, employing limited offensive action and deception to do so. It was a stark acknowledgement that the Italian campaign had been relegated to a holding action and that Fifth and Eighth Armies were no longer the offensive weapons of the previous summer. There was to be one last offensive, however, in the spring of 1945, to destroy the German armies south of the Po.

For three months the Allies prepared for this blow. Plans were formed, troops trained and new equipment assimilated, ammunition stockpiled. There were some additions that emphasized the increasingly international make-up of Clark's two armies, providing a badly-needed augmentation of infantry strength. Eighth Army had long been cosmopolitan, with its New Zealanders, South Africans, Indians, Poles and, until their redeployment, Canadians, as well as British formations. Now a Jewish brigade arrived from the Middle East and two new Polish brigades. Many of the latter had been captured in Normandy while serving in the German army, screened and sent to join their compatriots; in this way the Poles recruited from the front line itself. United States' formations included Japanese Americans (Nisei), while from South America came a Brazilian Expeditionary Division to join Fifth Army. Italian formations came into the battle line to help cover some mountain sectors. Most significant of all was the arrival from the United States of the highly trained 10th Mountain Division. Truscott sent it into action to gain battle experience, supported by the Brazilians, in mid-February in an attack to clear dominating ground astride Highway 64 leading to Bologna and a jump-off position for the spring offensive. Spearheaded by specialist rock-climbing teams, and in one instance roping an entire battalion up a 3,000-foot ridge, the attack secured some daunting heights and made such progress that the 29th Panzer Grenadier Division had to be brought in to bolster the infantry trying to stop them. By then the 10th had achieved its objective. It was the old story – skilled mountain troops could achieve much in Italy, but there were never enough of them. Had the Allies possessed them in greater numbers and the knowledge of how best to use them at the beginning of 1944, the Italian Campaign would have been a very different story.

Also appearing in Italy in early 1945 was specialized armour that had proved itself in North-West Europe, for employment in the lower lying and waterlogged ground. These included two types of armoured personnel carrier: the Kangaroos, which were M-4 Sherman tanks with their turrets removed and extended crew compartments, and the amphibious Buffalo LVTs (Landing Vehicles, Tracked), which in Italy would be called Fantails. There were also Duplex-Drive amphibious Sherman tanks, and tanks with specially widened track links to enable progress over soft ground. And for the forthcoming offensive, bridging equipment and materials were made available on a heavy scale.

As he had done before, in early 1945 Kesselring waited for the Allies to attack him. His armies, Fourteenth opposite Fifth Army around Bologna and Tenth covering the Romagna in the path of Eighth Army, had some 23 divisions plus some Italian Fascist battle groups. Although in varying states of manpower and equipment, the German formations in northern

Italy were generally better placed than those fighting in North-West Europe or trying to hold the Soviet onslaught from the east. Their combat power remained formidable, and they were preparing to stand upon a number of river lines before the Po – the Senio, the Santerro and the Sillaro (codenamed the Irmgard, Laura and Paula Lines respectively), while the even more dramatically named Ghengis Khan Line lay in front of Bologna. To the rear was the River Po, and a contingency plan, 'Autumn Mist' had been drawn up for a withdrawal across it into a further and much stronger line, the Venetian Line along the River Adige at the very foothills of the Alps. Once again German military engineers and labour organizations were hard at work to the rear.

Kesselring and his commanders had little hope of holding south of the Po against a major Allied onslaught. Once again, as he had before, Kesselring had to keep a reserve – in this case those old stalwarts the 29th and 90th Panzer Grenadier Divisions – against the threat of an amphibious descent on his flanks. Whereas Kesselring hoped to pull back in good order over the Po once – and if – Hitler agreed to a timely 'Autumn Mist', Alexander and his commanders were determined to destroy his armies before they could do so. In the weeks before their offensive, the Allied air forces, including the heavy bombers, whose strategic targets were by then fewer, conducted a relentless offensive against the German communications and supply lines. Though the Germans had substantial stockpiles of food and ammunition in place south of the Po, fuel was in critically short supply, and air attacks made deploying in or out of Italy a nightmare of losses, delays and disruption. This hardly boded well for 'Autumn Mist' if ever attempted in good flying weather. The Allied air forces had already driven the Luftwaffe into history.

Kesselring would never fight this last battle in Italy. At the end of March, Hitler appointed him to command the Western Front, presumably in the desperate hope that he could work a defensive miracle there as he had done in the south. He was replaced as Commander of Army Group C by von Vietinghoff, recalled from the grim Baltic Front where he had been posted earlier in the year. As an Army commander, von Vietinghoff was a fighter – he had proved that at Salerno and ever since – but in the fighting that was about to erupt for the last time in Italy his responsibilities would be far wider, and Kesselring's intuitive and sure touch would no longer be there to guide him.

In April the offensive began. It was Clark's battle and this could be seen in that he had made Truscott's Fifth Army the principal strike force to the west of Bologna; Eighth Army attacked first across the Senio to draw von Vietinghoff's reserves. The threat, induced by a deception scheme, of Eighth Army being the main attack force in conjunction with an amphibious landing north of the Po on the Venetian coast, was plausible enough to the Germans and raised the spectre of Anzio. The 29th Panzer Grenadier Division was held back watching the Venitian coastline while Eighth Army crashed over the Senio behind a weight of artillery and air support, including heavy bombers and phased fighter-bomber waves, that surpassed what had blasted it over the Sangro more than a year earlier. An amphibious flank attack to clear the Lake Comacchio area by Commandos supported the offensive on the right. On 14 April, also with a massive scale of air support including heavy bombers, Truscott attacked astride Highway 64. Several days of hard fighting broke the defence of XIV Panzer Corps around Bologna and on 22 April two armoured divisions, the 6th South African of Fifth Army and the 6th British of Eighth Army, linked up at the Po. Thereafter Army Group C's collapse was swift. With bridges downed by air attack and ferries destroyed, a trapped army dis-integrated. It was typical that the commander of the German I Parachute Corps, General Richard Heidrich, whose men had been such resolute opponents in Italy, should swim across the Po rather than be captured. It was a fitting end.[6] On 2 May, Army Group C formally surrendered to the Allies, the first of the German battlefronts to do so. That too was fitting.

16

FIGHTING IN ITALY:
THE VOICE OF EXPERIENCE

'On May 13, 1944, I moved out with a five-man patrol, down a deep draw running perpendicular to the enemy lines. This patrol was not a battalion order but independent action of the platoon. We moved out in a draw which was winding and affected good concealment in advancing. I informed my men that our mission was to investigate the draw for approximately 800 yards and fight only if necessary. It was my desire to capture a German, if possible, and I believed at that time of day he would not be alert since there never was any daytime activity on the beachhead. We proceeded in single file down the draw for approximately 600 yards until we came to a bend in the draw after which it straightened out for about 150 yards. At this point, I observed a German crawling into a machine-gun position up on the side of the bank about 150 yards away. I left three men behind at this point in position to place fire on that gun should they open up. My sergeant and I proceeded on down the draw. I instructed the men I left behind not to fire unless the enemy fired, or unless I opened fire. Using the available cover and concealment we advanced to within 50 yards of the gun emplacement. At this time, one of my men opened fire with a tommy-gun*. I found out later he had done so because he saw a German rise up and aim a rifle in the direction of the sergeant and myself. He hit the German, but at this point Jerry opened up with crossing machine gun fire and a rain of potato mashers**. The first grenade wounded me in the arm and leg, rendering my right arm useless. The sergeant was hit in the leg and couldn't walk. There were approximately 14 Germans in this position and they witnessed our approach and sucked us in. They came out of their position and got in behind us and drove off my three men. Then they started toward us searching through the grass. We decided we didn't have a chance to fight our way out and rather than surrender we decided to take our chance on their not finding us. They walked through us but did not find us. When they had all gone back to their position we decided we would have to stay until dark because we were wounded and could not fight effectively if observed moving out. Too, there was no wind blowing and trying to crawl out through tall grass would have attracted attention. We lay still until 10 o'clock that night, at which time we got out safely and returned to our lines.'[1]

* Thompson submachine-gun. ** German long-handled stick grenade.

Narrative campaign histories refer to the operations of divisions and battalions to paint a broad picture of battle, but they necessarily sweep over a mass of detail and experience that affected the individual soldiers. What did it really involve, for example, to take out a fighting patrol during the stalemate period of the Anzio beachhead, or to 'clear' a mountain feature of the enemy or to 'secure' a position? It is not the main purpose of this chapter to try and convey the horror and futility of war, or even for that matter the appalling conditions under which men were compelled to fight, though of course these emerge and it takes very little reading 'between the lines' to find them. Rather, it is intended to allow the soldiers of the Italian campaign to speak for themselves, to describe the nature of their war and the tactical methods they employed to overcome an enemy whose skill they had learned to respect but whom they now knew they could beat in the field. It is the voice of the young battle-hardened professional whose combat experiences and opinions were urgently required at the time by their armies' training organizations who were busily preparing men to face a similar test.

Mountain Warfare

You have an abnormal situation in mountains like these. You can't scale the peaks and you can't use the valleys which are mined. This means you must work the slopes. You must concentrate on taking one terrain feature. When you get that you must decide the next one to tackle. You can only learn these special tactics by going in and applying them.[2]

With the exception of the Indian divisions and the North African soldiers of the French colonial divisions, and later in the campaign the arrival of the superb US 10th Mountain Division, most Allied infantry were neither mountain-trained nor suitably mountain-equipped. They had to learn their mountain fighting the hard way, though without question they became increasingly proficient in understanding and exploiting such terrain. The basic problem was penetrating often complex defence zones to secure the dominating heights that controlled much of the surrounding area, while avoiding the valleys and natural approaches, such as trails, that had been mined extensively or which were covered by well-sited and difficult-to-locate strongpoints. This meant that infantry had to learn how to move and fight along the ridges and slopes, to overcome not only the physical but also the psychological barrier imposed by such terrain. Experience taught them how to recognize and exploit the potential of such ground, but they had to become 'mountain goats' in order to do so. To outflank and approach German positions by unexpected routes not previously identified by the Germans and registered by their guns usually meant hours of extreme exertion as men climbed, and sometimes crawled, in order to attain the ground from which to attack. It was work for small units and it depended upon good preliminary reconnaissance of the ground, an ability to use concealment and cover, and close coordination of small parties moving across dispersed and narrow frontages dictated by the terrain.

Movement and fighting in the mountains caused difficulties in a number of ways. The most apparent in Italy during 1943–4, and in contrast to the Sicily experience, was the effect of extreme physical exertion in winter weather conditions. In Sicily, in a comparatively short campaign during July and August 1943, Allied soldiers had to cope with mountains in very hot and very dry conditions. In a more prolonged period in Italy during the following winter, they had to move, fight and live for days and sometimes weeks at a time in mountains under conditions of very low temperatures, heavy rain and pervading damp, mud, frequently high winds, sleet and snow – and often with only the most rudimentary of shelters. This pushed men to the very limits of physical endurance, and Allied reports stress again and again that only the very fittest could stand up to it:

> Among all ranks physical hardening and conditioning to meet excessive strain of the mountain campaign have been paramount to the success of operations ... Only the highest level of hardening and stamina can resist the physical strain of combat operations under these conditions. The high percentage of non-battle casualties as a result of exhaustion and physical breakdown as well by sickness has demonstrated this fact only too clearly in Italy.[3]

> The importance of the highest standard of physical fitness has been brought out in the last few months. Mtn Arty personnel have got to be of real A1 standard in order to stand up to the strain.[4]

Even the toughest among the Allied troops were severely tested, as the commanding officer of an American Ranger battalion reported:

The Battalion relieved an RCT* in the sector north of VENAFRO and after splitting the Battalion due to the terrain, attacked and took the heights in their sector. The terrain was extremely rugged and heavily mined, and the weather was cold and wet. The enemy constantly shelled and counter-attacked the positions. Under such circumstances there were many cases of physical and mental exhaustion, especially among replacements. The action was such that even the older (battle hardened) men were affected.[5]

Prolonged periods of exposure and immersion in water brought again such debilitating problems as atrophy of the limbs and, particularly, the old scourge of the First World War, 'trench foot'. The following advice from a US 34th Infantry Division veteran indicates the basic measures taken to ward off the worst effects of wet and cold, but equally clear is the fact that there was little enough that could be done:

> You cannot smoke very often as your wind becomes cut. The neglect of the feet leads to trenchfoot. The socks have to be dried, if possible, and changed. Even though the shoes are damp or wet, dry socks and the feet dried by rubbing well with a towel and massaging with hands, feel much better and blood circulates again thus taking the cold and pain out of them. New men or replacements are the persons who have the most trouble. The clothing, when wet, should be wrung out for a damp piece of clothing is not near as miserable and discomforting as a soaking wet piece. For the bed, instead of lying on the cold, damp ground, you can gather up dry leaves, straw, long grass or cardboard upon which blankets can be placed. This keeps the cold from penetrating the body, thus causing aches and pains and cases of rheumatism.[6]

Men could not hope to survive at all in the mountains without adequate supplies of food and water. Infantry advancing in mountains had to take with them what they could in the hope that re-supply by mules or by porters would catch up with them sooner, rather than later, and not too late. The same was true of the essentials for fighting – ammunition and medical supplies to treat the wounded. All were held in limited amounts that were soon depleted, which affected fighting efficiency. A man might function for a time while he was hungry and thirsty, but a machine-gun or mortar badly needed for fire support would be no more than lumber

* Regimental Combat Team.

without ammunition. Casualties had to be evacuated for proper medical attention, but in mountain warfare stretcher bearers (sometimes referred to as litter bearers by the Americans) faced acute difficulties in getting their charges down the mountain slopes. In an example quoted by the US 34th Division, the time estimated to evacuate casualties from the mountains was two casualties per litter squad per day; not surprisingly men had to be taken from the rifle companies to assist, which in turn weakened the firing line.[7]

In addition to the problems of movement in the mountains, the attackers also had to locate the enemy positions. One lesson learned early was that the Germans favoured rear slope defences, which it had their advantages in that positions were protected from Allied observation.

> The German puts more men on the reverse slope than on the forward. The tendency of our infantry has been to use the forward slope and be easily observed and get the hell shelled out of them.[8]

Close fire support to deal with well-constructed German bunkers, strongpoints, gun and mortar positions was essential. As in Sicily, and despite the paucity of good roads and difficulties caused by weather, the Allied artillery very rarely failed to keep the battle front within the range of its guns. Nevertheless, because of terrain and difficulties of observation in dead ground, artillery could not always be brought to bear, or at least not with the necessary accuracy, upon specific targets. This task fell to the infantry's own close-support weapons, their heavy machine-guns and, particularly, their mortars, which became increasingly important as the mountain fighting progressed. Experience brought forth a high level of skill in using them and in exploiting their effect. Here, for example, an American infantry company commander reports how his unit captured a strongly defended German hill position by effective use of his supporting 81mm mortars:

> I pushed on with the leading platoon to a small hill just south of HILL 760 (the objective), but we met with heavy fire as soon as we tried to move forward towards HILL 760. First, I called for a mortar concentration on HILL 760. There was quite a pause after that. Then I called for another concentration on the same area, but this time I arranged for the 81's to start

firing about two minutes after this concentration lifted. The 81's caught the Germans just coming out of their shelters, we could tell by the screams that we got a lot of them.

My object was to work on the Germans until I could count on their staying in their shelters for at least five minutes after a concentration. So I kept mixing up the fire. Sometimes I would throw in my 60's to hit an area where I figured they were taking cover from the heavier stuff. Several times this drove the Germans out in into the open where we could shoot them down with rifles and BAR's.*

Finally I had worked them over long enough to be pretty sure that they wouldn't poke their heads out of their shelters for five or ten minutes after a concentration had lifted. I gave orders for the leading platoon to move forward as far as possible under the next concentration and to charge HILL 760 as soon as the concentration stopped. Then I called for another concentration on HILL 760. The concentration came down and the leading platoon moved forward. When the concentration lifted they charged and caught the Germans just coming out of their shelters and took them prisoner in about thirty seconds. We captured our objective with almost no casualties.[9]

Adept use of supporting fire certainly saved the lives of the American company commander's men in this attack, and his account indicates the psychological ascendancy that his possession and use of firepower gave him over his enemy. Quite clearly too his mortars were not short of ammunition. Such fire was usually directed by observers, unobserved fire being far too wasteful of precious ammunition; indeed ensuring ammunition stocks and their replenishment in the Italian mountains was a major problem in itself:

> An expenditure of thirty to fifty rounds per mortar per day is fairly common over here. One company has fired as much as 250 rounds of 60mm mortar ammunition in one day. Remember that all this has to be carried up a mountain by hand ... [10]

It was found more effective with the advancing infantry to have fewer mortars, which could keep firing for longer, than a larger number of mortars that quickly used up all the ammunition, leaving the infantry without their fire support. When infantry were moving as fast as they

---

* Browning Automatic Rifles.

could in the mountains, the mortars, carried on mules, could not keep up, with obvious implications for the responsiveness of fire support. For example, the US 504th Parachute Infantry, serving as conventional infantry with Fifth Army, reported that, although its companies' mortar platoons were each equipped with six 81mm mortars, they carried only two, with six mules per mortar, one for the mortar and the others each carrying eighteen rounds. Over a move of two or three miles, these mules would fall about half an hour behind the infantry, a significant time lapse. Nor was it wise to try and hurry mules, as to do so risked them slipping and falling, perhaps to their death, and the loss of their loads. As in Sicily, mules were a precious commodity.[11]

Although not available in great quantity, mountain artillery could also provide close support that the field and medium artillery sometimes could not, because it was able to engage targets in difficult ground and in close proximity to friendly troops with more precision. This was the experience of the British 85th Mountain Regiment (Royal Artillery), which reported that it had been employed 'constantly and usefully' in the close-support role, and in providing fire support to more mobile troops engaged on flank protection moving through difficult terrain. Movement depended upon mule and jeep transport, and it had one battery equipped with four 75mm pack howitzers (9,500 yards range) and two batteries each with four 3.7-inch pack howitzers (5,500 yards range). The latter weapons proved inadequate in range, compelling the gunners to take up often hazardous forward-slope positions under German observation in order to keep the infantry supported. Ammunition supply was also a problem, with stocks all too rapidly diminished. The Regiment reported that it really required at least double the amount of 75mm airburst rounds and 3.7-inch smoke rounds, useful for their incendiary effect, and that shortages prevented the guns from participating in divisional and corps fire plans.[12]

Neither mortars nor even mountain artillery could be depended upon actually to destroy some of the extremely well-constructed German bunkers and strongpoints, many of which were heavily protected. Even direct hits were more likely to just blow away some of the outer protection, and usually the infantry had to close with the position and put it out of action themselves. Supporting fire was important in enabling them to close with such positions by temporarily neutralizing the enemy fire and forcing the German troops to take cover. As in the example cited above, Allied infantry learned to exploit such effects, to 'lean on' their supporting fire by advancing under its cover so close as to sometimes catch German troops emerging from shelters before they could man their fire positions.

Firepower in Support of the Infantry Attack

Such exploitation of firepower had a resonance beyond mountain fighting, and, when the ground allowed, infantry attacked under the protection of heavy, moving concentrations of artillery fire, 'creeping barrages'. When successful, a defence could be blotted out by the weight of fire and prevented from reacting, and positions could be taken with few casualties providing the attacking infantry followed close upon the shells. The risk, however, was that of the attacking infantry suffering casualties from their own supporting fire. This was considered acceptable:

> Infantry advancing under a creeping barrage must keep up close to it, and prefer to accept the small risk of being hit by their own shells rather than the far greater risk they incur by lagging behind and subjecting themselves to the fire of an unblinded and recovering enemy. The barrage can be paused at any time at the commander's discretion.[13]

> In many instances our troops have not taken advantage of shock action and it has cost us many casualties. By the term SHOCK ACTION I mean artillery concentrations, mortar fire, bombing attacks, tank or TD* fire, bazooka fire and hand grenades. All must be followed aggressively and with no delay. Artillery concentrations and barrages are practically useless unless they are followed closely enough so that the rifleman can close with the enemy before the enemy front line soldier realizes that the fire has lifted and runs back to man his guns. In following the artillery closely you may have some casualties from your own artillery, but in the long run your casualties will be much lower.[14]

Success also depended upon the infantry keeping up with the creeping barrage, a challenge over broken ground. The British 78th Infantry Division, reporting on its experience in Italy between May and July 1944, reckoned on a rate of advance under barrage cover of 200 yards in 16

* Tank Destroyer.

minutes over broken country, and 200 yards in 12 minutes over easier ground. Fighting in Italy soon indicated to the Allies that only by a heavy use of firepower could they hope to overcome strong German defensive positions, and inexperienced troops gaining battle experience were particularly reliant upon its support.

Ammunition expenditure was phenomenal in Italy. In November 1943, Eighth Army literally blasted its way across the River Sangro, its 25-pounder field guns firing more than 600 rounds per gun in three days, and its medium artillery firing in excess of 300 rounds per gun. This was in addition to the Desert Air Force also attacking German positions ahead of the advance. During the Gustav Line battles at Cassino there were occasions when, to support an attack, British and American artillery fired at the rate of up to 800 rounds per gun in short periods of time.[15]

Through a comprehensive network of communications linking forward observers with the gun concentrations, the Allied artillery became a finely tuned and responsive weapon, able to lay down fire rapidly within minutes. The entire weight of a corps' artillery could be called down to support an attack in a particular sector, to engage an opportunity target spotted by observers, or to ensure that a defence could withstand a German counterattack. There were occasions when only the massed fire of the guns, and a lavish expenditure of shells enabled precariously-held positions, and especially unconsolidated bridgeheads during river crossing operations, to hold on against German tank and infantry counterattacks. An instance was the savage fighting to hold the initial bridgehead over the River Garigliano in January 1944, when the British X Corps infantry battalions only just across the river stood little chance against a determined onslaught by formidable German infantry and armour battle groups. The history of the Fifth British Division later recalled the

> solid steel wall of defensive Artillery fire that was invariably put round our positions when they were being counterattacked. No infantryman in the Division need feel ashamed or would be unprepared to acknowledge that the gunners probably held the small Garigliano bridgehead when called to do so at frequent intervals. So frequent were these demands for this that the Divisional Artillery fired practically unceasingly for many days …[16]

The other side of the picture was that such intensity of fire played havoc with the efforts to conserve ammunition stocks for later offensive action, and there were periods of local shortages and of imposed artillery famine when strict limitations had to be imposed on the number of rounds that guns could fire. Not long into the mainland campaign the British discovered that their artillery expenditure was far exceeding previous experience in Tunisia, to the tune of some 22,000 tons per month in Italy between October and December 1943 compared with the 10,000 tons per month used during the final months in Tunisia.[17]

Prolonged periods of heavy firing also increased the wear on the guns and equipment, so that there was an increase in the rate of maintenance, such as gun-barrel replacement. Rugged mountain conditions and severe weather also took their toll of equipment and of movement. Suitable gun positions had often to be blasted out of rock, and in the winter mud it was common for guns to sink and have to be subsequently winched out. The last word might well be left to a major of the US 34th Infantry Division's artillery:

> It is unnecessary to tell an experienced foot-slogging dogface how impor-
> tant artillery support is to him when he needs it. When he runs up against
> a Jerry strongpoint that is too tough to crack with infantry weapons the
> proper thing to do is to yell for artillery. He's got to be sure, however, that
> the target he sees is worth tossing a lot of cannonballs at because cannon-
> balls are the only reserve the artillery has and they cost sweat and blood. A
> single Heinie sunning himself or an Eyetie mule and cart is not worth an
> artillery concentration.[18]

German Counterattack and Allied Patrolling

The successful capture of a prominent terrain feature might unhinge a German defence zone, but it was equally important to be able to move fast to forestall the Germans from occupying adjacent ground from which their fire might make the captured height untenable. This was always a major challenge, especially when breaking into well-prepared defence zones of depth, which the Germans had occupied for some time, such as the Bernhardt Line positions and, especially, the Gustav and Gothic Lines. Even with efficient patrolling, when Allied infantry broke into the ground of such defence zones they frequently could not obtain a clear picture of the German positions and strength opposing them until actually in contact. The Germans were expert at concealing their positions, and the available maps did not always indicate the precise lie of the land and its concealment possibilities.

> Reports of patrols that a feature is unoccupied are not always reliable. The Germans frequently allow patrols to proceed unmolested, lying in wait to ambush the main forces.[19]

Unless attacking particularly strong defensive positions, Allied formations generally found the Germans barring their advance with defence localities covered by about a battalion of infantry, supported by a few tanks and self-propelled guns and, most often, large numbers of skilfully sited mortars. In favouring rear-slope defence in mountainous or hilly terrain, meaning that most of their troops and positions were sited on the reverse slopes of their defended features, the Germans were well positioned to bring down heavy fire on Allied troops as they advanced over the crests. Such positions were difficult to spot or to engage with artillery. Having occupied the ground usually for some time before the arrival of the Allied troops the Germans had a further advantage too: their guns and mortars were already registered on the ground over which the Allied troops were moving, and particularly upon its landmarks. Allied infantry soon learned that it did not pay to site their own positions or to dig in even temporarily near such sites as cross-roads, the junctions of roads and trails, or main stream beds, for these might – without warning – receive a sudden deluge of shells or mortar rounds:

> During one phase of the mountain fighting my platoon dug-in in the vicinity of a prominent trail junction. That evening Jerry threw some 170's at that trail junction. My platoon suffered three casualties. Results could have been worse. Lesson learned – avoid as much as possible all prominent land marks, which Jerry might have 'zeroed in' ... [20]

A particular threat to Allied infantry that had just secured a feature was a swift German counterattack, often preceded by a sudden heavy bombardment by artillery and mortars calculated to catch the Allied troops before they had consolidated. For reasons given above, it did not do for Allied infantry to occupy the slit trenches just vacated or captured from the Germans, and which had been 'zeroed in' by German guns and mortars. All too often Allied infantry found that their troubles only really began once they had secured an objective. An adequate defence with outposts established far enough forward to give warning of counterattack had to be established immediately. The British 78th Infantry Division gave the following warning:

> It is emphasised that troops who have captured and consolidated an objective can in no way be considered to be resting and are, indeed, frequently subjected to more intensive fire at such times than in the attack. Early relief, within 24 hours if possible, is important.[21]

The Germans were also adept at employing a spoiling attack to precede and cover a withdrawal. In particular, Allied troops learned to be wary of a late-afternoon attack, intended to cause shock and disorganization and thus enable a German withdrawal under the cover of darkness. In the words of an infantry captain of the US 34th Infantry Division referring to an action near Campoleone:

> The situation had been stabilized by quite a number of German infantry and tanks and we had been in approximately the same position for 48 hours. During that time there were heavy exchanges of artillery and mortar fire plus machine gun and sniper fire whenever a soldier exposed himself.
>
> Just at dusk on the second evening Jerry had decided he had taken enough punishment (as we learned later) and made a withdrawal. The general method that he uses to throw us off balance is to make two or three small attacks accompanied by much artillery. This particular evening he hit us with two simultaneous attacks each composed of approximately one platoon of infantry and one tank. He drove in our outposts and the enemy infantry came right to our MLR* before it was stopped. Then he immediately withdrew out of the zone of our defensive fires. The whole operation did not take 15 minutes at the most. The confusion and excitement that follows every attack by the enemy was intensified by the darkness, and, needless to say, it was at this time that the enemy completed his withdrawal. In spite of our continual heavy harassment the Germans managed to take all their equipment and wounded with them, although they left about 100 dead on the field.[22]

* Main Line of Resistance.

Often the fighting in Italy devolved into actions by small units, especially in mountainous terrain where the difficult ground restricted movement and attack frontages. Control, particularly when attacks were being carried out in darkness to maximize surprise and minimize casualties, was often difficult to maintain and could easily break down. It was then, much as Lieutenant Colonel Wigram had already observed in Sicily, that the outcome of battle depended upon a comparatively few men. The American infantry captain quoted above provides a graphic description of the problem, while urging the necessity of training companies for night attack:

> small groups must attack a limited objective simultaneously and reorganize into their company organization upon reaching the objective. There often are not enough trained men capable of guiding groups across strange ground and of recognizing their objective in the dark. Consequently, the few men that are capable have to do most of the fighting for a company while the rest of the unit comes along in a column of twos, each man keeping so close to the man in front of him that he steps on his heels for fear that he and all the men behind him will get lost if he breaks contact.[23]

Fundamentals of infantry fighting – thorough reconnaissance by active and aggressive patrolling to detect the German positions and minefields, plus the use of cover for approaches and concealment – had to be adapted. The individual soldier had to adapt too, to show a greater degree of initiative and resourcefulness. Allied formations generally responded well to these demands, which were important to mountain fighting but by no means restricted to it. Methods were much as Wigram had advocated after the Sicily experience. For example, in the British 78th Division the Royal West Kent battalion established a system of patrolling by specialist picked men commanded by a single officer who was allotted a proportion of men from each company. They were employed only for patrolling, raiding and providing protection for sappers and forward reconnaissance by tanks.[24] Other formations tended to follow suit. Following observer visits to the British 56th Division, 7th Armoured Division and 23rd Armoured Brigade serving in Fifth Army, a British report of November 1943 observed the particular difficulties in communications and maintaining contact with the enemy in difficult terrain, and noted of 56th Division:

The Division, in an effort to solve both these difficulties, is thinking very much along the same lines as 78 Division with its Battle Patrols. The object is to get behind the enemy in order to cut off his retreat and also prevent him blowing the bridges, demolishing the buildings across the roads, and making craters.[25]

The Americans developed similar tactics. The 34th Division recorded that during its spell in the Anzio beachhead it had to find ways of increasing patrol efficiency in order to obtain data on the German positions across large sectors of the Division's front:

> To remedy the situation a special patrol group was organized in each regiment of volunteer men. Given names such as the 168th Infantry Rattlesnakes, the 133rd Infantry Red Raiders and the 135th Infantry Blue Devils, the men lived and rehearsed their operations in the rear area. In a relatively short time the new organizations proved their worth and provided the Division with a wealth of information.[26]

This was a clear echo of Wigram's Sicily experience and suggests an increased efficiency followed from greater initiative and psychological affinity with a specialist aggressive role.

Casualties and Replacements

Casualties in the infantry rifle companies were heavy throughout the Italian campaign, and the battle losses among junior officers and the consequent effect upon small-unit leadership became a serious concern in the Allied armies. A British report stressed the need for officers to avoid being conspicuous and thereby a favoured target of snipers:

> The need for officers to wear dress and equipment indistinguishable from that of O.R.s is once again stressed. Only so will officer casualties be kept down.[27]

The Americans also acknowledged the need for the infantry units to have a means of filling gaps in battle leadership at critical times and at very short notice. In a sober acknowledgement of the rate of officer casualties, the US 45th Infantry Division reported:

The battalion commander problem is serious. The way to train battalion commanders is to take one out and send him visiting other battalions where he can learn and teach. Meanwhile the executive gets command and gets trained. Organizations are frequently too much a one-man job – he gets killed and the organization lacks leadership. The same situation is true of company commanders. Every lieutenant should know he is going to be a company commander.[28]

A similar report later in 1944 raised the same issue:

The casualty rate in platoon leaders is high. For this reason platoon sergeants must be trained as reserve platoon leaders.[29]

Filling gaps caused by casualties in formations committed to the battle posed the serious problem that, until they gained some experience, the raw replacements were far more vulnerable than veterans, and it frequently happened that the veterans took additional risks to keep them from making foolish and fatal mistakes. It was also the point at which shortfalls in training became glaringly apparent. An experienced Sergeant of an American infantry regiment recorded the following incident:

I have witnessed many fellow GI's in action. In one case we were going through the brush in the mountains and a machine-pistol opened up on us from our flank and we all hit the ground. We had a few new men with us that had just come in. No one had to tell them to get down, they just did. I asked one later how come he got down and he said it came natural. He took cover and good cover. He got behind a big rock, but the trouble came after that. He got down and then started trying to figure out just where the fire was coming from. He went around the rock twice, until I finally got close enough to point out the direction in which the bullets were coming from. I, myself had the same experience when I first came in and had to learn the hard way.

In an unconscious echo of Wigram's report on the Sicily fighting, this particular soldier called for better training to enable men to discern the direction of fire. There were other lessons learned the hard way, including knowing when to open fire, and when not to. Another example graphically described by an American Sergeant:

On the night of July 7, 1944, Company "G" attacked and took HILL 163, completely surprising the Jerries. We immediately began to dig in the hard rock for dawn would soon overtake us. Dawn broke and everything was quiet, too quiet. To our front a single Jerry jumped up, started running like "hell" to his lines. One of our riflemen fired and missed. Then another took upon himself to fire. Soon the whole company was placing its whole fire power on the single Jerry. The whole Jerry army let loose with small arms and 88's,* resulting in many casualties and deaths just because we had given away our position, strength and fire power on a single Jerry. We learned by experience to hold and control your fire until it is needed. [30]

The Urban Battle

It is often wasteful and unnecessary to commit troops to street and village fighting where towns and villages do NOT lie on main axis of advance and can be by-passed. The very fact of being by-passed and outflanked is often enough to make the enemy withdraw. When by-passing is not practicable, troops should be used lavishly, on about the scale of one platoon per five or ten houses.[31]

The time-consuming and potentially costly urban battle was avoided when possible but there were occasions, most notably when the Canadians reached the port town of Ortona in December 1943 and in the fighting at Cassino in February–March 1944, when Allied troops had to clear urban areas deliberately turned into strongpoints for a prolonged defensive battle. These occasions saw the employment of special tactics to clear individual buildings and entire streets turned into miniature fortresses forming part of a complex and interlocking defence zone.

The Canadians cleared Ortona with their infantry working in small teams to overcome building strongpoints and blocks of buildings systematically, working sector by sector. Although artillery assisted the assault troops (which were drawn from principally two battalions) to break into the town, once inside the battle became one of small units closely coordinated with their own close-support arms. These were heavy machine-guns, mortars, anti-tank guns and also tanks, and they proved essential in suppressing German defensive fire and blasting gaps in walls through which the assault troops could enter the buildings. The Canadian infantry also found their man-portable PIAT (Projector Infantry Anti-Tank) anti-tank weapon, of questionable value in its intended role, to be an invaluable

---

* 88mm artillery.

close-support weapon for close-in street fighting. Once inside the buildings, the infantry were engaged in savage close-quarter fighting from room
to room in which the submachine-gun and, especially, the grenade,
became the favoured weapons. The Canadians also soon learned that the
best way to clear buildings was from the top down, employing a technique
called 'mouse-holing', using explosive charges to blast holes through
connecting walls into adjacent buildings and avoiding the obvious routes
covered by German guns:

> It was found that to clear a house from the bottom to the top was appallingly
> expensive and for every German killed going up the stairs it cost us one of
> our own men.[32]

Gradually, in a week of fighting, the Canadians gained the upper hand,
clearing systematically and consolidating their hold on each block and
sector before moving on to the next, and ensuring against German re-
infiltration through concealed tunnels by leaving sufficient troops in possession of what had been gained. It was a time-consuming and intensive
battle, lulls occurring at night when both sides used darkness for re-supply,
relief and redeployment.

The US 34th Infantry Division became heavily engaged in street fighting in Italy, and particularly at Cassino, in the early part of 1944. The
following graphic accounts recorded in 1944 by some of its officers and
NCOs indicate strong comparisons with the Canadian experience at
Ortona, and in particular demonstrate the 34th Division's verdict on street
fighting: 'there is no easy answer to the problem. The enemy can only be
evicted by hard work.' An infantry Major provided a very comprehensive
picture of the fighting in Cassino:

> In discussing street fighting in Italy the reader must first realize that most of
> the Italian towns do not have regular well laid out streets, and that all the
> buildings are close together and have thick stone walls and usually very few
> doors and windows. In CASSINO the Germans had every building in the
> line of our advance fortified. Gun emplacements also were camouflaged in
> piles of rubble presumably created by our own artillery and tank fire. Their
> fires were well planned and coordinated so that each gun was covered by
> another.

To gain our first foothold in the town we used smoke and tanks supported by infantry. The infantry under unobserved fire removed mines and filled in anti-tank ditches to assist the advance of the tanks. On gaining the first foothold we got the men in buildings and consolidated our positions with particular attention to getting bazookas in large numbers placed in the most forward positions. German tanks in this sector had been giving us trouble, but the German armor didn't bother us in CASSINO because we had so many bazookas well forward. The bazookas proved to be a very effective weapon in street fighting. It was the squad leaders' direct fire artillery and with very little instruction and experience can be fired with surprising accuracy. Since all doors and lower windows were covered by fire, at times we had to make other entrances to these buildings through thick stone walls. If tanks could be maneuvered to shoot holes in these walls, it was done. Otherwise, the bazooka was used. In one instance it took nine rounds to get a hole big enough to go through. After an entrance was found or made a grenade always preceded the infantryman into the room if there was any possibility of Germans being there. In cases where a house could not be approached, tank fire was used to level the building to the ground. Of course, this gave the Germans some wonderful rubble piles to build camouflaged emplacements but they lost the overhead cover for artillery and mortar fire. We also used an 8" howitzer on some buildings. It can be fired with precision and changes as small as ten yards can be made so we used it on targets within 50 yards of our own troops. We called it sniping with an 8" how. Mortars were not too effective against the buildings and were used mainly to harass and interdict paths.

Snipers were employed freely by both sides and sometimes I am inclined to think the Germans had more success than we did. During the lulls our men got careless and became excellent targets. On the beachhead at ANZIO the opposite seemed to hold true.

In the house-to-house fighting or room-to-room fighting most of the men preferred the Tommy-gun and because of its size preferred the carbine to the rifle for working in close quarters. For defense, machine guns, both light and heavy, and BAR's were placed with the forward elements.

When we were in CASSINO the nights were very dark so little offensive action was attempted. At times we would have a very limited objective of say the next house. In many cases 'No Man's Land' consisted of about a 10-yard space between two houses; this was ideal for playing catch with grenades. A grenade that explodes on impact could have been used. At night we would make re-adjustments, reliefs, bring up supplies, and evacuate killed and wounded. The hand carry was only about 200 yards. Except in the most forward positions movement was comparatively safe.

This officer also noted the problem of maintaining communications in the town, vitally important for retaining control of the battle. As the Canadians also found in Ortona, radios functioned poorly and wire was continually being cut by artillery and mortar fire so that much reliance was placed upon runners and linesmen. The same American officer also referred to the Cassino fighting when stressing the importance of infantry exploiting their fire support properly, and once again a vivid picture of the battle in the town emerges through his account:

> One day at CASSINO we had a coordinated attack planned to get Company 'L' across the main street to gain a foothold on that side of town. Tanks were to fire a preparation on known and suspected targets and, as a signal to the riflemen that the tanks were to cease firing, the command tank was to fire four rounds in a doorway that was visible to all. Then the infantrymen were to dash across the street immediately and gain entrance to the buildings before the enemy had recovered. However, the riflemen waited 10 minutes before they started and by that time the Germans were back on their guns and stopped the attack. There is no fire more devastating and morale shattering than well-directed tank fire. At CASSINO the Germans knew the location of my battalion observation post and tried continually without success to knock it out with machine gun, mortar and artillery fire.
>
> German tanks gave us very little trouble in CASSINO but at dawn one morning they drove up one Mark VI* and started firing at my OP. Needless to say I was scared and was sitting in a corner saying my prayers and trying to call the artillery. I stayed in that corner, too, until five minutes after the last round was fired before I went back down the trail with the phone to try and splice it on the line. During those five minutes the enemy could have come in the building and found me in the corner with very little fight left.
>
> In CASSINO the battalion used, on the average, 500 grenades a day. One of our methods of advancing was to throw a grenade into a room and then to get into the room with a Tommy-gun right after the grenade went off. If there were any Germans in the room, those who were still alive were found lying on the floor with no fight left.[33]

The difficulty of clearing an urban area was well exemplified in the Cassino fighting, for the same battleground in the town that the US 34th Infantry Division came to know in January–February 1944 was also fought over by New Zealand troops in March, and despite bitter fighting

* The Mark VI was the Tiger.

the German paratrooper defenders retained a hold in the labyrinth of shattered buildings, craters and rubble.

Air Support

Allied possession of air superiority and the availability of large tactical air forces gave their armies a significant advantage in Italy, though not in itself a decisive one. Air power alone could not win the Italian campaign for the Allies, but when appropriately applied in concert with ground operations it could achieve an effect that could be exploited to achieve success. This effect of air power was most apparent when closely coordinated with ground action in an integrated plan, such as in the breakthrough following the 'Diadem' offensive when Allied fighter-bombers harassed the retreating German armies and disrupted their cohesion; also in the final offensive in April 1945 when Allied aircraft effectively pinned the Germans to the ground and cut off their retreat across the Po; there were numerous other examples. The diversion of the heavy bomber forces from their strategic role to the more unfamiliar one of close support of ground operations followed the imperative to overcome particularly formidable and stubborn German positions at less cost in lives and resources. Expectations of this form of air support had to be revised in the light of experience – such bombing could be counterproductive, as acknowledged in a report on the bombing of Cassino town in March 1944:

> The bombing achieved surprise and undoubtedly caused enemy to take shelter. At the same time the extra heavy bombing hindered our own advance by cratering and blocking of routes with debris ...
>
> In spite of heavy bombing and artillery fire, enemy machine guns, mortars and artillery were only partially neutralised. It is apparent that we cannot hope for any degree of complete destruction by bombing and artillery fire on a heavily fortified position. The lesson we can again draw is that infantry in sufficient quantity must follow the artillery barrage quickly to take advantage of the partial destruction of enemy works, the surprise effected and the shock to his troops caused by the weight of combined fires.[34]

The Allied tactical air forces, the RAF Desert Air Force and the US XII Air Support Command, became highly proficient partners to Eighth and

Fifth Armies, and as the campaign in Italy progressed close air support became a responsive and flexible weapon. The critical factors to success were that air and ground commanders learned how to integrate their operations. It was necessary to have a comprehensive communications system linking ground and air forces, including forward air controllers with the troops at the battlefront able to direct air strikes on to targets, and the availability of large numbers of fighter-bombers. This latter enabled the provision of aircraft kept over the battle front, able to be called down on to targets as required, a system known as 'Cabrank'. An example of the integration achieved and its success was seen in a British armoured attack in April 1945: In Operation Cygnet the 7th Armoured Brigade employing 2nd Royal Tank Regiment and the 10th Hussars, supported by a battalion of infantry (2/6th Queens) mounted in Kangaroos, attacked to clear a German pocket along the River Senio just to the north of Faenza. The pocket was held by some four battalions of German infantry supported by several tanks and self-propelled guns, and the ground was close and dotted with farm buildings, the principal roads mined. The attack plan determined to make the most of the frozen ground and achieve surprise by attacking along an unsuspected axis; there could be little artillery support because ammunition was in very short supply, but RAF Desert Air Force agreed to make up for this by providing a heavy scale of fighter-bomber support, including cabranks overhead, throughout the attack in close contact with forward controllers with the Brigade.

A closely coordinated plan was produced in which the fighter-bombers would sweep down to bomb and machine-gun strafe targets immediately ahead of the two leading tank squadrons, enabling the tanks to close-in upon strongpoints and overcome them by fire to in turn allow the infantry in Kangaroos to dismount and mop-up. Cygnet was a complete success, the pocket was cleared and some 300 German prisoners taken along with much equipment; there were only five British tank losses, two of which were subsequently recovered. The German defence had been paralysed by the combination of tank and air attack, in the words of the Armoured Brigade report:

> The efficiency of the CABRANK bombing was remarkable and has given very great confidence to the Tank crews in air support they are likely to get

in future operations. CABRANK was called down on groups of houses on the axes of the two leading Sqns whenever they were held up or suspected the presence of concealed A/Tk weapons ... Some targets were bombed within 200 yds of the leading tanks, and targets had to be adjusted quickly to conform with the forward movement of the tanks. On one occasion a target on the immediate front of the tanks was changed within five minutes of the time the aircraft were to attack, since the tanks reported they were occupying it. The aircraft were switched to another target a few hundred yds up the road and bombed with great success. Whenever air support was given it caused a temporary disorganisation of the enemy in the houses and enabled the tanks to close in without casualties ... There is no question that the accuracy, flexibility and speed of the CABRANK bombing contributed very largely to the success of this operation.[35]

Armour

There were comparatively few opportunities in the Italian terrain to maximize the effectiveness of armour en masse in sweeping attacks or pursuit operations. Much of the work conducted by tanks was in helping the infantry forward by overcoming stubborn defensive positions with their main armament and machine-guns. For both the British and Americans, the bulk of campaign experience reflected the need to learn how to best integrate the tank and its potential in this work of supporting the infantry, in both attack and defence. That there were problems in tank-infantry coordination, and that this was a learning process for both, is evident in the contemporary reports. In particular, there was a strong tendency for infantry commanders to want supporting tanks to remain with the forward troops, not only for fire support and protection but also to stiffen infantry morale. Yet this, as an outspoken report on its experience by British 7th Armoured Brigade in November 1944 observed, was

contrary to all teaching. Tanks should be relieved into forward rally at the earliest possible moment and anti-tank guns, SP and towed, must reach the objective in order that this may take place. It must be realised by all concerned that the tank has not yet been designed which can operate indefinitely without maintenance ... There is a tendency to look upon a tank as a SP anti-tank gun, as a heavy machine- gun and as a morale-raiser by its mere presence, in addition to its normal role. It is considered that full use is not made of the various arms which were designed for at least two of these roles. Tanks remaining on an objective during daylight for a length of time invariably attract artillery and mortar fire which causes casualties not only to tanks but also to the infantry. It is, therefore, not understood why it should be so popular.

Another problem in action was liaison, the report noting:

> Liaison between tanks and infantry was frequently established by tank commanders dismounting and going in search of infantry commanders on their feet. This, though essential at times, is extremely bad practice since the tank commander is away from his set and unable to receive fresh orders from his superior commanders. Infantry commanders in slit trenches, ditches, etc, are extremely difficult to find and it has been known that as much as an hour of fruitless search has been spent in this way. When tanks are in close proximity to the infantry it is considered that the infantry commander can clearly see the tank, can distinguish the troop leader's tank by the white mark on the barrel, and can time his movements, having regard to shelling and mortar fire, and liaise with the tank commander and make use of the tank telephone designed for this purpose.

Needless to say there was an infantry side to these issues, but clearly there were problems that only familiarity could solve. It was lamented that all too frequently infantry and tank commanders were given too little time for coordinating their battle and for information to be exchanged, and that on many occasions tanks simply 'motored into battle' with increased risks, and opportunities for mutual exploitation lost.[36]

Time, in any war and in any campaign, is a precious commodity, and this was true in Italy – the Allied soldiers learned as they fought. In this section providing snapshots of the war in Italy that Allied soldiers knew, here finally is the lament of an American Staff Sergeant: 'There have been too many instances of rushing into a situation without full knowledge of what is happening.'[37]

17

A HARD WAY TO MAKE A WAR:
THE ITALIAN CAMPAIGN IN RETROSPECT

To argue a case condemning or justifying the Allied strategic decisions leading to their campaign in mainland Italy, and the conduct of the campaign by Allied commanders once it was under way, is not the purpose of this book. Those who study the Italian campaign will arrive at their own conclusions as to whether it should have been fought at all, and if so whether it could have been handled better. They are interesting, indeed important, questions, especially for those who would learn the nature and pitfalls of formulating coalition war strategy and of how a theatre of war, and a campaign once under way, can generate its own imperatives and momentum. In these respects, the Allied strategy in the Mediterranean and the eventual campaign in Italy that followed from it are among the richest banks of experience offered by military history. Those questions are not straightforward, however, and must not be addressed simplistically as if the issues were matters of clear and distinct choice, either for strategic planners or theatre commanders and their subordinates. They were not. It was not that simple – war never is.

This book, therefore, would be incomplete without offering some considerations that might assist readers to arrive at their own conclusions about the strategic path followed by the Allies, which led their armies to mainland Italy and the campaign they subsequently fought there.

In a study of the Second World War completed shortly after its end, that most stimulating and forthright British soldier and military commentator, Major General J. F. C. Fuller, comprehensively damned the Allied campaign in Italy by describing it as 'a campaign which for lack of strategic sense and tactical imagination is unique in military history'.[1] In his much more recent (2001) study of the Italian campaign, Field Marshal Lord Carver, himself a veteran of Italy, subtitled his book 'A vital Contribution to Victory in Europe'.[2] Both these views reflect perceived realities, which an assessment of the Allied campaign must encompass, and they are not necessarily contradictory.

What was the 'strategic sense' of the Allied campaign? This is bound to be elusive, for the campaign was founded upon compromise and opportunism and its purpose, both before it became a reality and once Allied soldiers were actually fighting in Italy, was variable. What consistency is discernible follows from the conviction that Italy was the 'weak link' in the Axis and would prove a strategic liability to Germany. This is a theme underpinning British strategy from Mussolini's ill-considered entry into the war in the summer of 1940 through to the end of 1941, when the war took on global proportions. Thereafter British strategy could only be framed within the context of coalition warfare, and it was not long before a dissonance appeared between the British and Americans in their interpretations of the strategic significance of the Mediterranean theatre and of Italy. British successes against the Italians in 1940–1 reflected the seizing of an offensive opportunity that was impossible in Western Europe against Germany. Economic blockade offered little chance of affecting Germany's war effort. Indeed Britain herself was more vulnerable to such a strategy once Hitler controlled the European coastline from occupied Norway to neutral, but generally pro-Axis, Spain and the additional bases from which the U-boats could strike at her sea communications. Strategic bombing, Britain's only means of attacking Germany directly, would have to wait until RAF Bomber Command had been built up sufficiently to deliver effective blows against her economy and industry. Fostering subversion in the occupied countries offered little prospect of weakening the main strength of the Wehrmacht, and, while a possible corollary to a main war offensive strategy, it could hardly in itself substitute for one. These were the harsh realities within which British strategy had to be framed. In addition to the vital strategic importance of the Mediterranean to Britain, for its access to oil and its imperial communications, which had to be safeguarded, Mussolini's turning of the Mediterranean into a theatre of war offered Britain the opportunity to take the offensive that had been foreseen in those Anglo-French staff discussions in the spring of 1939.

To their own strategic discomfiture in 1941, the British proved the belief that pressuring Italy would compel Hitler to respond to support his ally and this would draw forth German strength. Hitler's intervention in North Africa and the Mediterranean to bolster Italy, and his invasions of

Yugoslavia and Greece, revealed a commitment to ensuring Mussolini's political survival in order to keep the Axis alliance a reality, and an imperative to secure the Axis flank in southern Europe and the Balkans. His decisions indicated that the retention of Italy in the Axis and in the war, and the security of the Balkans, so vital to Germany's war effort, robbed him of strategic choice. The result, however, was that, throughout 1941 and into 1942, Britain, with its early North African victories against Italy overturned and its venturing in support of Greece repulsed, was fighting to retain its hold in the Mediterranean and Middle East. Nevertheless, the conviction held firmly by Churchill that Italy constituted the vulnerable 'weak link' in the Axis, which would give way under sufficient pressure, remained unshaken. Hitler's invasion of the Soviet Union in the June of 1941 gave Britain the major continental ally she had lacked for a year since the fall of France. Yet, despite the imperative to support the USSR and keep her fighting, there was little direct military assistance Britain could provide, and certainly not the opening of the 'Second Front' in France that Stalin was demanding of Churchill within a month of the invasion. Only in the Mediterranean could an offensive be contemplated that might draw German strength, and this inevitably would primarily focus upon Italy. The 'Crusader' offensive of November 1941 in the Western Desert and the strategic opportunities that were believed might follow from its success; the inducement of the French North-West African colonies to enter the war against the Axis ('Gymnast') and even a British invasion of Sicily ('Whipcord'), were conceived not only to defeat Rommel in North Africa but also to intensify pressure on the weak link – Italy – and thereby undermine Germany's strategic position.

The widening of the war and the entry of the United States provided Britain with an ally of immense military and industrial power, but which had yet to be mobilized for a global, and total, war. The Americans brought into the war the strong imperative to defeat Germany as rapidly as possible in order to turn their war effort to the Pacific against Japan. There was every reason to concentrate force at the decisive point against Germany, and as 1942 unfolded this looked to American military thinking to be North-West Europe and the launching of a major cross-Channel offensive from the most logical base, Britain. The problem in 1942 was that the

Americans found themselves the inheritors of a European war already well under way and a campaign against the Axis in the Mediterranean that was far from concluded, and upon which not only vital British, but also Allied, strategic interests depended. While the Americans acknowledged the need to secure North Africa, British focus on the Mediterranean looked too much like 'Italy First' rather than the 'Germany First' and its strategic logic to which they had signed up at the 'Arcadia' Conference in December 1941. British inability and unwillingness to launch a cross-Channel offensive front against Germany in 1942, the fact that American mobilization and operational commitment had not yet reached the stage to provide the determining voice in strategy, and the imperative to get American forces into action against the European Axis before the end of 1942 led to the 'Torch' decision, and the commitment of sizeable American forces to the Mediterranean theatre. Hitler's decision to stand and fight in Tunisia, not least reflecting the imperative to protect Mussolini from catastrophic defeat for as long as possible, meant a prolonged campaign.

With the Casablanca conference and the decision to invade Sicily came an acknowledgement that there would be no cross-Channel offensive in the summer of 1943. The Mediterranean imperative asserted itself in the form of a sound military logic: the prospect of a cross-Channel offensive would be under-resourced and its success questionable set against the likelihood of a major blow against Italy that would likely hasten her collapse and lead to the significant diversion of German strength from the Eastern Front and the West to protect southern Europe and the Balkans. It was the short- and near-term means of demonstrating to Stalin that his Western Allies were committed to meaningful offensive action against Germany in the period until the cross-Channel offensive could be launched. With an increase in American strength and firmer adherence to their strategic interpretation of the importance of a cross-Channel offensive as the lynchpin of Allied strategy came a change in the interpretation of the Mediterranean and Italy. Faced with the commitment to a cross-Channel offensive in 1944, the British saw the Mediterranean and its offensive opportunities, still focused upon Italy, as a means of weakening Germany, for them the essential pre-requisite of a campaign in North-West Europe. To the Americans this approach looked likely to threaten the resources essential to the cross-

Channel invasion, by then known as 'Overlord'. By the 'Trident' Conference in May 1943, the Americans were able to set limitations on the strength that would be left in the Mediterranean theatre following the conclusion of the Sicily invasion. Troops, shipping and air power would be removed from the theatre for 'Overlord'.

Compromise had triumphed. Further Mediterranean opportunities could only be taken within this framework, despite British urging. With the fall of Mussolini in July 1943 as the Sicily campaign was under way, and with their strategic priorities fixed, the Allies were caught off guard by the situation within Italy and the likelihood of its defection from the Axis. In September 1943 the Allies were ready to move into mainland Italy with limited forces in the expectation of a German withdrawal to the north, as their intelligence indicated would occur – and as, at the time, Hitler intended to do. They were also willing to induce the Italians to change sides, while yet keeping from them just how limited Allied strength deployed to Italy would be. The game of bluff and prevarication was played out too long for either the Italians or the Allies to benefit from the Italian surrender when it came about, if indeed there ever was the likelihood of a feasible organized Italian military move against what had become significant German strength in the country prepared for just such a contingency.

By then the Allied rationale behind landing forces in Italy was to exploit the Italian collapse and the anticipated German northward withdrawal, and to gain the mainland airfields from which to intensify the strategic bombing of Germany. A campaign of hard fighting was not anticipated, though pressuring the Germans along their defensive line in northern Italy was envisaged. A different reality was imposed upon the Allies once Hitler, at Kesselring's urging, decided not to withdraw to the north of the country after all, but to stand and fight south of Rome. This presented the Allies with a campaign in Italy of a nature, and a potential drain on their resources, that had not been anticipated. One need look no further than General Alexander's sober assessment in October 1943 of what now faced the Allies in Italy to detect just what a shock Hitler's decision had been. Yet the situation demanded that the Allies maintain an offensive, despite the terrain and the likelihood of the weather being against them. Hitler's commitment to defend Italy south of Rome offered the possibility of draining his strength before

'Overlord', but this could not be achieved by a static battlefront south of the Italian capital surrendering the initiative to the Germans. As Eighth and Fifth Armies battled their way forward, the rationale of the campaign increasingly became one of helping to weaken the Germans in preparation for 'Overlord', and it was this link to the principal cross-Channel offensive that gave Alexander the forces he needed for 'Diadem'.

Once the Allies had broken through the Gustav Line and gained Rome, the Allies were ashore in Normandy and the 'Second Front' in North-West Europe was a reality. This ensured that British urging for flexibility in the forces allocated to Italy to enable further major offensives ran into obstinate American opposition. Instead the decision to launch an invasion of southern France saw, once again, the Mediterranean theatre denuded of experienced formations and air power. It would have been as politically and militarily unacceptable for Alexander to stand before the Gothic Line as it would have been for him to have stood before the Gustav Line. In Italy the attack had to be maintained, but the denuding of his forces for the invasion of southern France seriously compromised whatever chance Alexander may have had of achieving another 'Diadem'. As the fighting on the Gothic Line drew down in the autumn of 1944, the rationale of the campaign in Italy became one of containing the German forces in Italy and preventing their deployment to the main battlefronts in the West and in the East. It was no longer the theatre of strategic opportunity.

The 'strategic sense' of the Italian campaign is elusive because initial optimism and opportunism in the wake of the Italian surrender led the Allies into a campaign for which they were unprepared but in which their imperatives were fixed and their options limited. Once ashore in Italy, they could only go forward, however unfavourable the circumstances and the likely cost – there could be no going back.

What of the campaign's lack of tactical imagination? This is a resource-dominated question. 'Avalanche' and 'Shingle' were both bold enterprises hamstrung by being under-resourced in assault shipping, 'Shingle' perilously so. The principal German fear, and Kesselring's gamble in urging a defence south of Rome, was that the Allies' naval power would enable them to outflank any defensive line established in their path – Rommel had been convinced of it. Yet the demands of 'Overlord' for assault shipping ensured that once the Allies were confronted with a campaign in which they could only batter their way forward in terrain that might have been purpose-designed for a defender, the one logical amphibious alternative was denied them.

This reality robbed Allied commanders of the principal means necessary for the waging of an imaginative campaign in Italy that would have soon made military nonsense of Kesselring's defensive concept. If 'Shingle' had not been mounted on a shoestring, its intended success would not have been so dependent upon a bluff, of which the commander entrusted with it was not fully in the picture and which the evidence of his performance suggests he would have proved unwilling and incapable of attempting. Without sufficient assault shipping, but still under an imperative to maintain offensive pressure, the Allied commanders had to make the best of a militarily bad job, and there was little scope for imagination when predominantly mechanized armies were confronted with the Bernhardt and Gustav Lines. To unlock the Liri Valley for their armour, and the road to Rome, meant battering away at Monte Cassino. Did those battles lack tactical imagination? If one accepts that they did, one must also accept that there was little alternative at the time, other than attrition, and that Allied intelligence available indicated the perilous state of the German defence and its nearness to breaking-point.

Battles, like strategies and like campaigns, can generate their own momentum; the conviction that just one more push will get through can be a compelling one. It caused four very fine Allied divisions, two American, one Indian and one New Zealand, to be all but fought into the ground trying to get through at Cassino, yet they very nearly did it; the extent of their failure can be measured in yards. It is true that the Allies were slow to exploit the potential of their mountain troops in these battles, and that a greater degree of imagination might have been shown, but their numbers were limited. Ironically, just as Allied planning intended to maximize their potential for the attack on the Gothic Line, they were removed from Alexander's order of battle for the campaign in France. 'Diadem' showed tactical imagination, but its success was founded upon the attrition that had already been imposed upon the Germans on the Gustav Line and around the Anzio beachhead, and much of its initial fighting was attritional and costly until Kesselring's line was finally cracked open and his armies compelled to retreat to avoid destruction. It was not a radical departure from the pattern of fighting in Italy into which the Allies were locked and in which they would remain until the end. Superior ground and air fire-power, numbers, the ability to withstand greater attrition, all ultimately told – but so they did in North-West Europe and in the East as well.

'A Vital Contribution to Victory in Europe'? Here the evidence must be that the German forces committed to defend Italy between September 1943 and May 1945 could well have been employed elsewhere, that the imposition of a third major battlefront placed such manpower, equipment and logistic strain on the Germans that still offset the fact that the Allied armies in Italy and their air power might also have been used elsewhere. The question is also wider than that, for, as two leading military historians have pointed out, the presence in Italy of sizeable Allied armies and their potential threat was also a factor in fixing significant German strength in the Balkans. At the very least, this removed flexibility in Hitler's options by emphasising a threat which he was always disposed to take seriously.[3] This is important, because there is a general consistent balance in the Allied and German forces committed to the Italian campaign between 1943 and 1945. Although divisions varied in their actual strength to the extent that identifying a formation at a given time as a 'division' might belie the fact that its battalions might have been reduced by casualties to little more than companies, it is still a worthwhile measure. The table on the opposite page is based on General Sir William Jackson's summary compiled as an Appendix for his book *The Battle for Italy*, which cannot be bettered. The balance of forces was clearly not such as to enable the Allies to exert an overwhelming superiority and indicates how terrain and the weather, when added to the equation, enabled the often seriously weak-ened German Divisions to hold on for prolonged periods of fighting. The casualty figures also are fairly balanced:

Allied killed, wounded, missing (September 1943 – May 1945)
312,000 (188,746 Fifth Army/ 123,254 approx in Eighth Army)

German killed, wounded, missing
434,646 (48,067 killed, 172,531 wounded, 214,048 missing)[4]

This, as Dominick Graham and Shelford Bidwell observe, disposes of the theory that defence, even in Italian terrain, was more economical than

†††††††††††††††††††

The Balance of Forces during the Italian Campaign

Time Frame	Allied Divisions	German Divisions	In Battle Zone	
			Allied	German
Salerno – Volturno Oct 1943	8 British 2 Commonwealth 9 US	12 mobile* 7 Infantry**	19	12
Bernhardt Line Dec 1943	4 British 3 Commonwealth 1 French 5 US	7 mobile 11 Infantry	13	11
Gustav Line & Anzio Jan 1944	5 British 5 Commonwealth 1 Polish 2 French 5 US	9 mobile 14 Infantry	18	15
End of Winter Offensive March 1944	5 British 5 Commonwealth 2 Polish 3 French 6 US	9 mobile 15 Infantry	21	17
'Diadem' May 1944	5 British 7 Commonwealth 2 Polish 4 French 7 US	8 mobile 15 Infantry	25	18
Fall of Rome June 1944	5 British 7 Commonwealth 2 Polish 4 French 7 US	9 mobile 17 Infantry	25	19
Gothic Line Aug 1944	6 British 7 Commonwealth 2 Polish 5 US	8 mobile 18 Infantry	20	22
End of Autumn Battles Dec 1944	4 British 6 Commonwealth 2 Polish 1 Brazilian 6 US	6 mobile 21 Infantry	19	20
Final Allied Offensive April 1945	3 British 4 Commonwealth 2 Polish 1 Brazilian 7 US	5 mobile 18 Infantry	17	19

* Panzer, Panzer Grenadier and Parachute Divisions.

** Infantry, Mountain and Jaeger Divisions.

Note that German divisions in the battle zone are fewer than the total in Italy, this reflecting the German need to secure against partisan activity in the North of Italy. Note also that seven Allied divisions were withdrawn in December 1943 for 'Overlord' and six in August 1944 for 'Dragoon'.

attack. Certainly there were times when Kesselring took the offensive, as he did against the Anzio beachhead, and then he lost hard-to-replace combat troops every bit as quickly as Clark and Alexander could lose them. Allied firepower, particularly in artillery, was throughout superior, and the Germans, while they could defend robustly, learned that even local counterattacks could be a costly option and one that could only be undertaken sparingly. Equally clear is that there is no evidence to suggest that the Germans, while they successfully denied Allied progress for prolonged periods, imposed a disproportionate attrition upon them. For both sides, the Italian Campaign was a hard way to make a war.

NOTES

Introduction

1. Quoted in *US Army Report: Lessons from the Sicilian Campaign, 1943*. A copy is in the National Archives (UK), TNA WO 232/16.

1. The Strategic Context of the Italian Campaign

1. Allied Combined Chiefs of Staff. This remarkable organization came into being in February 1942 and welded together the British Chiefs of Staff and the American Joint Chiefs of Staff responsible to President Roosevelt and Prime Minister Winston Churchill. Only at the major Allied war conferences could full meetings take place, but permanent British representation in Washington was effected by the creation of the Joint Staff Mission headed by Field Marshal Sir John Dill and, after his death in 1944, by Field Marshal Sir Henry Maitland Wilson.

2. See Trumbull Higgins, *Soft Underbelly: The Anglo-American Controversy over the Italian Campaign 1939–1945*, p. 3; Macmillan, New York, 1968.

3. Louis Morton, 'Germany First: The Basic Concept of Allied Strategy in World War II' in Kent Roberts Greenfield (ed), *Command Decisions*, Harcourt, Brace and Company, New York, 1959.

4. The paper produced by the Allied Combined Chiefs was entitled 'WW1' and is detailed in Michael Howard, *Grand Strategy*, Vol. IV, pp. xv–xvi; HMSO, London, 1972.

5. Dwight D. Eisenhower, *Crusade in Europe*, pp. 50–2, Heinemann, London, 1948.

6. Marshall's memorandum for President Roosevelt outlining the cross-Channel attack concept is reproduced in Michael Howard, op. cit., Vol. IV, p. xvi.

7. Howard, op. cit, p. xxii.

8. Churchill is quoted in Norman Gelb, *Desperate Venture: The Story of Operation Torch*, p. 88; Hodder & Stoughton, London, 1992.

9. Martin Gilbert, *Road to Victory: Winston S. Churchill, 1941–1945*, pp. 137–40, Heinemann, London, 1986.

10. N. H. Gibbs, *Grand Strategy*, Vol. I, p. 668; HMSO, London, 1976; F. H. Hinsley *et al*, *British Intelligence in the Second World War*, Vol. 1, p. 200; HMSO, London, 1979.

11. Howard, op. cit., pp. 212–13; Ronald Lewin, *Churchill as Warlord*, pp. 170–1; Batsford, London, 1973.

12. Alex Danchev and Daniel Todman (eds), *War Diaries 1939–1945: Field Marshal Lord Alanbrooke*, p. 349, entry for 16 December 1942; Weidenfeld & Nicolson, London, 2001.

13. Howard, op. cit., p. 219.

14. Gilbert, *Road to Victory*, pp. 303–4; Winston S. Churchill, *The Second World War*, Vol. V: *The Hinge of Fate*, pp. 608–9, Cassell, London, 1966.

15. C.C.S. 155/1, 19 January 1943, is reproduced as Appendix III(D) in Howard, op. cit., p. 621.

16. See for example Elena Agarossi, *A Nation Collapses: The Italian Surrender of September 1943*, pp. 25–6 and notes p. 147; Cambridge University Press, Cambridge, 2006.

17. Churchill, op. cit., pp. 613–14.

18. Howard, op. cit., p. 419; G. A. Shepperd, *The Italian Campaign: A Political and Military Re-assessment*, p. 14; Arthur Barker, London, 1968.

19. Brigadier C. J. C. Molony, *The Mediterranean and Middle East*, Vol. V, p. 194; HMSO, London, 1973.

20. Churchill, op. cit., p. 741.

2. 'Husky': Commanders and Controversy

1. Brigadier C. J. C. Molony, *The Mediterranean and Middle East*, Vol. V, pp. 10–11; HMSO, London, 1973.

2. Figures in brackets are maximum estimates allowing for the effects of bombing and deliberate Axis demolitions based on data extracted from the North African campaign experience. In Molony, op. cit, p. 15.

3. W. G. F. Jackson, *Alexander of Tunis as Military Commander*, p. 212; Batsford, London, 1971.

4. Molony, op. cit, p. 14.

5. Jackson, op. cit., p. 212.

6. Molony, op. cit, p. 14.

7. This planning staff became known as 'Force 141' from the room number of the hotel where it first convened.

8. W. G. F. Jackson, *The Battle for Italy*, p. 30; Batsford, London, 1967.

9. Gairdner's experience would be to an extent mirrored by General Morgan in Britain, appointed by the Allies as 'Chief of Staff to the Supreme Allied Commander (COSSAC) and who had his own problems of 'absentee landordism' throughout much of 1943.

10. Danchev and Todman (eds), *War Diaries 1939–1945: Field Marshal Lord Alanbrooke*, p. 365; Weidenfeld & Nicolson, London, 2001.

11. Carlo D'Este, *Bitter Victory: The Battle for Sicily, 1943*, p. 72; Collins, London, 1988; also this author's *A Genius for War: A Life of General George S. Patton*, pp. 491–2; HarperCollins, London, 1995.

12. Jackson, *Alexander of Tunis as Military Commander*, p. 213; Batsford, London, 1971.

13. Molony, op. cit, p. 18.

14. Quoted in Nigel Hamilton, *Monty: Master of the Battlefield*, p. 241; Hodder & Stoughton, London, 1985.

15. Molony, op. cit, p. 19.

16. Tedder, *With Prejudice*, p. 428; Cassell, London, 1966.

17. Hamilton, op. cit., p. 243.

18. D'Este, *Bitter Victory*, p. 87.

19. Churchill's minute to the British Chiefs of Staff, 8 April 1943, is quoted in D'Este, op. cit, p. 86.

20. Quoted in ibid., p. 87.

21. Quoted in Hamilton, op. cit, pp. 244–5.

22. Molony, op. cit, p. 20.

23. Danchev and Todman, op. cit., p. 394.

24. Major General Sir Francis de Guingand, *Operation Victory*, p. 275; Hodder & Stoughton, London, 1947.

25. Hamilton, op. cit, p. 247.

26. Hamilton, op. cit, pp. 250–2.

27. Jackson, op. cit., p. 215.

28. It probably did not help that, while outlining his view during one meeting, Montgomery unwittingly referred to Admiral Ramsay as 'General' Ramsay. See Bernard Ferguson, *The Watery Maze*, p. 222; Collins, London, 1961.

29. *The Memoirs of Field Marshal the Viscount Montgomery of Alamein, K.G.*, p. 177; Collins, London, 1958.

30. Molony, op. cit, p. 24.

31. D'Este, op. cit, p. 123.

3. 'Husky': Planning the Allied Invasion of Sicily

1. Lieutenant Colonel G. A. Shepperd, *The Italian Campaign, 1943–45: A Political and Military Re-assessment*, pp. 43–4; Arthur Barker, London, 1968.

2. Combined Operations Headquarters, Bulletin No. Y/1, *Notes on the Planning and Assault Phases of the Sicilian Operation (October 1943)*, p. 9; copy held by Combined Arms Research Library, Fort Leavenworth, Kansas, and available online; accessed in July 2007 at: http://cgsc.cdmhost.com/u?/p4013coll8,60

3. Ibid., p. 4.

4. Combined Operations Headquarters, *Digest of some Notes and Reports from Operation 'Husky' (November 1943)*, p. 11; copy held by Combined Arms Research

Library, Fort Leavenworth Kansas and available online; accessed in July 2007 at: http://cgsc.cdmhost.com/u?/p4013coll8,51

5. Combined Operations Headquarters, op. cit, p. 3.

6. Ibid., p. 3.

7. Ronald Lewin, *Ultra Goes to War*, pp. 280–1; Hutchinson, London, 1978). The US II Corps was informed of the location of the Hermann Göring Division for its planning.

8. William O. Darby and William H. Baumer, *Darby's Rangers: We Led the Way*, p. 88; Presidio Press, San Rafael, California, 1980.

9. Brigadier C. J. C. Molony, *The Mediterranean and Middle East*, Vol. V, p. 42; HMSO, London, 1973.

10. Scenario quoted in Michael Howard, *British Intelligence in the Second World War*, Vol. V, *Strategic Deception*, pp. 86–7; HMSO, London, 1990. Details on 'A' Force operations are from this source.

11. The story of 'Mincemeat' is told by its architect, Ewen Montagu, in *The Man Who Never Was*, Evans, London, 1955. See also Ralph Bennett, *Ultra and Mediterranean Strategy, 1941–1945*, pp. 222–5; Hamish Hamilton, London 1989; Carlo D'Este, *Bitter Victory*, Chapter 9, pp. 181–91; Collins, London, 1988; and F. H. Hinsley, British Intelligence in the Second World War, Vol. 3, Part 1, pp. 78–9; HMSO, London, 1984. Speculation has persisted for years on the real identity of the corpse. Suggestions have included a suicide victim and, with possibly more plausibility, the body of a sailor from the ill-fated aircraft carrier HMS *Dasher*, which was lost in the Clyde, cause uncertain, in March 1943 with heavy loss of life only a few weeks before 'Mincemeat' was carried out.

12. Howard, *Strategic Deception*, p. 92.

13. Michael Howard observes that Hitler was already strongly inclined to reinforce the Balkans and that the success of 'A' Force and 'Mincemeat' should be seen in this context; *Strategic Deception*, p. 92.

14. Ralph Bennett, op. cit., pp. 225–6.

15. General Fridolin von Senger und Etterlin, *Neither Fear nor Hope*, p. 127; Macdonald, London, 1963.

16. *The Memoirs of Field Marshal Kesselring*, p. 160; London, Purnell, 1974.

17. Ibid., p. 158.

18. Ibid., p. 164.

19. Von Senger und Etterlin, op. cit, p. 148.

20. Ibid., p. 129.

21. Molony, op. cit, footnote, p. 40 and p. 42.

22. D'Este, *Bitter Victory*, p. 199

23. Molony, op. cit, p. 41.

24. Tanks were the French Renault R-35, and the Italian CV3. The R-35 was a good light tank in the late 1930s but seriously under-gunned by 1943, with only a 37mm main gun. It was also slow, and further hampered in combat by the fact that the commander also had to be the gunner in the one-man turret. Its maximum armour was 45mm. The Germans converted many R-35s to self-propelled guns by removing the turret and fitting a 47mm Czech gun in an open-top superstructure. This also proved obsolete for the main fighting fronts by 1943, but it seems likely that some of the Italian units on Sicily were equipped with them. The Italian CV3 hardly rated as a tank, being little more than a tracked machine-gun carrier similar to the British Army's Bren Gun Carrier, though unlike the latter the CV3's driving and fighting compartments were fully covered with armour plate. However, with armour of no more than 14mm, the CV3 was vulnerable to the anti-tank weapons carried by the US and British infantry; its armament was two 8mm machine-guns.

25. Most accounts of the Sicily campaign rightly refer to the 15th Panzer Grenadier Division. However this designation was apparently not in effect during the early period of the Allied invasion. On 1 July 1943 what had been termed on Sicily as the 'Sizilien Panzergrenadier Division' was reorganized as the 15th Panzer Division, but on 15 July the designation was again changed to the 15th Panzergrenadier Division. It seems, therefore, that between 10 and 15 July this German formation fought on Sicily as the 15th Panzer Division. See George F. Nafziger,

The German Order of Battle: Panzers and Artillery in World War II, p. 268; Greenhill Books, London, and Stackpole Books, Pennsylvania, 1999.

26. British and American troops first encountered the Tiger (Panzer Mark VI) in Tunisia. With armour up to 110mm thick, it was impervious to most British and US tank and anti-tank guns, certainly from the front, while its own 88mm gun could destroy any Allied tank. British and US tanks had to 'stalk' the Tiger to get within range and hit a vulnerable point, a hazardous enterprise at best, whereas a well-sited Tiger could dominate that part of the battle area under the range of its gun. Under such circumstances, it would require concentrations of artillery fire, or directed air attack by Allied fighter-bombers, to knock-out a Tiger or compel its withdrawal. Because of its sheer bulk and weight, the Tiger lacked manoeuvrability for the close-in tactical battle, and its mechanical reliability and maintenance were always problematic.

27. Von Senger, op. cit, pp. 132–3; Molony, op. cit, pp. 42–3.

28. Wesley Craven and James L. Cate, *The Army Air Forces in World War II. Europe: Torch to Pointblank, August 1942 to December 1943*, p. 445; University of Chicago Press, Chicago, 1949.

29. Molony, op. cit., p. 46.

30. Hinsley, op. cit., Vol. 3, Part 1, pp. 84–5.

31. Allied Force Headquarters, 12 July 1943, *Lessons from Operations against Pantelleria*, TNA WO 232/54, in UK National Archives. Army Air Forces Historical Study No 52 (May 1947), 'The Reduction of Pantelleria and Adjacent Islands 8 May – 14 June 1943; available online, accession 22 April 2008: http://www.ibiblio.org/hyperwar/AAF/AAFHS/AAF-HS-52.pdf

32. Tedder, 'With Prejudice', p. 443; Cassell, London, 1966.

33. E. R. Hooton, *Eagle in Flames: The Fall of the Luftwaffe*, pp. 224–6; Arms & Armour Press, London, 1997.

34. Ibid., p. 227.

4. Husky: the Battle for Sicily

1. Dwight D. Eisenhower, *Crusade in Europe*, p. 190; Heinemann, London, 1948.

2. Ibid., p. 190.

3. For a detailed account of the airborne landing, see Michael Hickey, *Out of the Sky: A History of Airborne Warfare*, pp. 99–102; Mills & Boon, London, 1979; and D'Este, *Bitter Victory: The Battle for Sicily*, pp. 238–53; Collins, London, 1988; Brigadier C. J. C. Molony, *The Mediterranean and Middle East*, Vol. V, pp. 79–84; HMSO, London, 1973.

4. Molony, op. cit., p. 58.

5. Bernard Fergusson, *The Watery Maze: The Story of Combined Operations*, p.236; Collins, London, 1961.

6. Combined Operations Headquarters, Bulletin No Y/1, *Notes on the Planning and Assault Phases of the Sicilian Operation (Oct 1943)*, p. 28; copy held by Combined Arms Research Library, Fort Leavenworth, Kansas, and available online; accessed in July 2007 at: http://cgsc.cdmhost.com/u?/p4013coll8,60

7. Molony, op. cit., pp. 65–6; and Army Historical Branch Narrative, *The Sicilian Campaign*, TNA AIR 41/52.

8. William O. Darby and William H. Baumer, *Darby's Rangers: We Led the Way*, p. 89–90; Presidio Press, San Rafael, California, 1980.

9. Account of the Gela beachhead battle from Lieutenant Colonel Albert N. Garland and Howard McGaw Smyth, *Sicily and the Surrender of Italy*, pp. 154–6; Washington, 1965; and D'Este, op. cit., pp. 282–300.

10. Quoted in D'Este, op. cit., p. 294.

11. Molony, op. cit., p. 85.

12. Ibid., p. 87.

13. Tedder, op. cit., p. 450.

14. Hickey, op. cit., p. 104; Molony, op. cit., pp. 95–6

15. The Agira battle is detailed in Lieutenant Colonel G. W. L. Nicholson, *The Canadians in Italy, 1943–1945*, pp. 120–34; Edmond Cloutier, Queen's Printer and Controller of Stationery, Ottawa, 1956.

16. Cyril Ray, *Algiers to Austria: A History of*

78 Division in the Second World War, p. 67, Eyre & Spottiswoode, London, 1952.

17. Detailed accounts of the Centuripe battle are in Brigadier Nelson Russell, 'The Irish Brigade in Sicily: July to August 1943' in *The Faugh-a-Ballagh*, July 1944; see also Richard Doherty, *Clear the Way: A History of the 38th (Irish) Brigade, 1941–1947*, pp. 68–70; Irish Academic Press, Blackrock, County Dublin, 1993.

18. Ray, op. cit, p. 69

19. Quoted in Sir Basil Liddell Hart, *History of the Second World War*, p. 465, Pan, London, 1977.

20. Quoted in US Army Report *Lessons from the Sicilian Campaign*, p.18; TNA WO 232/16.

21. Ralph Bennett, *Ultra and Mediterranean Strategy, 1941–1945*, pp. 235–8, Hamish Hamilton, London, 1989.

22. D'Este, op. cit., p. 535.

5. Sicily: The Voice of Battle Experience

1. US Army Report, *Lessons from the Sicilian Campaign, 1943*. p. 2; TNA WO 232/16, copy in the National Archives (UK).

2. A comprehensive and vivid summary description of Sicily in 1943, to which the above is indebted, is provided in the relevant volume of the British Official History, Brigadier C. J. C. Molony *et al*, *The Mediterranean and Middle East*, Vol. V, pp. 11–12; HMSO, London, 1973.

3. US Army Report, *Lessons from the Sicilian Campaign*, p. 3.

4. Molony, op. cit., p. 10.

5. Sir David Cole, *Rough Road to Rome: A Foot-Soldier in Sicily and Italy 1943–44*, p. 41; William Kimber, London, 1983; Sir David's battalion was the 2nd Inniskilling Fusiliers.

6. US Army Report, *Lessons from the Sicilian Campaign*, pp. 4–5.

7. Lieutenant Colonel A. E. C. Bredin, 'The Malta Brigade Strikes Back: I. Sicily and Italy', in *The Army Quarterly*, Volume L, No. 1, April 1945, p. 121. The battalions of the 231st Infantry Brigade had been part of the garrison of the island of Malta before joining Eighth Army for the invasion of Sicily – hence the title of this piece.

8. US Army Report, *Lessons from the Sicilian Campaign*, p. 5.

9. Report by Lieutenant Colonel M. P. Bogert, Commanding Officer, West Nova Scotia Regiment, to Canadian Historical Officer, 5 August 1943. Quoted in Lieutenant Colonel G. W. L. Nicholson, *The Canadians in Italy, 1943–1945*, p. 141; Edmond Cloutier, Queen's Printer and Controller of Stationery, Ottawa, 1956.

10. Cyril Ray, *Algiers to Austria: A History of 78 Division in the Second World War*, pp. 63–4; Eyre & Spottiswoode, London, 1952). The British Official History notes that an improvised pack train with some 400 mules and donkeys collected from the local area was formed for the 78th Division: Molony, op. cit., p. 152.

11. US Army Report, *Lessons from the Sicilian Campaign*, p. 8.

12. Account by Major A. R. Campbell and Captain N. R. Waugh, 'War Diary, Hastings and Prince Edward Regiment for 21 July 1943', quoted in Nicholson, op. cit, pp. 104–6.

13. War Diary, West Nova Scotia Regiment, 10 May 1943, quoted in Nicholson, op. cit, p. 33.

14. Lieutenant Colonel L. Wigram, reporting on the lessons of the campaign in Sicily in a letter to Brigadier A. G. Kenchington, Director of Military Training, British North African Forces, 16 August 1943. Copy in TNA WO 231/14. All references to Wigram's report are from this source.

15. Quoted (anonymously) in US Army Report, *Lessons from the Sicilian Campaign*, p. 6; TNA WO 232/16, copy in the National Archives (UK).

16. Ray, op. cit., p. 62.

17. US Army Report, *Lessons from the Sicilian Campaign*, p. 58.

18. Ibid., p. 58.

19. Quoted in US Army Report, *Lessons from the Sicilian Campaign*, p. 59.

20. Ibid., p. 58.

21. Captain D. L. C. Price, R.A., (124 Field Regiment) quoted in S. W. C. Pack, *Operation 'Husky': The Allied Invasion of Sicily*, p. 143; David & Charles, London and Newton Abbot, 1977.

22. US Army Report, *Lessons from the Sicilian Campaign*, p. 56.

23. Ibid., pp. 35–6.

24. Quoted in ibid., p. 31.

25. Quoted in ibid., p. 32.

26. Quoted in ibid., p. 31.

27. Molony, op. cit, pp. 151–2.

28. US Army Report, *Lessons from the Sicilian Campaign*, p. 9.

29. Ibid., p. 32.

30. Ibid., p. 45.

31. Ibid., p. 34.

32. Ibid., p. 36.

33. Nicholson, op. cit, p. 97 (from information supplied by Major the Lord Tweedsmuir, the Hastings' second-in-command at the time).

34. Ibid., p. 143.

35. Quoted in US Army Report, *Lessons from the Sicilian Campaign*, p. 37.

36. Ibid., pp. 32–33.

37. Quoted in ibid., p. 27.

38. Ibid., p. 26.

39. Ibid., p. 44.

40. Quoted in ibid., p. 26.

41. Major John North, British Army Directorate of Military Training, Reporting from Sicily, August 1943. Extract from Major North's DO letter dated 11.8.43, TNA WO 231/11; quoted in Timothy Harrison Place, *Military Training in the British Army, 1940–1944*, p. 68; Frank Cass, London, and Portland, Oregon, 2000.

42. Headquarters Royal Canadian Artillery, 1st Canadian Division, 'Barrage Notes', 26 July 1943; Account by Lieutenant Colonel R. A. Lindsay (Officer Commanding Princess Patricia's Canadian Light Infantry), 30 July 1943; The Royal Artillery Commemoration Book, *Canadian Gunners in Sicily*, p. 424. Referred to in Nicholson, op. cit, p. 129, and references pp. 708–9.

43. US Army Report, *Lessons from the Sicilian Campaign*, p. 26.

44. Discussion on Lessons Learned During the Year of Fighting from El Alamein to Messina, in TNA WO 231/16; Quoted in Harrison Place (see next note), pp. 68–9.

45. 'Battle Drill' is fully examined in Timothy Harrison Place's important study: *Military Training in the British Army, 1940–1944: From Dunkirk to D-Day*, Chapters 4 and 5; Frank Cass, London, 2000.

46. US Army Report, Lessons from the Sicilian Campaign, op. cit, p. 19.

47. Nicholson, op. cit., p.131.

48. 15th Panzer Grenadier Division Experience Report for the Campaign in Sicily, 4 September 1943, quoted in Nicholson, op. cit, p. 106.

49. See Harrison Place, op. cit, pp. 69–70.

50. US Army Report, *Lessons from the Sicilian Campaign*, p. 14.

51. Ibid., p. 23.

52. Ibid., p. 10.

53. Lieutenant Colonel A. E. C. Bredin, 'The Malta Brigade Strikes Back: I. Sicily and Italy', in *The Army Quarterly*, Volume L, No. 1, April 1945, p. 124.

54. Lieutenant Colonel A. E. C. Bredin, *Three Assault Landings: The Story of the 1st Bn. The Dorsetshire Regiment in Sicily, Italy and N.W. Europe*, p. 24; Gale & Polden, Aldershot, 1946.

55. Incident related in *Rough Road to Rome: A Foot-Soldier in Sicily and Italy 1943–44*, pp. 48–9; William Kimber, London, 1983.

56. US Army Report, *Lessons from the Sicilian Campaign*, pp. 10-11.

6. Planning the Next Move: The Decision to Invade Mainland Italy, June–August 1943

1. Quoted in Michael Howard, *Grand Strategy*, Vol. IV, p. 500; HMSO, London, 1972.

2. Tedder, *With Prejudice*, pp. 435 and 454; Cassell, London, 1966; Howard, op. cit., p. 500.

3. Martin Blumenson, *Salerno to Cassino*, p.13; US Army Center of Military History, Washington, DC, 1993 edition.

4. Quoted in Howard, op. cit., p. 502.

5. Ibid., p. 503.

6. Lieutenant Colonel G. A. Shepperd, *The Italian Campaign: A Political and Military Re-assessment*, pp. 90–1; Arthur Barker, London, 1968.

7. Quoted in Hamilton, *Monty: Master of the Battlefield*, p. 376; Hodder & Stoughton, London, 1985.

8. Major General Sir Francis de Guingand, *Operation Victory*, p. 311; Hodder & Stoughton, London, 1947.

9. Hamilton, op. cit. p. 381.

7. The Surrender of Italy, August–September 1943

1. General Walter Warlimont, *Inside Hitler's Headquarters*, p. 343, Weidenfeld & Nicolson, London, 1964.

2. Elena Agarossi, *A Nation Collapses: The Italian Surrender of September 1943*, p. 50; Cambridge University Press, Cambridge, 2006; and Denis Mack Smith, *Mussolini*, p. 342, Paladin, London, 1985.

3. See Sir Basil Liddell Hart (ed), *The Rommel Papers*, pp. 435–6; Collins, London, 1953.

4. Quoted in John Strawson, *The Italian Campaign*, pp. 96–7, Carroll & Graf, New York, 1988.

5. General Walter Warlimont, op. cit., p. 335; and *The Memoirs of Field Marshal Kesselring*, p. 168; Purnell Books/William Kimber, London, 1974.

6. Kesselring, op. cit., p. 168.

7. Strawson, op. cit., pp. 114–15.

8. Kesselring, op. cit., p. 122.

9. F. M. Hinsley, *British Intelligence in the Second World War*, Vol. 3, p. 102, HMSO, London, 1984.

10. Howard, *Grand Strategy*, Vol IV, pp. 515–16; HMSO, London, 1972.

11. Ibid., p. 521.

12. Ibid., p. 521.

13. Hinsley, op. cit., pp. 102–3.

14. Howard, op. cit., pp. 523–4.

15. Quoted in Howard, op. cit., p. 528.

16. Incident related in Harold Macmillan, *The Blast of War, 1939–1945*, London, Macmillan, 1967; and quoted in W. G. F. Jackson, *Alexander as Military Commander*, p. 235; Batsford, London, 1967; see also Nigel Nicolson, *Alex: The Life of Field Marshal Earl Alexander of Tunis*, p. 210; Weidenfeld & Nicolson, London, 1973.

17. Maxwell Taylor, interview, 17.10.81, quoted in Nigel Hamilton, *Monty: Master of the Battlefield, 1942–1944*, p. 390; Hodder & Stoughton/Coronet, London, 1985.

18. In addition to Chapter XXVII in Michael Howard's *Grand Strategy*, the surrender of Italy is comprehensively detailed by Elena Agarossi in *A Nation Collapses: The Italian Surrender of September 1943*, Cambridge University Press, Cambridge, 2000 and 2006.

8. Ashore in Italy

1. Major General Sir Francis de Guingand, *Operation Victory*, p. 318; Hodder & Stoughton, London, 1947.

2. George Aris, *The Fifth British Division, 1939 to 1945*, p. 143; Fifth Division Benevolent Fund, London 1959.

3. Ibid., p. 152.

4. An account is in Lieutenant Colonel A. E. C. Bredin, *Three Assault Landings: The Story of the 1st Bn. The Dorsetshire Regiment in Sicily, Italy and N.W. Europe*, pp. 38–41; Gale & Polden, Aldershot, 1946.

5. General Mark W. Clark, *Calculated Risk*, p. 189, Harrap, London, 1951.

6. Ibid., pp. 173–4.

7. Brigadier C. J. C. Molony, *The Mediterranean and Middle East*, Vol. V, p. 253; HMSO, London, 1973.

8. Martin Blumenson, *Salerno to Cassino*, p. 26; US Army Center of Military History, Washington, DC, 1993 edition.

9. Quoted in F. H. Hinsley *et al*, *British Intelligence in the Second World War*, Volume 3, Part 1, p. 107; HMSO, London, 1984).

10. Molony, op. cit., footnote, p. 267; Blumenson, op. cit., pp. 66–77; Hinsley, op. cit., p. 108.

11. Quoted in Blumenson, op. cit., p. 69.

12. Brigadier J. A. Gascoigne, '201st Guards Brigade at the Battle of Salerno', in *The Army Quarterly*, Vol. XLIX, No. 2, January 1945, p. 165.

13. Molony, op. cit., p. 255.

14. Blumenson, op. cit, pp. 49–50.

15. Molony, op. cit.; Blumenson, op. cit.; Hugh Pond, *Salerno*, William Kimber, London, 1961; Eric Morris, *Salerno*, Hutchinson, London, 1983; George F. Nafziger, *The German Order of Battle: Panzers and Artillery in World War II*; Greenhill, London; Stackpole, Pennsylvania, 1999; Historical Division, War Department, *Salerno: American Operations From the Beaches to the Volturno (9 September – 6 October 1943)*, *American Forces in Action* series, 1944, reprinted 1990.

16. Brigadier T. B. L. Churchill, 'The Commandos in Action at Salerno', in *The Army Quarterly*, Volume LI, No. 2, January 1946, p. 255.

17. Pond, op. cit., pp. 73–4; Morris, op. cit., p. 108.

18. Molony, op. cit., p. 286.

19. Blumenson, op. cit., p. 92.

9. 'Avalanche': The Landing Battle Experience

1. US Army Report, *Lessons from the Italian Campaign*, March 1944, p. 9; TNA WO 204/7564, copy in UK National Archives.

2. Ibid., p. 10.

3. Hugh Pond, *Salerno*, p. 93, William Kimber, London, 1961.

4. US Army Report, op. cit., pp. 9–10.

5. Ibid., p. 11.

6. *Pioneers in an Opposed Landing – Lessons Learnt, 18 October 1943*, in TNA WO 231/15; copy in UK National Archives.

10. The Salerno Beachhead Battle, 10–16 September

1. W. G. F. Jackson, *The Battle for Italy*, p. 112; Batsford, London, 1967.

2. Brigadier T. B. L. Churchill, 'The Commandos in Action at Salerno', *The Army Quarterly*, Volume LI, No. 2, January 1946, pp. 255–6.

3. Nigel Nicolson, *Alex: The Life of Field Marshal Earl Alexander of Tunis*, p. 223; Weidenfeld & Nicolson, London, 1973. General Lemnitzer is quoted on p. 222.

4. *The Rise and Fall of the German Air Force, 1933–1945*, p. 262; Air Ministry, 1948; Arms & Armour Press, 1987.

5. Quoted in Martin Blumenson, *Salerno to Cassino*, p.143; US Army Center of Military History, Washington, DC, 1993 edition.

6. Brigadier C. J. C. Molony, *The Mediterranean and Middle East*, Vol. V, p. 325; HMSO, London, 1973.

7. Winston S. Churchill, *The Second World War*, Vol. V, *Closing the Ring*, p. 127; Cassell, London, 1952.

11. Autumn Frustration

1. Brigadier C. J. C. Molony, *The Mediterranean and Middle East*, Vol. V, pp. 332–3; HMSO, London, 1973.

2. F. H. Hinsley *et al*, *British Intelligence in the Second World War*, Volume 3, Part 1, p. 115–16; HMSO, London, 1984).

3. Ralph S. Mavrogordato, 'Hitler's Decision on the Defense of Italy' in Kent Roberts Greenfield (ed.), *Command Decisions*; Harcourt, Brace & Company, New York, 1959; see also Lieutenant Colonel G. A. Shepperd, *The Italian Campaign: A Political and Military Re-assessment*, p. 140–1; Arthur Barker, London, 1968.

4. Hinsley, op. cit., p. 173.

5. Telegram Prime Minister to President Roosevelt, 10 October 1943, TNA Premier, 3/124/3; UK National Archives.

6. Alexander's Report is given in full in Winston S. Churchill, *The Second World War*, Vol. V, *Closing the Ring*, pp. 216–20; Cassell, London, 1966.

12. The Mainland Campaign to the 'Winter Line'

1. Cyril Ray, *Algiers to Austria: A History of 78 Division in the Second World War*, p. 95, Eyre & Spottiswoode, London, 1952.

2. Ibid., p. 98.

3. *The Memoirs of Field Marshal Kesselring*, p. 187; Purnell Books/William Kimber, London, 1974.

4. F. M. Hinsley, *British Intelligence in the Second World War*, Vol. 3, Part 1, pp. 175–6; HMSO, London, 1984.

5. Quoted in Martin Blumenson, *Salerno to Cassino*, p. 264–5; US Army Center of Military History, Washington, DC, 1993 edition.

6. Ibid., pp. 266–7.

7. Ibid., p. 285.

8. Lieutenant Colonel G. W. L. Nicholson, *The Canadians in Italy, 1943–1945*, p. 333; Edmond Cloutier, Queen's Printer and Controller of Stationery, Ottawa, 1956.

13. The Gustav Line

1. *The Memoirs of Field Marshal Kesselring*, p. 192; Purnell Books/William Kimber, London, 1974.

2. Quoted in Martin Gilbert, *Road to Victory: Winston S. Churchill, 1941–1945*, p. 619, Heinemann, London, 1986.

3. Winston S. Churchill, *The Second World War*, Vol. V, *Closing the Ring*, p. 385; Cassell, London, 1966.

4. W. G. F. Jackson, *The Battle for Italy*, p. 169; Batsford, London, 1967.

5. Churchill and Alexander, quoted in Nigel Nicolson, *Alex: The Life of Field Marshal Earl*

Alexander of Tunis, pp. 229–30; Weidenfeld & Nicolson, London, 1973.

6. Kesselring, op. cit., p. 194.

7. Alexander's notes, 9 January 1944, quoted in Nicolson, op. cit., p. 230.

8. F. M. Hinsley, *British Intelligence in the Second World War*, Vol. 3, Part 1, p. 185, HMSO, London, 1984; see also Ralph Bennett, *Ultra and Mediterranean Strategy*, pp. 262–3

9. Eisenhower's signal is quoted in W. G. F. Jackson, *Alexander as Military Commander*, p. 257; Batsford, London, 1967.

10. Quoted in Martin Blumenson, *Salerno to Cassino*, p. 355; US Army Center of Military History, Washington, DC, 1993 edition.

11. Lucas's diary, quoted in Blumenson, op. cit., pp. 355, 356; see also Julian Thompson, 'John Lucas and Anzio' in Brian Bond (ed.), *Fallen Stars: Eleven Studies of Twentieth Century Military Disasters*, p. 195; Brassey's, London, 1991.

12. Brigadier C. J. C. Molony, *The Mediterranean and Middle East*, Vol. V, p. 604; HMSO, London, 1973.

13. General Fridolin von Senger und Etterlin, *Neither Fear nor Hope*, p. 190; Macdonald, London, 1963.

14. Ibid., p. 192.

15. Quoted in Blumenson, op. cit., p. 332.

16. Ibid., p. 346.

14. Anzio and Rome

1. German reconnaissance Bf. 109 pilot, reporting on the Anzio landings; message intercepted by Signals Intelligence Field Unit with RAF Desert Air Force, 8.20 a.m., 22 January 1944, quoted in Aileen Clayton, *The Enemy is Listening: The Story of the Y Service*, p. 327; Hutchinson, London, 1980.

2. For example, Field Marshal Sir Gerald Templer (a divisional commander at Anzio), and General Clark himself, who both gave their views to Nigel Nicolson and are quoted in his book *Alex* (pp. 232–3), and General Truscott in his own book *Command Missions*, 1954, quoted in the same source.

3. See Major F. Jones, Report on the events leading to the bombing of the Abbey of Monte Cassino on 15 February 1944, 14 October 1949, TNA WO 204/12508; UK National Archives.

4. Lieutenant Colonel G. A. Shepperd, *The Italian Campaign: A Political and Military Re-assessment*, pp. 276–7; Arthur Barker, London, 1968.

15. TO THE GOTHIC LINE AND BEYOND

1. Quoted in Lieutenant Colonel G. W. L. Nicholson, *The Canadians in Italy, 1943–1945*, p. 461; Edmond Cloutier, Queen's Printer and Controller of Stationery, Ottawa, 1956.

2. *The Memoirs of Field Marshal Kesselring*, p. 207; Purnell Books/William Kimber, London, 1974.

3. Nicholson, op. cit., p. 463; W. G. F. Jackson, *Alexander as Military Commander*, p. 297–8; Batsford, London, 1971

4. Alex Danchev and Daniel Todman (eds), *War Diaries 1939–1945: Field Marshal Lord Alanbrooke*, pp. 561–2, diary entry 23 June 1944; Weidenfeld & Nicolson, London, 2001.

5. Jackson, *Alexander as Military Commander*, p. 302.

6. Nicholson, op. cit., p. 676.

16. Fighting in Italy: The Voice of Experience

1. Report on a patrol action, Anzio beachhead, by an Infantry First Lieutenant, US 34th Infantry Division; Headquarters US 34th Infantry Division, September 1944, *Lessons Learned in Combat*, pp. 16–17; TNA WO 204/4635, copy in UK National Archives.

2. US 45th Infantry Division, quoted in US Army, Training Memorandum No. 3, *Lessons from the Italian Campaign*, 10 March 1944, p. 22; TNA WO 204/7564, copy in UK National Archives.

3. Quoted in US Army, Training Memorandum No. 3, op. cit., pp. 20–1.

4. British Army Headquarters R.A. (V Corps), 13 October 1944, *Lessons from Ops – Mountain Artillery*, p. 4; TNA WO 204/8164.

5. Quoted in US Army, Training Memorandum No. 3, op. cit., p.21.

6. Headquarters US 34th Infantry Division, September 1944, op, cit., p.17.

7. Ibid., p. 6.

8. US 3rd Infantry Division, Quoted in US Army, Training Memorandum No. 3, op. cit., p.23.

9. Quoted in US Army, Training Memorandum No. 3, op. cit., p.25.

10. US Battalion Commander, 179th Infantry Regiment, quoted in US Army, Training Memorandum No. 3, op. cit., p.28.

11. US Army, Training Memorandum No. 3, op. cit., p. 25.

12. British Army HQ R.A. (V Corps), op. cit., p. 4.

13. British Directorate of Military Training Report, *78 Division in the Pursuit Battle, August 1944*; TNA WO 204/8164.

14. Infantry Major, quoted in Headquarters US 34th Infantry Division, op. cit., pp. 16–17.

15. Details from J. B. A. Bailey, *Field Artillery and Firepower*, footnotes, p. 190; The Military Press, Oxford, 1989.

16. George Aris, *The Fifth British Division 1939 to 1945*, p. 186; Fifth Division Benevolent Fund, London, 1959.

17. Brigadier C. J. C. Molony, *The Mediterranean and Middle East*, Vol. V, p. 390; HMSO, London, 1973.

18. Quoted in Headquarters US 34th Infantry Division, op. cit., p. 46.

19. Headquarters US Fifth Army, 15 July 1944, *Lessons Learned in the Battle from the Garigliano to North of Rome*, p. 18; TNA WO 204/7572, copy in UK National Archives,

20. Infantry First Lieutenant, quoted in Headquarters US 34th Infantry Division, op. cit., p. 7.

21. British Directorate of Military Training Report, *78 Division in the Pursuit Battle, August 1944*; TNA WO 204/8164.

22. Quoted in Headquarters US 34th Infantry Division, op. cit. pp. 4–5.

23. Quoted in Headquarters US 34th Infantry Division, op. cit., pp. 4–5.

24. British Directorate of Military Training Report, *78 Division in the Pursuit Battle, August 1944*; TNA WO 204/8164; and Cyril Ray, *Algiers to Austria: A History of 78 Division in the Second World War*, p. 98, Eyre & Spottiswoode, London, 1952.

25. British Military Training Directorate (North Africa), 18 November 1943 *Lessons from Operations*, p. 2; TNA WO 231/15, UK National Archives.

26. Headquarters US 34th Infantry Division, op. cit., p. 15.

27. British Directorate of Military Training Report, *78 Division in the Pursuit Battle, August 1944*; TNA WO 204/8164.

28. US Army, Training Memorandum No. 3, op. cit., p. 30.

29. Headquarters US Fifth Army, 15 July 1944 *Lessons Learned in the Battle from the Garigliano to North of Rome*, p. 18; TNA WO 204/7572, copy in UK National Archives.

30. Both incidents quoted in Headquarters US 34th Infantry Division, op. cit., pp. 36, 37.

31. British Directorate of Military Training Report, *78 Division in the Pursuit Battle, August 1944*; TNA WO 204/8164.

32. Street Fighting (report based upon Canadian experience at Ortona); TNA WO 32/11458, in UK National Archives.

33. Both incidents quoted in Headquarters US 34th Infantry Division, op. cit., pp. 1, 3.

34. Directorate of Military Training, 17 May 1944, *Lessons from Cassino Operations*; TNA WO 204/7566, copy in UK National Archives.

35. Account of Operation 'Cygnet' (1945); TNA WO 204/7989, copy in UK National Archives.

36. Details from British 7th Armoured Brigade, 11 November 1944, *Notes and Lessons on Recent Operations Including the Breach of the Gothic Line and Subsequent Fighting Advance to the Line of Fiumicino River*; TNA WO 204/8164, copy in UK National Archives.

37. Headquarters US 34th Infantry Division, op. cit., p. 35.

16. A Hard Way to Make a War: The Italian Campaign in Retrospect

1. Major General J. F. C. Fuller, *The Second World War*, p. 261; Eyre & Spottiswoode, London, 1948.

2. Field Marshal Lord Carver, *The Imperial War Museum Book of the War in Italy 1943–1945: A Vital Contribution to Victory in Europe*; Sidgwick and Jackson, London, 2001, and Pan *Grand Strategy* series, 2002, in association with the Imperial War Museum.

3. Dominic Graham and Shelford Bidwell, *Tug of War: The Battle for Italy 1943–1945*, p. 402, Hodder & Stoughton, London 1986.

4. US Army Official History quoted in Dominick Graham and Shelford Bidwell, op. cit., p. 403.

APPENDIX:
GERMAN AND ALLIED DIVISIONS

This appendix briefly summarizes the organization, strength and principal equipments of Allied and German divisions. It is important always to remember that, while the following details give full establishment figures, divisions were very rarely at full strength. Periods of intensive fighting saw heavy casualties to the infantry on both sides, and replacements frequently could not make up for them. This was particularly so for the Germans, whose divisions in Italy suffered from the increasingly severe manpower shortage affecting the Wehrmacht during 1943–5. The oft-mentioned campaign stalwarts in Kesselring's order of battle, and upon which his campaign relied, were the 16th and 26th Panzer Divisions, the Hermann Göring Panzer Division, the 3rd, 15th, 29th and 90th Panzer Grenadier Divisions, and the 1st and 4th Parachute Divisions. Often they fought as mere shadows of their theoretical strength.

German Infantry Divisions
Divisional headquarters
3 × infantry regiments, each with 2 × battalions and intrinsic 6 × 75mm and 2 × 150mm infantry guns plus anti-tank guns. Each battalion had a heavy support company
Reconnaissance battalion
Anti-tank strength 12 × 75mm towed or self-propelled (SP) guns
Divisional artillery 30 × 105 mm gun/howitzers and 9 × 150mm howitzers
Plus support units
Varying numbers of motor and horse-drawn vehicles
Total personnel 12,772.

German Parachute Divisions (These were Luftwaffe formations)
Approximately 16,000 troops liberally equipped with machine-guns and automatic weapons.
3 × infantry regiments, each with 3 × battalions
Artillery regiment
Anti-tank battalion
Reconnaissance battalion

Panzer Grenadier Divisions (motorized or mechanized infantry)
Divisional headquarters
2 × motorized infantry regiments
Armoured reconnaissance unit
Tank or assault gun battalion (strength varied)
Anti-tank regiment including 43 × 75mm guns and 12 × dual-purpose anti-aircraft/anti-tank guns

340

Artillery regiment 30 × 105mm, 18 × 150mm, 6 x 150mm rocket projectors
Vehicles 3,500
Total personnel 14,000.

Panzer Divisions
Divisional headquarters
1 × armoured (panzer) regiment (2 × tank battalions)
2 × panzer grenadier regiments
Armoured artillery regiment
Anti-tank battalion
Tank strength approximately 200
Vehicles approximately 4,000
Personnel approximately 14,000
The principal German tanks deployed in the Italian campaign were the Panzer (Panzerkampfwagen) IV and Panzer V (Panther) both with 75mm guns.
Numbers of the Panzer VI (Tiger) with 88mm main armament were attached on occasions.

British Infantry Divisions
Divisional headquarters
3 × infantry brigades (each of three infantry battalions)
An infantry battalion consisted of four rifle companies totalling some 360 men, organized into platoons and rifle sections, while a further 360 men were in supporting or non-combatant units.
Reconnaissance regiment (with an anti-tank platoon of 6-pounder guns)
Machine-gun battalion
Divisional artillery 3 × field regiments with a total of 72 × 25-pounder gun/howitzers
Anti-tank regiment 32 × 17-pounders and 16 x 16-pounder anti-tank guns
Light anti-aircraft regiment
Plus engineer, signals, medical and supply units
Total personnel 18,347
Total vehicles: 4,330
Rifles 9,437
Infantry anti-tank weapons 436
Machine-guns 1,322
Mortars 359.

United States Infantry Divisions
Divisional headquarters
3 × infantry regiments each of 3 × battalions, each with a heavy weapons company
Divisional artillery 3 × light artillery regiments with 54 × 105mm gun/howitzers, plus 3 × medium batteries with 12 × 155mm howitzers
Reconnaissance, engineer and signals units
Total personnel 14,037
Total vehicles 2,113
Rifles 6,518

Machine-guns 636
Mortars 144
Infantry anti-tank weapons 557.

British Armoured Divisions
Divisional headquarters
1 × armoured brigade (three armoured regiments)
1 × infantry motor battalion
1 × armoured reconnaissance regiment
1 × infantry brigade
1 × independent machine-gun company
Divisional artillery 1 × towed field regiment of 25-pounders and
1 × self-propelled regiment, with a total of 48 x 25-pounders
1 × anti-tank regiment of 48 x 17-pounder guns
1 × anti-aircraft regiment of 40mm guns
Plus support units
Total personnel 14,964
Tank strength 244 (310 after May 1944)
Total vehicles 4,267
Independent armoured brigades 3 × armoured regiments, each with 78 tanks).

United States Armored Divisions
Divisional headquarters
2 × combat command headquarters
3 × armored battalions
3 × armored infantry battalions
3 × armored field artillery battalions of self-propelled 105mm howitzers
1 × reconnaissance squadron
Plus support units
Tank strength 195 medium tanks, 77 light tanks
Total vehicles 2,650
Total personnel 11,304
The principal Allied tank was the Sherman M-4 armed with a 75mm gun.

Main Sources: Appendix B to G. A. Shepperd, *The Italian Campaign: A Political and Military Re-assessment* (London: Arthur Barker Ltd, 1968) pp. 395–8; John Ellis, *Cassino: The Hollow Victory*, (London: André Deutsch, 1984) Appendix One.

BIBLIOGRAPHY

Agarossi, Elena, *A Nation Collapses: The Italian Surrender of September 1943*, Cambridge University Press, Cambridge, 2006.

Air Historical Branch Narrative, *The Sicilian Campaign*, TNA AIR 41/52.

Air Ministry, *The Rise and Fall of the German Air Force 1933–1945,* based upon German documents, London, 1947; Arms & Armour Press edition, London, 1983.

Aris, George, *The Fifth British Division 1939 to 1945*, Fifth Division Benevolent Fund, London, 1959.

Belchem, David, *All in the Day's March*, Collins, London, 1978.

Bennett, Ralph, *Ultra and Mediterranean Strategy, 1941–1945*, Hamish Hamilton, London, 1989.

Blumenson, Martin, *Salerno to Cassino*, US Army Center of Military History, Washington, DC, 1969; 1993 edition.

Bullock, Alan, *Hitler: A Study in Tyranny*, Odhams, 1952.

Butler, J. R. M., *Grand Strategy,* Vol. II, HMSO, London, 1957.

Churchill, Brigadier T. B. L., 'The Commandos in Action at Salerno' in *The Army Quarterly*, Vol. LI, No. 2, January 1946.

Churchill, Winston S., *The Second World War*, Vol. III, *The Grand Alliance*, Cassell, London, 1950.

— *The Second World War*, Vol. IV, *The Hinge of Fate*, Cassell, London, 1951.

— *The Second World War*, Vol. V, *Closing the Ring*, Cassell, London, 1952.

Clark, Lloyd, *Anzio: The Friction of War*, Headline, London, 2006.

Clark, Mark, *Calculated Risk*, Harrap, London, 1951.

Combined Operations Headquarters Bulletin No. Y/1, *Notes on the Planning and Assault Phases of the Sicilian Campaign (October 1943)*. Copy held by Combined Arms Research Library, Fort Leavenworth Kansas and available online.

Combined Operations Headquarters, *Digest of some Notes and Reports from Operation 'Husky' (November 1943)*. Copy held by Combined Arms Research Library, Fort Leavenworth Kansas and available online.

Craven, Wesley, and Cate, James L., *The Army Air Forces in World War II. Europe: Torch to Pointblank, August 1942 to December 1943*, University of Chicago Press, Chicago, 1949.

Danchev, Alex, and Todman, Daniel, (eds.), *War Diaries 1939–1945: Field Marshal Lord Alanbrooke*, Weidenfeld & Nicolson, London, 2001.

Darby, William O., and Baumer, William H., *Darby's Rangers: We Led the Way*, Presidio Press, San Rafael, California, 1980.

Doherty, Richard, *Clear the Way: A History of the 38th (Irish) Brigade, 1941–47*, Irish Academic Press, Blackrock, County Dublin, 1993.

D'Este, Carlo, *Bitter Victory: The Battle for Sicily, 1943*, Collins, London, 1988.

— *A Genius For War: A Life of General George S. Patton*, HarperCollins, London, 1995.

Ehrman, John, *History of the Second World War: Grand Strategy*, Vol. V, HMSO, London, 1956.

Eisenhower, Dwight D., *Crusade in Europe*, Heinemann, London, 1948.

Fergusson, Bernard, *The Watery Maze*, Collins, London, 1961.

Fraser, David. *Alanbrooke*, Atheneum, New York, 1982.

Garland, Lieutenant Colonel Albert N., and Smyth, Howard McGaw, *Sicily and the Surrender of Italy*, Office of the Chief of Military History, Department of the Army, Washington, DC, 1965.

Gascoigne, Brigadier J. A., '201st Guards Brigade at the Battle of Salerno' in *The Army Quarterly*, Vol. XLIX, No. 2, January 1945.

Gelb, Norman, *Desperate Venture: The Story of Operation Torch*, Hodder & Stoughton, London, 1992.

Gibbs, N. H., *History of the Second World War: Grand Strategy*, Vol. I, HMSO, London, 1976).

Gilbert, Martin, *Winston S. Churchill*, Vol. 7, *Road To Victory, 1941–1945*, Heinemann, London, 1986.

Guingand, Major General Sir Francis de, *Operation Victory*, Hodder & Stoughton, London, 1947.

Gwyer, J. M. A., and Butler, J. R. M., *Grand Strategy:* Vol. III, HMSO, London, 1964.

Hamilton, Nigel, *Monty*, Vol. 2, *Master of the Battlefield, 1942–1944*, Hamish Hamilton, London, 1983.

Hecks, Karl. *Bombing, 1939–45*, Robert Hale, London, 1990.

Hickey, Des, and Smith, Gus, *Operation Avalanche: The Salerno Landings, 1943*, Heinemann, London, 1983.

Higgins, Trumbull, *Soft Underbelly: The Anglo-American Controversy over the Italian Campaign, 1939–1945*, Macmillan, New York, 1968.

Hinsley, F. H. *et al*, *British Intelligence in the Second World War*, Vol. 1, HMSO, London, 1979.

— *British Intelligence in the Second World War*, Vol. 3, Part 1, HMSO, London, 1984.

Historical Division, War Department, 1944. *Salerno: American Operations From the Beaches to the Volturno (9 September – 6 October 1943)*, American Forces in Action series, reprinted 1990.

†††††††††††††††††††

Hooton, E. R., *Eagle in Flames: The Fall of the Luftwaffe*, Arms & Armour Press, London, 1997.

Howard, Michael. *Grand Strategy*, Vol. IV, HMSO, London, 1972.

— *British Intelligence in the Second World War*, Vol. V, *Strategic Deception*, HMSO, London, 1990.

Irving, David. *Hitler's War*, Hodder & Stoughton, London, 1977.

Jackson, W. G. F., *The Battle for Italy*, Batsford, London, 1967.

— *The Battle for Rome*, Batsford, London, 1969.

— *Alexander as Military Commander*, Batsford, London, 1971.

Kesselring, Field Marshal A., *The Memoirs of Field Marshal Kesselring*, William Kimber, London, 1953.

Lewin, Ronald, *Churchill as Warlord*, Batsford, London, 1973.

Matloff, Maurice, and Snell, Edwin, *United States Army in World War II, Strategic Planning for Coalition Warfare, 1941–1942* (Washington, DC, 1953.

Mediterranean Allied Air Forces, *Preliminary Report on Operation 'Husky' July 9 to July 17 1943*, TNA AIR 23/1702.

Meyer, Leo J., 'The Decision to Invade North Africa (Torch) (1942)' in Kent Roberts Greenfield (ed), *Command Decisions*, Harcourt, Brace & Company, New York, 1959.

Molony, Brigadier C. J. C., *The Mediterranean and Middle East*, Vol. V, HMSO, London 1973.

Montgomery, Viscount, *El Alamein to the River Sangro*, Hutchinson, London, 1956.

— *Memoirs*, Collins, London, 1958.

Nafziger, George F., *The German Order of Battle: Panzers and Artillery in World War II*, Greenhill, London, and Stackpole, Pennsylvania, 1999.

Nicholson, Lieutenant Colonel G. W. L., *The Canadians in Italy 1943–1945*, Ottawa, 1956.

Nicolson, Nigel, *Alex*, Weidenfeld & Nicolson, London, 1973.

Pack, S. W. C., *Operation 'Husky'*, David & Charles, Newton Abbot, 1977.

Pond, Hugh, *Salerno*, William Kimber, London, 1961.

Ray, Cyril, *Algiers to Austria: A History of 78 Division in the Second World War*, Eyre & Spottiswoode, London, 1952.

Roskill, S. W., *The War at Sea*, HMSO, London, 1954.

Russell, Brigadier Nelson, 'The Irish Brigade in Sicily: July to August 1943' in *The Faugh-A-Ballagh*, July 1944.

Senger und Etterlin, General Fridolin von, *Neither Fear Nor Hope*, Macdonald, London, 1963.

Shepperd, G. A., *The Italian Campaign 1943–45*, Arthur Barker Ltd, London, 1968.

Smith, Denis Mack, *Mussolini*, Weidenfeld & Nicolson, London, 1981.

Strawson, John, *The Italian Campaign*, Secker & Warburg, London, 1987.

Tedder, Lord, *With Prejudice*, Cassell, London, 1966.

Warlimont, General Walter, *Inside Hitler's Headquarters*, Weidenfeld & Nicolson, London, 1964.

US Army Report, *Lessons from the Italian Campaign, March 1944*, copy in UK National Archives, TNA WO 204/7564.

INDEX